STAR MYTHS:
Show-Business Biographies on Film

by

Robert Milton Miller

The Scarecrow Press, Inc.
Metuchen, N.J., & London
1983

Library of Congress Cataloging in Publication Data

Miller, Robert Milton
 Star myths.

   Filmography: p.
   Bibliography: p.
   Includes index.
   1. Entertainers in motion pictures. 2. Biographical films--History and criticism. I. Title.
PN1995.9.E77M5 1983   791.43'09'0935279   83-14292
ISBN 0-8108-1643-1

Copyright © 1982, 1983 by Robert Milton Miller
Manufactured in the United States of America

DEDICATION

In memory of two inspiring educators who gave their wholehearted support to the start of this project ... and are sorely missed at its conclusion:

Paddy Whannel, who taught me the value of the popular arts, with film as the primary text.

Martin Maloney, who revealed to me the amazing interrelatedness of all forms of popular culture.

CONTENTS

Acknowledgments		vii
Introduction		ix
I	Sound and Music	1
II	Barnum and the Business	11
III	The Ziegfeld Success	17
IV	Bring Back the Old Songs	44
V	The Form Takes Shape	76
VI	The Songwriters	98
VII	The Bandleaders	133
VIII	The Singers	158
IX	The Actors	212
X	The Dancers	271
XI	The Comedians	294
XII	Celebrity Miscellany	335
Conclusion		361
Filmography		362
Bibliography		388
Index		391
About the Author		406

ACKNOWLEDGMENTS

A sincere note of thanks is hereby expressed to the following organizations and individuals for their generosity and cooperation in facilitating screenings of the films analyzed in this text and in supplying stills.

Audio Brandon Films
Budget Films
Capitol Communications
Clem Williams Films
Films Incorporated
Hurlock Cine-World
Roa's Films
Swank Motion Pictures
Universal Pictures
Wisconsin Center for Film
 and Theatre Research

WBBM-TV
WFLD-TV
WGN-TV
WMAQ-TV
WSNS-TV
WTTW-TV

Dick Anderson
Barbara Benja
Mike Caisson
George Crittenden
Susan Dalton
Dorothy Desmond
Alan Estrin
Maxine Fleckner
Al Green
Ron Hall
Bob Koester
Hania Kuzmik
Doug Lemza
Alice Necker
Mark Nelson
Cathy Plant
Bill Rapp
Ron Roloff
Joe Savage
Elena Shapiro
George Shumacher
Harry Trigg

I don't think anybody cares about the facts of my life. Names, dates, places--I'll give you a bunch of them and you can juggle 'em around any way you want. What really matters is the singing--and the story....
    --Al Jolson in Jolson Sings Again, advising the screenwriters of The Jolson Story.

Entertainment is not reality. If people wanted truth--they'd stay home!"
    --Florenz Ziegfeld explaining show business to his father in Ziegfeld: The Man and His Women.

INTRODUCTION

A myth is not a lie. Although many people confuse the terms, there is a very important difference between them. Lies are instantaneous; they occur whenever one person tries to deceive another. Myths are ancient; they represent not humanity's pitiful attempts at deception, but the age-old struggle to understand and explain the human condition, to shape the bewildering chaos of life into ordered, predictable, comprehensible patterns of events--patterns which then allow the mind to perceive a kind of pre-scientific meaning, or answer, to the riddle of existence. Myths function as the basis of all storytelling, but captured in this delimited, linear state, they can be put to all sorts of uses, both noble and ignoble. Myth-infused stories have the power to point people toward God, but they can also set nation against nation in a cataclysm of destruction and death. Midway between these two extremes lies the power of the myth-infused story to entertain--to amuse, shock, inspire, reassure, or satiate humankind's natural curiosity.

When such stories are written, dramatized, enacted, possibly told abstractly in music or dance, possibly recorded and duplicated, and ultimately offered to the public as commercial products in a capitalist society, the attendant process is called ... show business. This book is a study of what happens whenever that business packages and sells to its customers not just any story, but little mythic pieces of its own history, carefully wrapped in celluloid. This is the story of the stories of the show business biographical film. The book was written in accordance with certain contemporary principles of literary and film criticism, which can be explained as follows.

Star Myths is a product of applied generic (grouping by shared characteristics) structural analysis. While many other modes of analytical criticism (auteurist, Marxist, humanist, Freudian, etc.) yield useful information when applied in the study of a number of related films, the body of work analyzed herein (because of its superficial sameness or surface uniformity as perceived by the movie-going public) seems to lend itself best to an investigation which employs the tools of genre-directed criticism. Therefore the theoretical foundation of this book is derived from the writings of C. G. Jung, Northrop Frye, Vladimir Propp, Claude Levi-Strauss, Joseph Campbell, Tzvetan Todorov, and John Cawelti as taught in literature and film courses at Northwestern University by Professors Frank McConnell and Stuart Kaminsky and unified and exemplified in their respective books, Storytelling and Mythmaking and American Film Genres.

In researching and writing Star Myths I have identified, located, and screened a group of more than 125 theatrical and television dramas which purport to tell the life stories of prominent figures in the history of American show business. These films are analyzed in terms of their continuing similarities across a span of five decades (1930-1982) of American popular culture, counterpointed by the films' evolutionary differences which reflect a modifying process in cultural values and audience expectations.

In keeping with the principles of bias exclusion first codified by Northrop Frye in his Anatomy of Criticism, this study is intentionally non-evaluative. Every attempt has been made to avoid hierarchical pronouncements of personal taste which would rank so-called "good" films above "bad" ones or champion works of "genius" or "political daring" while denouncing the supposedly "retrograde" genre from whence they emerged. Such critical forays in this context would only tend to impede my primary goal of analytically dissecting and categorizing the characters, plots, themes, motifs, icons, settings and underlying myths employed and displayed within each film's diegesis (the enclosed world bounded by the borders of the frame).

An aesthetics-based evaluation of the genre might even risk drowning in its own denunciations, in light of the fact that established critics have mercilessly maligned most of the past half-century's worth of show business bio-films with mock-anguished cries of "maudlin," "distorted," "sensationalized," or "contrived." Yet the American public has enthusiastically continued to support these films with an ongoing sense of curiosity proved through regular viewership. Today such motion pictures form an integral ritual in the mass media-facilitated process of fame worship. This book is an investigation into the myth-powered mechanism of that ritual.

CHAPTER I

SOUND AND MUSIC

Biographical films (dramatic narratives ostensibly based on the lives of real people) have been a staple of American film production since the industry's beginning. Outlaws, statesmen, peace officers, generals, rascals and saints from both recent and ancient history were depicted in early movies as part of the cinema's post-Lumierean practice of either adapting story material directly from books and plays, or composing original screen drama with characters and plots similar to those which had already proved popular in earlier media.

The silent cinema, perhaps because of the specific location of its span of existence within the much wider boundaries of the chronological evolution of American show business, did not offer biographical depictions of professional entertainers in the manner which became a regular practice in the sound era. Anomalies exist, such as THE LIFE OF BUFFALO BILL in which the hunter-turned-showman appears as himself in quick vignettes depicting his alleged adventures as chronicled by Ned Buntline and others. However, a more frequent method of biographical drama based on an entertainer's life appeared late in the silent era. It was the fictitious narrative (about a show business luminary) which bore strong similarities to portions of the real life of the performer cast in the starring role (Al Jolson in THE JAZZ SINGER, Texas Guinan in QUEEN OF THE NIGHT CLUBS, George Jessel in LUCKY BOY, or the somewhat earlier adventure serials about a master escape artist which starred Harry Houdini). These were films exploiting the fame and popularity of a performer who was still alive and active, a personage whose public acceptance was roughly contemporaneous with the release of the film. The name of the performer was most often not the same as that of the character in the drama, but the public could easily see the similarities. This practice bridged the changeover to sound, as exemplified by John McCormick in SONG OF MY HEART, Ted Lewis in IS EVERYBODY HAPPY? and Fanny Brice in BE YOURSELF.

Show business in America, circa 1929, had already amassed a considerable tradition and history, but little had been written to digest, summarize and historicize this subject for the contemporary audience. All of the most widely acclaimed performances from earlier years in vaudeville and the legitimate theatre, in the center ring or on the concert stage, were lost to fading photos and to memory, save for the primitive reproduction of old phonograph records or the fleeting glimpses of legendary performers captured on silent film when they were far past their prime (Sarah Bernhardt in QUEEN ELIZABETH, William Gillette in SHERLOCK HOLMES). Show business nostalgia was not the highly marketable item it would eventually become, although nostalgic exploitations of the other paraphernalia of popular memory, such as war ethos, had already proved quite successful (cf. the spate of books, plays and films about the Great War which won wide acceptance from American entertainment consumers in the years just preceding the onset of the Depression and the era of the talkies).

In 1930, amidst the flurry of film musicals made possible by the recent conversion to sound and the seeming public demand for screen drama punctuated with songs, MGM concocted a vehicle deemed suitable for highlighting the voice of a performer who had won success in both Metropolitan Opera productions and popular Broadway musicals. Grace Moore, who went on to continued acceptance in film musicals with fictitious heroines (all of whom were opera stars), made her film debut in the suggestively titled A LADY'S MORALS. For export, the studio titled the picture after its real-life heroine, the famous mid-nineteenth-century concert vocalist and stage star, Jenny Lind.

The film's narrative, while not a life-spanning, cradle-to-grave biography, did center on a few crucial years in Lind's career. Moore starred as the famous singer, and actual names, dates, and places from Lind's personal history were incorporated into the screenplay. The story employed one of the most tried-and-true mythic formulations in all of drama and fiction, that of a love which is lost and then found. Its embellishment with biographical details from the life of a major show business personality appears to have been a genuine innovation, one which would be copied, reworked, altered by changing social custom, and continued in more than 125 feature films during the succeeding half-century of cinema and television history.

The central love story of A LADY'S MORALS begins with the performer already a celebrated artist in her home country, Sweden. Stopping for a visit to her home town on the eve of what is to be her first major concert tour of the capitals of Europe, she is dismayed to learn that the last available room at the local inn has been taken by an arrogant young composer named Paul Brandt. Following a flirtatious argument with the visiting diva over whether he will relinquish his room for the night, Brandt agrees to do so on condition that Lind sing his latest song. He rewards her rendition of his composition with an uninvited kiss, and over her protestations announces that they "haven't met by accident," and will surely "meet again."

Smitten with unrequited love for the lady, Brandt dutifully follows her across the Continent, attending each of her performances. During a run of the opera "The Daughter of the Regiment" at the Royal Opera House in Malmö, Brandt summons the courage to invite himself to Lind's hotel room following a performance, and orders dinner for two. Another flirtatious argument ensues when she discovers him, culminating in her singing "Oh Why (Do Men Run After Me?)." Brandt explains his own obsession by displaying a picture of her (at age 15) that he has long carried with him. "You can't find out about life except by living," he admonishes the virginal stage star. "And that means men!" she replies in anguish. As she begins to realize his romantic interest in her is reciprocated, the two discuss marriage, but she is shocked to learn that his designs on her stop short of any formalized commitment. He defends his indecent proposal by explaining, "You're married to the world," but she will have none of such an arrangement. Brandt stalks out of his bungled tryst after issuing a parting warning: "You've given your life to the crowd, and when the fire dies out and youth is gone, you'll find out that they're in love with somebody else ... but I'll never care for anyone but you." Thus the film's curious title is given a measure of relevance.

Some time later, at the conclusion of what has been an arduous tour, Lind's exquisite voice is put to the ultimate test as she appears before a hypercritical audience in the land of opera's birth, Italy. Just before the curtain rises on a performance of "Norma," Brandt pays a surprise visit to Lind backstage and repeats his indecent proposal, only to be rebuffed again. The reigning local diva, a haughty woman called "La Rosatti," is in the audience that night, and the crowd is rife with hushed discussions as to whether Lind will be able to surpass Rosatti's previous triumph in the leading role. Lind appears to do just that, winning a powerful ovation from the theatre's patrons. Pressed for an encore she feels too weak to deliver, Lind tells her offstage company members that she fears another aria will seriously damage her voice. The jubilant audience is insistent, however, and Lind reluctantly agrees. The strain does prove to be too great and her voice breaks; the fickle crowd then jeers her distress and calls for the return of Rosatti, who is only too happy to oblige. When an outraged Paul Brandt, seated in the gallery, chides the crowd for its rudeness, a brawl erupts and he is knocked unconscious by a blow from an empty wine bottle. Backstage, the distraught Lind stands alone, deserted by the entourage which had attended to her distress moments earlier, but is now eagerly peering from the wings at her replacement. "Amazing, isn't it," she remarks, "just a few words of sympathy, then everyone's gone."

Lind's career thus grinds to a painful halt. She has succumbed to the great dread of all opera performers--she has damaged her voice and can no longer sing. The devoted Brandt eventually manages to intrude upon her remorseful seclusion, bringing with him his uncle, the famous Maestro Garcia, who is alleged to be one of Europe's best vocal coaches. Following Brandt's hasty departure, Garcia informs his new pupil that the proud Brandt has become blind as a result of the head injury he suffered in the theatre brawl. Sounding a proper note of sacrifice to characterize this drama built on the mythic pattern of romantic separation and reunion, Garcia explains, "All failure, all success, all life as we know it is built and founded upon someone truly loving someone else." "I feel so selfish," replies the penitent and soon-to-be-healed Lind, as she considers how to make amends to the young man who has lost his sight while defending her talent in the face of an angry crowd.

Having regained her voice under the kind tutelage of Maestro Garcia, Lind sets off to search for her defender/benefactor/suitor and soon locates him in a secluded Tyrolean village. There the two spend a loving idyll prior to his undergoing eye surgery. Presaging what is to become one of the show business biography's most recurrent dramatic themes, Brandt observes, "We think we're pretty big ... until a couple of things happen to us." Lind counters his notation of the need for ego deflation with another future show-business-on-film aphorism: "But we must believe in ourselves." As the next half-century of such films will show, the ladder to the top is rarely ascended without massive doses of self-confidence and an indefatigable will to succeed.

Brandt's operation turns out to be only a marginal success and he is thus doomed to a life of faint shadows and threatening dependency. Despite Lind's wry announcement that she has decided to accept his "invitation" (to become his mistress), Brandt conceals his distressing fate and slips out of her life with only a terse letter of farewell.

At this point the narrative leaps forward to Jenny Lind's famous American debut under the sponsorship of master showman P. T. Barnum. An advertising poster fills the screen, announcing that the event is scheduled to take place on September 11, 1850 at New York City's elegant Castle Garden Theatre. Lind's air of European refinement is pointedly contrasted with the American brashness of Barnum as they are seen conversing in her dressing room on the night of the auspicious event. "New York's a grand town--when you wake 'em up," announces the egregious impresario to the Swedish ambassador, who has come calling backstage to pay his respects. The American penchant for celebrity merchandising, a phenomenon which permeated the decade preceding the film's release, is shown to date at least as far back as the middle of the previous century when Barnum points out the peculiar charm of such bizarre items as a "Jenny Lind teakettle" and a "Jenny Lind cigar."

Invoking some of the best-remembered aspects of the popularly received memories of Barnum and his troupe, the narrative then has the showman introduce Lind to an assortment of performing freaks (a midget, a fat lady, an "India Rubber Man," etc.) and warn her to expect the customary Barnum ballyhoo in the press. "Don't be surprised if you read in the papers that you've been disappointed in love," advises Barnum as he departs from Lind's dressing room, leaving her to ponder the ironic accuracy of the remark and her only partially concealed state of melancholy longing for her lost love. Lind's long-time personal manager/companion,

a crusty older woman named Josephine, remarks that her
employer's secret sadness has begun to work some very unwelcome changes on Lind's personality and disposition.

At this point Olaf, an eccentric Swedish fan of Lind's
(who has also become a drinking buddy of Brandt's) literally
bursts through a backstage window and presents the startled
Josephine with a copy of a new song written by his friend,
who is currently working as a blind street musician in the
city. Upon hearing this news, Lind immediately resolves to
find him, but first she must proceed with her New York debut. Without a moment's hesitation, her opening night repertoire is expanded to include Brandt's new composition,
which is actually an original song written for the film and
entitled "Lovely Hour."

Although the men Lind hires in an attempt to find a
blind musician among New York City's 600,000 population
(noted with the contrastive humor of historical hindsight)
yield no results, Brandt's Swedish friend nevertheless
tricks Brandt into journeying to Lind's hotel, where an emotional reunion of the parted lovers fulfills the mythic pattern
and concludes the drama. "Why didn't you tell me that
you're blind," Lind tearfully asks the man who had feared
becoming a "burden" to her. Overcome with joy, his only
answer is, "My Jenny ... My Jenny Lind!"

Although A LADY'S MORALS was not a giant box-office hit (Grace Moore returned to the New York stage and
did not resume her Hollywood career until four years later),
it stands as a landmark film by virtue of its initial combination of certain crucial attractional factors. The subject matter, allegedly taken from the real life of a major entertainer
who had thrilled an earlier generation, was infused with historical and curiosity value. Jenny Lind's popularity had far
exceeded that of a mere concert star. Her voice, like Enrico Caruso's, had taken on something of a legendary quality
in the years since it had last been heard by an adoring public. (She retired from the stage well before the turn of the
century.) Old-timers boasted to younger music fans of the
unmatchable beauty and purity of the "Swedish Nightingale's"
vocalizing. It had been the elders' unique and unrecapturable
pleasure to hear the great Jenny Lind in her prime, and
memories of that experience later became something of an
unofficial standard by which to judge even the most gifted of
aspiring sopranos. To announce to the movie-going public of
1930 that they could now see and hear the life of Jenny Lind

on film (albeit in a dramatic recreation) was to offer the potential audience a chance to investigate the past, to witness the birth of a legend. D. W. Griffith's ABRAHAM LINCOLN was released that same year, and what success it enjoyed in attracting patrons to the ticket window was very likely for similar reasons. However, there was an important and crucial difference in the appeal of these two films.

All through recorded history, socio-political control of the masses has been facilitated in part by giving the public officially designated heroes, the study of whose lives becomes a part of the formal education of youth. While the tendency toward hero-worship may stem from longings in the collective unconscious and from the primary parent-emulation behavior patterns of early childhood, it has always remained for the managers of society to select those heroes whose lives would be officially taught as ideal patterns of behavior. Popular entertainers, on the other hand, are creatures of the semi-official mass media (some might even say creations of the media), and their accomplishments have yet to be made a significant part of school curricula.

Despite their absence from formal programs of societal instruction, entertainment figures (particularly since the rise of newspapers and magazines) have become part of the public consciousness without official sanction. They become heroes and heroines of the masses not through bold and noble deeds for God and country, but by providing diversions, more skillfully and pleasurably than their competitors. By wont of essentially favorable and intensive publicity in the media over a sustained period, they are eventually perceived as embodying popular ideals of desirability, wit, grace, beauty, physical prowess, and social success. As the industrial revolution, modified by the union movement and reform legislation, ended the "full day of work" and gave the public "leisure time," the entertainment industry ("show business") grew and flourished, providing various means of filling the increasing hours no longer devoted exclusively to work.

What appeared in the United States by the early years of the twentieth century was a burgeoning entertainment industry (vaudeville, legitimate theatre, popular songs on records and sheet music, burlesque, cabarets, circuses, movies and radio) offering "stars" to the public. The most favorably received entertainers became the recipients of much the same sort of adulation that was previously showered only upon military, political and religious heroes. One might argue that such an array of diversionary personalities was offered to the masses only to deflect their attention from the less than heroic activities of their elected leaders at this time (consorting with and eventually becoming the captives of the most powerful economic interests who sought to establish monopoly capitalism in America under the guise of Fabian social reform). Whether by design or by psychosocial destiny, the hero-worship of entertainers was a highly visible phenomenon by 1930, the year the generic category of films under investigation appears to have begun forming.

Because of the number of years which had elapsed between the cessation of Jenny Lind's concert appearances and the release of A LADY'S MORALS, most of the audience for the film knew of her only indirectly, through word-of-mouth from an earlier generation. The chances of public disappointment arising from unfavorable comparisons between Grace Moore's performance and memories of Lind in person were slight. Rather than employ only vocal selections from the authentic Lind repertoire, several new songs were composed for the film. Scenes of operatic performance were chiefly limited to two works: "Daughter of the Regiment" and "Norma." With the addition of songs composed to appeal to popular taste circa 1930, the film was definitely geared to a much wider audience than one composed solely of classical music devotees. Since the real Jenny Lind's repertoire did include some of the popular ballads of her day, the commissioning of new songs for the film was more in keeping with the spirit of Lind's concert work than with creating a precise replication of her performances.

Taking this principle one step further, as we shall see in the many screen biographies of show business figures which followed, re-creating the "spirit" of a famous entertainer's career rather than the details was to become a prime concern of Hollywood's myth-makers. Determining the specifics of such a spirit was not so much a task of dramatizing the subject's life as it was a job of exploiting for dramatic effect the major facets of how that life was publicly perceived.

The highest echelons of show business in America encompassed a community of performers, authors and impresarios centered first around the theatrical district of New York City, and later spreading to the largest cities on the major vaudeville circuits and to the growing colony of film makers in southern California. Through the coincidences of working together "on the same bill," performing in the same stage or film vehicle, or collaborating in the writing or production of a show, this community of entertainers, when viewed in its historical context, includes many overlapping careers. Friendships, alliances, even rivalries and antagonisms abound, providing grist for the writer's mill when turning the life of a celebrity into screen drama. These overlapping careers are quite evident in the body of films under investigation. A character who forms the center of one film often turns up or is referred to in several others, thereby linking a large group of films together in an extended diegesis. This linkage of characters becomes a narrative linkage of considerable complexity, as it is clearly coupled with frequently recurring and specifically identified settings (major theatres, movie studios, talent agencies, publishing companies, and hit songs, plays and films of the past).

The linkage is already operative between the first film under study and the second one, taken in the chronological order of their release to the public. Following the appearance of A LADY'S MORALS in 1930, four years went by before the release of another show business biography on film. In the interim America's movie screens were populated with dozens of "backstage dramas," always overtly fictional in nature but often based loosely on the adventures of real stage and film entertainers who were never named in the films.

This cycle of motion pictures actually predates A LADY'S MORALS by a year and has antecedents extending far back into the silent era. The coming of sound, however, allowed film makers to integrate popular songs into screen comedy and drama on a much more widespread basis than had been possible with silent films (cf. WHAT PRICE GLORY's "Charmaine," LILAC TIME's "Jeanine, I Dream of Lilac Time," or SEVENTH HEAVEN's "Diane"-- all examples of popular songs introduced and promoted by silent films). THE BROADWAY MELODY, THE GREAT GABBO, the GOLD DIGGERS films and their many imitators in the earliest years of sound relied heavily on contemporary show business settings and character types while propelling song after song onto the national hit parade. (Each major studio controlled its own music publishing firm, thus making the production of such films doubly lucrative.) The public demonstrated that its appetite for popular songs could be whetted by films with an extensive musical content, and the use of show business settings allowed for facile integration of songs and story. (Previously, authors of stage musicals, as differentiated from revues, had customarily tailored song lyrics to enhance points made in the dialogue or to further the plot.)

Buying and adapting stage musicals for the screen was expensive and not always successful. Creating original musicals for film was more economical, and the use of a show business setting allowed for the "dropping in" of studio-commissioned songs at will, without regard to dramatic appropriateness. One song could easily be substituted for another without altering the script, thus allowing studio executives to do a great deal of last-minute tinkering, packing each new release only with tunes deemed to have the greatest hit potential. Songs which had little relevance to the dialogue could always be sung by an actor playing a singer who was either rehearsing or giving a performance.

CHAPTER II

BARNUM AND THE BUSINESS

The next motion picture which specifically proclaimed to be telling the life story of a prominent show business figure was released in 1934. THE MIGHTY BARNUM was ostensibly based on the career of the famous showman Phineas T. Barnum, a museum, freak show and circus operator who mastered the technique of generating widespread publicity from hokum and whose name became synonymous in the public vernacular with ballyhoo, exaggerated spectacle, and his apocryphal remark, "There's a sucker born every minute." The phenomenon of linkage between show business biographical films is already operative in this picture, with Jenny Lind, the central character of the previous film, appearing as a secondary figure in THE MIGHTY BARNUM. P.T. himself had appeared in A LADY'S MORALS as the promoter who arranged for Jenny Lind's American debut. Reinforcing the linkage on a visual level is the fact that Wallace Beery portrays Barnum in both films.

THE MIGHTY BARNUM uses a different dramatic formula, eschewing its predecessor's lost-and-found love plot (with pride and sacrifice complications) for a "stick with what you do best" resolution to what in Jungian terms would be an adventure of the inflated ego coming to terms with self. Barnum is depicted as a crude and vulgar (though amiable and amusing) huckster who aspires to rise from the trade of exhibiting freaks for the gullible to the profession of presenting highbrow artists for the cultured. A native of Connecticut with roots in the provincial culture of small-town New England, Barnum has moved to New York City as the film begins, and he is the proprietor of a store in the Bowery. He aids in the rehabilitation of an alcoholic named Walsh (who fits the stereotype of the has-been Shakespearian actor) and the two become fast friends and partners. (Walsh has romantic designs on Barnum's young ward Ellen but he is too old for her.) Barnum's fascination with freaks is already in evidence. His wife explains her having borne no children by expressing her fear that any baby of the Barnums' would probably have five legs. Her husband's response: "Think of the crowds it would draw."

Disappointed with his career as a shopkeeper, Barnum purchases tickets to Connecticut, then sells them when a promoter named Skiff offers to relinquish his contract to exhibit "George Washington's Nurse" in return for some quick cash. After buying the services of the "nurse," Barnum opens a freak museum in partnership with Walsh. Their next star attraction is a bearded lady, "Madame Zorro," imported from Italy. Barnum's promotions are subjected to a stinging series of newspaper attacks launched by a newspaper editor named James Gordon Greeley (a composite of real-life editors James Gordon Bennett and Horace Greeley). A corrupt local sheriff tries to extort money from Barnum, is rebuffed, and then conspires to make the bearded lady appear a fake (by substituting an imposter) when Greeley's newspaper stages a public examination (by lady judges) of Madame Zorro's true gender. Barnum loses a large wager made with Greeley (the proceeds go to charity) and the museum is destroyed by a riot of outraged customers. Impoverished and disgraced, Barnum answers his wife's demand that they return to Connecticut by expressing his confidence that Walsh will return from a freak-scouting trip with "something to make you shiver." The result--Barnum's newest attraction --is "Colonel and Mrs. Tom Thumb," a pair of perfect midgets. Barnum goes on a world tour with these and other attractions, and what is popularly known as a "Hollywood Montage," a rapid succession of lap-dissolved shots depicting extensive activity and suggesting the passage of sizable blocks of time, follows, informing us that Barnum's "Greatest Show on Earth" has played the major European capitals and appeared before the Queen of England.

As his ego continues to inflate, Barnum quips, "I'm a big success ... I'm sitting on top of the world." His less than enthusiastic wife responds, "But the world turns round every twenty-four hours." The course of Barnum's initial rise has been charted in the narrative, and the seemingly inevitable fall follows. Back in America he announces the imminent arrival of the world's largest captive elephant, the 33-ton "Jumbo," which Walsh has arranged to purchase from the London Zoo. When Walsh returns from his European "shopping trip" for new attractions, he tells Barnum that although the zoo refused to sell the beast, Walsh has signed up an even more spectacular creature--Jenny Lind, "The Swedish Nightingale." At a gala reception following the docking of Walsh's boat, Lind is introduced to the crowd that has been waiting for the famous elephant. After he hears her sing "Believe Me, If All Those Endearing Young Charms," Barnum is so impressed that he immediately proclaims her "his discovery" and makes plans for her American debut at the Castle Garden Theatre.

As Barnum becomes increasingly involved with promoting an American concert tour for Jenny Lind, his social aspirations soar. He neglects both his museum and his wife, believing them to be too "low class" for his new public image. After he offhandedly insults Tom Thumb, telling the midget that an impresario has no time for freaks, the small but feisty performer protests, "You belong with us ... someday you'll eat those words."

Jenny Lind's presentation to the cream of New York society is scheduled to occur at a formal banquet, attended by such notables as Henry Wadsworth Longfellow and Mr. and Mrs. John J. Astor. Under Barnum's direction as Master of Ceremonies, the event rapidly becomes a social disaster, with the orchestra playing the Swedish national anthem far too many times and Barnum comporting himself in an outrageously boorish manner. When he unwittingly insults Jenny Lind by addressing her with a stream of obscenities in Swedish (taught him by a masseur), the horrified dignitaries and the guest of honor storm out of the banquet hall. Humiliated, Barnum goes on a drunken binge. His wife leaves him, his museum closes in bankruptcy, and he winds up on skid row, only to be rescued while lying in a gutter by a solicitous Tom Thumb.

The midget takes his former boss home (Thumb's quarters are rather cramped with P.T. as a guest) and reunites him with his still loyal freaks, who agree to work for free until Barnum can make his business a paying concern again. (Skiff, Barnum's longtime competitor, has been trying to hire them for his new museum on Canal Street.) Barnum's "Greatest Show on Earth" reopens, his wife returns, and Walsh, whom Barnum had bitterly accused of "stealing Jenny Lind away," turns up drunk and reciting Shakespeare. While Walsh hides in a mummy case with the intention of surprising Barnum, the envious Skiff sneaks onto the premises and starts a fire. Informed that his errant friend has returned and is trapped in the burning building, Barnum rushes into the flames, forces open the case, and rescues Walsh. The pair jump from a high window into a firemen's net with Barnum exclaiming, "In my old age I turn acrobat."

A multiple happy ending concludes the film, with Walsh again paying court to Barnum's ward Ellen, P.T. and his wife reconciled, all the freaks safely surviving the fire (though Mme. Zorro's beard is singed), and Barnum and Walsh thrilled with the last-minute delivery of Jumbo, a gift from the forgiving Jenny Lind. The entourage walks away from the fire in parade-like fashion, with the two partners leading the way and excitedly discussing their next venture. After remarking, "Shucks, I'm no impresario, I'm a showman," Barnum suggests that they put on future exhibitions in a tent, one that can be moved from place to place when business slacks off. They consider calling the show "Barnum and Walsh," but P.T. rejects the idea, claiming "it don't rhyme." Then he asks Walsh what his first name is. Walsh protests that it has always been a family secret, but he relents and says it is "Bailey." P.T. has the last line in the film, exuberantly prophesying, "That's it! Barnum and Bailey present The Greatest Show on Earth. Why, a hundred years from now people will still be talking about us."

The first two American show-business biographical films, produced at the beginning and end of a cycle of fictional backstage, or "let's put on a show," motion pictures, both recreated an era from the previous century. Close comparisons by the public of the genuine with the artificial were impossible. Jenny Lind, known in her time for the beauty of her voice far more than for her only marginal physical attractiveness, could easily be impersonated by the glamorous Grace Moore (in the first film) or the spectacularly beautiful Virginia Bruce (in the second picture). Since little of Lind's private life had become mingled with the accumulated legends recounting her singing ability, the screenwriters were free to invent subsidiary characters and details while relying on a dramatic formula with proven audience response. Technical improvements in the practice of dubbing by 1934 even allowed the makers of the second film to cast two performers (one for acting, the other for singing) as Jenny Lind in order to obtain the desired combination of appearance and voice. P. T. Barnum, considerably less remembered as a performer but preserved in popular legends by the events and exhibitions he directed, had become with the passing of time even more the sort of amorphous character who could be freely crafted and shaped at will by the film makers to fit a convenient (or appropriate) mythic plot of fall and rise, and thus arouse positive audience response. No matter if the real Barnum had been a cynical exploiter of the physically distorted victims of birth defects, callously sensationalizing their oddities to satiate the morbid curiosity of a simple-minded public that was hungry for reassurance of its own assumed "normalcy." Whether or not this was the case might be the concern of an academically inclined researcher compiling a sociological history of the nineteenth century. It was very likely not a major worry of the authors of THE MIGHTY BARNUM. What was operative in the delineating of the Barnum character as portrayed by Wallace Beery was the employment of a type, a benign source of amusement and wonder whose filmic adventures involved the learning of a lesson handed down from ancient folklore--"Stick to your own kind" and "Do what you do best."

Audience sympathy for the Barnum character was automatic to a certain extent because of the popularity of Wallace Beery by 1934. Already a frequent screen performer for more than a decade, his initial typecasting in villainous roles was giving way to a kind of "lovable rascal" character often written especially for him. Possessed of the weaknesses, vices and desires of an adult, the Beery persona also exhibited the shyness, sentimentality and awkwardness of an early adolescent. Coupled with plots in which his failing larcenous schemes, transparent lies and lack of malice fit into a comic framework, this persona ultimately reinforced contemporary morality by burlesquing the character's attempts to violate it. The portrayal of P. T. Barnum by Wallace Beery thus mitigated the harsher facets of the historical Barnum, rendering the less than admirable nature of his career (even as it survived the transition to screenplay) innocuous. The extension of Barnum's de facto family circle to include his ultimately loyal freaks even lends his character (by film's end) a note of nobility. Nowhere in the screenplay is he depicted as an outright fraud, despite attacks by a suspiciously motivated newspaper editor, and the apocryphal remark about "suckers" is never uttered. The film's creators, rather than show the audience how its forebears were repeatedly tricked by a skillful charlatan, chose to craft an historical fiction along formula lines and offer it under the guise of depicting the life of a famous showman. The film's positive response was followed, two years later, by the filmic lionizing of yet another showman--Florenz Ziegfeld.

CHAPTER III

THE ZIEGFELD SUCCESS

Florenz Ziegfeld, who had died in 1932, was a much more contemporary figure than Barnum or Lind, but his name had also come to signify in popular usage both a standard of comparison and a distinctive style of entertainment. The cycle of "backstage musicals" which was so active in the early 1930s had abated but not ceased by 1936, and thinly veiled fictional dramas based on the escapades of contemporary celebrities (RECKLESS, BROADWAY THROUGH A KEYHOLE, WHAT PRICE HOLLYWOOD?) were continuing in popularity, with the public actively participating in the guessing game as to whom the film was really about. THE GREAT ZIEGFELD, the two-million-dollar spectacular which, as we shall see, played a major role in defining the form of the show business biographical film, was in itself a combination and extension of these earlier ventures. The key innovation was the exploitation of the public's curiosity about celebrities within a formula which allowed for the concomitant attractions of popular music, choreographic spectacle, and the illusion of truth (real names and places) rather than fiction.

That the narrative was heavily fictionalized, despite the plethora of biographical detail to come, was implied by an introductory title card which read: "Suggested by romances and incidents in the life of America's greatest showman." This disclaimer was an "up front" announcement in large type, altogether different in tone from the standard "any similarity to actual institutions, places or persons, living or dead, is entirely coincidental," which began appearing in the fine print of most opening credits shortly after the first libel suits were filed against the film industry.

While this is to be an essentially generic analysis of

the films selected, concerned more with the synthetic world of the diegesis than with the historical lives of the real-life subjects, it must be noted for proper understanding of the filmic material that legal constraints and precedents were established early on, which prevented film makers from arbitrarily portraying real persons in photoplays. Costly damage settlements soon convinced the industry to obtain prior consent (via sworn affidavits and usually for the payment of a fee) from individuals before portraying them by name in a film. In filming biographical dramas with contemporary or near-contemporary settings, the rule of thumb in Hollywood became clear: obtain legal clearance or disguise the identities of the characters. The only exception to this rule was the relatively free hand allowed by the courts to film makers in the re-staging of legitimate, public news events. All private transactions and relationships had to be cleared with the persons portrayed, if they were still living.

If this could not be done (because the individuals in question held out for too much money or demanded unacceptable script changes), the film makers faced certain difficult choices: 1) omit the uncooperative persons from the story entirely; 2) keep them in the story but give them false names; or 3) combine two or more such persons into one composite character. Choice number one could lead to the filming of a biographical drama bearing little resemblance to the real life of the main character. Choice number two ran the risk of distracting the audience from the unfolding narrative by fostering excessive speculation if the disguised characters were highly recognizable from their actions and dialogue. Choice number three, while likely to arouse more confusion than suspicion, did allow for the simplifying of complex careers into concise dramatic form and proved the most popular of the three; film makers frequently opted for it in advance, thus saving themselves the trouble of locating and seeking clearance from the numerous minor figures who played some part in the real life story being dramatized.

Other factors leading to the fictionalization of screen biographies include the deliberate invention of dramatic episodes geared to stimulate favorable audience response and the outright granting of real-life persons' demands for script changes, particularly requests made by a story's main characters or their heirs. With these forces at work in the shaping of the narratives of many show-business biographical films, it is little wonder that some of the examples to be analyzed in later pages, while surprisingly accurate in period detail and historical time frame, tell almost nothing about the title figure's life as it really happened.

This study attempts to construct no hierarchy vaunting the "true" biographies over the "false" ones; rather it is designed to detect how this body of work interrelates, from example to example, building a mythic framework of success and failure in the diegetical world of "show business," crafted by the film makers and perceived by the public. Even when a film can be exposed through precise historical research to be patently false from start to finish, if it bears the trappings of truth (purporting to tell a celebrity's life story to a curious crowd), it may be mythic twin to a film which promises historical truth and delivers with uncanny accuracy. Neither veracity nor verisimilitude carry great significance in this analysis. Rather, it is the shared patterns of myth presented as history and covered by a common iconography which call for deeper investigation.

THE GREAT ZIEGFELD, assisted in no small measure by its three-hour running time, is an attempt to span nearly the whole of its central character's adult life. This stands in contrast to the film's two direct predecessors, which dramatized events from only a few years during which the protagonist ascended (with setbacks) to the top of his/her profession. The film opens with its credit sequence blazing forth from a series of electric signs designed to appear like those which used to adorn the tops of Broadway theatres, announcing the latest stage attractions. The title music is a medley of hit songs from Ziegfeld shows, played under the credits as if it were an overture to a stage musical. The parallels between THE GREAT ZIEGFELD and one of his own Broadway shows begin at this point and continue through to the musical reprise which accompanies the ethereal concluding sequence. Punctuated with lavish production numbers, hit songs and guest star appearances throughout its 179 minutes, THE GREAT ZIEGFELD is truly a filmic replication of the style in which Ziegfeld presented his famous revues and musical plays. Yet beneath the unique opulence and grandiosity of the physical production runs a narrative pattern of rise-and-fall dating back to the earliest quest myths, a pattern which became an integral part of many show business biographical films in the years following the phenomenal box-office success of this motion picture.

Exploding fireworks come into view at the conclusion of the credits, and a sign passes across the screen announc-

ing the 1893 Chicago World's Fair. The first glimpse we
get of the hero is in a show-business setting. Ziegfeld,
played by the forty-three-year-old William Powell but made
up to look as young as possible, is a carnival barker and
proprietor of his own side show. His direct competitor, a
barker named Billings, is attracting much more of the crowd
to his tent than Ziegfeld is drawing into his. The problem--Billings is running a "girlie" show, with the notorious
dancer Little Egypt swiveling her hips to the delight of many
more customers than Ziegfeld can attract with the weightlifting exploits of "Sandow the Strong Man." The dilemma
posited by the narrative is both simple and crucial. Ziegfeld is a failure because he is offering the public strength
instead of sex appeal. While walking down the midway with
Sandow, Ziegfeld recounts his (phallic) superstition that if
you touch an elephant's trunk and he immediately raises it,
then you're in for a run of good luck. Following Sandow and
Ziegfeld's encounter with an elephant who not only raises his
trunk but squirts water at Sandow in the process, the pair
ponder whether the public would like to touch Sandow's muscles while he is displaying his strength. Physical contact
with the customers, particularly ladies who faint when Sandow (dressed in a new, more sexually enhancing costume)
ripples his muscles for them, causes Ziegfeld's side show
to become a success. Ziegfeld has learned the crucial value
of sex appeal in attracting a crowd.

Significant facets of Ziegfeld's character are displayed
early in the narrative. While lunching with Billings, Ziegfeld pays extraordinary attention to Billings' lady friend
Claire, going so far as to criticize her wardrobe in detail
and suggest how she might make herself more attractive.
Billings tries to diminish Claire's growing interest in "Ziggy," as his friends call him, by warning, "You wouldn't like
him; he's up one day and down the next." Soon a romance
develops between Ziegfeld and Claire, but after he gives her
a ring he decides to take Sandow on a European tour.

Prior to his departure with Sandow, Ziegfeld pays a
visit to his father, Professor Ziegfeld, director of the Chicago Musical College. We learn that the younger Ziegfeld
has been something of a disappointment to his high-minded
parent, rejecting the world of classical music for the sawdust of the carnival. A diploma on the wall from Leipzig
University reveals that the professor is an old-world scholar,
and his sadness is compounded by his having no other son to
inherit and manage the prestigious school he has founded. A

third party to the poignant exchange between father and son is a little girl, about eight years old, to whom the professor has been giving a piano lesson when the prodigal arrives for an unexpected visit. The little girl, very likely a friend of the family since she is receiving instruction from the school's director, has a childhood crush on her teacher's son Florenz (called "Flo" when he is not called "Ziggy"). The child proclaims that when she grows up she intends to marry Flo. He demurs gently, explaining, "I'm the funniest kind of fellow; I like all the girls." Ziegfeld then shares with the eager child his grandest plan: "Someday I'm gonna take all the beautiful girls like you and put 'em all together ... and make pictures of them!" The professor, resigned to his son's commitment to culture on a less lofty plane, wishes him good luck on his tour with Sandow.

A montage sequence follows, with newspaper headlines lap-dissolving into shots of railroad cars, tracks, engines, and show-business activities. We learn that even before his tour extends to Europe, Ziegfeld is drawing huge crowds and making news in one American city after another by skillful staging of publicity stunts. When one San Francisco promoter's announced public fight between a lion and a bear threatens to upstage Sandow's opening night in a deluxe vaudeville theatre, Ziegfeld calls on the SPCA to stop the fight. Then the wily showman makes more headlines by announcing that Sandow will tackle the giant cat. This particular stunt comes a cropper when the lion is discovered to be tame, and Ziegfeld and Sandow leave town separately in disgrace. While Sandow soon lands a role in Lillian Russell's Broadway production of "As You Like It," Ziegfeld sails for Europe, his plans uncertain. The notion of the master showman as gambler, first outlined in the uneven fortunes of P. T. Barnum, is echoed in THE GREAT ZIEGFELD, presaged by Billings' characterization of Ziggy as "up one day and down the next."

Billings, who acts as a composite of many other rival promoters who matched wits with Ziegfeld, reenters the narrative during the ocean crossing, and a transactional pattern between the two begins to emerge. First it was Ziegfeld's drawing away Billings' crowd by matching female allure with male sex appeal. Then it was Ziegfeld's winning the heart of Billings' girl friend Claire, only to depart quickly in pursuit of greater show-business success. No sooner have the rivals met on board the ocean liner than Ziegfeld starts pumping Billings for information about the latter's plans to sign up a new entertainer about whom he has been boasting but has not named. Proving himself to be as devious as he is ambitious, Ziegfeld hires away Billings' valet, a dutiful Britisher named Sidney, and Sidney sets about making a "gentleman" out of the over-eager Ziegfeld.

After the boat docks in England, Ziegfeld learns by tricking a hotel doorman that Billings is planning to sign up a French songstress named Anna Held. Trying to beat his rival, Ziegfeld charms his way into the performer's dressing room at the London theatre where she is appearing to great public acclaim. Although he has recently lost what remained of his fortune through gambling, Ziegfeld has lost none of his nerve. Warning Anna Held that unless she embarks upon an American career under his guidance she is doomed to failure, he observes, "Foreigners come into New York every day, and what happens to them? They open at Tony Pastor's theatre and they get the hook!" Ziegfeld then offers to merchandise Held into a national byword: "Why, there'll be Anna Held corsets, Anna Held shoes...." Although she is impressed by his flowery and enthusiastic presentation, she becomes furious when he admits that he has no money to match Billings' formal offer of a ten-thousand-dollar contract. Nevertheless, as is implied by the opening of the following sequence, she succumbs to his seductive rhetoric and makes her American debut at the Herald Square Theatre in a play called "The Parlour Match," produced by Ziegfeld on borrowed money.

The Ziegfeld we have seen so far is a dreamer, entranced by an ideal of feminine beauty but driven by an overpowering desire to succeed in entertaining the public. He is a charmer, a fast talker, and a devious conniver. Like Barnum he has a special conception of what he thinks his audience will respond to most favorably, and he devotes all of his time and energy to realizing that vision in the grandest terms possible. Yet despite his burgeoning ambition, there is no malice in him. The film makers have crafted a character with whom one can sympathize even as he tricks his way to the top. Perhaps there is a mythic quality in such a hero which puts him, if not above the bounds of morality, at least outside the strictures of fair play. After all, his goal is to entertain the public much more than it is merely to enrich himself.

Anna Held's opening night is indicated in the film by shots of the exterior of the theatre where "The Parlour

Match" is playing. A stream of patrons exits, indicating the play's conclusion, and audience comments are overheard, identifying the VIPs who have been in attendance. Famous bankers and industrialists are in the crowd, including "Diamond Jim" Brady. Lillian Russell is seen leaving the theatre just a few steps ahead of Brady; surprisingly, she is accompanied by some other gentleman. The VIPs' comments are not very favorable. Some complain that Held's accent was too thick to understand. Others remark about the large number of empty seats in the house.

The implications of this sequence are complex, arising from the air of authenticity generated by the use of the names of contemporary historical personages. A direct parallel with THE MIGHTY BARNUM would relate this sequence to Jenny Lind's debut. In both instances the cream of New York society is in attendance; each occasion marks the hero's first bid for recognition by the "best people." Both events are less than successful, but the public disdain, which crushes Barnum's societal aspirations (due to his behavior at the reception), only spurs Ziegfeld to try harder to please the taste-makers. The essential difference between the Barnum and Ziegfeld characters surfaces at this common point. Barnum aimed too high, was brought low, and went on to success on a middle plane (circus for the masses). Ziegfeld, as we shall see, continues to aim higher and higher with each passing year.

The poor reception given Anna Held does not persuade Ziegfeld to close her show, even though it continues to lose more of its producer's borrowed money with each performance. Instead he embarks upon a crafty publicity campaign designed to increase public curiosity over his French discovery. Ziegfeld orders hundreds of gallons of milk delivered to Held's hotel suite and spreads the rumor that she takes daily milk baths to preserve her beauty. After these stories appear in the press, he refuses to pay the enormous milk bill, thus generating still more news coverage. To improve Held's accent Ziegfeld employs a vocal coach for her, and during the sequence of her practicing with the instructor we learn that she is falling in love with her producer. A production number follows this revelation, with Anna Held singing "It's Delightful to Be Married." Because she had complained to Ziegfeld that she wanted to dress in costumes as fancy as those adorning Lillian Russell, he counters her request by "putting eight Lillian Russells on the stage" behind Held as she sings. (The eight are chorus girls dressed in replicas of the famous Russell hourglass figure costume with matching blonde wigs in the upswept Russell style.) Ziegfeld has thus shown his initial devotion to Anna Held and her career, sparing no expense to make her a major star of the Broadway stage. As we see, her response to his personal attentiveness and concern is to become romantically infatuated with her mentor.

The narrative omits any depiction of Ziegfeld actively courting Held or even becoming aware of her private feelings for him. Instead the story skips ahead to the first anniversary of their marriage, announced to the viewer by means of a congratulatory telegram read aloud by Held in her dressing room following her performance in the still-running show. Accompanying the message are expensive pieces of jewelry, presents from husband to wife to mark the occasion. Held visits the chorus girls' communal dressing room (she is still quite naive and child-like) to share her excitement over the expensive presents. All the girls are joyously exuberant but one. The narrative halts at this point for a specialty number, performed by eccentric dancer Ray Bolger in the character of a stagehand who yearns to be a performer. While sweeping the stage after the show, he breaks into a dance routine featuring the dizzy and broken-leg steps which were Bolger's trademarks in numerous Broadway shows of the 1930s and beyond. A phantom orchestra (unseen and not identified) accompanies him--the first use of such a convention in this otherwise more realistically framed narrative.

The story resumes with Ziegfeld discussing financial matters with a man named Sampson. Although never directly introduced to the audience, Sampson is, as we learn gradually through his reappearances in subsequent scenes, Ziegfeld's business manager. Anna Held enters the conversation, shows off her new jewelry to Sampson, and she and Ziegfeld go off to talk in her dressing room. This is the first time we see the pair together following their marriage, and already Ziegfeld is tiring of what has become his first successful Broadway show. Held assumes he is tiring of her as well, and her response to his discussing plans for a new show is a mixture of anger and disappointment. Moments earlier she had exclaimed, "Sometimes I think I'm too happy!" After learning that Ziegfeld does not want her in his next production, she suspects their relationship is doomed. The interrelatedness of private and public passions in the Ziegfeld character, implied in this sequence, becomes overt in the next sequence.

In the Manhattan office of Klaw and Erlanger, producer-backers of some of the most lavish theatrical events of the time, Ziegfeld outlines his plans for a new kind of stage revue. He describes it as basically a girlie show, but with much higher aspirations than the regular fare in burlesque houses, or even on the legitimate stage of the day. (The narrative has been vague as to exactly how many years have passed since the story began in 1893.) Ziegfeld speaks of his intentions to dress his girls in costumes of the finest silk and lace, "not for the bald heads in the front row, but for the ladies in the back." Then, as if struck by a sudden inspiration, he proclaims what will be the unifying theme of the show--"Glorifying the American Girl." His title for the new revue is "The Ziegfeld Follies."

Ziegfeld's introduction to Klaw and Erlanger has been arranged by one of their top employees, who just happens to be Ziegfeld's old rival, Billings. Even though he has numerous reasons to resent Ziegfeld, Billings is portrayed as recognizing Ziegfeld's talent for attracting and pleasing a crowd. Billings dutifully supports the plans of his nemesis and helps win the vital Klaw and Erlanger backing for the Follies.

A theatrical marquee shot opens the next sequence, with the sign announcing the New Amsterdam Theatre's engagement of the Ziegfeld Follies, starring Will Rogers and Eddie Cantor. A great amount of factual condensation occurs at this point in the narrative, giving the viewer the impression that nearly all the famous performers discovered and promoted by Ziegfeld made their initial appearances in the first year's edition of what was to become his annual revue. Shots of the opening night crowd milling into the lobby follow, with patrons stopping to gaze at oil portraits of the "Ziegfeld Girls" displayed on the walls. On stage we see an actor (in blackface and with white horn-rimmed glasses) who is supposed to be Eddie Cantor. Clapping his white-gloved hands and prancing in the famous Cantor style, he sings "If You Knew Susie." The voice is also an imitation. Within the bounds of a dramatic re-creation for film, his performance may be no more false than the portrayal of other real individuals by actors in this and the two previous features covered by this study. However, the real Eddie Cantor was very much alive and in the public eye at the time of THE GREAT ZIEGFELD's release. Audience comparisons of the real with the simulation become inevitable at this point. An underlying dialectic between the two perceptions is thus introduced in this film and, as we shall see, continues as the formula is repeated and expanded upon by film makers in the years which follow.

Shots of backstage commotion accompany the Cantor number as other performers prepare for their acts. A stage manager is heard to call out the name of Bert Williams (a Ziegfeld star comedian and a black man who nevertheless did his songs and jokes in blackface), but Williams is never seen. "Shine on Harvest Moon" is heard in the background as the next act takes the stage, but they are only seen in long shot from the wings. Amid the backstage hubbub someone mentions Bayes and Norworth, the vaudeville headliners. The viewer is left to make the connection, which is dependent upon the knowledge that "Harvest Moon" was the team's long-time theme song. A costume merchant appears in the wings, demanding payment from Sampson (a plot device greatly used in the putting-on-a-show film musicals of the early 1930s). Meanwhile Ziegfeld has a dressing room conference with Will Rogers, the cowboy philosopher-comic. Rogers is portrayed by a close lookalike, and as was the case with the Cantor character, his voice is supplied by an offscreen mimic. The Rogers character expresses his uncertainty about appearing on stage, and Ziegfeld reassures him. Rogers professes humility as to his expertise on contemporary affairs, explaining, "All I know is what I read in the papers."

This integration of a famous phrase or slogan into what is ostensibly spontaneous conversation (cf. Ziegfeld's discussion with Klaw and Erlanger) epitomizes the screenplay's deliberate attempts to exploit material with which the audience is likely to be familiar, even to the point of structuring dialogue to contain easily identifiable points of reference. The aforementioned dialectic between perceptions of the real and the simulated sometimes yields the most virulent alienation among certain viewers (witness the critical disdain of show-business biographical films in general), and the employment of familiar phraseology is one of several narrative strategies to ameliorate possible viewer hostility. That this can be done with visible lack of subtlety (albeit a subjective perception) prevents at least some film makers from relying heavily on this specific device.

Rogers had been dead barely a year when THE GREAT ZIEGFELD first appeared, and his immense popularity, amounting almost to reverence (he was once seriously considered by the bosses as a presidential candidate), made his inclusion in the narrative both an essential and a highly delicate maneuver.

Any widely perceived disparity between William Powell's portrayal of Ziegfeld and the actual showman, although he is the central figure of the film, was a less crucial problem, Ziegfeld never having been a performer. The mass of the movie-going public could only compare the screen image with memories of journalistic accounts of his activities and a few published photos. Since there was a basic similarity of facial structure and profile between Powell and Ziegfeld, the casting of Powell actually assisted the film's illusion, abetted by the skilled craftsmen in MGM's makeup department.

The Ziegfeld Follies, however, were widely known. Memories of the original stage shows, the touring shows, the star performers who went on to individual success and the presentations offered by other showmen in the "Ziegfeld tradition" were still fresh in the minds of the public. It was to this conjunction of imagery that the film had to be most faithful in order to reap the benefits of exploiting the favorably familiar.

Although the narrative patterns of fiction can most easily be traced if one looks for the outlines of a quest myth and a seasonally identified time frame, when dealing with a decidedly less linear form of popular diversion such as the stage spectacle the emerging patterns can sometimes group themselves into concentric circles instead. If we think of THE GREAT ZIEGFELD as a conventional narrative (one man's quest for beauty, realized in its ultimate form on the "Great White Way") overlaid with the circular structure of the stage spectacle (specialty acts of wide variety surrounding a dazzling series of tableux vivants), then the cynosure of the film arrives with Ziegfeld's realization of his Follies dream. Condensing several years of successive Follies presentations into one opening night, the frenetic backstage activity and star impersonations culminate in an elaborate production number set to the song, "A Pretty Girl Is Like a Melody."

Staged for the opening night audience in the film but explored intimately for the film's audience by a widely swooping and craning motion picture camera, this set piece offers a series of tableux enacted on the steps of a huge conical

tower. The tower, swathed in plush tapestries which are
gradually lifted to display each successive group of costumed
players, revolves as the camera ascends from setting to setting, the style of the musical accompaniment changing as the
costumes and decor change. Scenes from opera ("Madame
Butterfly"), classical forms of dance (a minuet at the French
court), and more modern attire and melodies (a Gershwin
figure plays part of the "Rhapsody in Blue") appear on the
staircase as the camera reaches the pinnacle. In a most
curious vocal transposition, singer-actor Dennis Morgan uses
singer Alan Jones' voice to address the "Pretty Girl" song
to the bevy of Ziegfeld Girls who throng the staircase, but a
close shot of the top girl reveals who it is that epitomizes
Ziegfeld's ideal of beauty--a chorus girl named Audrey. The
actress portraying her (and here is the peculiar linkage phenomenon again) is Virginia Bruce, who portrayed Jenny Lind
in THE MIGHTY BARNUM.

    Audrey is the same girl who was singularly unemotional when Anna Held was showing off her new necklace and
diamond bracelet. Her only response had been to coldly declare, "I'd sell my soul for diamonds like that." The viewer is left to conclude that she had subsequently carried out
the threat (after a fashion), for in the sequence following the
"Pretty Girl" number we see her basking in expensive jewelry courtesy of her boss. Anna Held visits backstage and
catches a glimpse of the attention now being showered on
Audrey by Ziegfeld. The stage is set, figuratively, for the
breakup of Ziegfeld's first marriage.

    Again we do not see Ziegfeld actively pursuing a girl;
we are only given clues that he has formed a new attachment.
The manipulation of audience sympathy is a particularly difficult business for biographical film makers in regard to divorce proceedings. The easiest solution is simply to omit
first, second, or third wives from the screenplay and rely
on the formula of boy-meets-girl only once in the course of
a screen lifetime. In cases where early, unsuccessful marriages are too well-known to ignore and there is no libel obstacle (all clearances having been obtained), the breakup of
the couple need not be portrayed as stemming from the faithless nature of either spouse. Irreconcilable (career-linked)
differences or the dangerous interposition of an outside,
third-party force can be blamed. The character of Audrey,
a disguised version of Ziegfeld "favorite" Lillian Lorraine,
is invested with just such a divisive force, almost Faustian
in its cold determination and underscored by Ziegfeld's

obsessive weakness for ideal beauty and by the extraordinary attractiveness of former Ziegfled showgirl Virginia Bruce.

Although THE GREAT ZIEGFELD, with its revue-like infrastructure, has production numbers spotted throughout its lengthy narrative, not all the numbers are halts in the flow of vital action or diversions from the dramatic points being made. The songs require closer scrutiny in their direct bearing on the plot. Anna Held is seen singing "It's Delightful to Be Married" immediately before we learn that she has been wed to her producer for a whole year. The "A Pretty Girl Is Like a Melody" lyric culminates in establishing who has taken Held's place in Ziegfeld's affections.

In the original theatrical release version of the film, an intermission occurred at the conclusion of this song, with the action picking up just prior to a series of production numbers taking place in a rooftop cabaret operated by Ziegfeld above the New Amsterdam Theatre. Ray Bolger, in his character of a stage-struck stagehand, was seen in a specialty number just preceding the "Pretty Girl" spectacle. Now he returns to do another bit in the rooftop show. The lyric of the opening number, sung in chorus by a bevy of Ziegfeld Girls holding crepe paper streamers and riding movable platforms which thrust out into the audience and back to the proscenium stage, comments on how Audrey has become the star of the rooftop show. The song's title: "You Gotta Pull Strings."

Another number, more in the style of Busby Berkeley's dance routines at Warner Brothers, follows immediately, giving explicit visual emphasis on "how" to pull those figurative strings. Dozens of Ziegfeld Girls appear on stage, each clad in undergarments and doing identical dance routines on top of individual beds. The accompanying song is "You (Gee, But You're Wonderful)." A dress parade climaxes the activity, with the girls modeling an array of exotic and sequined revue costumes, replete with oriental and peacock-spread headdresses. Audrey, the centerpiece of this display, receives a thunderous round of applause. A shot of Ziegfeld and his wife, watching the show from the back of the cabaret, reveals him to be graying at the temples, visual shorthand in movies that a character is entering middle age. That Anna Held has not mistaken the show's implicit message is demonstrated by this exchange: Ziegfeld: "Lovely, isn't it?" Held: "Yes, isn't she!"

Although Ziegfeld's extra-marital activities are given an oblique and somewhat excused treatment, his deviousness in business matters continues to be sketched with bold strokes. During the altercation with the anxious costume supplier, Ziegfeld uses verbal sleight of hand to convince the merchant that the showman was doing him a favor by using the costumes at all, let alone pay for them at some later date. After the conclusion of the rooftop show, Audrey, tipsy from drinking, makes an impromptu and embarrassing curtain speech, thanking Ziegfeld for backing the show. Acknowledging the tribute and trying to divert the audience's attention, he offers a toast to a guest in the crowd, an actress named Sally Manners, who is appearing in a hit show elsewhere and has signed up with Billings. Says Ziegfeld as he asks her to take a bow, "I hope Billings has you under a long contract." A montage of publicity photos and newspaper headlines then dissolves into view, indicating that Ziegfeld has just signed Sally Manners to appear in his next show.

Although the character of Sally Manners may be a composite of several performers whose services Ziegfeld obtained by buying them away from other producers, the actress who plays her in the film does bear a definite resemblance to Marilyn Miller, a major Ziegfeld star. The viewer's possible association of the fictional actress with the real life star is intensified by the fact that Marilyn Miller's greatest success was as the lead in Ziegfeld's production of "Sally." Thus, even in the case of fictional or composite characterizations, the film is making bids for audience recognition.

The next sequence sketches in more lines of the Ziegfeld character, now fast approaching the height of his career. Relating to the ambitious, restless young man we saw discussing his plans with his music-teacher father, the sequence recalls that early dialogue by reintroducing Mary Lou, the little girl who was a third party to the conversation. Now she has grown up and Ziegfeld does not recognize her, although he roguishly feigns they "must have met somewhere before" and starts to flirt with her as if she were just

---

Opposite, two scenes from THE GREAT ZIEGFELD (1936), starring William Powell. Top, note the elephant statues in Ziegfeld's office. Bottom, Ziegfeld with Fanny Brice, playing herself. Photos courtesy of Wisconsin Center for Film and Theater Research.

another showgirl begging for a part in his next production. (Ziegfeld's office is emphatically decorated with at least nine elephant statuettes, all with their trunks raised.) He is taken aback, almost as if seized by the hint of an incest taboo, when she reveals her identity, and he resists her amorous attentions by protesting that he can't get mixed up with other women because he is married. Her reply ironically points up a central tension in the Ziegfeld life story and a major obstacle faced by the film's authors in making the character sympathetic to a mass audience of the 1930s. As she fondles the man she has idolized for years, she coos, "Being married in New York doesn't mean anything, does it?" Ziegfeld's startled response is to brusquely send her out of the office with the promise of an audition.

Yet another bid for the familiar follows with the introduction of the uniquely gifted "torch singer" and Yiddish comedienne Fanny Brice. The sequence is played for comedy and contrast, with Ziegfeld attending a sleazy burlesque house upon the recommendation of his business manager. There Ziegfeld views an incredibly unattractive and inept chorus line populated by fat and blowsy women who sing off key while prancing about in hideously grotesque costumes. This presentation, no less voyeuristic but a far cry from the beauty and grace of a Ziegfeld show, is capped with a performance by Fanny Brice, the show's headliner. At this point the film departs from its so far consistent practice of dramatic re-creation through impersonation. The surprise (although not so much if one has read the credits) is that Fanny Brice is played by Fanny Brice. Here then, is the ultimate in authentic characterization. From a strictly narrative point of view it makes no difference, but iconographically the shift in the intensity of visual references is marked. It could be argued that this is merely an associative and time-linked difference, quite meaningless when the film is viewed by an audience not familiar enough with Fanny Brice to note the extreme authenticity of her portrayal. However, so many of the films yet to be studied rest so strongly upon roughly contemporary associative references as their <u>raison d'être</u> (exploiting the public's curiosity about show business figures with whom it is already somewhat familiar) that to deny the significance of congruent performances (playing oneself) is to be blind to the life-simulating processes of the narrative film in its most heightened state of transcending the boundary between the diegesis and the real world. The inevitable falsity of dramatically structuring what were once the coincidences of a life pattern or tangential events prevents this act of transcendence from extending to encompass an entire film, but in moments where it does occur, such as the introduction of Fanny Brice, the foundation of associative references upon which a film like THE GREAT ZIEGFELD rests is both altered and strengthened.

Ziegfeld, attending the burlesque show with his attentive Audrey, displays his egalitarian view of show business with the comment, "Some of the greatest stars have come from places like this." Backstage he introduces himself to Brice and offers her an expensive fur coat as a gift. Unable to believe that such a high-class showman as Ziegfeld could be interested in her (she had earlier been joking with her dressing room-mate about a stocking salesman who called himself Belasco), Brice concludes that Ziegfeld is a fur merchant and tries to buy the coat from him. She is not convinced that he is genuine until she later receives a note from him refunding her money and inviting her to be in the Follies. The sequence is played for laughs, and it stands out as a rare comic episode in a film which generates most of its humor from ironic observations of the world of Broadway and Forty-Second Street.

Ziegfeld's sharply defined ideas about costumes and feminine appeal are underlined again when Brice starts rehearsals for the Follies. He objects strongly to her fancy black dress with a long train. The show's costume designer (an effeminate stock character, familiar from numerous putting-on-a-show film musicals) obsequiously removes the dress's train and frills so that Brice can do her torch songs (sad and submissive, dedicated to the memory of a departed man) in more humble attire.

A business conference in Ziegfeld's office reveals his plans to move from plotless revues into operettas and musical comedies. One of the men he confers with is introduced as Victor Herbert (yet another invocation of the familiar, the famous, and in Herbert's case the beloved, as judged by popular taste at the time of the film's release). Ziegfeld explains that for a performer as special as Sally Manners he wants plot, as well as glamor. A songwriter (supposedly Jerome Kern) sits down at the piano and plays a song which is being considered for the new show. As he renders "Look for the Silver Lining," a lap-dissolve introduces the opening night of "Sally" with a milling throng of patrons entering under the theatre marquee which announces the show. The identification process is complete. Now there can be no doubt that Sally Manners is Marilyn Miller. The song which became her theme, so identified with her that it became the title of her own film biography in 1949 (LOOK FOR THE SILVER LINING), has been taken up by the theatre orchestra.

Backstage we see Ziegfeld as the eternal gambler once more. The costume and scenery suppliers are after him for money and he has to bluff his way along until the box-office receipts can restore him to solvency. At this moment of minor crisis the narrative tackles the delicate task of confirming for Anna Held her suspicions about Ziegfeld's possible infidelity while allowing viewers to believe the man to be either innocent or guilty. Depending on the strictness of each viewer's moral code, the Ziegfeld character could have lost valuable audience sympathy here, thereby jeopardizing the picture's commercial success. However, the possibility of Ziegfeld being perceived a "heel" (to use 1930s popular jargon) is obviated. Held notices Ziegfeld kissing Audrey backstage and believes the worst. We see a lengthier version of the incident. Audrey has been imbibing and is visibly intoxicated. Ziegfeld shows a fatherly concern for her, sternly admonishing her to avoid ruining her promising career through too much drinking. He kisses her out of solicitude, to cajole her to promise she will try to stay sober in the future. Confronted with his wife's sudden intrusion into the scene, Ziegfeld is at a loss to explain his behavior in the instant she allows him to respond, and she is enraged. Newspaper headlines fill the screen: "Anna Held Leaves Ziegfeld."

The film's narrative has thus provided ample suggestions of Ziegfeld's infidelity, but in the crucial confrontation scene the audience (to say nothing of the Hays Office censors of the day) is allowed to believe that his first marriage dissolved because of a misunderstanding. This ambivalence and calculated uncertainty regarding the moral flaws of the central character would not have been necessary had this been a purely fictional drama with a show-business setting. Personal vices and weaknesses of character (at least as perceived by the "moral guardians" of the era in which this film was released) can be found in the heroes of many other screen dramas of the time, of course, but there they appear at the behest of an author who invents them, or who borrows from and enhances earlier mythic patterns and personages, for a dramatic purpose. In creating THE GREAT ZIEGFELD the authors had to dramatize the life of a specific and well-known individual whose private life had overlapped into the public record. They faced the choice of either grossly falsifying his story by omitting his first marriage and his reported affairs with many showgirls, or depicting these relationships in a condensed and ambivalent manner which would not jeopardize the then-crucial element of audience sympathy. The enforced morality and audience expectations of the era mitigated strongly against a third option: namely, portraying Ziegfeld as an insatiable satyr who catered to the lascivious tastes of a repressed public under a thin veneer of expensive frills and cultural pretensions. The unflattering show business biographical film was still nearly two decades in the future.

In THE GREAT ZIEGFELD the central character is a heroic figure, driven by ambition, to be sure, but lacking in the malice, cruelty, indifference or blatant moral turpitude which in 1936 could invite audience revulsion and disapproval. The Ziegfeld character is witty, charming, debonair and, most of all, highly appreciative of other people's talent. Nearly all the major stars whose careers he boosted were either still performing at the time of the film's release or fresh in the public's memory from earlier triumphs. The name Ziegfeld was like Sterling on silver. It represented a widely admired standard of what was popularly considered to be quality entertainment. To expose the man behind the name as sex-obsessed, ruthless and manipulative (as done by his most recent biographer in print) would have been an unwelcome insult to his admiring public. The existing perceptions of a mass audience are more efficiently exploited when reinforced (people willingly cooperate in the strengthening of their illusions) than when brutally challenged. The subversion and alteration of mass perceptions is much too gradual a process for a single film to tackle. However, once set in motion, by a complex mix of societal forces which may include numerous films over several years, such a changing of public perceptions (and this is happening all the time) may be an ongoing dynamic or process which can also be exploited (for a favorable response) by an individual film released at a convenient point in time. In 1936 it was much more advantageous to bolster a popular and heroic conception of a show-business legend, as the phenomenal success of THE GREAT ZIEGFELD (including an Oscar for Best Picture) testifies.

Following the archetypal formula of a protagonist's rise, fall, evanescence and renewal, the film continues the ascendant phase of Ziegfeld's life (after conveniently ambiguous circumstances have disposed of his first wife) by quickly introducing the woman who was to become "the great love of his life." First, however, the troublesome Audrey is jettisoned as well. On the morning after his row with Anna, Ziegfeld mopes about his lavish apartment, shaken by the fact that she has left him. Sitting down to the piano, he picks out the melody to "It's Delightful to Be Married" (again a popular song commenting upon the narrative, this time in an ironic mode), and is surprised by the sudden intrusion of a very angry Audrey. The perplexed showman, surrounded by a menagerie of plaster elephants, has little defense for the tirade she delivers. Outraged over losing the title role in "Sally" to Sally Manners, Audrey smashes a large elephant-shaped planter and departs for good.

Ziegfeld's financial brinksmanship leads him to the eve of yet another opening night without the cash to raise the curtain. Once more his respectful adversary Billings helps raise the cash to make another successful Ziegfeld show possible. A brief montage of theatre facades and electric signs reveals that his string of hit shows is continuing, the latest being "Kid Boots," starring Eddie Cantor.

The next visual is a shot of an invitation to a dress ball at the Astor Hotel. Ziegfeld attends, surrounded by the "cream of New York society," although unlike P. T. Barnum's foray into this territory, Ziegfeld's presence at such a soirée is peaceful and even fortuitous; he is treated as an equal. In the time which had passed between Barnum's era and Ziegfeld's, the upper-class prejudice against show people may have moderated. Even if such a feeling still existed among New York's "400" the film does not acknowledge it. Rather, the narrative offers us a Ziegfeld who is very much at home in the haunts of the very rich, many of whom have been front-row and box-seat patrons of his string of hit shows for several years. That the years have indeed been passing is indicated by Ziegfeld's changed appearance at the party. He is now much more gray-haired than before, but his eye for the ladies is undiminished. "Who's the gorgeous redhead?" he asks. The answer is--Billie Burke, a beautiful young actress. During a "Paul Jones" dance he arranges to end up with her as his partner each time the circulating music stops. The romance of Ziegfeld and Billie Burke, well-chronicled by the press and firmly implanted in the public memory circa 1936, allows the narrative to sketch the couple's courtship very briefly, and their marriage follows as no great surprise.

The altered time sequence (the real-life couple were married several years before the opening of KID BOOTS) is only one of numerous historical inaccuracies in the narrative, but such minutiae appear to have done little to detract from the public response to the story. As we shall see, chronological precision, absent from even the earliest films under study, would remain a low-priority item in the scores of show business biographical films to come. The underlying mythic structure and the invocation of familiarity would be far more important.

Ziegfeld's first conversation with Burke following their meeting on the dance floor is carried out on a secluded terrace, the smitten showman hesitant to reveal his identity for fear that his name will conjure up too many distracting, preconceived notions. We are at last seeing Ziegfeld the man, unsettled by his own public image, anxious to avoid the process by which his fame precedes him and makes it difficult to relate to others on a one-to-one basis. His success has actually isolated him; he is curious to learn what people outside his professional circle of entertainment figures say and think about him. No sooner has the terrace conversation swung around to "third person" talk of the famous Flo Ziegfeld than Billings interrupts and calls his old rival by name. We learn that Billings is the lady's escort for the evening; Ziegfeld has done his best to steal her away.

A moonlit, lakeside conversation between Ziegfeld and Burke a few days later reveals that they have been seeing each other secretly. A key passage underscoring Ziegfeld's lack of malice in the ending of his first marriage occurs when Burke inquires, "Didn't Anna Held take up a few of your years?" Ziegfeld: "Yes, she was a wonderful woman." Burke: "I love you for saying that." A newspaper headline dissolves into view announcing the Ziegfeld-Burke marriage.

The delicate matter of avoiding blame for Ziegfeld's divorce is tackled again by the film makers in the famous telephone scene which reputedly won Louise Rainer her first Academy Award. After reading of the marriage in the newspaper, Anna Held (Rainer) chokes back tears and tells her maid to get Ziegfeld on the phone. Held explains that she wants to congratulate him on the happy occasion. The conversation is shown only from Held's side; we do not hear Ziegfeld's responses. She tells him how happy she is for him and his new bride, forcing her voice to sound cheerful while we see a profound sadness appear on her face, overtake her composure, and convulse her whole body in grief as she ends the conversation and hangs up the phone. The sequence thus explains that she still loves him but has waited too long to offer her forgiveness and try for a reconciliation. In a final, magnanimous gesture she has given her blessing to his new union, freeing him from any residual guilt for their breakup. Two crucial elements, audience sympathy and the approval of the Production Code (which forbade promoting divorce as an easy solution to marital disharmony), are thereby reinforced one final time before the film's conclusion.

Ziegfeld's ultimate success, in the personal as well as the professional sphere of experience, is portrayed in the family sequence, which takes place in a Christmas setting. Flo and Billie are at home with their child, a little girl (no more than four or five) named Patricia. An ornate tree lights the Ziegfeld's living room, and presents are scattered all around. The proud father playfully asks his daughter, "Hasn't Santa Claus brought the elephant yet?" (The pachyderm imagery extends even into the Christmas celebration to stamp it as yet another link in the Ziegfeld chain of "good luck.") Husband asks wife to open her gifts, and she happily unwraps more items which conform with the high and customary standard of Ziegfeld largesse--diamond-encrusted jewelry and a new fur coat. Little Patricia's presents include a complete miniature-circus set, and her father identifies the various figures for her, relating them to his earlier associates on the carnival circuit. Says Ziegfeld, "Here's the strong man; we'll call him Sandow...." He identifies the bareback rider figure as specialty dancer Harriet Hoctor, and a circular wipe introduces the film's final production number, a circus spectacular with the real Harriet Hoctor flanked by chorus girls in circus costumes, a few dozen trained dogs, and a parade of circus horses appearing magically from the center ring floor.

At the conclusion of the number, as has been the case with each previous musical and choreographic interlude, a camera shot tracks backwards to frame the ensemble by means of the proscenium arch, thus identifying what we have seen as a stage presentation, a physical realization of what may have started as a vision born in Ziegfeld's imagination. The concluding shot of this number reveals the proud showman in the back of the theatre, as before, only now his companion is his second wife, Billie Burke.

The Ziegfeld Success / 39

Christmas with the Ziegfelds: Flo, Patricia, and Billie (William Powell, Joan Holland, Myrna Loy). Photo courtesy of Wisconsin Center for Film and Theater Research.

Shortly before the death of the real-life Ziegfeld, his wife had returned to acting, primarily in motion pictures, and by 1936 Burke had become a very familiar presence to moviegoers. But it was only later, after her 1937 appearance in TOPPER, that she became typecast in roles of flighty, whimsical and scatterbrained upper-class society matrons, complete with twittering voice and anxious mannerisms. The invocation of the familiar, as practiced in creating the screen portrayal of Billie Burke as a young woman, relies therefore not on mimicry, but on a previous cinema pairing of William Powell with a particular leading lady. In THE THIN MAN Powell had scored a huge hit with Myrna Loy as his co-star, and there was much public praise of the pair as the "perfect couple." Loy's performance as Billie Burke therefore benefits from resonances of a previous and immense popular success.

The cyclical pattern of rise and fall now shifts to the down slope of Ziegfeld's career. From the zenith of a happy second marriage, a child, and a string of hit shows on Broadway, the narrative turns to setbacks and failure. The practices of condensation and selective omission, used in varying degrees throughout the picture (so as to fit many years of activity into the running time of a feature film), are now applied to Ziegfeld's life with great intensity. A newspaper headline, seen in Variety (as are most of the headlines used as visuals), fills the screen, stating that the extravagance of Ziegfeld's shows is causing him severe financial problems. The accompanying story goes on to explain that Ziegfeld's refusal to sacrifice quality for quantity (he won't put more than one road company of a show on tour) is making it impossible to recoup the enormous costs of his stage spectaculars. The implication of such criticism is that Ziegfeld is almost martyring himself financially in order to deliver only the very best entertainment (by his standards) to the public.

A sequence in a barbershop gives a humorous touch to Ziegfeld's predicament, lightening the seriousness of it for the moment as well as illustrating his residual energy despite the passage of time. While he has his face wrapped in hot towels and is waiting for a shave, several other customers read about Ziegfeld's declining fortunes in the paper and begin discussing his downfall. With such expressions as "He's all through" and "He's washed up," the men indicate the quicksilver nature of public opinion--how the crowd can cheer a hero one day and boo him when he seems to be going out of fashion. Ziegfeld tears off his mask of towels, accuses the startled customers of trying to "bury him," and vows that within a year he'll be back on Broadway (apparently he has nothing running at present) with four hit shows playing simultaneously. The Ziegfeld we see emerge from the barber chair is now totally gray; how many years have passed since we last saw him is not specified, but his energy certainly seems undiminished.

At home with Billie Burke, Ziegfeld recounts the barbershop incident, seeking sympathy from the one who has been his faithful companion through all the "good years." Visibly depressed over the downturn in his fortunes, he pays her an odd compliment: "You know what makes me admire you? It's your sublime superiority." It seems that the "great" Ziegfeld of the title, long accustomed to being the center of other people's attentions, reserves his greatest admiration for the one person in his life who does not live

The Ziegfeld Success / 41

in constant awe of him and his success. Burke reassures him, suggesting that all he needs to return to the top of his profession is a little more of the courage which had sustained him from the beginning. "Don't be afraid of yourself," she tells him, and he promises, "I won't be afraid." This is the closest the film comes actually to moralizing or giving an overt "point" to Ziegfeld's career. Much of his theatrical wizardry and success had earlier been laid to his obsession with ideal female beauty and his compulsion to glorify and share it with the public because, as he said, "I love all the girls." Now we are told that obsession isn't enough; courage is necessary too. The narrative has turned from pathological case study to heroic struggle. Ziegfeld's quest for beauty becomes noble as well as compulsive.

Ziegfeld's prediction comes true very quickly (in filmic time, not real time, for no dates or years have been supplied to the viewer since the narrative began). A montage of electric signs reveals that four of his best-remembered stage productions are running at major New York theatres. None of them are Follies-type revues; all are musical plays. "Rio Rita" is playing at the Majestic; "Whoopie" is at the New Amsterdam; "The Three Musketeers" is running at the Lyric, and "Showboat" is on the boards at the theatre named for its owner--the Ziegfeld. Under each shot of a sign we hear a few bars of a hit song from the advertised show: the title tunes from the first two plus "We Are the Musketeers" and "Old Man River." Even though each show and song are given only the briefest of inclusions in the film, the invocation of the familiar is functioning at a peak level of intensity. Ziegfeld's comeback is an accomplished fact.

As both a prank and a gesture of self-affirmation, Ziegfeld uses his considerable influence in metropolitan New York to have the police identify and round up the men who had earlier pronounced his demise in the barbershop. Escorted into his presence by the city's finest, and roundly surprised by a reward of prized tickets to each of the new shows, the men graciously accept the incident without rancor and even thank their conniving benefactor. The implication is that good seats at the latest Ziegfeld shows are so valuable as to smooth over even the insult of a false arrest. Financial advisor Sampson later admonishes Ziegfeld that he could have been sued for a great deal of money in damages. Ziegfeld's carefree response is: "There's nothing to worry about; I've been buying stock, million after million." Such a line of dialogue, spoken into the ear of an American audience of 1936, could signal only one event on the horizon. Ziegfeld's comeback was to be short-lived.

A sequence portraying panic on the trading floor of the New York Stock Exchange, something of a stock item in dozens of film dramas from the early 1930s, indicates that the crash has arrived. Billings is on the trading floor, speaking agitatedly with business associates and revealing that he has already lost his own considerable fortune in the sudden downturn of market prices. Despite personal misfortune, Billings' main concern seems to be for Ziegfeld. "Ziggy'll be wiped out," he says, "and this is the one time he can't get more from me." Ziegfeld's ability to inspire loyalty in others is still operative, even in moments of extreme crisis.

The electric sign montage which signalled Ziegfeld's comeback is then reprised, only this time the blinking of the lights quickly decreases in frequency, then stops, as the sign for each show is extinguished. The orchestral accompaniment of show tunes is heard in a halting fashion, with each song ceasing abruptly when its sign goes out. The Ziegfeld era is over, its demise confirmed not in a spate of backstage dialogue, but in the extinguishing of the electric signs which had announced it to millions of passers-by at the "crossroads of the world," Broadway and Forty-Second Street.

The narrative itself comes to a full stop shortly thereafter, with an aging Ziegfeld, attended by a private nurse, sitting in an overstuffed chair and staring out the window at the dark theatre which still bears his name. Dialogue reveals that it is two years since the crash, that Ziegfeld has suffered a total breakdown, and that his wife has returned to acting. Says Ziegfeld to the now gray-haired Billings, who is visiting, "I wish she weren't ... but it helps." The two old-timers reminisce about their former days of glory, with Ziegfeld observing, "Why is it the world's so old and life's so short?" Both talk about taking another trip to Europe, each proudly denying that he was wiped out by the crash. Ziegfeld tells of his plan to do a new Follies. Billings promises to come up with the needed cash. Ziegfeld pays his old rival what sounds like the highest possible compliment, calling him "a real person." Staggering to the window, the feeble showman envisions the all-star lineup: "I must get Rogers, Fields,

Cantor..." Then he breaks off, chuckles painfully and explains, "I can't laugh any more, because I'm wrong ..." and he returns to his chair.

After a time transition Billings comes to call again but is turned away by the nurse, who explains that Ziegfeld is resting peacefully. Inside his room, an over-the-shoulder shot reveals Ziegfeld's visions of past glory. To the accompaniment of an orchestral medley of songs heard in the electric sign montage we see "ghostly" (transparent) images of what appear to be performers from his last shows. The old man cries out, "More steps ... got to get higher!" A flower he has been holding in his right hand descends to the floor. The arm falls limp. The orchestral music swells and the scene fades into the end titles. The implication is that the departing showman has ascended his imaginary staircase and has gone to seek for beauty on a higher plane. Ten years later, when the same studio releases the Technicolor revue titled THE ZIEGFELD FOLLIES, that is precisely where the public will find him.

Compared to THE GREAT ZIEGFELD, A LADY'S MORALS and THE MIGHTY BARNUM were for the most part experiments (not necessarily in intention but ultimately in effect), testing public reaction to the inclusion of show business figures in the pantheon of heroes and villains so frequently drawn on for biographical representation by the creators of the film segment of popular culture. With the release of THE GREAT ZIEGFELD the public's tendency towards positive response to such material was overwhelmingly confirmed. The mythic structure of popular biography (the hero's quest) could be used in delineating the lives of entertainers as well as statesmen and saints. The formula was becoming cast. The cycle had begun, but its start was to be a gradual one; it would not pick up speed until the turn of the decade.

CHAPTER IV

BRING BACK THE OLD SONGS

THE GREAT ZIEGFELD began its series of roadshow engagements at first-run theatres in April of 1936. As it moved into the neighborhood and second-run houses that summer and chalked up impressive grosses at the box office, there was still no word of any similar picture going into production in Hollywood. Even after it won the Oscar for Best Picture the following spring there was no "follow-up" in release from any studio. Hollywood continued to turn out only pseudo-biographies of entertainment figures, reserving the allegedly factual treatment for statesmen, inventors, generals, humanitarians, and scientists. Warner Brothers did offer a 1937 release with Brian Aherne as the famous English Shakespearian actor David Garrick, but the milieu was far from the worlds of Broadway, Tin Pan Alley, or the film capital itself. It wasn't really a biography anyway, since it dealt with only a single anecdote from Garrick's life. In 1938 Metro produced THE GREAT WALTZ, ostensibly telling how the waltz king came to write his famous melodies, but the music of Strauss was also the product of a bygone European culture in which support for composers came from nobility, not the hit parade.

The following year Twentieth Century-Fox released one of the most notorious of all pseudo-biographies, ROSE OF WASHINGTON SQUARE, with an unlikely Alice Faye portraying a fictitious singer whose offstage romance with a criminal dangerously paralleled the real-life relationship between Ziegfeld star Fanny Brice and gambler Nicky Arnstein. Since Faye and Brice shared little resemblance in appearance or singing style, the film was certainly no attempt at impersonation, as the large-type, opening disclaimer boldly proclaimed. Nevertheless, Brice's lawyers filed suit on the basis of Faye's rendition of the Brice-popularized song "My Man."

Another 1938 film from the same studio invoked the familiar at a still higher level, despite an overtly fictitious narrative. ALEXANDER'S RAGTIME BAND, had it been made a few years later, might have been called "The Irving Berlin Story," since it was a drama about a composer-musician who is shown writing or performing nearly the entire World-War-I-era Berlin catalogue of hit songs. Studio executives, in conference with Berlin himself, decided not to produce the film as Berlin's personal story, but rather as "the story of an era." Scores of tunes written by Berlin in the early years of the century (as well as three new Berlin songs) were woven into the narrative via performance situations. The plot was the familiar lost-and-found love story between a man and a woman, this time with a self-sacrificing and self-destructive second male lead added to form a romantic triangle before conveniently disposing of himself in order to facilitate the picture's happy ending. Real names, dates and places from Berlin's early career were used sparingly, but his extremely popular songs from the World War I era brought on what is euphemistically referred to as "a wave of nostalgia" among movie-goers old enough to remember the time. The film's huge commercial success supplied movie makers with the missing element from the GREAT ZIEGFELD formula: bring back the old songs in their entirety--not just as abbreviated accompaniment for the names and faces of earlier star performers.

Three years to the month following the opening of THE GREAT ZIEGFELD, RKO released a film which clearly profited from the lessons of both ZIEGFELD and ALEXANDER. THE STORY OF VERNON AND IRENE CASTLE was only the fourth authentic, specifically identified show business biography produced in the course of what was by then a full decade of filming in the sound era. However, the seeds had been planted, the harvest of public response was favorable, and by way of comparison, the next ten years would see the release of twenty-seven more filmed life stories of entertainment figures. With a new show-business biography appearing on the nation's theatre screens at an average rate of nearly one every four months, the subject matter soon became a staple of the industry's output in the 1940s.

A distinct parallel of personalities is operative in THE STORY OF VERNON AND IRENE CASTLE. Designed as a showcase for the studio's extremely popular dancing team of Fred Astaire and Ginger Rogers, the film was based on the lives of another highly successful and well-remembered pair of professional dancers who toured Europe and America in the years just preceding World War I. As told on the screen, the Castles' joint career is basically a public extension of their private love affair. Yet elements of earlier show business biographies are also evident, and the film's mythic structure transforms (by the narrative's conclusion) what started as a comic love story into a semi-tragic drama of sacrifice and remembrance.

The film's structure can be divided into four sections: courtship, marriage, separation, and fantasized reunion. Although no attempt is made to bestow godly or superhuman powers on what are essentially a pair of gifted dancers who made good use of some lucky breaks, the similarity between their story and ancient myths of dying gods might be noted as possible explanation for the film's sentimental power over an audience. (The picture has retained a reputation as a "tear jerker.")

The courtship phase of the drama is played out against a dual backdrop of backstage life in vaudeville theatres and the pastoral world of New Rochelle, New York, circa 1911. An opening title gives the date and goes on to read: "In a fabulous and beloved era, near enough to be warmly remembered ... Vernon and Irene Castle whirled across the horizon. This is their story." The iconography of the show-business biography is firmly founded on the means of billing--advertising signs, lobby cards, posters, theatre programs, billboards, and playbills. A LADY'S MORALS and THE MIGHTY BARNUM relied on such devices at frequent points in the narrative, and THE GREAT ZIEGFELD was filled with them, often announcing the arrival of new stars who had just joined the Ziegfeld constellation. Vernon Castle is introduced to the viewer by a shot of the playbill at the vaudeville theatre where he is "picking up time," as the professional expression goes.

As a procession of suffragettes passes by (more historical placement), the camera picks up the bill, on which Castle's name can be read at the very bottom. The message: he is far from success and barely getting by in the world of the theatre. His offstage life is a reflection of his career, as indicated by a sequence in which he is rebuffed by a showgirl to whom he has been paying court. At the beach he meets a new girl named Irene by way of saving her dog from drowning. Repeated visits to her family home in New Rochelle result in a romance, spurred on by the

Fred Astaire and Ginger Rogers in THE STORY OF VERNON AND IRENE CASTLE (1939). Photo courtesy of Wisconsin Center for Film and Theater Research.

girl's intense ambition to go on the stage. A humorous sequence in the family's parlor features Irene giving out with her amateur's imitation of a vaudeville star of the day, Bessie McCoy, singing and dancing to the "Yama Yama Man Song." Lengthy prattling about Irene's talents by her doting mother, plus a scrapbook of the girl's triumphs in school and little theatre productions, make it clear that she is enamored not only of her beau, but of his profession as well.

The Castles' climb to the heights of show business success starts out from rather humble beginnings: she is horrified to learn that he is working as the stooge in a low comedy act which requires him to suffer numerous indignities including a face full of shaving cream. Soon the pair are spending afternoons and his days off working on a duo dance routine in her parlor. With the full, almost over-encouragement of her parents and an eccentric family friend simply called Walter, the pair marry and begin a joint show business career.

As in previous entertainment figure biographies, the audition sequence portrays a crucial moment in the lives of the central characters. The Castles nearly lose their nerve, and only go through with the audition at the urging of the benevolent Walter. Real life vaudeville star Lew Fields (of Weber and Fields) plays himself, in his famous costume, as the owner of the theatre where the tryout occurs. Fields' appearance is a strong invocation of the familiar, combining with the authentic period songs which have been heard so far in the film, including one of the biggest hits of the time, "Oh, You Beautiful Doll."

The Castles' audition fails to impress the cynical Fields (indicative of the entertainment standards of his day), who dismisses their act with the rhetorical question, "Who wants to see a man dance with his wife?" Providential coincidence, adding to the mythic structure of the narrative, supplies two French stage producers who have been watching from the back of the empty theatre. The Parisian showmen offer the fledgling dance team a contract to appear at the prestigious Theatre Aubel. The leap from American obscurity to European fame (never mind how long it took in real life) is nearly instantaneous in the mythical realm of cinema biography. Once the team arrives in Paris, however, certain complications which provide dramatic conflict do delineate again the sometimes callous behavior of show-business entrepreneurs. The Castles are curtly told by their new employers to wait six weeks without advance salary until the new show goes into rehearsal (or at least until the Aubels finish their seemingly interminable chess game). When the show does begin preparations, Vernon is chagrined to learn that the Aubels want him again to play the stooge in a comedy act. The comedic presence of Walter as friend and advisor is complemented at this point by the introduction of his female counterpart, another aging eccentric named Maggie Sutton, who encourages the Castles to audition their dance routine at the Café de Paris.

Following a production number by the Café's regular performing troupe ("Darktown Strutters' Ball" sung in French), the Castles join the patrons in dancing to "Too Much Mustard" and quickly have everyone else standing and watching as they go into their specialty, which they call the "Castle Walk." Then the patrons (European royalty and members of socially prominent families are present) pick up the step, and soon the entire crowd is doing the Castles' invention. The implication: dance for the right people. The cream of society can sometimes do more for a performer than any agent or producer.

A montage sequence heralds the Castles' swift rise to fame and fortune, illustrated by their names in lights and shots of the couple dancing while outfitted in an assortment of costumes. Signs dissolve into view announcing the Castles' introduction of new dance steps--the tango, fox trot, and Castle Polka. Items merchandised via the Castle name pass in front of the camera--books, records, sheet music, designer frocks, hats, even face cream, shoes, cigars and candy. One shot reveals that they now have their own theatre, the Castle House. Another shot superimposes their dancing figures whirling across a sky thick with twinkling stars, and newspaper headlines extol their triumphs, one bearing the shocking news: "Irene Castle Cuts Her Hair!" The result--the Castle Bob. Sheet music covers advertise "Castles by the Sea" and "The Maxixe." A news item announces that the Castles are making an American tour which will cover 35 cities in 28 days. A shot of a map of the country features two small dancing figures traveling from city to city, and in their wake whole crowds of dancing couples spring up, showing off the steps they have learned from Vernon and Irene. In this brief sequence of only a couple of minutes' duration, the concentration of show-business-related images has been so intense and multiple-layered as to condense several years of activity into rapid-fire display of mounting successes.

A sequence on board a train reveals that Maggie, who is now their manager, wants them to begin a second nationwide tour, but Vernon and Irene want to settle down to conventional family life. The opposition between domestic and theatrical pressures, hinted at in THE MIGHTY BARNUM but no real problem in ZIEGFELD, is to play an increasingly important role in numerous show-business biographies to come, but before it can develop at this point, another pressure on the lives of the characters, the intrusion of war, enters the plot and the drama shifts into the separation phase.

In innumerable fictional dramas, as well as in scores of biographies of nearly all types, the outbreak of war marks an important transition in the narrative. Whether the news is barked out by a newsboy, blared forth as a radio bulletin, spread gossip-like through a crowd, splashed across the screen in a swirl of headlines or allowed surreptitiously to enter the mise-en-scène as an ignored newscaster's remark or discarded front page whose significance dawns upon the main character only at some later time, the information imparted to the film audience is unchanging and immediately clear: the hero and heroine's lives will soon be disrupted and possibly permanently altered by war.

In this instance the initial announcement occurs with a newspaper headline: "Germany Declares War," clearly visible while carried by someone in a train station and seen by the viewer through the window of the train compartment where the Castles and Maggie are discussing their future. Dialogue reveals that Vernon was born a British subject (although Fred Astaire's accent is quite American). His national loyalty begins to tempt him to enlist in the fight to defend his homeland. No further explanation is offered concerning how long he has lived in the U.S. Instead, the story skips ahead to preparations for a vaudeville benefit show for British Relief. Irene is fearful that her husband will go off to war, and Maggie, acting in her counselor/advisor capacity, observes: "Women are pathetic when they try to fight something bigger than they are.... War is men's business--women only do what they're told." This remark, occurring in a 1939 film set in 1914, may seem chauvinistic and era-limited when perceived through contemporary sensibilities, but the possibility exists that it was already an instance of anachronistic overstatement when recorded on film forty years ago. The process of selectively recreating the past in film biographies, like all creative exercise of memory, involves extensive omission, distortion and magnification, the latter often in an ironic mode. A significant difficulty in comprehending a period piece executed in an era which itself has become the subject of latter-day period pieces is to keep mentally segregated the popular attitudes of three disparate time frames, since history, whether semi-fictional entertainment or scholarly treatise, is never composed within a neutral context.[1]

Vernon Castle's separation from his wife and show-business career is motivated by a sense of duty (national loyalty) which transcends his dual love affair with his partner and his audience. He performs at the benefit while dressed in a British Army uniform. As he realizes that his stage routine is only pretense, while the recruits in the audience are about to depart America for combat in a real theatre of war, the motivation for his own enlistment in the Royal Flying Corps is visually underlined. A subsequent fade-in on a map of France and Belgium dissolves to shots of reconnaissance planes in flight, a blackboard with fliers' names on it, a hand erasing the names, and the notation that pilot Vernon Castle is overdue.

This first "war montage," ending on a suspenseful note, is followed by a sequence demonstrating Castle's bravery. He arrives back from his mission safely, only to learn that his photographic plates were destroyed by gunfire. He resolutely returns to the air to shoot them over again, this time without the protection of a convoy of fighter planes. In a drama where so far the boldest thing the hero has done is to set foot on a stage, this insertion of more cinematically conventional heroics serves both to quicken the pace of the film's concluding moments and to lift the story onto a nobler plane, more attuned to the imminent sacrificial denoument.

Vernon gets leave from the RFC and has a brief reunion with Irene and their surrogate "family," Walter and Maggie. Looking out from a New York hotel balcony, the Castles observe an uproar in the street below. Vernon has just remarked how lucky he feels, when the couple learn that America has entered the war and that it is now "practically over." (This type of anachronistic, ironic overstatement is less controversial than that mentioned above. It occurs frequently in all types of period drama and serves as a pleasure- or fear-inducing device for an audience possessed of even the most rudimentary hindsight and/or historical knowledge.)

A second "war montage" follows, with shots of the American flag, battlefield combat, and the drive to sell war bonds. Irene Castle is seen on a platform, wearing a uniform and extolling the benefits of bonds to the crowd. Her career as a motion picture actress is briefly delineated by shots of the gateway to "International Pictures," a poster advertising her starring role in the serial film PATRIA, and a traveling shot of Irene walking past the sets of several pictures being filmed simultaneously in the same studio. The passage of much time and activity is thus elided by means of convenient historical rearrangement (PATRIA was released while America was still neutral), a practice clearly on view in ZIEGFELD and soon to become something of a hallmark of the show-business biographical film, despite its already long-standing usage in dramatizing life stories of all types.

A final reunion of the Castles (he has been transferred to an Army base in Texas to teach flying to American soldiers) is thwarted when Vernon has his leave postponed and makes one more training flight. Dialogue reveals that he once survived a crash while training a young Canadian pilot because the boy sat in the front seat and suffered the severest impact. Since that time Vernon has insisted that each student sit in the back while Vernon gives instructions from the more dangerous forward position (another heroic manifestation). He crashes again.

In a private dining room in a nearby hotel, Irene is preparing to be reunited with her husband. The ever-faithful Walter enters with the news that Vernon has been killed. Through her tears Irene catches the sound of the hotel's orchestra and observes: "They were playing that song when I first met him." The film concludes with a cinematic denial of the finality of death which dates back well into the silent era (cf. John Barrymore as BEAU BRUMMEL and Douglas Fairbanks as D'Artagnan in THE IRON MASK), as Irene looks out the window in the hotel garden and sees a ghostly couple (herself and Vernon) dancing to the music, whirling down the garden path as the end credits dissolve into view.

THE STORY OF VERNON AND IRENE CASTLE, a four-phased romance ending on a mystical note of re-birth (perhaps in legend, the closing image symbolizing that the Castles live on in the spirit of the dancing they spread across the world), firmly laid the last bricks of the foundation of the show-business biographical film. Its popular success could no longer be considered an isolated incident in film history. Popular culture's historical recreations in BARNUM and ZIEGFELD, and the musical recycling of ALEXANDER'S RAGTIME BAND, effectively responded to a mass appetite for filmic confections selectively molded from a semi-synthetic past, and THE CASTLES proved that these attractions would not lose their appeal even when grafted onto the archetypal four-phased mythic cycle of drama with its requisite unhappy ending (albeit followed by a symbolic transcendence of death).

Before the cycle of show-business biographies, which was to be so evident during the next decade, really began in earnest, two rather hybrid narratives appeared on the nation's theatre screens. Both were essentially fictional dramas with show-business settings and therefore part of the earlier cycle of non-specific exploitations of the nostalgia phenomenon, but one of them invoked the familiar in a manner reminiscent of THE GREAT ZIEGFELD, and the other featured a decidedly "undisguised disguised" central character. HOLLYWOOD CAVALCADE and THE STAR MAKER, released within six weeks of each other near the end of 1939, each demonstrated the influence of the growing biographical trend in show-business-based screen drama.

HOLLYWOOD CAVALCADE was essentially a lost-and-found love story set in the early days of film production in California. Don Ameche played the hero, a fictitious director whose composite character was drawn from the widely publicized activities and appearances of D. W. Griffith, Cecil B. DeMille, Thomas Ince and Mack Sennett. One could almost say he dressed like Griffith, acted like DeMille, had the ambition of Ince and turned out Sennett-like comedies. The unusually strong invocation of the familiar in what was overtly a fictional story came in the casting of the players to be directed in silent comedies produced by the Ameche character. Buster Keaton, Chester Conklin, Ben Turpin and some surviving members of the Keystone Cops were among the actors shown going through their paces in new sepia-toned footage, specially shot for the feature and inserted at appropriate points into the Technicolor continuity. While these characters (none of whom was named in the dialogue) were shown walking into position or rehearsing for a take, they too were photographed in color. The question of whether Buster Keaton and the others were portraying themselves or simply non-specific representatives of the craft of silent comedy was not resolved.

THE STAR MAKER, on the other hand, tackled the representation question in a wholly different manner. Included in the opening credits, in large type and easily readable, was the declaration: "Suggested by the career of Gus Edwards." The drama which followed was indeed the story of how Edwards rose to fame and fortune by producing vaudeville shows built exclusively around the talents of teenage and pre-teen children. Names and places from Edwards' career (including theatres, cities, producers, music publishers, even the titles of his hit stage shows) were used freely, but the leading character (played by Bing Crosby) was called Larry Earl. Whatever the legal reasons for this decision, it is a matter of record that many latter-day celebrities got their start as juvenile performers in Edwards' shows. None of them (the group included such diverse talents as Walter Winchell, Bert Wheeler, George Jessel, Eddie Cantor and Mervin LeRoy) was identified by name in the film either.

Rather than use a lost-and-found love plot, the narrative instead traces Edwards'/Earl's career along a curvature of rise, fall and renewal. Early in the film he marries his sweetheart Mary, an attendant at an orphanage, and she continues to give him emotional support through good times and bad. The familial structure of character relationships, like those in the BARNUM and CASTLE films, is extended to include an eccentric older man. In the earlier films the part was filled by Adolphe Menjou and Walter Brennan, respectively. In ZIEGFELD Frank Morgan's portrayal of the friendly rival Billings functioned in a similar vein, and in the CASTLE story Edna Mae Oliver's Maggie character served to double the reinforcement. In THE STAR MAKER the role of Speed King, ace publicity man and confidant/advisor to Larry Earl, is filled by the no less eccentric Ned Sparks. His professed aversion to sentiment in general and children in particular operates as a comic counterpoint to the benevolent and paternalistic ministrations evidenced in Crosby's portrayal of Earl.

The film begins with Larry Earl as a ne'er-do-well, a recently resigned hotel night clerk who whiles away the hours entertaining orphanage children with songs he has composed but can't sell. A year of marriage doesn't change him, as is demonstrated by a later sequence in which he skips a job interview (for the position of dimestore floorwalker) and buys a new and far-too-expensive piano. He excuses his behavior to his wife by claiming to have had an inspiring conversation with stage and cabaret star Sophie

Tucker, and he compares his latest composition, which he performs on the new instrument, very favorably with "After the Ball" (a tune used in scores of show-business-set film dramas to give immediate reference to the turn of the century, a time when the song was immensely popular).

In addition to being a fictionalized biography of Gus Edwards, THE STAR MAKER was also very much a star vehicle for Crosby, showcasing his vocal talents in the same manner as most of the other films he made during his long tenure at Paramount. In keeping with the practice of integrating song and dialogue sequences in those films, no specific "performance situation" is needed to frame or justify his bursting into song with full (and unseen, or "phantom") orchestral accompaniment. While such "spontaneous" vocalizing was common and would continue to be so in the singer's star vehicles for years to come, it is worth noting that even in show-business biographies with singers as their central characters, phantom orchestral accompaniments and non-performance renditions of songs have tended to be the exception, thereby suggesting frequent attempts by film makers to construct more confining perimeters of perceived "realism" when working with historical/biographical material.

Larry Earl's epiphanic moment comes when he witnesses a group of Lower East Side newsboys performing an impromptu song-and-dance routine on a Manhattan street corner. Earl is struck by their raw talent and crowd-pleasing style (passers-by throw pennies). He invites the half-dozen urchins to his shabby apartment and begins hatching plans to take the vaudeville world by storm with "Larry Earl's Singing Newsboys." Earl's ambitious nature, a characteristic shared with his counterparts in previous show-business biographies, is on view in the excuse he gives his wife for missing another job interview: "Why should I work for someone else when I can have my own act?" Returning to the practice of performing songs to comment upon one's career, Earl sits down to his unpaid-for piano and sings "If I Were a Millionaire."

Entry into the limelight, shown to be difficult for the Castles, heavily dependent on financial credit for Ziegfeld, and directly related to the sensational nature of one's material for Barnum, is a formidable task for Earl as well. Rejected by talent agencies, unable to secure appointments directly with theatrical producers, Earl sinks into despair, but he is rescued by his wife's ingenuity and persistence.

She sneaks out of their apartment at 4 a.m., hurries to a night spot called Reisenweber's, and hides in the parked car of Mr. Proctor, owner of a string of first-rate vaudeville houses. When the blustery impresario departs his all-night revels, Mary surprises him with her passionate appeal that he give her aspiring husband a break and book the newsboys' act. The intense competition, first for opportunity and then for public approval, which confronts would-be entrants into the entertainment world, is definitely acknowledged but not centrally emphasized in the earlier films under study. It would soon become a major theme in show-business biographies. In THE STAR MAKER this highly competitive milieu is staked out and primally defined in Proctor's response: "My dear young lady ... everyone in New York has an act!" Another key theme, soon to become central in many similar biographies and already well established in numerous fictional show-business dramas (dating back at least as far as 1929's THE DANCE OF LIFE) is the imminent danger of an entertainer's wounded pride. After convincing Proctor to give her husband an audition, Mary also exacts a promise from Proctor not to tell the latter of his wife's intervention. Underscoring the inflated state of Larry Earl's ego while at the same time trying to ward off the danger of having oversold the merits of his act, Mary departs with the admonition, "Larry isn't as good as he'll tell you. Nobody could be that good."

The initial ascent phase of the narrative has Earl's Singing Newsboys moving right into the "big time" (a vaudeville phrase which has since become part of general American slang) with a guest appearance at Proctor's Theatre in Manhattan. Invocation of the familiar is already functioning at a high level, with the star names on the playbill including song-and-dance man Eddie Leonard, vocalist Blanche Ring, and the world-renowned female impersonator, Julian Eltinge. The newsboys' production number, "Go Fly a Kite," draws thunderous applause from the crowd; Earl signs for a long engagement and immediately begins planning to expand and compound his success. His ambition: to tour the nation with multiple "kid act" road companies. Subsequent shots depict Earl's mounting good fortunes. (One vaudeville playbill even has his singing newsboys billed above Harry Houdini.)

"Larry Earl Kiddie Productions" opens an office in Manhattan, publicity agent Speed King is hired to promote the enterprise, and the shrewd operator designs a nationwide talent hunt/tour with a private train (painted with Mother Goose characters and sponsored by a malted milk company) crisscrossing the continent and stopping in each major city to audition talented tykes for the next Earl stage show. The train carries the name "The Larry Earl Starmaker." This flurry of activity is sketched in by-now-familiar montage fashion, intercutting shots of rail travel with brief audition sequences featuring young talent. Newspaper ads are seen advising: "Are you a child? Do you have talent? See Larry Earl." The succession of visual imagery carries the unmistakable message that Earl's enterprise has become truly national in scope, insinuating itself into the American consciousness.

Despite the hectic pace of the narrative at this point, the Earl character, as portrayed by Bing Crosby, still takes time out at selected points to croon popular songs of the period, including "I Wonder Who's Kissing Her Now," sung while coaxing a reticent little girl to sing by herself at an audition.

An elaborate production number from the stage show, "Larry Earl's Vacation Days," follows, with several dozen pre-teen boys and girls dressed in rural costumes and performing "My Merry Oldsmobile" amid pasteboard and canvas props and scenery. As in ZIEGFELD, the film audience is actually presented with stylized re-creations of the sort of entertainment for which the central figure was noted, thus adding to the film's popular drawing power the attraction of witnessing crowd-pleasing spectacles from the past which have since passed from fashion.

Earl holds a press conference backstage at his next production, "Larry Earl's Nursery Frolics," revealing that he now has fourteen companies on the road. In the meantime his wife, who is still devoted to her orphanage duties, has returned there to look after things. Her now-successful husband is sending home generous financial support to improve living conditions at the institution. It is clear that THE STAR MAKER, despite its narrative pattern of rise and fall, does not echo the didacticism of THE MIGHTY BARNUM. Although Larry Earl is heading for a fall, he will not learn Barnum's lesson of "sticking to that which you do well." Earl has no false notions of his own importance in the world that lies beyond the foyer and box office. Nevertheless, a striking parallel with BARNUM does occur when Earl discovers a "classical" singer and takes a strong interest in her career.

Much younger than Jenny Lind and just starting out, the gifted performer is fourteen-year-old Jane Gray, escorted to a Larry Earl tryout by her failed-singer mother, who seeks to realize her own youthful ambitions in a career for her daughter. Hearing the girl sing an operatic aria, Earl barks out his dismissal response, and in doing so reveals his realistically limited opinion of his type of productions: "We can't use her; we cater to customers, not patrons." This sober distinction, separating the world of "serious music" from the popular taste of the mass audience, had long served as an operant tension in show-business-based fiction films, and would continue to do so well into the post-World-War-II era. Attempted violations of the taste barrier had, however, sometimes reaped rich box-office rewards (for example, the financial salvation of Universal Studios by the aria-filled films of Deanna Durbin just months before the release of THE STAR MAKER).

Introduction of the Jane Gray character causes the narrative to veer away for a time from the still-being-established cinema biographical formulae, revealing instead the influence of the Durbin films, as Earl takes the girl "under his wing" and makes her a star of a different sort. It should be noted that the Larry Earl/Gus Edwards character at this point in the story is, despite his success, a vaudeville showman with no pretensions toward acceptance in higher circles of culture. Earl declares, "Opera is not vaudeville," and tells the girl and her mother to see "highbrow" promoter Sol Hurok instead.

The classical versus popular dialectic is extended as the girl evades her mother's attention long enough to perform a "hot" vocal rendition of "Darktown Strutters' Ball," thus demonstrating to Earl the ability and savvy needed to please a mass audience. An ironic postscript to these proceedings occurs in Earl's buying off the mother's objections to her daughter's performing popular music by offering the older woman a performing spot in one of his touring companies. (Cultural pretensions are shown to be easily compromised by the promise of fame.) Earl's initial involvement with serious music devotees arouses objections from the acid-tongued Speed King: "Now ya wanna get in competition with Ziegfeld, Erlanger and Dillingham." Although the remark appears to be overstated (none of these famous showmen made their millions from staging operas and symphonies), it does strengthen the narrative's historical placement (the Ziegfeld era) and suggests the scope of Earl's broadening aspirations. (The gradations of social acceptance among burlesque, vaudeville, legitimate theatre and the concert hall function as a given in nearly all the films under study.) King's cynical observation reflects Earl's would-be expansion of his stage attractions to include popularizing serious music by inserting excerpts of it performed by concert artists in a mass appeal, show-business format. (Ziegfeld, Erlanger and Dillingham had already practiced this with considerable success.) This blending--its critics call it cheapening--of music from a higher social stratum with entertainment forms aimed at the broad public can be witnessed in a whole cycle of opera-influenced films of the mid-1930s as well, culminating in the aforementioned Durbin star vehicles which retained their popularity until the years following World War II.

Jane Gray becomes a star in Larry Earl's revue, "School Days," and the narrative pauses for another elaborate production number recreating the Gus Edwards style of entertainment. It includes the show's title song performed by pupils in a stage classroom, with Earl appearing as the teacher and Jane singing "An Apple for the Teacher," then introduces an audience sing-along via the "follow the bouncing ball" technique on a suspended movie screen. The apotheosis of Earl's career having been delineated, his initial rise is superseded by a devastating fall.

Suddenly Earl's traveling shows are cancelled in city after city, as a result of a concerted nationwide effort by Children's Welfare Leagues to enforce the child labor law. Because children under twelve are forbidden to work after 10 p.m., Earl's entire enterprise collapses in a matter of days. Jane Gray's career is safeguarded by the benignly paternalistic Earl, however; he secures for her an engagement to sing with a symphony orchestra at Carnegie Hall. Real-life conductor Walter Damrosch appears as himself, invoking the familiar--past the point of impersonation--and Gray's debut (with a vocal rendition of "The Waltz of the Flowers") is a success. The ironic depiction of how the public often misdirects its appreciation (soon to be a recurring motif in many show-business biographies) is exemplified in one concert-goer's remark: "Damrosch is a real star maker; I wonder where he found her."

Gloom pervades Larry Earl's extended family (Speed King included) as they reflect on their reduced situation. Larry dolefully plays a phonograph record of himself singing "If I Were a Millionaire" and observes, "Well, honey,

60 / Star Myths

here we are, right back where we started." The narrative cycle of rise and fall has plunged to the depths, but amid the despair Mary reminds her husband, "The fine things in life aren't written in bank books." She suggests he take a stroll down Broadway and see in lights all the star performers who got their start in a Larry Earl show. Despite the curious avoidance of invoking those names, the point is still made that Earl's many contributions to show business have paid no bankable, long-term dividends. He expresses his desire to leave the entertainment world and run a chicken farm in New Jersey. (The origin of this by-now clichéd remark seems likely to date from years before this film, but the words are delivered in sincerity rather than jest.) King, on the other hand, expresses a desire to enter the fast-growing field of commercial radio. No attempt has been made to locate the progression of the narrative within a specific time frame, but the dialogue (referring to the many stars who have emerged from Earl's shows and the ascendance of radio) suggests that the story has moved to the vicinity of 1925-27. The characters have not visibly aged, so the viewer can only make vague estimates as to how many years have passed. The film's emphasis is instead on the more cyclical-mythical nature of Earl's career.

From the bottommost point he is soon rescued by the possibilities of a new medium. As "Dardanella" plays on the radio, he is struck with a new idea: "The radio! An audience for show-business acts ... the radio ... everyone'll have one ... it's right out of heaven and it's made to order for me! I can use kids!" A quick dissolve leads to the first broadcast of "Larry Earl and his Stars of Tomorrow." Subsequent shots show Jane listening at her home and Mary and Ned discussing Larry's bright new future. Mary ponders what her husband will do next. Ned replies, "He's already done it--he bought the network!" Since there is no record of the real Gus Edwards owning a radio network, the film's fictionalized story-from-life comes to a decidedly fictitious conclusion, but the cyclical plot of rise, fall and rise is nevertheless true to familiar audience expectations.

THE MIGHTY BARNUM, THE GREAT ZIEGFELD and THE STAR MAKER, three of the cinema's earliest show-business biographies, each dealt with the life and career of a famous showman: Barnum exhibited freaks and animals to the patrons of sideshows, Gus Edwards/Larry Earl worked his kiddie shows on the nation's vaudeville circuits, and Ziegfeld provided lavish diversions for the more affluent

Allan Jones, Walter Connolly and Mary Martin in THE GREAT VICTOR HERBERT (1939). Photo courtesy of Wisconsin Center for Film and Theater Research.

theatre-goers in Broadway's poshest entertainment palaces. The central figure in each film fulfilled the functions of manager, promoter, visionary of the public taste, and father-figure to his performers. The last of these functions was emphasized to a far greater degree in the next show business biography to emerge from Hollywood, THE GREAT VICTOR HERBERT, a Christmas release from Paramount at the end of 1939.

The narrative centered on the stormy marriage of a fictitious, possibly composite tenor and prima donna whose careers are shown to be intertwined with composer Herbert and his long string of successful operettas, produced on Broadway in the early years of the twentieth century. The cantankerous but considerate Herbert, as portrayed by Walter Connolly, serves as a father-confessor to the troubled pair while their domestic drama unfolds.

Twenty-eight of Herbert's songs are included in the

picture, always presented in performance situations and strongly adding to the film's popular attractions after the manner of ALEXANDER'S RAGTIME BAND. Invocation of the familiar is kept at a high level throughout the narrative as most of the songs are linked by dialogue or visual device (electric signs, posters and theatre programs) to the stage vehicles for which they were originally written. In view of the fact that these operettas were still being revived circa 1939 by both professional and non-professional theatre companies (and some were even available in recent film adaptations), the score of THE GREAT VICTOR HERBERT benefited from a fairly current, as well as a nostalgic, presence in the public mind.

The plot is essentially one of lost-and-found love, but with the major complications of failed marriage, ardent second suitor and neglected child added. Louise Hall, the prima donna in the story, is given her "big break" (an introduction to Victor Herbert) by the egotistical tenor John Ramsey. The pair marry, ignoring Herbert's advice that they are unsuited, and become leading performers in Herbert's operettas. When Louise becomes a greater favorite with the crowd than John, he deserts her, their child, and the Broadway stage to sink into ignominy. Louise's old boyfriend from her small-town home, a dedicated children's doctor, tries to fill the void in her life, and the child, who wants to sing like her mother, grows to age fourteen hating her missing father. Despite all the good efforts of Victor Herbert to reunite the pair (he even offers the washed-up John a chance at a comeback, with Herbert secretly paying the singer's salary out of his own pocket), the sad situation continues until the fourteen-year-old makes an emergency stage debut as a last-minute substitute for her ailing mother in a revival of an early Herbert success. Choking with fear, the girl is unable to complete her big song until her long-lost father, donning an appropriate costume, steps out of the wings to sing a duet with her and restore her confidence. A tearful family reconciliation, set to Herbert's music, concludes the picture.

Counterpointing the subsidiary role of Herbert as kindly confidant and advisor is the character of Louise's agent, Barney Harris, whom John describes as having "a big heart, delivered every day by the ice man." This character, directly related to the humorous Speed King in THE STAR MAKER, is also comparable to the advisor roles in other early show-business biographies, but his cynical and calculating nature represents a departure into ironic territory which had previously been entered only in overtly fictitious show-business dramas (cf. the press agent in the 1937 A STAR IS BORN). The theme of wounded pride is given stronger emphasis in THE GREAT VICTOR HERBERT than in any previous film under study, but it too had already been well worked over in non-biographical entertainment settings, as noted previously.

Just as THE STAR MAKER hedged its self-presentation as a true-life story by giving the central figure a different name after announcing up front that the story was definitely related to a named celebrity's career, THE GREAT VICTOR HERBERT hedges its biographical representation. The surprise is that the admitted shift away from verisimilitude is reserved for an end-title disclaimer: "No attempt has been made in this picture to tell the actual life of Victor Herbert. The characters are fictitious. Only the mood is genuine." Whether some last-minute threat of legal action caused this appendix-like statement to appear is open to speculation, but its undeniable presence represents something of a public acknowledgment of the mythical nature of the enterprise at hand. The "actual story" is expendable; the "mood" (created by catering to audience expectations) is essential. In this singular case the ostensible central figure turned out to be nearly expendable as well. His name was exploited to attract public interest, and patrons attending the film were rewarded with a large dose of his still-popular melodies, intertwined with a conventional love story in a show business setting. The mythic structure of love lost and later found took precedence over any claim to historical re-creation of a famous man's life.

Until this point in the evolution of the show-business biographical film, no central character had been depicted as suffering from an ultimately fatal flaw. The films which ended with the hero's death, ZIEGFELD and THE CASTLES, showed the man's demise to be hastened by external forces (the stock market crash, the Great War). With the release of SWANEE RIVER, only two days before the beginning of 1940, a new element was added to the collection of mythic plots used in constructing these films. Since it can be identified in a wide array of dramatic/literary forms dating back thousands of years, the element (a fatal character flaw or personality trait) was new only in relation to its new context. In the case of SWANEE RIVER the flaw appears as alcoholism, unleashed by the unbearable pain of failed ambitions, but stemming from some dark recess of the soul which the screenwriters did not attempt to fathom. As Stephen Foster, the tragic hero, says to his wife when asked why he can't conquer his "one weakness," "Why must any of us be what we are?"

THE GREAT VICTOR HERBERT displayed its opening credits within the framing device of a proscenium arch, the words superimposed against a curtain, below which the Herbert character was shown conducting an orchestra in an overture of melodies from the film. SWANEE RIVER, the first show business biography in Technicolor, unfolds its credits in the form of embroidered samplers, with the various colored yarns spelling out names and titles. As was the case with the electric sign credits of THE GREAT ZIEGFELD, the iconographic references to the narrative's time and place precede even the beginning of the story. Stylized credits were, of course, not unique to biographical films, but the information imparted in this manner will, like the dramas themselves, begin to share a commonality as the generic cycle intensifies.

The sampler, popularly identified with the rural, home-centered living of an earlier era, provides immediate reference to the narrative's past-tense setting. The fore and aft disclaimers of THE STAR MAKER and THE GREAT VICTOR HERBERT are missing from this film, safely set as it is in an earlier century, with all its real-life characters long dead and no immediate heirs likely to sue. Instead, an assertive, uncompromising title supplies the most specific promise of historical "truth" yet presented in such a film: "This is the strange story of a northern youth to whom the Southland brought immortal inspiration. Though his stormy life is long forgotten, his simple words and simple music live on in the hearts of the whole American people."

SWANEE RIVER presents itself as the life story of Stephen Foster, an American composer of popular songs whose initial success came from the performance of his material for a nationwide audience via the traveling minstrel shows which toured the country in the years just preceding the Civil War. So many of Foster's compositions later became "standards" (perpetually revived popular favorites) that his work was still well-known to the public at the time of the film's release.* Therefore the public aware-

---

*In fact, since the entire catalog of Foster's songs   (cont.)

ness factor, which figured in the creation and appeal of all previous show-business biographies, still functioned in the case of SWANEE RIVER, despite the remoteness of the period depicted. However, invocation of the familiar could not function at a very high level, simply because of this remoteness. Roles could be cast at will, without regard to resemblance, and the names of theatres, publishing companies, popular singers of the day and producers (while they might all have been genuine) carried scant recognition value for a 1939 audience. The relative freedom from contradicting widely held memories of the era being depicted, shared with the earliest films in this study, A LADY'S MORALS and THE MIGHTY BARNUM, was limited mainly by certain popular conceptions about the Civil War, as taught in public school and dramatized in works of fiction.

Because he lent his name to the most successful of the minstrel companies, one which prospered and survived long enough to become something of a show-business legend in itself, the character of E. P. Christy stands as a singular exception to the above-mentioned historical remoteness of the mid-1800s entertainment world. This character's function in the plot of SWANEE RIVER combines the roles of confidant, eccentric friend/family member and opportunistic agent into a single personage, epitomizing the inflated ego and crowd-pleasing skill of what can best be described as the archetypal entertainer. He is portrayed by Al Jolson, whose own on- and offstage reputations embodied these

---

had long since fallen into the public domain, they had earlier been chosen by one of Hollywood's "poverty row" studios, Mascot Pictures, as the material around which to build a very low-budget historical musical entitled HARMONY LANE. Douglass Montgomery, on the downslide after a brief period of stardom as Universal's most histrionic of leading men, was cast as Foster in this first screen recounting of the composer's rise to fame. Doomed to only the sparsest of exhibition in third-rate theatres because of its humble origin, the 1935 production is unlikely to have had much influence on the development of the show-business biographical film, but is worth noting as a significant example of how the exploitation process inherent in the making and marketing of a show-business biographical film tended to cut across the economic hierarchy of the movie capital and unite both the mighty and the low in an early appreciation of the generic formula's potential.

qualities to an unparalleled degree. Thus a variation on the invocation of the familiar (almost in a reincarnational sense) functions in the place of more conventional replication. Also, a secondary linkage factor exists in the fact that Jolson's earlier career as a blackface entertainer carried on the style of performing which was originated in minstrel shows such as Christy's.

Although the historical period delineated in SWANEE RIVER predates those of all previous films under study, the iconography of the entertainment world is already on view. Sheet music covers, theatrical playbills, marquees, publishing companies, producers' offices, dressing rooms, and proscenium stages recur throughout the narrative as important locales and significant points of reference.

At the time of the film's release, no show-business biographical film had yet attempted to span the entire lifetime of its central character. Most had started with the hero as a young adult, either about to enter the entertainment business or having attained only a modest early success. An exception was THE GREAT VICTOR HERBERT, in which the nominal title figure was already well past fifty and solidly established at the head of his profession. SWANEE RIVER's opening sequences establish that Stephen Foster's family obligations compel him to work as a clerk in a shipping company office, while his true ambition is to write popular songs based on the spirituals and work chants of Negro slaves. The conflict between respectable employment and the lure of the footlights (a familiar theme in countless fictional show business dramas) appears early in the films under study when Florenz Ziegfeld forsakes training in classical music to promote carnival sideshows.

The precise statement of ambition, introduced into biographical film drama in THE MIGHTY BARNUM's remark to Walsh about buying a tent and moving his show from town to town, is exceedingly exact in SWANEE RIVER. After listening to slaves working on a levee, Foster remarks to his fiancée, Jane MacDowell, "It's music from the heart, from the heart of a simple people. By jingo, it's the only real American contribution to music. I wonder why no one's taken the trouble to write it down, develop, compose original music in the same mood." Jane replies, "Why don't you, Stephen?" His answer--"Well, why don't I? You'll have to take the blame. Without you I don't think I can write. I'd just die."

In one brief exchange the hero's grand ambition and
untimely end are both proclaimed with little room for compromise.
The narrative thereby takes on a fatal form of
unity, moving inexorably toward the composer's foreseen demise.
Opposition to the hero's plans, already evidenced in
several of the films under study, becomes more of a personal
attack in SWANEE RIVER. It is not just financial
troubles, critics' disapproval or the lack of a "big break"
which work at cross purposes to his ambitions. His fiancée's
family opposes their daughter's marrying a man who
"loses his mind when he gets a tune in his head." The
girl's father, apparently aware of the lax copyright laws of
the day and the financially precarious position of composers,
predicts that Foster will never make a dime writing songs
and bitterly denounces him as "a fool with a pennywhistle."

More subtle criticism of Foster's ambition comes
from Henry Kleiber, an old country/Viennese music teacher
and lifelong friend of the younger man. In a characterization
which strongly parallels that of old Professor Ziegfeld,
Kleiber expresses his disapproval of modern popular music
in general and Foster's later association with E. P. Christy
in particular. Kleiber's contempt for the vulgarity and
brashness of Christy is intense and remains an unresolved
conflict at the film's conclusion. Some justification for such
a strong dislike is provided by Foster's initial encounter
with Christy, a man who has achieved great fame and success
by distorting Negro culture for the amusement of white
audiences. Desperate for a foothold in show business, Foster
begs Christy to buy and perform a song, even if he requires
Foster to relinquish claim to the composition and allow
Christy to put his own name on the sheet music. Christy
struts and boasts in his dressing room, intimidating the
fledgling composer with statements such as "For ten years
I've held audiences in the hollow of my hand with any song
I care to sing. I don't write songs. One song more or
less is nothing in the life of E. P. Christy." As the selfimpressed
star dons blackface makeup, the linkage between
his role in the film and the actor portraying him (Al Jolson)
tightens into congruency. When Christy accepts Foster's
offer of forsaking songwriter credit, the singer-showman
caps his egomaniacal performance with the fatuous rhetorical
questions: "I am gifted. Does that allow me to become
completely heartless? The world calls me an artist. Must
I ignore its suffering?" Christy then purchases "Oh, Susannah"
from Stephen Foster for the sum of one dollar. In
dramatizing the negative aspects of show business in a far

68 / Star Myths

Don Ameche and Andrea Leeds in SWANEE RIVER (1939).
Photo courtesy of Wisconsin Center for Film and Theater
Research.

more bitter manner than its predecessors, SWANEE RIVER
portrays the entertainment world as fraught with dangers
and harmful characters, ever ready to take advantage of
the unwary aspirant.

The immense popular approval granted "Oh, Susannah" is delineated in familiar montage fashion (sheet music sales, people singing it while at work), but the public credit goes to Christy, not Foster. Inspired nevertheless by the song's reception, and spurred on by news that "the boys were singing it at the Camptown Races," Foster slacks off work at the shipping company and pens "Camptown Races." While Victor Herbert's many compositions were implied as having been made strictly in the business-like, orderly creation of stage shows, Stephen Foster becomes the first film-biographied popular composer to garner instant inspiration from momentary occurrences. (Film biographies of "serious" composers, such as Strauss in THE GREAT WALTZ, made a year earlier, had introduced this technique; for example, the carriage ride through the countryside which accompanies the in-motion composition of "Tales From the Vienna Woods.")

A parallel montage illustrates Foster's continued inability to get a song published under his own, unknown name. Rejection notices pile up, his landlady pesters him for back rent, and finally Foster writes a farewell note to the fiancée for whom he had promised to become a great success: "The dream is ended. Life with me will always be a squalid affair. Goodbye my angel." SWANEE RIVER's tragic structure, with its hero doomed to fall from grace because of a fatal shortcoming, has only begun to function, however. Spending his last cash on whiskey and telling the barkeep to throw him in the river when he passes out, the utterly dejected Foster is surprised to find E. P. Christy re-entering his life. The ebullient Christy lays the success of "Oh, Susannah" to inscrutable fate: "Nobody can tell if a song will hit or not," and says he has been looking for Foster for the past six months. Christy outlines his plan: "You write songs. I'll sing 'em. You are now the protégé of E. P. Christy."

SWANEE RIVER thus reiterates the old adage, "It's who you know that counts," as it displays Stephen Foster's rise to prominence. Although Foster, upon seeing Christy in the bar, had called him a thief and started a fight, the dejected composer (whose competence as a crowd-pleaser has been certified) is now treated by the showman as a friend and valuable asset to "Christy's World-Renowned Ethiopian Serenaders." Foster joins the company but soon becomes dissatisfied with Christy's refusal to perform Foster's ballads, preferring only his faster-paced tunes. In a backstage dispute over the merits of "My Old Kentucky Home," Christy upbraids Foster's confidence in his new song with the supremely ironic and anachronistic statement, "If there's anything I hate in a man, it's an inflated ego!" Yet Foster's ego is not the character trait which will destroy him. The mythic structure being worked out here is one of approaching doom brought on by a more ephemeral facet of the self.

Despite the historical fact that most popular songwriters of the pre-rock music era spent little time on stage performing their own material, SWANEE RIVER sets the pattern for many songwriter biographies to come by having Stephen Foster sneak on stage while Christy is napping and debut "My Old Kentucky Home" before a wildly appreciative minstrel show audience. The unmitigated professionalism of Christy (whatever his failings as an immodest human being) is demonstrated as his anger turns to approval when he wakes during Foster's performance, decides that it is going over well, and sends in a double quartet to harmonize with Foster on the last verse and chorus. As was the case in THE STAR MAKER, the casting of a popular singer in the lead role by itself led to audience expectation of his performing musically as well as dramatically. Don Ameche as Stephen Foster fulfills a similar function, albeit to a lesser extent than the phenomenally popular Bing Crosby, whose previous films had never failed to include songs sung by the star. Ameche was already a familiar performer in film musicals, but his non-singing roles still allowed producers the options of having him sing or not doing so, without violating the anticipatory response of the crowd.

The mythic pattern builds as the narrative shifts from Foster's upward struggle to the high plateau of success, from which he will eventually plummet. A series of positive images fills the screen, including a fat royalty check, a fast ride on horseback, a justice of the peace sign and a happy bride and groom. To the accompaniment of wedding music, we see the hopes of Stephen Foster fulfilled. On their honeymoon voyage up the river to Pittsburgh, Foster exclaims joyfully to his new wife, "I'm a success, even beyond my wildest dreams!" Yet on their wedding night, Stephen deserts Jane to compose a new song, inspired by the sound of a banjo on board the riverboat. To atone for the lovers' quarrel which results, he follows the composition of "Ring, Ring the Banjo" with "Jeannie with the Light Brown Hair," inspired, so he says, by the moonlight reflecting from his wife's auburn tresses. (Foster has begun to call his wife Jeannie, although her name is Jane.) Again the narrative can be seen supplying direct and specific inspiration for compositions which in real life may have come into being in decidedly different circumstances and chronology. The mythic/romantic notion that an author's compositions directly reflect his personal encounters is already functioning at a very perceptible level.

Foster's good fortune expands; he purchases a lavish town house in New York City and becomes involved in

extravagant social functions. Against the better judgment of
Herr Kleiber, who knows his friend lacks sufficient training
in classical composition, Foster announces plans to compose
a suite for piano and string quartet. Echoing the warnings
to P. T. Barnum when he tried to outstep his "class,"
Kleiber expresses to Jane his fear that Stephen will become
only a "tenth-rate Beethoven." Now that Foster is something of a celebrity, his activities are covered in the press,
and a shot of a newspaper column (already one of the most
standard information-carrying devices in show-business biographies) reveals that six months of rumor in New York
musical circles have given way to the announcement that
Stephen Foster will premiere his new work at Dodsworth's
Recital Hall on Broadway.

The fortuitous or fatal conjunction of crucial events,
long an established device of the craft of writing all sorts of
dramatic fiction, is to become an increasingly operative
force in restructuring history as the show-business biographical film evolves. On the night of the premiere concert,
Jane goes into labor with the Fosters' first child. The concert is a washout, with disgruntled serious-music patrons
walking out before the performance is concluded. Leaving
the theatre, the dismayed composer encounters his nemesis-
cum-benefactor, E. P. Christy, who, upon learning of the
disaster, responds with the moral of THE MIGHTY BARNUM: "I never attend my friends' funerals. Stick to what
you know best." Christy goes on to suggest, "There's a
silver lining in yonder saloon," and the pair repair to the
bar, where Stephen Foster commences his long slide to the
depths. A montage of beer mugs and whiskey glasses employs standard screen shorthand to emphasize the point.

The growing estrangement between Foster and his
wife is given a strong push when he deserts her in her
time of trial, and his pledge never to repeat the episode
is met by her skeptical warning, "Don't make promises
you can't keep." A visit to her parents' home is saddened
by the death of the faithful family servant, an elderly slave
named Joe. On his deathbed he speaks of "hearing the
voices calling" and asks if Mister Stephen has kept his
promise to write a song for the old fellow. A shot of his
tombstone (with the authentic footnote of giving him the
family's last name, MacDowell) is followed by a chorus of
other slaves surrounding the grave and singing "Old Black
Joe," still another Foster composition supposedly inspired
by a specific encounter in the narrative.

The interposition of war, acting as a life-disrupting force, was first witnessed in the films under study when Vernon Castle volunteered to leave show business for combat duty. The outbreak of the Civil War, announced in like manner by a newspaper headline and combat footage, prompts Stephen Foster to volunteer, but he is rejected by a Yankee Army physician who tells him he has heart disease and who echoes the earlier advice of Christy to "go on writing songs." However, the doctor adds, "Don't get excited. Walk, don't run." The intimations of doom have begun to intensify.

At a military ball for Yankee officers, we see Jane waltzing with Herr Kleiber, who has been a devoted family friend for years (he was the one who attended her the night the Fosters' daughter Marion was born). No less eccentric than Maggie and Walter in THE CASTLES or Speed King in THE STAR MAKER, no less dedicated than Bailey Walsh in THE MIGHTY BARNUM, Kleiber still can not countenance the presence of E. P. Christy, whose arrival at the party prompts the old music teacher to exclaim, "Now my evening is ruined!"

Although at this point in the narrative the character of Christy is not functioning as a malevolent obstacle to Foster's well-being, the showman's good intentions come to naught, and ultimately give a fatal shove to Foster on his downhill slide. In his customarily grandiose manner, Christy stops the orchestra and announces to the crowd the presence in their midst of "America's troubador composer." The assemblage's enthusiastic response swiftly turns to fury when the musicians begin a chorus of "Oh, Sussannah." Societal forces, beyond the control of the characters in the drama, intervene. A heckler shouts, "There's a war on, and that's a Rebel song!" Other guests chime in with angry remarks, and one asks if Foster sympathizes with the South. "Yes, deeply," he replies, and the crowd begins to act ugly, with shouts of "traitor" filling the air. While Kleiber berates Christy as a "windbag" and an "egomaniac" for causing the trouble, Foster slinks away to seek solace in liquor.

A drunken scene in her seven-year-old daughter's bedroom disgusts Jane to the point that she deserts Foster, taking the little girl with her. Even at this point the dialogue ties in with a song title when, on the morning of the mother and daughter's departure, the father tells little Marion he won't be going with her to the "Old Kentucky Home" because he has to stay in New York and "rattle out more

songs." The familiar notion of a psychological malady
called "writer's block," soon to become a recurrent motif
in similar films, grips Stephen Foster in the throes of his
despair. Meanwhile, Christy runs short of material and
puts ads in the personal columns, seeking the composer's
whereabouts. After a long search of the saloons of Manhattan, Christy finds Foster playing the piano for drinks in
a sleazy dive. After listening to the brash minstrel's tales
of performing before the "crowned heads of Europe" and being told by Queen Victoria that he had "real oscamazoola,"
Foster responds to Christy's question of "What went wrong?"
with the dour confession, "I just don't have it any more."
In a rare moment of candor Christy admits, "It was all a
lot of bunk about the crowned heads ... but we did pack 'em
in, and I owe it to you. Look what your songs have done
for me." Thus the roles are reversed, from the pair's
initial confrontation in which Christy denigrated the importance of composers in his own career and Foster pleaded
for an arrangement between them, to Christy's giving Foster the credit for the minstrel troupe's success and Foster
insisting that no future collaboration between them is possible. Gray-haired and despondent, Foster says he only wants
to sit and listen to his old songs sung the old way.

Alone and living in a hovel, Foster makes a feeble
attempt at composition but discards the note scratchings and
sinks into a drunkard's sleep. As the narrative draws to
its tragic conclusion, Foster appears to have reached the
nadir of his life's journey--yet a brief moment of renaissance occurs. A note comes from Jane, suggesting the
possibility of reconciliation. She has been advised by
Kleiber and disbelieves Stephen's pitiful attempts to pretend that he is well off. He meets with her in a hotel
lobby, and she tells him Christy is most anxious to feature
a new Stephen Foster song in the show he is about to open
on Broadway. Working all night with Jane's encouragement,
Foster pens a new ballad describing the time they once
spent "down on the river."

A sign outside New York City's Marble Hall announces:
"Tonight, first time on stage--a new song by America's
Troubador, Stephen Foster, sung by E. P. Christy, America's Ethiopian Minstrel King." Inside, Christy, proud as
ever, marvels at the size of the wartime crowd, then boasts
that "E. P. Christy could sing 'Marching Through Georgia'
in Atlanta and make 'em love it." Kleiber and Jane arrive
at the theatre, explaining that Stephen will be joining them

later. Outside, a crowd of agitators mills about, threatening to disrupt the performance because of their belief that Foster is still a Southern sympathizer. Back in his dingy apartment, he prepares to shave himself with a straight razor. While he is offscreen the sound of a crash is heard. Back at the theatre a messenger boy arrives with the news that Foster has had an accident. Christy and Jane rush to Stephen's bedside, where Christy prevaricates about the new song getting five encores. Not suspecting the deception, Foster compliments Christy on singing "our songs" better than anyone else. The conflict between the two collaborators is thus resolved, and to Jane the dying man apologizes, "I'm sorry, Jeannie ... it seems that something always happens...." The life of Stephen Foster is over. His accounts with those closest to him have been settled, and the narrative could end at this point in tragic fashion, but without sufficient emotional release the mythic pattern would be incomplete.

Back at the Marble Hall, Christy quiets the restive crowd with the announcement that "Stephen Foster's moment of triumph has become his memorial." The convenient conjunction of historical events effected once more, Christy introduces the film's title song to the startled crowd with the words: "He left us his new song ... it will endure long after the war is forgotten. He wrote it for all the American people." After Christy finishes singing "Swanee River," the crowd stands and sings it again with him, and a concluding montage of Southern scenes dissolves into view, ending with a shot of two slaves standing by a tar paper shack along the river bank. Finally the film's end titles appear, spelled out in the sampler style of the opening and visually closing the mythic cycle.

SWANEE RIVER's narrative offers few definite clues to the specific nature of the flaw(s) which destroyed its hero. Even the circumstances of his death are rendered ambiguously. The messenger boy mentions both a heart attack and Foster's having fallen on his razor, thereby raising the possibility that the distressed composer tried to cut his throat and died from shock. Foster's bitter disappointment at failing to conquer the serious music world certainly played a part in his growing depression and self-destructive behavior; his displaying greater concern for his music than for his wife clearly played a crucial role in the dissolution of his marriage. If an obsession with his career appears at the center of Foster's slide into an alcoholic miasma, then it presages the spate of success-crazed figures whose lives would be dramatized on America's movie screens in the years to come. Yet SWANEE RIVER is no tale of an artist making personal sacrifices for his craft. The line between sacrifice and self-destruction, while it would become decidedly thin in later biographies, is still quite distinct at this point. Thus the element of fate must also be considered as operative in the mythic structure. SWANEE RIVER is an affirmation of the power of Stephen Foster's music, but a testament to his own powerlessness as well.

Note

1. The caveats of Edward Hallett Carr, as set forth in What Is History? apply remarkably well to the study of show-business biographical films. This study, without contradicting its stated methodology of examining the films themselves as primary texts, does take notice of industrial forces and popular beliefs whose imprints can be found within the filmic texts under examination. The goal of better comprehending a generic grouping by delineating how individual works interrelate and evolve over a period of years cannot be achieved in a void. If one is to undertake the task at hand without prejudice, then one must be cognizant of and on guard against the pre-existing forces which tend to color one's understanding.

CHAPTER V

THE FORM TAKES SHAPE

The first two show-business biographies to arrive on the nation's theatre screens following the turn of the decade were based on the lives of famous actresses who were at the height of their popularity at the turn of the century. LILLIAN RUSSELL and THE LADY WITH RED HAIR (both 1940) differed primarily in that the former fit the generally accepted definition of a "musical" (a drama interspersed with songs), while the latter did not. LILLIAN RUSSELL, however, invoked the familiar to a somewhat greater extent than did LADY, starting with the choice of film title and extending to the inclusion of a larger number of once-famous celebrities as subsidiary characters. While not a "cradle-to-grave" biography (the narrative ends with the title character embarking on her last marriage), LILLIAN RUSSELL does begin with her birth and a "childhood signifier of future greatness." The offscreen sound of the baby's wailing is greeted with a relative's remark, "I'll say one thing for her--she's got a good voice." Born in Iowa in the midst of the Civil War, and to a family of four daughters and no sons (her father disappointedly refuses to look at the newborn), the girl derives little affection from her cold father and politically obsessed mother. Lillian is closest to her sharp-tongued but amusing grandmother (a recurrence of the familiar eccentric companion/advisor) because the girl's mother is preoccupied with suffragette politics.

A subsequent signifier of destined notoriety comes in the remarks of opera impresario Leopold Damrosch (a forebear of the Damrosch visited by Larry Earl/Gus Edwards), for whom a teenaged Lillian (still called by her real name, Helen Leonard) auditions with hopes of a career on the stage. "I feel sorry for you," says the operatic starmaker. "Because of your beauty ... you may never know which man loves you for yourself."

Alice Faye in the starring role, Don Ameche (at piano), and Edward Arnold (r.) in LILLIAN RUSSELL (1940). Photo courtesy of Wisconsin Center for Film and Theater Research.

The numerous love affairs and marriages of the historical Lillian Russell are severely condensed in the film narrative, with a great deal of screen time given over to period musical numbers rendered in performance situations. The plot essentially becomes a variation on the standard lost-and-found love story, with Russell meeting a young newspaperman named Alexander Moore when he rescues her from a runaway horse-carriage as she is leaving her audition for Damrosch. This coincident conjunction of events foreshadows Moore's "waiting on the sidelines" while the girl is courted by the rich and powerful, and his last-minute "rescue" of her (via a "good" marriage) when her romantic fortunes have collapsed.

The dialogue repeatedly emphasizes the emotional price she has to pay for being a matchless beauty and a sought-after celebrity. At one point she and financier Diamond Jim Brady console each other's broken hearts, and Brady observes, "We're very much alike, aren't we?

We have everything life could give us except what we really want." As had been a standard Hollywood depression-era practice in photoplays about the rich, the possibility of audience envy and resentment of their "betters" is obviated by revealing the suffering and heartbreak which allegedly stud the road to fame and fortune.

Invocation of the familiar in LILLIAN RUSSELL functions with heavy dependence on the nostalgia factor (re-creating the memorable and recognizable to the supposed delight of audience members whose first immersion in popular culture was during the period depicted). A somewhat peculiar linkage to an earlier (1935) non-show-business biography occurs with the performance of Edward Arnold as Diamond Jim, a role he first essayed in the film of the same name (in which his unsuccessful courting of Russell was only a subplot).

As in THE GREAT ZIEGFELD, celebrity iconography via both close impersonation and congruent reality of performance enhances the invocatory process. Eddie Foy, Jr. appears as his famous father and does one of the elder Foy's vaudeville routines, "Going to Church on Sunday." The (by 1940) elderly comedy team, Weber and Fields, perform as their younger selves (from 40 years earlier) and do their famous "Casino-Casino-Casino" stage turn. Songs identified with the "gaslight era," with Tony Pastor's Manhattan theatre-restaurant, and with Russell's stage successes fill the sound track, including the tune which was to become an instantly identifiable anthem for evoking the milieu in dozens of factual and fictitious films to come: "After the Ball." Even Russell's unsuccessful attempt at starring in a Gilbert and Sullivan operetta in London is briefly sketched, with the actors who appear as the composers seen (characteristically) quarreling with each other.

While the film's narrative functions centrally in imposing a lost-and-found love plot on the warmly invoked memory of Russell's public image and career, the mythical founding of a fact-based, yet nostalgically re-worked surrounding era is ultimately a larger creation of the film when analyzed as merely another fictive device interfacing with the public mind circa 1940. The film LILLIAN RUSSELL, unreeling in the nation's projection booths at that fixed point in time, was laying at least some of the building blocks of a more discrete, less linear mythic perception--not about a famous performer's life so much as about her times. Just as THE GREAT ZIEGFELD had refined and offered to the public the supposed essence of theatrical excitement and opulence in the generation that preceded the crash, LILLIAN RUSSELL served up a distillation of sights and sounds capsulizing what the stage ensemble sings about in the film's concluding production number: "The Gay Days of Old Broadway," part of a period which by 1940 was already popularly referred to as the "Gay Nineties." Suffragettes marching, Lillian and two of her robber-baron boyfriends gliding through Central Park on a three-seat bicycle, mountains of food at Tony Pastor's saloon, horsecars and carriages on Fifth Avenue, stage door Johnnies waiting in full evening dress with handfuls of furs and diamonds at the ready, the enormous feathered hats and bulging bustles of the fashionable ladies-- these are some of the images of the mythical past which the film transmits concomitantly with its mythical plot, carved into familiar shape from bits and pieces of historical fact and dramatic tradition.

While Lillian Russell was known more for her glamorous appearance, rich beaus and "way with a song" than for her acting ability, Mrs. Leslie Carter, whose career chronologically paralleled that of Russell, was a dramatic actress of the highest repute. The story of her celebrated career, allegedly told in THE LADY WITH RED HAIR, employs a rather unique variation on the lost-and-found love plot. Not only does she lose and regain the affection of the second-rate actor who ultimately becomes her second husband, but she also enters, exits and re-enters the most profitable professional relationship of her career: acting under the Svengali-like tutelage of theatrical impresario and wizard David Belasco.

The theme of an actress having to sacrifice her hopes for a home and family in order to achieve success on the stage, underlined quite clearly in the dialogue of LILLIAN RUSSELL, is here given the most explicit recitation and repetition yet in a specifically biographical show business film. Carolyn Carter, a notorious divorcée whose highly publicized separation from her wealthy husband has left her impoverished and devoid of the custody of her young son, makes a somewhat late-in-life decision to go on the stage. After creating a scene at her son's boarding school, she is sarcastically advised by astonished onlookers that she should be an actress. Later she tells her mother, "I can walk and talk and shout as well as any of them." While deprecating the acting profession, the younger woman also announces her decision to take the advice seriously.

Claude Rains (l.) as David Belasco, with John Litel and Mona Barrie in THE LADY WITH RED HAIR (1940). Photo courtesy of Wisconsin Center for Film and Theater Research.

Entrance into the guarded halls of Broadway success is, according to the accumulating genre custom, difficult at first, partially dependent upon luck, and finally awarded on the basis of the gatekeepers (producers, directors, agents, publishers) perceiving some natural talent. Lillian Russell was fortunate enough to have a friend arrange for Tony Pastor to hear her singing at a beer garden. Carolyn Carter, despite the use of a letter of introduction from a family friend, is not able to attract the serious attention of the man she wants to start her "at the top" (Belasco) until she manages to be camped on his front porch just at the time he happens to need an extra body to read lines and walk through stage movements while they are being timed.

Implicit in Belasco's "discovery" of Mrs. Carter are the elements of chance and perseverence. There is also a suggestion of her being "touched" by the quasi-divine muse of Belasco himself, already a theatrical legend at the time of their meeting. When the lady expresses misgivings about her ability to live up to her director's expectations, her boastful mentor replies: "David Belasco could make an actress out of a telephone pole."

Invocation of the familiar functions throughout the narrative in regard to what members of the 1940 public might previously know about Carter and Belasco. Montage sequences prominently display the titles of plays in which the historical Mrs. Carter starred; Belasco is overheard in pompous discourse while extolling the virtues of and utter necessity for "realism" on the stage.

As in the film's generic predecessors, the mythic plot of lost-and-found love binds the historic and invented details together, but the duality of the Carter-second husband and Carter-Belasco relationships is rendered not by congruence, but in a sequential, causal mode. Carter's rise to stardom under Belasco's direction is halted when she violates the director's dictum against combining personal with professional life. Her disobedient (in the master's view) and long-delayed marriage to actor Lou Paine causes the arrogant showman to cease his guidance of her career. When Carter's romance with Paine (cut off when Belasco told her she had to become "married to the theatre") is resumed, it costs her her success. Without Belasco she fails in stage ventures of her own choosing. Even though she has attained romantic fulfillment with Lou Paine, her career continues a downward spiral until Paine seeks out Belasco and begs him to assist Carter, who has undertaken a difficult part in what could be her last play. Deceived into believing that the request comes from a repentant Carolyn, Belasco helps the actress master the role and save her career.

Whether Belasco's jealousy of Paine has a sexual subtext is difficult to ascertain from the film's overt assertions. The dialogue denies such a motivation, yet the oppositional relationships of the main characters echo the romantic triangle permutations of some of the most familiar of dramatic plots. Romantic considerations aside, the film's plot can also be analyzed in terms of the actress' professional rise, fall and renaissance, thus increasing the picture's reliance on the formula used by THE MIGHTY BARNUM and THE GREAT ZIEGFELD.

LILLIAN RUSSELL and THE LADY WITH RED HAIR, although released during the year 1940, actually marked the close of the show-business biographical film's formula-establishment phase, a period rightly identified with the 1930s. In LILLIAN RUSSELL the invocation of the familiar functions quite broadly, with the popular conception of the title figure as symbol of <u>fin-de-siècle</u> glamor exploited to achieve maximum audience interest and positive response. In the latter film such invocation is more limited (as evidenced by the choice of an ambiguous, referent-reduced title). It is not the re-created images of Belasco and Carter that are being sold to the public. Rather it is their names, personal histories and surroundings that are, in effect, being used to dress up, or outfit a formula-cast romantic drama of rise-and-fall. The story is then pitched to the public as the latest "star vehicle" for Miriam Hopkins and Claude Rains, two salable personalities who, despite their second-rank star status, were (at that time) able to command sufficient audience interest and loyalty to make the project economically feasible to its backers.

Only once before, in the production and promotion of the anomalous STAR MAKER, was the show business personage being portrayed treated as of secondary importance to the actor playing the lead. In the next phase of development of the show-business biographical film the promotional (audience-grabbing) emphasis becomes decidedly more diffused. While invocation of the familiar continues to be a most important factor in the stimulus-response interaction between film and audience, an increasing number of show-business biographical films are conceived and executed primarily as "star vehicles" and only secondarily as potentially profitable projects liable to succeed because of the public's susceptibility to exploitation of its continuing celebrity-directed curiosity and nostalgia.

As noted earlier, in the 1940s the show-business biography becomes almost a staple in Hollywood's assembly-line output of entertainment product, with a new entry appearing on the nation's theatre screens about as often as the seasons change. Large-scale, big-budget depictions of major celebrities' lives such as THE GREAT ZIEGFELD and THE STORY OF VERNON AND IRENE CASTLE continue to be filmed during the next phase, but many smaller-scale biographies of lesser-known, even relatively obscure entertainment personages are also filmed. The mythic narrative underpinning, beneath an attractive overlay of familiar-nostalgic details and settings, continues as in the earlier phase, although it becomes a far more frequent occurrence that the star is of greater importance (in terms of interest generation) than the historical character he is playing.

Central to this transition or broadening of the formula is the rise of the songwriter biography. No new show-business biographical films were released in America for a full year preceding the nation's entry into World War II. Yet shortly after Pearl Harbor the cycle began to resume. By the end of 1945 eleven more "life stories" of show-business celebrities had been released, including one British import. Only two of these utilized the central character's name in the title, but eight of the eleven took their titles from popular songs.*

In May of 1942, two show-business biographies were released, both taking their titles from popular songs rather than from the names of the real-life composers whose lives were being dramatized. YANKEE DOODLE DANDY, based on the career of songwriter-playwright-performer George M. Cohan, was produced on a lavish scale rivaling that of THE GREAT ZIEGFELD. Promoted as a "Five Million Dollar Production," the Cohan biography re-created numerous sequences from his long string of hit stage shows, interspersing them with a flashback-framed narrative which was itself quite linear, showing the upward progress of the central character from birth to retirement, moving from success to success, and topping off a well-spent life with a greatly acclaimed comeback and the nation's highest award. The mythic pattern, therefore, is essentially one of straightforward quest, not of rise-and-fall or lost-and-found love. To sustain dramatic interest, the plot does digress for a series of minor setbacks and conflicts with subsidiary characters, but at no point does the Cohan character suffer a

---

*Despite reduced budgets, the loss of many major male stars to military service, and the loss of revenue from exhibition in much of Europe and Asia, the American film industry prospered during the war years with many urban theatres playing twenty-four hours a day to a de facto captive audience of ration-bound and travel-restricted citizens. It was said that "every movie made a profit," but the proliferation of show-business biographies after a year-long dearth indicates they must have enjoyed a substantial cumulative profit.

84 / Star Myths

painful fall from the high road of success. Nor does he become estranged from his "one true love" (although the historical Cohan had three wives).

The linear narrative is wide-rangingly chronological enough to take Cohan from the date of his birth (as a newborn, given a flag to wave in his cradle) to his twilight years (as a raspy-voiced, gray-haired old trouper receiving a special honor from the president). It begins with Cohan in perhaps the most apropos of all show-business settings, backstage in his dressing room. Aged but still energetic, the veteran actor reacts to a telegram inviting him to the White House by deciding to walk there from the District of Columbia theatre where he has just completed a road show performance of his successful comeback vehicle (a gentle spoof of the presidency written not by him but by Kaufman and Hart), "I'd Rather Be Right." While invocation of the

James Cagney and Eddie Foy, Jr. in YANKEE DOODLE DANDY (1942). Photo courtesy of Wisconsin Center for Film and Theater Research.

familiar functions in the film's opening sequence only for those viewers who (in 1942) might still remember Cohan as he appeared in his last stage work, the invocational process soars to an extremely high level when the Cohan character reaches the Oval Office. There a series of reverential, over-the-shoulder shots (Roosevelt's face is not revealed to the camera) and the dubbed voice of a mimic signify that Cohan has come into the presence of the nation's commander-in-chief. The invocational process exercises in this sequence a significant concatenation of inherently contradictory stimuli: although the Roosevelt figure is clearly sitting at his desk, only a few feet from the Cohan character, the Roosevelt voice speaks not in an intimate, conversational mode, but rather in a decelerated, declamatory style, akin to that used in making a speech, which was the way in which most Americans were used to hearing the voice of the real-life President Roosevelt.

The president praises Cohan for his (and the Irish people's) contributions to American culture, and asks the old vaudevillian to share the story of his life. The succeeding narrative, in flashback, begins with George's birth on the Fourth of July, 1878, a time which a printed title tells us is the "Beginning of the Horatio Alger Age." The popular conceptualizing of an era employed in this instance gives a convenient and comfortable identity to a relatively unfamiliar time in American history. The late 1870s had, with the exception of western adventure stories, been the subject of much less screen drama than, say, the 1860s (the Civil War) or the 1890s (the "Gay Nineties"). The familiar iconography of the show-business biography is not far away, however, and the second image the camera dwells on (the first was an Independence Day Parade) is the vaudeville bill of acts appearing at the "Colony Opera House." The featured performers are "The Irish Darlings--Mr. and Mrs. Jerry Cohan."

Young George is born into a family so wrapped up in the trade of performing that even his middle name, which his father had intended to be Washington, is changed to Michael to facilitate easier placement on a theatre marquee. The linear narrative of the extended flashback which makes up the body of the film is augmented at major leaps in continuity by spoken, offscreen narration in the voice of the central character who is supposedly (in the duality of a flashback-framed diegesis) still telling his story to the president.

What follows is, essentially, a series of successes. We see first a montage of appearances on the "tank circuit" of small-town music halls by the family song-and-dance act billed as "The Four Cohans." (George's four-years-younger sister Josie joins the act as soon as she can walk and learn a few dance steps.) By the time George is thirteen, he is a hit as the star of a Brooklyn production of the stage perennial about juvenile misbehavior, "Peck's Bad Boy." When the lad's premature success causes him to carry the cockiness of his stage character offstage, a group of neighborhood boys rough him up, and his father consoles the battered, fledgling star with not just the moral of the lad's comeuppance, but also the heroic/adulatory message of the entire film: "Most actors give their whole lives to the profession without scoring a hit. You're a hit at thirteen ... but I've never known any that wouldn't rather be a great guy than a great actor."

As in LILLIAN RUSSELL, the first of these films which actually starts with the birth of the central character, the intimation of future greatness is mingled with a warning. While still in her teens, Lillian was alerted to the possibility that her great beauty would bring her great sadness. Now George is cautioned that because he has embarked upon a life in the theatre, his character (in the virtuous sense) will always be in danger of being sacrificed to the aggrandizement of his character on stage. The "big break" so often spoken of in show-business parlance, and a significant turning point in many of these films, comes immediately after this lecture (the convenient conjunction of circumstance) when the head of the "big time" Albee theatre circuit enters the Cohans' dressing room and offers them booking in the best theatres in the country.

Ten years pass, via montage shots and voice-over narration; a key image is the dissolve shot of George's legs, transforming the knee britches of childhood into the long pants of a young adult. At this point in the linear, upward progression of his life and career he meets his "one true love," an eighteen-year-old aspiring actress who, having been totally convinced by George's stage characterization, asks what she thinks is a very old actor if he has any advice for her. Her surprise when he kicks up his heels, does a very lively dance step, and then removes his makeup, turns to admiration/attraction, and the pair go off to dine together. Their choice of restaurant is the famous nightspot which has by this point in the evolution of the show-business biographical film become virtual screen shorthand for the ultimate in Gay Nineties socializing--Tony Pastor's. While 1878 might have been so unfamiliar to movie audiences as to require its identification with the heroes of Horatio Alger, the era the film's narrative is now outlining overlaps with several predecessors in our group of targeted films.

Although there are to be no major/tragic setbacks to the fictionalized career of George M. Cohan, and while the element of spectacle (musical production numbers re-created from successful Cohan productions) is to dominate much of the balance of the picture, the customary secondary conflicts necessary to maintain dramatic interest still occur at scattered points in the narrative. One such conflict stems from George's excessive efforts to further his sweetheart Mary's career. (She has joined the same vaudeville troupe as the Four Cohans, but as a specialty dancer, not as part of the family act.) George's managing to get the trainer of the dog act drunk so that Mary could do a longer number causes him to be temporarily blacklisted from the circuit, and he tries his hand at selling his songs to various music publishers in New York City. The multiple rejections that plagued Stephen Foster in SWANEE RIVER return to buffet the young Cohan, until he learns how to exploit the obvious covetousness and rivalry of the "show biz types" who have been unresponsive to his pleadings. (The portrayal of bickering, petty-minded producers, particularly those who are partners, was especially notable in THE STORY OF VERNON AND IRENE CASTLE.)

In the midst of "conning" a producer named Schwab into backing a Broadway show Cohan has written--the pretext is that another, rival impresario wants it--George joins forces with struggling songwriter Sam Harris, who coincidentally enters the scene just when Cohan needs a "shill" to back up his story. The two young composers become fast friends and partners (with Harris turning from tunesmithing to business managing), and the show, "Little Johnny Jones," becomes a Broadway success. While the character of George M. Cohan, like that of Florenz Ziegfeld, is shown not to be above using trickery in attaining his objectives, at no time is Cohan actually depicted crossing the line between good-natured chicanery and criminally dishonest behavior. His father's concern that the boy grow into a "great man" is echoed in the screenplay, and audience sympathy for the central character is not jeopardized.

One unusual alteration in the emerging formula of the show-business biography occurs in the portrayal of Cohan's subsequent close friend and advisor, Sam H. Harris. The part is not played for humor, and the actor cast as Harris has none of the eccentric mannerisms or speech patterns of a Frank Morgan, Walter Brennan or Ned Sparks. Instead, Richard Whorf enacts the role of Harris in a most sober and self-effacing way. Balancing this alteration, however, is the portrayal of the befuddled producer Schwab, who backs Cohan in his initial Broadway success. Schwab's crucial line of dialogue, which okays Cohan and Harris' "con" and makes the launching of "Little Johnny Jones" possible (and ameliorates any audience unease about the trickery involved), is spoken by the veteran cinema buffoon S. Z. "Cuddles" Sakall. The line: "Why is Dietz's wife's money better than my wife's money?"

Another key line, thoroughly in keeping with the ambition proclamations spoken by nearly every central figure in the films under study since P. T. Barnum, is uttered by Cohan while trying unsuccessfully to obtain backing from the producing team of Dietz and Goff. Says Cohan, "I'm gonna have my name plastered up and down Broadway, till I'm as well known as Coot's Sarsaparilla." The fulfillment of this prediction begins with the immensely successful opening of "Little Johnny Jones," Cohan's musical drama about an American jockey who becomes involved in a British racing scandal. The narrative pauses at this point to make way for what has become (by way of the excerpting process in numerous compilation films) one of the most-seen production numbers in the history of the musical film, the "Yankee Doodle Dandy" song-and-dance routine performed by James Cagney in a close approximation of the vocal and choreographic style of the real-life Cohan. Invocation of the familiar (for those who knew Cohan's style) thus functions at a much higher level when the Cohan character is seen performing, than when he is observed interacting with others in the steady progression of the dramatic continuity. At those times the behavior of actor Cagney is much less distinguishable from his long line of "star performances" than it is when he is mimicking Cohan to the point of capturing the exact intonation patterns and movements of the famous entertainer's stage routines.

Another invocational episode which verges on the near-congruency of the Will Rogers and Eddie Cantor portrayals in THE GREAT ZIEGFELD occurs when Cohan boasts

The Form Takes Shape / 89

his way through a street corner confrontation with rival bigtime vaudevillian (and "family act" performer) Eddie Foy. Pretending not to know one another, the two meet by chance in front of a billboard advertising Cohan's latest show. The pals playfully argue about whether the performer whose face appears on the sign is as good an entertainer as the famous Eddie Foy. Eddie Foy, Jr. closely impersonates his father in this exchange, which stresses the intense but benign competition that supposedly existed in the theatrical kingdom over which Cohan was to reign for several seasons. Indeed, even the titles of his subsequent hit shows echo the motif of Cohan's goodnatured supremacy: "The American Idea," "The Little Millionaire," "Hello Broadway," and "The Man Who Owns Broadway."

The identification of a show-business figure's public creations and accomplishments with persons and events in his private life functions very clearly in YANKEE DOODLE DANDY. One of Cohan's most famous and long-lasting songs, "Mary's a Grand Old Name," is depicted as having been written for his sweetheart, although the exigencies of stage politics force him to give the song to star vocalist Fay Templeton to introduce in the Klaw and Erlanger production of "A Little Bit of Everything." A testy exchange with the haughty Templeton (who lives in New Rochelle, forty-five minutes' drive from the "noisy and neurotic people" of the Broadway show district) then inspires Cohan to write "Forty-Five Minutes from Broadway," which opens at the New Amsterdam Theatre as a hit show starring Templeton and Victor Moore.

That Cohan is building a heroic legend of success about himself is summarized in a remark by Templeton's manager: "He's the whole darn country squeezed into one pair of pants. Hitch your wagon to his star ... now! He's found every American's private dream." Here the mythic infrastructure of the narrative sharpens into focus, its highly linear progression outlining the rudiments of the quest. Cross-identification between Cohan's achieving popular success and the cultural ethos known as the "American Dream" becomes exceptionally strong in the production number set to the tune "You're a Grand Old Flag," which features the entire Cohan family (he has retrieved them from their continuing career in vaudeville and has married Mary) plus a large chorus, costumed in variations of the best-known patriotic symbols.

Despite the aforementioned linearity, vestiges of rise-and-fall stories from previous show-business biographical films do surface following a success montage, but at no time is any serious threat to Cohan's happy marriage or Broadway supremacy given credence. What little rise-and-fall plot curvature and "stick to what you do best" thematic emphasis survive in YANKEE DOODLE DANDY manifest themselves in Cohan's isolated and ill-fated attempt to write a "serious," non-musical stage drama. Its dismal failure with both audience and critics barely dents Cohan's growing fortune and continuing career. (Concurrent with the play's opening, Cohan is also shown to be backing a new minstrel show and starring in yet another musical comedy.) When Stephen Foster in SWANEE RIVER failed at creating "serious" music, his self-esteem crumbled, but Cohan steers clear of the pit of self-pity by placing his obligation to "the public" above his temporary mortification. He immediately purchases newspaper advertisements warning New York theatre-goers to stay away from his flop and apologizing for disappointing those who attended the opening night. This apparently noble act is shown to have a pragmatic basis in Cohan's private explanation: "You can't disappoint the public --they'll never forgive you."

Catering to the public's expectations, anticipating and attempting to satisfy their needs for emotional gratification (curiosity satiation in regard to celebrity figures) is, of course, what the show-business biographical film has been about since its inception, although the manufacturing of nostalgia stimuli (bringing back the old songs in seemingly authentic settings) is a parallel process in popular culture which, as shown, begins to intersect and concur with the biographical process fairly early in the appearance of the films under study. Both fictive creative processes combine in the musical show-business biographical film, depending, as they did when separate, upon a long-standardized group of myth-plots as the basis for individual narratives.

In YANKEE DOODLE DANDY, however, a third process makes its influence felt at this point in the narrative, modifying the diegesis (which has been somewhat vague as to precise, historical chronology) with the intrusion of war. In THE STORY OF VERNON AND IRENE CASTLE the outbreak of war was just as clearly depicted, but there it functioned only as a plot device to separate the lovers before their mystical reunion in the narrative's mythic fourth phase or season. World War I becomes part of the diegesis of

YANKEE DOODLE DANDY as a thinly disguised representation of the new war which was strongly re-shaping all of American popular culture during the months in which the film was in production. In earlier films analyzed by this study, the phenomenon of the hindsight-influenced historical-social pronouncement was observed as a pleasure-inducing stimulus, gratifying viewers by allowing them to imagine themselves as enjoying a superior position to the characters in a history-limited diegesis. George M. Cohan's hindsight-influenced pronouncement, stemming not only from the failure of his play, but also from the subsequent announcement of the sinking of the Lusitania (the coincident conjunction of events, once again) carried an unmistakable message to every viewer who saw the film at the time of its initial release, less than six months after Pearl Harbor. Says George: "It always happens. Whenever we get too high-hat and sophisticated for flag-waving, some thug nation thinks we're a pushover!"

Marxist critics would likely identify all show-business biographical films produced within a capitalist economy as representational parts of an industry-wide, continuing propaganda effort to suppress class revolt and divert the working population's attention from the realities of the economic struggle. Be that as it may, YANKEE DOODLE DANDY marks a shift from whatever "background propaganda" infuses the Hollywood-produced, fictional narrative film as a whole, in so far as it is a rare example of overtly promoting wartime patriotic fervor via the discrete (and usually time-distanced) medium of show-business biography.

Cohan is portrayed as volunteering for military service but being turned down by an army major, who explains, "We need you here more than we do over there." Thus the Cohan character's exemption from the soldiering which all forms of popular culture in both wars promoted (by inducing national guilt feelings about "shirking one's duty") is accomplished without jeopardizing audience sympathy. The inspiration-from-events motif recurs immediately following Cohan's service rejection, when, outside the recruiting office, he hears a bugler sound three notes. Later, seated at a piano on a bare stage, Cohan recalls the three notes (E-G-C) and promptly composes "Over There," which a subsequent montage sequence depicts as becoming something of a national anthem in support of American intervention in European combat. As in the corresponding montage from THE STORY OF VERNON AND IRENE CASTLE, selling war bonds and entertaining the troops are shown to be very appropriate activities for first-rank entertainers in time of war. The invocation of familiar components from the iconography of show business continues, therefore, even in the midst of the above-mentioned montage. At one point in the rapid succession of images, Cohan is seen at a YMCA-sponsored army camp show, accompanying on a piano a linkage figure from THE GREAT ZIEGFELD, vaudeville headliner Nora Bayes, whose former partner Jack Norworth is not appearing (possibly because he, unlike Cohan, was needed more "Over There").

Neither success (he was cured of a "swelled head" at age thirteen) nor failure (he always had other irons in the fire) nor world-wide war can halt the upward progression of Cohan's life and career. (A post-war montage displays a whole new string of his hit shows.) Only the dissolution of the family unit, George's wellspring of inspiration and energy, finally induces him to retire from performing and composing.

That the Cohan story is representative of something much larger than one man's spectacular career is suggested by a doctor's remark outside the bedroom where George's father lies dying. Noting that this is the last time the Four Cohans will be together, the physician observes, "A whole theatrical era is dying in there, but he lived long enough to see his son become an American institution."

Whatever the real-life reasons for the much-publicized breakup of the Cohan and Harris producing team, in the idealized, myth-infused diegesis of YANKEE DOODLE DANDY their "perfect partnership" is severed (symbolized by the tearing in half of a business card) simply because of melancholy. With a tear in his voice, Cohan explains, "It was the only firm with two senior partners, but after Dad died all the fun went out of it." Show business to George M. Cohan was, above all, fun. Even though the real-life Cohan appears to have been possessed by some driving need to perform continually, to win public approval, to promote the brassiest brand of American patriotism, and to advertise to the nation the harmony and strength of his family ties, the narrative of the film skirts these complex motivational issues to offer the more easily comprehensible (via obfuscatory simplification) motivation: fun. This observational analysis is not to fault the picture, for indeed, most of its predecessors took the need to perform as a "given" in establishing

The Form Takes Shape / 93

the rudiments of their characters. Rather, the "fun" aspect of Cohan's story, specifically the delight he is shown to experience in performing with his family whenever possible, supersedes all other themes in the narrative, even that of wartime morale-boosting, to become the dominant force behind the singularly upward progression of his career. His repeated phrase (something of a stage trademark) at the end of his performance sequences makes this quite clear: "My father thanks you ... my mother thanks you ... my sister thanks you ... and I thank you."

Cohan quits while he is on top. His last string of Broadway hit performances is shown via montage to include such shows as "Disraeli," "Little Nellie Kelly," "Song and Dance Man," "The Tavern," and "Ah, Wilderness." Understandably, the question arises at this point whether (in the mythic infrastructure of the narrative) he has succeeded in his quest, or whether his hiatus from the stage is some variation of rise-and-fall after all. Since, as Todorov has demonstrated in The Morphology of the Folktale, it is possible for storytellers to overlay one myth upon another without creating any essentially new forms, a more useful explanation is that a seasonal pattern is co-existent with that of the quest when Cohan retires from Broadway to "rubberneck like a tourist" on an extended world tour/vacation with his wife Mary. It is in the winter of his career.

Because of the film's flashback framework, investing the diegesis with a contemporary chronological point of reference, the passing of the years between his departure from the stage and his return (culminating in a visit to FDR's office) are implied by a sequence showing Cohan and his wife living a life of retirement in a modest rural home near a country road. When a group of "jitterbug-happy" teenagers drive up in a "jalopy" and converse with Cohan while asking for some water, it becomes clear that they have never heard of him--that he has become a forgotten man in the popular culture of the "swing era." The historical fact that the real-life Cohan enjoyed no such retirement and continued to appear in Broadway shows all through the 1930s makes it clear that this invented episode was not included in the narrative by force of fact. Rather, the episode serves to strengthen the seasonal nature of his "retirement" and by contrast pave the way for his triumphant "comeback" in the long-running Rodgers and Hart/Kaufman and Hart musical comedy "I'd Rather Be Right." Thus the winter is followed by Cohan's theatrical re-birth as a Broadway star for a new generation.

Cohan agrees to play the lead, the President of the United States, at the urging of his wife (who berates him for having retired too early) and as a personal favor to Sam Harris, who is broke and can get financial backing only if Cohan accepts the role--because "he's the only actor in the world who can play it."

Although the actual play opened in 1937, the excerpt shown in the film has Cohan speaking lines which include: "We'll knock the axe off the Axis!" and "We'll take it back from Hitler and put ants in his Japants!" With propagandistic invocation of the present functioning as the strongest influence upon the narrative at this point, the flashback framework of the film's opening recurs, just as FDR informs the visiting Cohan that he has been awarded the Congressional Medal of Honor for composing and popularizing "Over There" and "You're a Grand Old Flag," two songs, the President says, which have proven to be "just as important as guns." Underlining the political content of this key sequence, Cohan responds with his traditional four-part thank-you and then asks, "Where else in the world could a plain guy like me come in and talk things over with the head man?" The quest has concluded with the nation's highest award going to the hero as the ultimate in public recognition.

The cyclical construction of the flashback closes with the gray-haired, scratchy-voiced Cohan tap-dancing down the White House steps, walking vigorously out onto Pennsylvania Avenue, and joining stride with a singing parade of troops, presumably on their way to combat overseas. Noticing that Cohan is not singing along with the soldiers, a young GI asks, "What's the matter, old timer? Don't you remember this song?" Of course he does. The full circle of the closing narrative echoes the seasonal nature of history, as the nation's newest Congressional Medal-winner joins the young men in the next chorus of "Over There."

As mentioned earlier, YANKEE DOODLE DANDY was not the only show-business biography released in 1942 which took its title from a popular song rather than from its central character. The rise of the songwriter biography (traceable to SWANEE RIVER) really began in earnest with 1942's MY GAL SAL. The multi-talented Cohan, even though his bio-film's producers chose to employ one of his best-known songs rather than his name as a title, had been a familiar figure to much of the American public. By contrast, Paul Dresser, the composer-hero of MY GAL SAL, was a near-

The Form Takes Shape / 95

nonentity to the movie-goers of 1942. Yet many of his hit songs, popularized in the prime nostalgia years (for 1942) of the early twentieth century, had become "standards," with a strong public recognition factor at the time of the film's release. The musical nostalgia process which had proved so successful in ALEXANDER'S RAGTIME BAND (without biographical data) had also been shown to be effective in SWANEE RIVER and THE GREAT VICTOR HERBERT (with the narrative overlay of an ostensible "real life"). The release of MY GAL SAL renewed the exploitational emphasis on familiar songs as the prime-attraction factor and initiated a meta-cycle of "composers' lives" (within the broader generic formula of show-business biographies) which continued to make regular appearances on America's theatre screens until the late 1950s, when the rise of "format radio" signalled the irreversible fragmentation of American popular music. By then a total of fourteen more songwriter biographies had been produced, not one of them employing the composer's name in the title.

Before considering the songwriter biography as a subgeneric, or meta-formulaic category, it would be appropriate to assess and summarize the basic characteristics of the show-business biographical film in general, as it coalesced and took shape in the first phase of its development (1930-1942).

1. The ambitious hero is surrounded by an extended family of fellow professionals and assistants; his environs frequently include the entertainment "hub" of Manhattan.
2. An eccentric, older character provides companionship and advice, often in a humorous vein; an agent, on the other hand, is shrewd, cynical and city-wise.
3. The exceptional talent of the hero is a given; entry into the realm of success, however, is difficult (publishers, agents, producers, established stars are hard to convince) until the lucky "big break" occurs.
4. A class tension between "high-brow" and "low-brow" forms of entertainment is an important source of dramatic conflict; work performed with cultural pretensions strongly contrasts with that which is primarily executed for commercial rewards.
5. The more life-spanning the biographical treatment, the more a cyclical/mythic pattern of rise-and-fall is employed in the structure of the narrative, often with a "lesson" learned by the hero before the conclusion.

6. Montage sequences condense segments of a career via headlines in the trade press, entertainment columns in daily newspapers, excerpts from germane radio broadcasts, plus shots of theatre marquees, billboards, sheet music covers, record albums and singles, concert performance excerpts, applauding crowds, map graphics (animated lines connecting cities on a tour) and road signs (with the names of cities where the hero is appearing).
7. Incidents from the hero's life are shown to be directly related to examples of his creative output.
8. Multiple crucial events in the hero's life often coincide, both for dramatic impact and for purposes of narrative telescoping.
9. Characters with whom the hero interacts in both personal and professional life are frequently composites of several individuals.
10. Facts and events from the hero's real life are bent or omitted at will in fitting the character's story to the pattern of one or more traditional narrative myths (conventional dramatic construction takes precedence over precise reportage). Audience sympathy is thus maintained.
11. The public's taste is portrayed as unpredictable; popular approval is therefore fleeting, and the fickle masses often can be seen misdirecting their applause when they are ill-informed as to the identity of the "creative genius" who is actually responsible for their pleasurable sensations.
12. Roles may reverse after the hero achieves success.
13. The drive for success (the desire for ego inflation) often supersedes all other motivating forces in the hero's behavior, yet he is rarely placed at odds with conventional morality.
14. Linkage between films is extensive; settings and characters overlap as they correspond to real show business persons and places.

It would be incorrect to imply that these points of observational analysis are wholly unique to the show-business biographical film. In many respects they reflect the strong influence of widely held attitudes towards the entertainment business as expressed in other media of the time (fan magazines, newspaper columns and feature stories, radio gossip shows), as well as in hundreds of "backstage" novels and plays. Overtly fictional show-business dramas created for the screen (the closest relative to the category under study) reflect these attitudes and ideas as well, but always through the conscious filtering device of an alternate reality. That is to say, overtly fictional heroes may be similar to real-life celebrities in the entertainment business, but the device of dramatic congruence with life/history is not employed. Hence, popular attitudes toward the figures portrayed cannot be fixated upon the central characters with anything approaching the force of specificity available in the biographical mode. And it is this specificity (no matter how violated its accuracy may become through dramatic distortion) which must be kept in mind in abstracting and analyzing the interrelatedness of the films considered here.

CHAPTER VI

THE SONGWRITERS

As is the case in all forms of capitalist commerce, the division of labor by specialization functions to support the economic order by maintaining parallel hierarchies, trade by trade. The economic sub-system of show business as practiced in America has followed suit with its own specializations, and the show-business biographical film paradigmatically charts these divisions concurrently through its second phase of development, beginning with a rapid period of expansion following the outbreak of the Second World War.* A broad overview of the qualifying films produced in the second phase reveals distinct "families" of biographies which can be easily identified by their central character's specializations. These are dealt with in this and subsequent chapters according to the historical order in which each specialized cycle emerged.

Before examining the mythic patterns of the first of the specializations, it is useful to consider the existence of certain singular economic conditions which also underlie the creation of the songwriter biographies of the 1940s. Whatever their intrinsic appeal to the mass audience, the films functioned as a strategic maneuver in a commercial conflict raging behind the scenes of American popular culture. The new generation of songwriters, allied with the major broad-

---

*Sports biographies and films based on the lives of classical composers, two types of motion pictures which clearly stem from the show-business biographical film and flourish during the period, have been excluded here. These films extend beyond the world of commercial show business to fields of contention where the quest myth can be fulfilled only by following the rules of sport of the politics of court.

casting interests in the compensation-for-use agency called BMI, had begun to dominate the airwaves and sales charts in the aftermath of the "ASCAP war" (a period of time at the close of the former decade when the older compensation agency, representing the established authors and publishers, banned ASCAP tunes from all radio exposure in an effort to force broadcasters to agree to substantially higher royalty rates). The flock of songwriter biographies that followed can therefore be viewed as ploys to revive interest in many older ASCAP songs, the rights to which had come to be owned by the major studios through their publishing company subsidiaries. Had the campaign not been effective, the regular recurrence of songwriter biographical films might have ceased soon into the cycle, but the nostalgia phenomenon tested in the late 1930s functioned aptly here as well. Even catalogs of old songs not already controlled by studio-connected publishing houses were acquired and fitted into screenplays about the "good old days," and many of the stories were biographical.

MY GAL SAL, the first of the songwriter films to follow in the wake of YANKEE DOODLE DANDY, was based on "My Brother Paul," one of the least-known stories of the celebrated author Theodore Dreiser. Invocation of the familiar centered on the composer's hit songs; Paul Dresser's relationship to his literary sibling (who retained his name's original spelling) played no significant part in the narrative. Essentially it was a lost-and-found love tale, complicated by the inflated ego syndrome of early success. Curiously, the relationship between Dresser and his one true love (conjunctively named in accordance with the title song) is depicted in a humorous vein as an ongoing battle (interrupted by Paul's infatuation with a European countess), with Paul and Sal supposedly attracted to each other by a mutual love of bickering and throwing breakable objects.

The class tension aspect of the narrative is nearly archetypal in its polarity. In the opening sequence, Dresser is shown leaving home for the specific purpose of avoiding his parents' plans for him to become a minister. Instead, he finds employment hawking phony jewelry and soon graduates to performing in a tawdry, traveling medicine show. Ashamed of his low station when he is struck by the beauty of a high-style actress in big-time vaudeville, he attempts to win her over by composing a hit song for her. Just as happened when Stephen Foster wrote material for E. P. Christy, Dresser's song is wrongfully appropriated by Sal as her own. His emphatic protestations and additional compositions lead to a similarly profitable show-business partnership, but the heterosexual attraction factor (complicated by the team's love of amatory conflict) eventually leads the narrative in a direction distinctly different from the tragic denoument of SWANEE RIVER. Dresser's aspiration to "social acceptance" in the company of a predatory noblewoman is only a minimally conflictive digression on his path to romantic reunion with Sal and popular success as the author of such songs as "Back Home Again in Indiana," and "On the Banks of the Wabash Far Away."

The influence of SWANEE RIVER is even more strongly apparent in DIXIE, the 1943 biography of composer-performer Dan Emmett. While MY GAL SAL invoked the familiar/nostalgic era of the turn of the century, DIXIE set its narrative directly in the last years before the Civil War. Not just the story of one of the leading show business figures of that time, DIXIE also purported to be something of a history of the birth of the entertainment form which functioned as the centerpiece/spectacle of SWANEE RIVER's performance segments. DIXIE's narrative conveys the impression that the blackface minstrel show began by accident, with a group of white musical performers attempting to conceal their bruises and black eyes (received in a brawl) by donning burnt cork and singing their songs in "darkie style." The performers' impromptu change of appearance and manner, while initially shocking to their white Southern audience, is quickly perceived by the crowd as harmless and highly amusing. Dan Emmett and company rocket to nationwide success, the journey interrupted, of course, by the customary dramatic complications.

Rather than employ the familiar lost-and-found love formula, the narrative cuts short Emmett's budding romance with an attractive girl singer in his minstrel troupe when she, in an act of self-sacrifice, rejects him so that he will return to his crippled, long-suffering wife. The hero's aspiration to greatness is, however, much more in keeping with the established generic pattern. When Emmett quits the minstrel troupe and tries to make it on his own as a songwriter in New York City, publishers repeatedly turn him away. In desperation he eventually sells the rights to several of his songs for a mere ten dollars apiece.

Success returns when Dan rejoins his former partner and salvages the latter's failing minstrel troupe by composing new material for it, thus echoing the "stick to what you do best" maxim propounded as early as THE MIGHTY BARNUM. Indeed, the minstrel performance segments, with their forty blackface performers decked out in striped red and yellow trousers, polka-dotted red and white waistcoats, oversize blue ties, extra-large wing collars, shiny white spats, sparkling gold vests and high-gloss boots, provide the overriding attraction factor of spectacle. Shot in Technicolor (as was its direct predecessor, SWANEE RIVER), DIXIE was only the second show-business biographical film to employ the process.

Though overtly biographical and easily identified by the public as a "musical," DIXIE also bore a curious resemblance to the "road" pictures of Hope and Crosby which the same studio, Paramount, was also producing in the 1940s. Bing Crosby is the singer/hero of this film, Dorothy Lamour is his (albeit thwarted) love interest, and Crosby's "partner" in show business is portrayed as a cowardly, boastful, often dishonest but comical rival for the affections of the Lamour character (and is the man whom she ultimately agrees to wed at the story's conclusion). The performance of actor Billy DeWolfe (his screen debut) as Crosby's counterpart lacks the effeminate mannerisms which later became DeWolfe's stock-in-trade, and his role in the narrative echoes several of those written expressly for Bob Hope.

Dan Emmett's best-known song (and the film's title), although not depicted as being composed in response to a specific or crucial event in the hero's life, does become crafted into the style of performance from which the public came to know it, by a dramatic conflict played out in the picture's closing minutes. Thus the link with "creational events" in other biographies is maintained. Earlier in the narrative the song is performed as a slow ballad, one which elicits little emotional response from its listeners. A running motif throughout the film, Emmett's tendency to start accidental fires through the careless use of his pipe, recurs when Dan is about to perform "Dixie" before a packed theatre audience. Urged to speed up his rendition in order to conclude the show quickly so that the building can be emptied in an orderly fashion without someone yelling "Fire!," Emmett reels off the song at a much faster tempo than before and is met with a thunderous ovation, plus several "rebel yells." What had been an unsuccessful song becomes an "instant hit," and the narrative reaches a full stop on a note of triumph. The mythic quest, the hero's striving for success outside the confines of the minstrel show, has been achieved, for the "Concert of Songs by Dan Emmett" in which he has just performed has been taking place not in some second-rate theatre, but on the stage of the New York Civic Opera House. Unlike the tragic Stephen Foster, however, Emmett lives to see his dream realized.

IRISH EYES ARE SMILING, a 1944 songwriter biography, returned to the then-prime nostalgia years of the turn of the century for its setting, and again the hero's name was eschewed for title usage in favor of one of his best-known songs. While DIXIE can be viewed as a singular reworking of the key elements of SWANEE RIVER, IRISH EYES ARE SMILING much more generally resumes the eulogization/exploitation of American "pop music" history which began in earnest with ALEXANDER'S RAGTIME BAND. Most closely related to its immediate predecessor MY GAL SAL, IRISH EYES invokes the familiarity of its hero's famous compositions ("Mother Machree," "A Little Bit of Heaven," "Let the Rest of the World Go By") and invents a rather simple, myth-infused plot of lost-and-found love to fill the intervals between its numerous performance segments.

As in MY GAL SAL, the class tension between differing levels of cultural aspiration motivates the hero's initial departure on his quest for show-business success. Fired from his position as an instructor at the Cleveland Conservatory of Music (he is accused of "degrading the classics and turning them into love songs"), composer Ernest R. Ball moves on to the sleazy world of the burlesque theatre, where he finds employment as an accompanist and spends his off-hours composing. A "success pact" with a burlesque star's personal maid leads Ball to take up boxing as a sideline in order to raise cash for a try at crashing the music publishing world in New York City. In keeping with the established formula of a talented artist's need for a lucky "big break" in order to be discovered by the public, Ball is fortunate in convincing a vaudeville headliner to introduce "Let the Rest of the World Go By," and a success montage quickly capsulizes Ball's rise to fame and fortune as he turns out one Ireland-tinged ballad after another.

Curiously, no business difficulties with producers, agents or publishers plague Ball's ascendance. Dramatic conflict is instead maintained by his arduous pursuit of the maid-turned-singer, who precedes him to New York. The inspirational/creational axis between biographical events

The Songwriters / 103

and the hero's creative output functions (as in MY GAL SAL) primarily via the title song; the love interest is nicknamed "Irish." Ball himself is never referred to as a "son of Erin," and the Gaelic material in many of his other compositions is presented without explicatory comment.

The "misunderstanding" so crucial to lost-and-found love plots is heavily bound up in the narrative not with Ball's own quest for success, but with his conniving to promote a successful performing career for the former ladies' maid with whom he had earlier pledged to share his success. The misdirection of public accolades then serves as the key motivational factor in reuniting the lovers when the girl (assisted by a crafty agent) stages a Broadway musical employing previously unpublished Ball songs without giving him credit. The wandering and temporarily disillusioned composer reads of the fraud in Variety (his friends knew he would never lose touch with show business) and rushes back to New York from the other end of the continent, dead set on preventing the usurpation of his material. When he learns the trick was played out of love, a tearful reunion ends the narrative with traditional romantic stasis and closure.

Although it is impossible to identify and categorize all of the attractional factors in a commercial entertainment film designed and promoted to attract a characteristically discretionary audience, certain of these factors are highly visible and change markedly from one generic category to another. As noted early on, public curiosity about celebrities' lives and the promise of its (partial) satiation constitute a key segment of the attractional process which accompanies each theatrical release of a show-business biographical film. The implied (and sometimes overt) offers of spectacle, romance, nostalgia, drama, exposé, humor, and pleasing melody which are concomitant with the key promise of a "true-life story" are often delivered, however, to a far greater degree. Most songwriter biographies have been able to shift this answer-emphasis unobtrusively, since their subject-heroes were nearly anonymous apart from their creations.

Two Warner Brothers releases of the mid-1940s (when the cycle was approaching its zenith in terms of frequency) practiced this cinematic equivalent of "bait-and-switch" to a degree far in excess of most other songwriter biographies. The challenge to the film makers arose from the unavoidable fact that the real-life heroes of RHAPSODY IN BLUE (George

Gershwin) and NIGHT AND DAY (Cole Porter), despite their not being composer-performers, were very visible, well-known and written-about celebrities. It is in these two films that the transformational, hagiographic practice more common to all other branches of filmed show business biography (and begun with THE MIGHTY BARNUM and THE GREAT ZIEGFELD) zeroes in at full intensity upon the otherwise wholly malleable figure of the traditionally invisible tune-smith. George Gershwin, the brilliant but overbearing, egomaniacal master of melody, and Cole Porter, the impeccable sophisticate whose clever and infectious songs celebrating heterosexual love thinly concealed his decidedly alternate passions, had to be turned into mythic heroes, capable of arousing and sustaining 1940s audience sympathy during their dramatized quests for love and success.

Unless the real-life hero is still living, the translation of personal/career history into popular myth always confronts the issue of death. Even in the earliest films under study, the film makers dealt with the passing of their central historical characters in varying ways, depending on the specific mythic pattern imposed upon the primary historical material of a life once lived. THE MIGHTY BARNUM's fall-and-rise cycle ceased with his decision to join Bailey Walsh in founding a spectacular traveling circus; thus Barnum was allowed to live well beyond the narrative's limits. THE GREAT ZIEGFELD (whose historical passing was much closer to the film's release date) spiritually transcended death as his season-keyed life ebbed away in the final reel. The showman simply moved on to stage glorious new spectacles of beauty "on a higher plane."

George Gershwin had been dead only seven years when RHAPSODY IN BLUE went into production, and the pain of his early departure (when he was only in his thirties) was still felt by the millions of people who had come to love his music. Rather than craft Gershwin's life story into the more familiar mythic molds of lost-and-found love, rise-and-fall, quest-for-success, or even passing-of-the-seasons, the film makers structured a narrative based on a much more arcane myth which muted the blunt shock of dying young by imposing the hand of inexorable fate. Gershwin was portrayed in the film as a man engaged in a desperate race with time--with death waiting at the finish line. This is not to say that RHAPSODY IN BLUE marked a radical departure from the generic formulae--many elements in the film relate directly to its predecessors: the "old world"

Robert Alda (r.) as George Gershwin with Albert Basserman in RHAPSODY IN BLUE (1945). Photo courtesy of Wisconsin Center for Film and Theater Research.

music professor who gives young George his first lessons and advice, the intimations of future greatness ("there's all this music in my head"), an unsatisfactory early stint as a song plugger, the crucial and lucky audition for a big producer, "success montages" featuring Gershwin's hit shows and songs, and even the zenith of "cultural recognition" signified by a triumphant concert at Carnegie Hall. Yet all through the lengthy narrative (which includes many extended performance segments) the dialogue contains repeated references to the danger of "burning out" early in life, Gershwin's crowding too many activities into a short expanse of time, and the young composer's not having "time for flops." One particular sequence on board a speeding train sums up the thematic drive of the narrative. As Gershwin is shown listening to the rhythmic sound of the rails beneath his train car, he interprets the auditory pattern with the words: "Gotta make time ... gotta make time ..." With his career (and life) zipping along at this point--he has just premiered "Porgy and Bess"--George ecstatically exclaims, "Speed--I love it!"

Todorov's principle of mythic overlap is especially operant in RHAPSODY IN BLUE, for congruent with the "death race" plot is Gershwin's lost-and-found love affair with a showgirl named Julie, whom he meets in the cast of a musical he has written for Broadway star Al Jolson. Friends and family attest repeatedly that she is "right" for George, but Gershwin instead becomes enamored of a cold, haute couture American expatriate named Christine. Even though she does play a part in his being inspired to compose "An American in Paris," Gershwin realizes his error and attempts a reconciliation with Julie in the closing moments of his life.

Ameliorating the pain of Gershwin's early passing, the narrative asserts that despite the alleged fact that his own life was essentially unhappy, loveless, and devoid of human warmth, his music brought much beauty and joy to others. Whether this functioned as propitiation for the real Gershwin's semi-private reputation as a self-involved, bisexual braggart is difficult to determine, but a clue seems apparent in the dialogue passage where he explains his sorrow: "Maybe I'm just a family man without a family." When told that his deteriorating health will require him to refrain from work for many months, he sets the stage for his departure and even supplies some pained justification for the early arrival of death: "It's only in my music that I can prove my right to live." One of the preparatory dialogue exchanges (pointing the way towards a fated early demise) involves a warning to Gershwin to beware the example of classical composer Franz Schubert, who devoted himself so intensely to composing that he "fizzled out" at 32. In the filmed biography of Schubert, NEW WINE (1942), the composer's death is an offscreen event mentioned almost in passing by characters with whom he has not conversed for some time. The shock is also softened by the film's contemporary flashback structure which warns the audience of the hero's fate by referring to it as a distant, historical (in the schoolbook sense) event.

The death of George Gershwin, while also an offscreen occurrence, is presented as a much more immediate and personal tragedy, as seen through the eyes of one of his closest friends, pianist-composer-wit Oscar Levant, who (in a congruent invocation of the familiar) plays himself. Levant is about to perform in a live radio broadcast of Gershwin's title composition, with the orchestra conducted (also congruently) by the real-life Paul Whiteman. A news bulletin announcing Gershwin's death reaches the concert stage just prior to the start of the performance, and, in an impromptu eulogy, the audience is told that the performance will be a tribute in memory of its composer. Though Gershwin lost his race with time, the film still allows him a moment of transcendence closely related to the conclusion of SWANEE RIVER, where another coincident concert becomes an instant memorial. A saddened Levant tells the shocked listeners, "George Gershwin will forever sing to us--through his melodies." A shot of an empty piano bench is followed by a quick reprise of the main Rhapsody theme; then a rapid crane shot up and out of the outdoor stadium where the concert is being held dissolves into the spiritual imagery of celestial clouds. Gershwin, too, has joined the immortals.

With real-life composer Cole Porter still alive, the challenge of making the central character of NIGHT AND DAY an appealing figure in the midst of a dramatically effective plot was decidedly different from the problem of dealing with inevitable death which so strongly affected the narrative construction of RHAPSODY IN BLUE. Yet as was the case with Gershwin, Porter's not-so-secret real life had to be discarded first in order to avoid a commercially impossible assault on the titular morality and ingrained sensibilities of popular culture circa 1946. In short, there was no way a major-studio feature film of that time could have portrayed the life of Cole Porter as that of an active and happy homosexual, whose marriage of convenience to a woman who adored high living substituted "understanding" for love. In fact, other than exploiting the box-office draw of shocking revelations, there would have been little point to filming such a story until a time when popular values had modified enough to allow the standard romantic myths to be recast on film with homosexual, lesbian, or bisexual characters. *

Instead, the mythic infrastructure of NIGHT AND DAY, ageless as are all myths, was cloaked in a narrative construction much more appropriate for and familiar to its day and audience. The story can be analyzed as essentially a quest-for-success tale, overlaid with certain lost-and-found

---

*THE FOX, SUNDAY, BLOODY SUNDAY, MAKING LOVE, NIJINSKY, DEATHTRAP, and TV's THAT CERTAIN SUMMER are each products of a time and culture considerably removed from the mid-1940s.

Monty Woolley, Jane Wyman and Cary Grant in NIGHT AND DAY (1946). Photo courtesy of Wisconsin Center for Film and Theater Research.

love complications which fall short of dominating the dramatic emphasis but do perform an essential function in maintaining audience sympathy. As is continually the case in songwriter biographies, performance segments of familiar and successful compositions abound as a prime attractional factor. Aspirational class-tension opens the film, with young Porter defying his well-to-do midwestern family's hopes for him to become a lawyer. He much prefers the writing of musical stage shows. A significant contrast is visible here between Porter's beginnings and those of George Gershwin, who starts out his life-on-film as the son of a Lower East Side New York family whose parents want him to become a "serious musician." Porter's initiation to the musical theatre is by way of writing college shows at prestigious Yale University; young Gershwin first supports himself as a "Tin Pan Alley" song plugger and soon becomes dazzled by the bright lights of Broadway. Yet both go into show business in opposition to the elevated aspirations of their greatly differing families. The parental interdiction before the quest, a key mythic component first identified by Todorov in his morphological analysis of the Russian folktale, thus unites the dramatized careers of two composers from opposite ends of the sociological spectrum.

Another parallel between the two films can be seen in the congruent performances of real-life friends of the composers. Just as Oscar Levant enacted the role of himself in RHAPSODY, the comparably sharp-tongued Monty Woolley appears as Monty Woolley, Porter's long-time crony and former professor at Yale. The fact that both films were produced on the same studio lot and within a year of each other does not necessarily indicate a direct relationship between their narratives, but the interrelatedness of the pair becomes obvious when the diegetic, attractional and mythic elements are compared. This is not to say that the second film is an exact duplication of the first, however. Gershwin's race with time and early death are replaced in the second film by the hero's protracted struggle with physical pain, loneliness and pride. Porter's obsession with composing scores for musical comedies reaches a peak of intensity while he is recuperating in a French hospital from a wound suffered in the First World War.

The nurse who attends Porter (convenient conjunction of events) turns out to be a friend from the States who later marries him. Her admiration for his talent leads her to back one of his shows secretly before he has become a success, but when he does achieve public acclaim, ambition drives him to devote so much time to composing that she is sorely neglected. Porter's repeated postponing of their honeymoon in order to work on each new show leads to his estrangement from the new Mrs. Porter. When she leaves him for yet another of her jaunts across Europe, he simply continues his wholehearted devotion to composing until he is struck down by crippling pain, the end result of multiple bone fractures he suffers when a horse falls on his leg. Too proud to admit his helplessness (and re-stage his period of wartime recuperation during which his wife-to-be first attended him), Porter conceals the news of his injury from her and devotes himself entirely to more composing, amid an excruciating series of 27 surgical operations performed in hopes of restoring his ability to walk. When at last Porter is able to employ two canes and hobble down the aisle to accept a tribute from his <u>alma mater</u> during a

110 / Star Myths

choral concert of his most famous songs (which stands in for the prestigious New York concert hall finales of other songwriter biographies), his estranged wife surprises him-- an event arranged by friend Monty Woolley--and the pair are reunited for an emotional climax to the narrative.

The heroes of NIGHT AND DAY and RHAPSODY IN BLUE both "learn lessons" prior to the close of their filmed life stories, just as did many of their counterparts in earlier show business biographies. Unlike the knowledge imparted to P. T. Barnum or Stephen Foster, however, the lesson in these instances does not concern the futility of excessive aspirations, but rather the artist's need for self-integration by familial sharing of both the trials and rewards of creation. Whereas George Gershwin uses his own words to express his plight of being "a family man without a family," the lesson for Cole Porter is spoken as an admonition from his dying grandfather: "Success, Cole, has to be shared...."

While NIGHT and RHAPSODY relate so closely to each other that one can classify them as mirror image/companion pieces in the evolutionary development of biographical show business films, a subsequent pair of songwriter biographies made at MGM during the next three years (1946-48) mined similar historical material but offered the finished dramatic product to the public via very dissimilar modes of filmic interpretation. TILL THE CLOUDS ROLL BY purported to tell the story of composers Jerome Kern and Oscar Hammerstein II; WORDS AND MUSIC performed the same task in regard to Richard Rodgers and Lorenz Hart. Although the latter-day team made up of their survivors, Rodgers and Hammerstein, had already begun its long and successful collaboration before either film went into production, each picture's narrative concentrated only on the years of the prior compositional partnership before death claimed one of its members. (Hart died in 1943, Kern in 1945.) Just as was the case with Cole Porter and George Gershwin, the central characters of these two subsequent songwriter biographies had transcended the relative obscurity enjoyed by most writers of American popular songs, almost to the point that their names were as well-known as their compositions. Yet the titles of their bio-films still invoked the familiarity of the creation in preference to that of the artist.*

---

*An anomaly occurs in the case of the Rodgers and   (cont.)

Both films' narratives confront the issue of the recent historical death of one of their central characters, but the problem is surmounted in very different dramatic ways. TILL THE CLOUDS ROLL BY ignores the recent death of Jerome Kern entirely, closing its narrative on the night of Kern and Hammerstein's "greatest success," the opening Broadway performance of "Show Boat." WORDS AND MUSIC, on the other hand, makes the early death of Lorenz Hart a tragic event of the greatest dramatic importance and closes the narrative with a star-studded memorial concert dedicated to "the little guy who thought he was alone." The mythic infrastructure of CLOUDS' plot is clearly lost-and-found love, albeit de facto parentis rather than of the conjugal variety. WORDS' plot relates most closely to that of SWANEE RIVER, employing the tragic mode to enact the rise-and-fall of a gifted lyricist who was supposedly devastated by his lack of success with women (whereas Stephen Foster was crushed by his lack of success in the world of "serious" music). Hart's long-term homosexual liaison with a notorious "physician" is, of course, omitted.

Although both films de-emphasize the life of one member of each composing team in favor of concentrating upon the activities of the other, CLOUDS' narrative goes the furthest in centering audience attention on Jerome Kern to the almost total exclusion of Oscar Hammerstein II until well into the final third of the picture. WORDS begins from the viewpoint of the Richard Rodgers character, even has him perform voiceover narration, but eventually centers its dramatic conflicts on the eccentric and self-destructive behavior of Lorenz Hart, a near-midget in real life who is shown to be obsessed with his lack of height. When he rises from his sickbed and staggers down Broadway to attend the opening of his final "great success," he collapses fatally in the gutter in front of a store that sells elevator shoes.

TILL THE CLOUDS ROLL BY structures its lost-and-found love plot around the relationship between middle-aged composer Kern and the orphaned daughter of Kern's

---

Hart biography's title. Although not a specific popular song, it was a reference to the overall result of their partnership, the general product of their efforts by which the audience knew them best. A 1932 Broadway revue of songs and sketches penned by Noel Coward used the same title, but it bears no relation to the film.

"old world" music teacher. Despite Kern's sincere attempts to be a "second father" to the stage-struck girl, she flees the company of Kern and his extended family of theatre people when she is denied the chance to star in a show her father-figure has ostensibly written just for her. (Box-office pressures necessitate the casting of Ziegfeld star Marilyn Miller.) This wholly invented central conflict is resolved when Kern and the girl are reunited on the set of a Hollywood musical the composer has been brought west to write. By sheer (fictive) coincidence, an MGM talent scout has selected her to be the star.

Both films' narratives do converge, however, in their concluding sequences, lavish production spectacles featuring a medley of their respective composers' best-known songs. Another factor relating the two films is the numerous "guest appearances" featuring then-current Metro musical stars who appear as ambiguously identified period performers, singing and dancing to the music of the composer-heroes. Thus the attractional factors and basic subject material of the two films overlap, even to the point of covering essentially the same historical period and locale, while the functional myths of each narrative diverge markedly.

Despite the success of filmed biographies of popular songwriters who actually achieved celebrity status, and whose own names easily invoked the familiar, the American film industry continued to devote considerable attention to the supposed lives of the traditionally anonymous tunesmiths of Tin Pan Alley. As was the case in such earlier efforts as MY GAL SAL (1942) and IRISH EYES ARE SMILING (1944), the film makers again invoked the familiarity of a composer's best-loved song (for title purposes) and drew upon reliable plot devices and more once-popular songs to fill out each succeeding nine or ten reels of product. Joe Howard, Fred Fischer, Burt Kalmar & Harry Ruby, Gus Kahn, and the trio of Buddy DeSylva, Lew Brown & Ray Henderson were each given their moment of fame in the cinema spotlight as the subjects of, respectively: I WONDER WHO'S KISSING HER NOW (1947), OH, YOU BEAUTIFUL DOLL (1949),

---

Opposite: two composer movies. Top, Robert Walker, Judy Garland and Paul Langton in TILL THE CLOUDS ROLL BY (1946). Below, Marshall Thompson, Tom Drake and Mickey Rooney in WORDS AND MUSIC (1948). Photos courtesy of Wisconsin Center for Film and Theater Research.

114 / Star Myths

THREE LITTLE WORDS (1950), I'LL SEE YOU IN MY DREAMS (1951) and THE BEST THINGS IN LIFE ARE FREE (1956).

These five films read quite clearly as successive variations on a central theme: that the journeymen songwriters of New York's Tin Pan Alley performed a valuable and needed service for the country--providing millions of tongue-tied couples with the right words with which to say, "I Love You." A key piece of professional advice offered (via the linkage phenomenon) by Victor Herbert to Jerome Kern in TILL THE CLOUDS ROLL BY sums it up. The elderly Herbert, predicting that Kern will become the next "dean" of popular music, reminds the younger man that people need to have "songs for their lives."

Each of these five films opens its narrative with a scene-setting device to locate the diegesis as falling in the prime nostalgia years of one or two generations earlier.

June Haver and Mark Stevens (r.) in I WONDER WHO'S KISSING HER NOW (1947). Photo courtesy of Films Incorporated.

I WONDER WHO'S KISSING HER NOW provides a title card that reads: "Joe Howard--that ageless troubador who wrote and sang the nation's songs at the turn of the century...." OH, YOU BEAUTIFUL DOLL begins in a bar just off Tin Pan Alley, with a flashback keyed to a conversation about a wall of framed portraits of the most successful songwriters of the early 1900s. THREE LITTLE WORDS sports the succinct title: "1919--A couple of fellows met in Tin Pan Alley. Their songs became part of America." I'LL SEE YOU IN MY DREAMS, the story of composer Gus Kahn, whose biggest life crisis was making the decision to forsake his beloved Chicago in order to take up residence near "the Alley," begins not with a title card, but with a long crane/tracking shot down Wabash Avenue. Yet the horse cars, fashions and shop windows quickly fix the time as the turn of the century, and the first dialogue is spoken in the Chicago offices of a local music publisher, where a lady song plugger is explaining to delivery man and would-be songwriter Kahn why the most important and successful tunes are always love songs. THE BEST THINGS IN LIFE ARE FREE, the last of the series, filmed on the eve of rock and roll's ascendency, repeats the formula one final time with an opening title that reads: "1920: Three men from different parts of the country (despite or because of their differences) for seven years wrote the song hits of the nation--This is the story of those hits and those years."

I WONDER WHO'S KISSING HER NOW was an exceptionally close reworking of the lost-and-found love plot of IRISH EYES ARE SMILING, with its hero leaving a mundane job to write songs for a popular female vocalist, gaining early success, becoming involved with the rich and powerful, but eventually curing his "swelled head" and marrying "the sweet little girl from back home" who turns out to be a gifted performer in her own right. Even the plot device of retrieving the hero from his self-imposed "exile" by publicizing his latest composition as the work of another is employed to similar effect. As an added irony, several years after the film's release Tin Pan Alley yielded up the truth-- that the historical Joe Howard had falsely claimed credit for another composer's work.

OH, YOU BEAUTIFUL DOLL relies on the high/low culture dichotomy of SWANEE RIVER for plot conflict, depicting the failed attempts of "old world" classical composer Alfred Breitenbach to get his operatic scores published and performed until a Tin Pan Alley song plugger revises the

main melodies into a series of hugely successful popular
songs, published under the pseudonym of "Fred Fisher."
Breitenbach's agony over his dual identity eventually causes
him to go into hiding from his "monster self," and only a
"serious music" concert of his famous melodies, performed
at prestigious Aeolian Hall, brings him back from exile.
Amidst thunderous applause, Breitenbach/Fisher delivers
the exculpatory blessing operant in all of these films: "Popular
music is good music." Essentially employing a narrative
structure based on the quest (for success) myth, OH,
YOU BEAUTIFUL DOLL turns a variation on the "stick to
what you do best" motif by having its hero learn rather late
in life that the pursuit at which he excels is one which he
had never previously attempted. Due to the advanced age of
the hero in the years spanned by the narrative, as was the
case in THE GREAT VICTOR HERBERT, Breitenbach/Fisher
is not depicted as pursuing romantic/sexual fulfillment himself,
but instead serves as a father-confessor figure to a
younger couple involved in the film's romantic sub-plot.
This, of course, is a convention common to much of myth
and fiction--that romance is for youth, but that wisdom
comes with age.

THREE LITTLE WORDS is yet another lost-and-found
love story given a show-business biography setting, but a
significant inversion in the character relationships marks it
as an innovation, not in film narrative per se, but definitely
so in the motion pictures under study. The interrupted love
relationship which supplies material for the necessary dramatic
conflict is a fraternal one, between two male composer-collaborators
whose differing gifts and temperaments lend
themselves to bursts of successful creativity interspersed
with stretches of hostile conflict. WORDS AND MUSIC, despite
its prime emphasis upon the emotional conflicts of the
tortured Lorenz Hart character, pointed in this direction by
way of the strain Hart's eccentricities and long absences
placed upon his collaboration with Rodgers. In THREE LITTLE
WORDS such conflicts are central to the unfolding
drama. Songwriters Burt Kalmar and Harry Ruby, following
an earlier encounter in which the latter accidentally sabotages
the former's vaudeville magic act, are paired by a
music publisher and assigned to write songs. Although their
first musical collaboration ends in a rancorous re-hashing of
the earlier episode, Ruby salvages a crumpled song sheet
from the waste basket, submits it to the publisher, and the
tune becomes a hit. Reunited by success, the team survives
recurring spats and its members' contrary ambitions (Kalmar

wants to be a vaudeville performer and Ruby yearns to play pro baseball) through years of hit songs, Broadway shows, and movie scores. The two men learn to care deeply for each other's well-being, with each meddling in the other's romantic affairs to make certain both partners meet and marry "the right girl." Such benevolent meddling eventually leads to the misunderstanding that causes the team's breakup, when Kalmar learns that Ruby has subverted Kalmar's plans to produce a "serious" stage play that Ruby believed was doomed to fail. The "stick to what you do best" motif, familiar from earlier show-business biographies, thus recurs in THREE LITTLE WORDS, but its endorsement by the Ruby character serves as a divisive plot instrument rather than as a lesson to be learned by either hero.

The historical fact that the team of Kalmar and Ruby actually did split up could have been sidestepped by the film makers, had the narrative employed some other mythic framework, but since the lost-and-found pattern was chosen, a joyous reunion concludes the story, with the pair coerced by their conspiring wives to perform an "And Then I Wrote ..." routine together on Phil Regan's radio show, "Songwriter's Parade." This invocation of the familiar, with flagrant disregard for historical accuracy in favor of mythic continuity, depicts the estranged collaborators finally completing the film's title song, supposedly a composition they first tackled unsuccessfully at the beginning of their partnership.

I'LL SEE YOU IN MY DREAMS, the story of Chicago-based songwriter Gus Kahn, fitted selected details of Kahn's life and career into a rise-and-fall format, at the same time emphasizing the price he allegedly was forced to pay by resisting (for a time) and then yielding to the siren calls of the show-business biography's twin meccas, New York City and Hollywood. Kahn marries his "one true love" early in the narrative, and it is her expertise (she is an experienced song plugger) and ambition that propel him to the heights of commercial success. The historical Gus Kahn was an untutored poet, strictly a purveyor of lyrics who collaborated with many different tunesmiths in his lifetime, and the film's narrative does not shy away from this fact. His wife's pleadings that he collaborate with only the best melody makers is depicted as just another of the pieces of sound business advice she gives him in the course of his career. Dramatic conflict arises not from the obstacles he must confront during his climb to the top, but rather from his reluctance to relinquish being what he calls a "big frog in a little pond" and depart his beloved Chicago.

It is only a personal invitation from Florenz Ziegfeld that proves persuasive enough to bring the reluctant Kahn to Manhattan, and his decision not to uproot his family leaves him alone in the Eastern show business capital, subject to the customary temptations of high living and ambitious showgirls. Significantly, Kahn has just completed the lyrics to the score of WHOOPIE! when his wife rushes to New York to rescue him from the engulfing decadence, even though it was she who encouraged him to venture there in the first place. The historical fact that the nationwide sales of sheet music took a precipitous drop with the emergence of network radio and just prior to the ascendance of talking pictures is attendant to Kahn's dramatized 1929 rejection of all his regular collaborators' urgings that he move to Hollywood and cash in on the demand for movie musicals.

Here the rise-and-fall cycle approaches its nadir, with an impoverished Kahn reduced to writing lewd parodies of his earlier hits, so that they can be performed in Chicago's sleaziest burlesque theatres. When Kahn finally does move to Hollywood, he is so far off his stride that he quarrels with "studio hacks" and collapses from a heart attack. Here the renaissance phase of the operant myth makes its appearance, and Kahn is feted with a testimonial dinner staged by several of his concerned former collaborators and attended by a host of entertainment celebrities and popular music's most successful composers. A concluding linkage factor adds a humorous touch to the proceedings: Kahn almost misses his surprise testimonial because of an invitation to attend a baseball game with Harry Ruby.

The extent to which a songwriter biography could employ a narrative which contained only the barest minimum of historical accuracy was demonstrated by a 1952 release, I DREAM OF JEANNIE. As was the case with Mascot Pictures' 1935 production of HARMONY LANE, I DREAM OF JEANNIE emerged from one of Hollywood's lowest-budgeted studios (in this case, Republic Pictures) and managed to save thousands of dollars in copyright clearance/performance fees by concentrating on the work of a still-popular composer whose work was safely in the public domain--Stephen Foster. In light of the fact that in the interim Twentieth Century-Fox had produced its "A" picture-budgeted, Technicolor-enhanced SWANEE RIVER, the makers of I DREAM OF JEANNIE probably took great pains to make sure that the copyrighted screenplay of the Fox picture was not infringed upon. Yet since that picture had freely adapted the historical facts of Foster's life anyway, the path was clear to invent a markedly different, yet still myth-infused life for the composer depicted in Republic's "Trucolor" production.

Basic similarities between these narratives are limited to a few historically verifiable facts of Foster's career. He was without close rival, the most popular American songwriter of the mid-nineteenth century, a northerner influenced by the work songs and spirituals of black slaves and a frequent contributor of musical material to the immensely popular minstrel shows of the day, particularly those staged by Edwin P. Christy, who bought and published Foster's early compositions under Christy's own name. Apart from these essential points of historical agreement, and the inclusion of many of the same songs, the narratives of the Foster bio-films differ extensively.

I DREAM OF JEANNIE employs the lost-and-found love formula by way of the familiar (from other dramatic and fictional works) "mistaken affections" variation. The Stephen Foster of this story is a Cincinnati bookkeeper who frequently neglects his job to compose bits of melody and lyric, which he jots down in the margins of his business ledger. For some time he has been courting a haughty, wealthy girl named Inez, who is the "toast" of Cincinnati society by virtue of her musical cotillions, at which she invariably gives vocal recitals featuring her own splendid talents as a coloratura. She is frequently at odds with her beau over his preference for the folk music of slaves, and her disagreeable personality is contrasted sharply with the sweetness and sympathy of her younger sister, Jeannie, who encourages Foster in his songwriting avocation. Thus the traditional dichotomy between high and low music is established as a prime element in the dramatic conflict.

Edwin P. Christy's exploitation of Foster's talent, sharply emphasized in SWANEE RIVER, receives similar treatment in I DREAM OF JEANNIE, but with the added expository material of a discussion between characters which more clearly outlines the near-defenseless position of composers during the years when America's copyright laws favored the publishing interests almost exclusively. Coming to the defense of the rather passive Foster is yet another character (besides the girls) who was unmentioned in the earlier films--Stephen's older and more pugnacious brother, a feisty riverboat captain named Dunning.

Although the determined efforts of Dunning win Stephen a measure of the respect and compensation he deserves for composing a series of songs which virtually sweep the country in popularity (the obligatory concert in tribute to the composer and his songs occurs early in the narrative), Stephen's romantic troubles take up the balance of the story as he becomes estranged from Inez for inadvertently participating in the disruption of one of her musical evenings. Distraught at the collapse of his dream of love, Stephen flees for escape to the real South, where he hopes for the first time in his life to encounter the actual locales about which he has been writing so successfully.

Stephen Foster's disappearance prompts his friends to search the South, first by the traditional means of "sending out the bloodhounds," and later by an even more appropriate method--following the trail of songs he has left behind after teaching them to the rural folk. At last the errant composer is discovered, down on his luck in a seedy, Southern barroom. Jeannie is the first to find him, drawn by the sound of the musical instrument he has always carried with him--a flute. The narrative attains its dramatic climax by means of a barroom brawl which Christy manages to quell simply by distracting the combatants with a Stephen Foster song, embellished by Christy's masterful baritone, just as another riotous situation was quelled in SWANEE RIVER. Foster's reunion, not with Inez but with little Jeannie, is capped by the realization that not only is she the girl he should have been courting in the first place, but her name fits perfectly into a certain song lyric he has long been struggling to finish.

I DREAM OF JEANNIE, despite its broad factual disagreement with Foster's earlier film incarnations, retains the previous mix of performance situations drawn from the composer's repertoire and causational anecdotes, in the latter case including Foster's writing and singing "Old Dog Tray" for an actual dog and his composition of the title tune (a delayed climax event comparable to the conclusion of THREE LITTLE WORDS) for his own true love.

A passing element of ironic historical hindsight/humor, more common in bio-films set several generations in the past, has Christy contemptuously referring to a "friend" of his who is supposedly writing a story about fugitive slaves which is called "Uncle Bob's Cabin." "No one will buy that," says Christy, in regard to the decidedly unfelicitous title. Linkage to prior bio-films, A LADY'S MORALS and THE MIGHTY BARNUM, occurs in the sequence in which Foster tries to smoothe Inez' ruffled feathers by telling her, "You're better [at vocalizing] than Jenny Lind ever thought of being." Later he is seen buying tickets to take Inez to a Lind concert.

Although none of the performers in this modestly financed Republic production was particularly well-known or a box-office attraction, an unusual quirk of casting had singer-actor Ray Middleton (whose biggest successes had been in the original Broadway productions of "Roberta" and "Annie Get Your Gun") billed above singer-actor Bill Shirley, even though Shirley played the leading role of Foster and Middleton was given the subsidiary part of Christy. While Shirley was an accomplished vocalist himself (he had divided his time in Hollywood during the previous decade between appearing in minor films and dubbing songs for non-singing actors), his perfectly adequate voice was just as easily upstaged by the powerhouse singing of Middleton as was the vocalizing of Don Ameche by that of Al Jolson when the latter pair appeared as Foster and Christy in SWANEE RIVER.* Much to Jolson's chagrin, however, he was not top billed in the earlier film.

THE BEST THINGS IN LIFE ARE FREE, the last of the Tin Pan Alley-based songwriter biographies, appeared in 1956 and again dealt with the formation, breakup, and reunion of a successful composing team. This time, instead of the usual composer twosome, the film dealt with the famous creative trio of DeSylva, Brown and Henderson.** Although the personal commitment of a composing team to each other is not stressed as deeply in the dialogue and situations as it is in THREE LITTLE WORDS, the basic form of the narra-

---

*A form of subliminal linkage occurs here, for it was Shirley who provided the unbilled singing voice of actor Mark Stevens when he appeared as composer Joe Howard in I WONDER WHO'S KISSING HER NOW.
**The visual compositions are expanded in like manner. With its three heroes, THE BEST THINGS IN LIFE ARE FREE was the only songwriter biography to be filmed in CinemaScope.

Ernest Borgnine, Gordon MacRae, Sheree North and Dan Dailey in THE BEST THINGS IN LIFE ARE FREE (1956). Photo courtesy of Films Incorporated.

tive follows the rudiments of lost-and-found plot construction quite closely.

    The three composers have their ultimately divisive disagreements, as was the case with Kalmar and Ruby, but DB&H's differences stem less from an archetypal "misunderstanding" than from a clear case of contradictory side interests. DeSylva is a playboy who can't get enough of show business parties and nightclub atmosphere. Brown is an ex-hustler from the slums, an inveterate poker player accustomed to the company of gamblers and thugs. Henderson is a former schoolteacher, a family man with a suspicious wife who expects him home for supper every night. They join forces during rehearsal for a musical show tryout in Atlantic City. (DeSylva and Brown are already a team; Henderson impresses them with his own compositions and is asked to join them.) They spend the first years of their combined career writing scores for the Broadway productions of Ziegfeld's ace rival, George White.

Familiar sub-plot motifs include the team's interest in a talented understudy who is more qualified than the show's star (a similar situation occurred in THREE LITTLE WORDS) and the enactment of narrative incidents supposedly linked to the creation of well-known songs. In one such instance, invocation of the familiar employs the portrayal of Broadway headliner Al Jolson, having just begun his new career in talking pictures, telephoning the boys from Hollywood and imploring them to write him an extremely sentimental ballad. Taken aback by Jolson's excessive importuning, DB&H resolve to compose an equally excessive "sob song," so maudlin as to be a joke. The pleasurable perception of historical irony afforded to a 1956 audience viewing the film at this point lies in the knowledge that the resultant song, "Sonny Boy," became one of the biggest hits of Jolson's career, a song so popular that the public later often mistook it for the actual title of the film (THE SINGING FOOL, his biggest commercial success) in which it was introduced.

When DB&H move to Hollywood to write for the early movie musicals, a crisis in their relationship soon ensues, paralleling the West Coast crises which imperiled Gus Kahn and split up Kalmar and Ruby after each heeded the call of the talking picture. In this case, however, the threat is from neither heart failure nor hurt feelings. The adulation heaped upon the team's first film project, SUNNY SIDE UP, simply causes Buddy DeSylva to suffer the "swelled head" malady of ego inflation first endured, among this group of films, in THE MIGHTY BARNUM. A fist-fight with his partners seals the breakup (conveniently telescoping events and ignoring the team's later collaborations on such films as the 1930 JUST IMAGINE and 1931's INDISCREET) and sends Brown and Henderson back to Broadway to compose the score for a revue titled "Strike Me Pink."

A circular overlay to the lost-and-found plot construction assists in providing the narrative with a closure sequence, returning to the Atlantic City rehearsal hall of the opening, only this time it is a repentant DeSylva who bursts in upon the harried Brown and Henderson with just the advice they need to make the troubled show a hit: toss in some of their old "surplus songs," written for, but not used in, their earlier collaborations. The implication of the emotional reunion sequence is that the historical DB&H became a team again, although the introductory title card referred to their partnership as lasting but seven years. In addition, while Lew Brown and Ray Henderson never did equal on their own the successes of their early years, Buddy DeSylva later became B. G. DeSylva, motion picture producer and eventually head of Paramount Studios. None of this is dealt with in the narrative of THE BEST THINGS IN LIFE ARE FREE. The mythic framework of lost-and-found love (read partnership in this case) is necessarily limiting. Reunion must fall by age-old custom in a linear position penultimate to conclusion.

To date there have been no other film biographies devoted to the lives of show-business figures whose careers concentrated upon the composing of popular songs of the Tin Pan Alley variety, commercial products often introduced in stage musicals or motion pictures, but aimed at maximum marketing and exploitation via sheet music and record sales, prompted by repeated performances on the vaudeville stage, by dance orchestras, and on the radio. Some five more songwriter biographies do exist however, but their central characters functioned historically apart from the Tin Pan Alley context. Three of these motion pictures must be classified as borderline cases which, were it not for the historical fact that their central characters are known to posterity for their compositions much more than for their performances, would qualify as musician biographies.

STARS AND STRIPES FOREVER, the 1952 biography of John Philip Sousa, chronicles its hero's accomplishments from late middle age until the last years of his life. As was the case in THE GREAT VICTOR HERBERT and OH, YOU BEAUTIFUL DOLL, the central character therefore functions as a father figure to a pair of young lovers whose lost-and-found love subplot unfolds against the background of the older man's ascending career. In this instance the Sousa character, who begins the story as the sergeant major conductor of the U.S. Marine Band, watches over and advises the romance between a tuba player from his ensemble and a burlesque show vocalist who aspires to be a star of the legitimate musical stage. Dramatic conflict arises from their need to keep their marriage a secret, as no married men are allowed in the traveling aggregation Sousa forms when he leaves the service.

Sousa's career is presented in a manner akin to the upward progression of the quest myth operant in YANKEE DOODLE DANDY. A key component of the narrative is the recurrent voice-over narration by an anonymous announcer, who at one point summarizes the height of the Sousa career:

The Songwriters / 125

Clifton Webb (as Sousa) and, at his right, Finlay Currie, in STARS AND STRIPES FOREVER (1952). Photo courtesy of Wisconsin Center for Film and Theater Research.

"Then followed the really fabulous years. Honor upon honor, performing with all the great soloists of the day, always new ... progressive ... and entertaining." Even the less-than-minor setback of a bout with typhoid fever, suffered when Sousa re-enlists upon the outbreak of the Spanish-American War, places barely a dent in the upward curve of his success. He uses his recuperation during a sea voyage to write the score for his immensely successful stage operetta, "El Capitán."

Most of Sousa's best-known and most-performed marches are included in the performance segments, following the pattern established in the decade of songwriter biographies which preceded the film, and directly relating incidents from his life to individual acts of composition. Invocation of the familiar even parallels the diegetic insertion of a presidential character in YANKEE DOODLE DANDY, when president Grover Cleveland asks Sousa to make a march out of a ballad he is premiering at a political gathering. Sousa is portrayed as originally wanting to compose love songs but forced by circumstance into "doing what he does best," writing and performing march music. Once he resigns himself to this specialty and dedicates himself to the task fully, however, the future holds only a long string of successes before him.

ST. LOUIS BLUES, released in 1958, became the first show-business biographical film with a black man as its hero. Like Sousa, W. C. Handy was a performing musician whose compositions gained popularity with untold millions of people who had never heard him play his own works. Both penned sheet music that sold exceedingly well all over

Nat King Cole (at piano), Eartha Kitt and Cab Calloway (r.) in ST. LOUIS BLUES (1958). Photo courtesy of Wisconsin Center for Film and Theater Research.

the western world, but neither came out of, or functioned in, the New York/Broadway-based Tin Pan Alley tradition. Their dramatized careers on film, however, were infused with significantly differing mythic structures. Handy's life is presented as much less of an uninterrupted, upward quest for successes of greater and greater magnitude. Instead, it is a quest preceded by an archetypal paternal interdiction, followed by sharply alternating periods of rise and fall, and culminating in an equally archetypal vindication/veneration ceremony performed in an august concert hall before a crowd of society's leading tastemakers.

Echoing the departure from home of Paul Dresser in MY GAL SAL, young W. C. Handy also fails his father's aspirations for the boy to become a minister. This time the interdiction is even more strongly expressed, for the elder Handy specifically warns his son to beware the temptations of jazz, "the Devil's music." The polarities of supposed good and evil are thereafter personified by the characters of the evil temptress/vocalist at a local black nightclub in Memphis, and the home-loving childhood sweetheart who wants to save W. C. from the dangers of gin and bad women. Handy is torn between the two women, and what they represent, in alternating dramatic episodes, interspersed with attempted family reconciliations and periodic bursts of success and failure, such as selling his first songs, being swindled by crooked recording entrepreneurs, getting his "big break" to perform in New York City, and losing the engagement when he discovers he is going blind.

The miraculous restoration of his sight while accompanying a hymn in his father's church nearly convinces Handy never to stray from the fold again, but a powerful inner drive to "express the music of his people" leads him back to the world of early twentieth-century Chicago jazz clubs, even though it means forsaking the love and companionship of those he loves most dearly. This inner drive, or vision, most strongly emphasized among songwriters in RHAPSODY IN BLUE, is to become archetypal also in films based on the lives of other jazz musicians. The customary tearful reunion with friends and family which conludes the vindicating concert of Handy's music at Aeolian Hall (now that he has been given recognition by the elite as a "great composer") ends with Elizabeth, the "good girl" from back home, telling Handy's father (in an exculpatory admission directly related to the ending of OH, YOU BEAUTIFUL DOLL): "We sinned against him!"

Nineteen years later the basic subject matter of ST. LOUIS BLUES was re-worked in a 1977 TV-movie, SCOTT JOPLIN. The parental interdiction against young Joplin is not for religious reasons, however, but because his grieving father associates music with his recently deceased wife. Nevertheless, Joplin is forbidden to play the piano at home, so he retreats into the neighborhood bordello to play for his board and room. Like Handy, Joplin is driven by an inner need "to be heard by the whole world," and he works late into the early hours of each following day to set the music in his head down on paper.

Although moral advice (which Joplin, like Handy, also disregards) does not come from a stern father, a surrogate father figure provides it, appearing in the character of St. Louis music publisher John Stark, who is so impressed with Joplin's performance at a piano roll cutting contest while in Sedalia that the older white man hires the gifted black composer to "write rags for white folks." Stark promises Joplin a wide and receptive audience, but warns, "Stay away from alcohol and whores." The myth-infused plot of rise-and-fall then runs its course in a truly seasonal dispersion of events, with Joplin's courtship of and marriage to a beautiful young widow paralleling the states of his career. Sales of his sheet music become increasingly brisk, minstrel shows and vaudeville troupes popularize his latest compositions with turn-of-the-century audiences, and in 1901 the press acclaims him as the "King of Ragtime." A curious linkage with STARS AND STRIPES FOREVER occurs when Stark arranges for a ragtime orchestra to perform Joplin's music in alternating performances with John Philip Sousa's band at the 1903 St. Louis Exposition. When the press ignores Joplin in favor of Sousa, Joplin's inflated-then-damaged ego explodes: "I want to write opera, not Broadway jig-time and coon show music!"

Overreaching ambition of the same stripe that brought down Stephen Foster in SWANEE RIVER takes its toll on Scott Joplin as the drama shifts into the autumn phase and he finds it impossible to obtain financial backing for his final and most elaborate composition, an all-black, plantation-set opera called "Tremonisha." Joplin's close friend and former fellow bawdy house pianist, Louis Chauvin (whose failure to write down his own compositions has fated him for obscurity), dies of venereal disease, Joplin's infant child dies of perhaps the same cause, and his marriage falls apart. Publisher Stark, upon closing his New York

office (the competition was too fierce) and moving back to
Missouri, observes the ruination of Joplin's own career, for
Joplin too is now dying of syphilis and has lost the muscle
coordination necessary to play the piano. At this point
Stark makes (perhaps because of the late date of the film's
creation, written in the wake of so many earlier show-business biographies) what is one of the most self-conscious, generically self-referential statements in the entire body of
work here being analyzed: "You almost turned out to not
fit the myth ... the Black Illusion ... Carnegie Hall." Joplin's rejoinder, his last and most significant utterance before
his approaching demise, goes to the heart of the romantic
illusion underpinning so many of these films: "You said I
was a genius. I want everybody to know it!"

Yet despite this remarkably anti-romantic interruption
of the seasonal/rise-and-fall myth being played out upon the
screen, the narrative's epilogue returns dead center to the
track of custom, telling the audience: "In 1974 Scott Joplin's music won an Oscar. In 1975 his opera 'Tremonisha'
was finally produced to great critical acclaim. In 1976 his
work was awarded the Pulitzer Prize. He died in 1917."
The mythic need for a concluding epiphany of redemptive
renaissance, it seems, could not be denied.

Despite the occurrence of the cultural avatar SCOTT
JOPLIN in 1977, the mid-1950s clearly mark the end of the
songwriter biography cycle. The sharp changes in and fragmentation of the American popular music industry that followed led to a downgrading of the image of the behind-the-scenes pop songwriter, in favor of the singer-songwriter as
media hero. Two final biographical films, despite the "semiclassical" nature of their subject's compositions, qualify for
inclusion in this chapter. THE GREAT GILBERT AND SULLIVAN, a 1953 British import which received wide exhibition
in America, distinctly shows its relation to the "partnership"
films, WORDS AND MUSIC, THREE LITTLE WORDS, and
the subsequent THE BEST THINGS IN LIFE ARE FREE. A
noticeable difference is the employment of its subjects' names
in the title, a practice not used in America for composer
biographies since 1939's THE GREAT VICTOR HERBERT.
The stormy relationship between songwriting partners, nevertheless, traverses many parallels with several of its American counterparts in the intervening fourteen years. Performance segments, a key attractional factor in all songwriter biographies, overwhelm (in terms of screen time) the narrative
of THE GREAT GILBERT AND SULLIVAN, but the underlying

myth-infused plot shines through as a duality of lost-and-found love (again, close friendship between two men) and the quest (for cultural recognition). The high-brow/low-brow dialectic is operant in Arthur Sullivan's painful unease about postponing his ambition to write serious concert music, and when he does attempt a non-comic, grand opera on his own, the elite reject it with a chorus of boos and jeers even fiercer than the hostile reaction to Stephen Foster's great failure.

The petty bickering between the two partners, over so mundane a matter as a roll of carpet, leads to their famous estrangement, but in the diegetic world of the narrative, the pair are joyously reunited just prior to a late-in-their-lives revival of one of their earliest comic opera successes. Although Sullivan dies shortly thereafter (a concession to historical record), Gilbert, the more "common" of the pair, sees his successful catering to the tastes of the middle-brow audience rewarded with an honor not available along the Broadway/Hollywood axis of similar motion pictures covered by this study. In America the apotheosis of cultural recognition for a songwriter has been shown repeatedly on film to be a dedicatory concert of his music at one of the iconic temples of social respectability, a prestigious concert hall. In the concluding sequence of THE GREAT GILBERT AND SULLIVAN, the surviving member of the team is knighted at Buckingham Palace.

America's two masters of the operetta (which, like comic opera, is also a direct antecedent of the Broadway musical comedy) were Victor Herbert (bio-filmed in 1939) and Sigmund Romberg. Just as the works of Gilbert and Sullivan were still being revived for contemporary audiences of the mid-1950s, Romberg's operettas continued to be stage perennials at that time, with two of them, THE DESERT SONG and THE STUDENT PRINCE, being re-filmed as major Hollywood productions in the year preceding the late-1954 release of the Sigmund Romberg biography, DEEP IN MY HEART. Therefore the attractional quotient of the film's subject matter was relatively high, despite the passing of the years since the initial popularity of Romberg's music. Invocation of the familiar is straightforward and to the point. The introductory title card reads: "To all those who love the music of Sigmund Romberg."

The narrative unfolds as a variant on the quest myth; Romberg begins life in America as a fresh-off-the-boat

Austrian immigrant who finds his first New York City employment as a piano player in a Second Avenue beer garden. His ambition is to write music for the Broadway stage in the tradition and style of the popular, romantic operettas of Old Vienna. A Tin Pan Alley song plugger convinces Romberg that in order to establish himself as a composer and earn a decent living, he should first write what, in the parlance of the World War One era, is called "hotsy totsy" music. In the narrative's streamlined simplification of his early career, Romberg does just that, but with only mediocre results. Like the songwriters of MY GAL SAL and IRISH EYES ARE SMILING, he gains his first real success by writing songs specifically for a female star vocalist who is a headliner in big-time vaudeville. In this case the singer (the historical character Gaby Deslys) "jazzes" up his music to fit popular taste, and Romberg is disconsolate about his success until musical stage star Dorothy Donnelly and talent agent Bert Townsend take a proprietary interest in the composer's career and guide him through his new association with impresario J. J. Shubert.

In addition to invoking several famous names and characters from show business history, the narrative of DEEP IN MY HEART utilizes a wide variety of other familiar motifs from the body of film work which precedes it. The oft-employed cultural dialectic appears in Romberg's struggle, during his years with the Shubert organization, to win approval for a softer, more orchestral and less "brassy" kind of musical score. His eventual triumph in composing "Maytime" is followed by the failure of overreaching, trying to be his own producer and director for the disastrous "Magic Melody." His infatuation with his "one true love" is followed by an exceptional ten-year "misunderstanding," caused by her mother's disapproval of what she believes are vulgar, show-business people. It is only with the artistic triumph of "The Student Prince" that Romberg finally wins her hand, and their happy years together are spelled out in terms of a standard Ziegfeld/Cohan-type montage of his continuing string of hit shows, often composed in collaboration with Dorothy Donnelly, and later with Oscar Hammerstein.

When the latter-day shows written with Hammerstein, such as "East Wind" and "May Wine," do not equal Romberg's earlier successes, his wife Lillian comments, "You've graduated from Tin Pan Alley; you should be in Carnegie Hall." The film's final sequence, concluding the quest for public acceptance via the strongest archetype of all musical show-business biographies, takes place in just that location, with a concert of Romberg's best-loved melodies, conducted by the composer. As was the case with the studio's previous songwriter biographies of Kern and Hammerstein (TILL THE CLOUDS ROLL BY) and Rodgers and Hart (WORDS AND MUSIC), MGM's current roster of musical performers is called on to populate the staged tribute. Yet since the era being re-created is long before their time, they can not be said to be portraying themselves, except in the most extradiegetic sense.

CHAPTER VII

THE BANDLEADERS

Show-business biographies of famous musicians began their own cycle with a rather deviously constructed 1943 film, IS EVERYBODY HAPPY? The inquisitive title, long the identifying catch-phrase of bandleader/clarinetist Ted Lewis, had previously been employed for an overtly fictional 1929 motion picture in which Lewis portrayed a jazz band leader named Ted Todd. While that film's narrative distantly echoed certain aspects of Lewis' real-life career, the picture rightly belongs in the more amorphous category of fictitious show-business dramas which feature a popular performer in a diegetic milieu similar to that of his own environs. The second IS EVERYBODY HAPPY?, on the other hand, actually subjected, albeit via a circuitous narrative route, the historical personage of entertainer Lewis to the ongoing process of filmed biography. It is this certain hesitance in the mode of exposition, due to a diversionary narrative device, which calls for closer analysis of the 1943 HAPPY.

The opening credits include an easily read disclaimer notice: "The characters and incidents portrayed and the names used herein are fictitious, and any similarity to the name, character, or history of any person is entirely accidental and unintentional." Such an unequivocal declaration of non-biographic intent would seem to settle the matter up front, without cause for audience uncertainty or subsequent legal action by parties perceiving themselves to be portrayed without prior consent. The story that follows, however, works to undermine this introductory notice in such a manner as to call into question its essential veracity.

The main body of the narrative concerns the World-War-I-era efforts of two young musicians, a clarinetist and a piano player, to start their own orchestra and introduce Southern jazz to New York City audiences. A romantic triangle involving the pair and their female vocalist is resolved when she chooses the pianist, but the intervention of war and the pianist's disabling loss of one arm separate the friends and lovers until an emotional reunion while the clarinetist's band is performing at a veterans' hospital. The wounded soldier-musician is then persuaded to take up the trumpet.

What is of special significance is the positioning of the story within a contemporary 1943 flashback frame. Ted Lewis, appearing as himself, dressed in his standard bandleader costume, complete with top hat and title phrase, opens the film by performing one of his theme songs, "Just Around the Corner." Then he befriends a young soldier-musician and regales the lad and his fiancée with the tale of two of Lewis' "buddies," who helped introduce jazz to the

Michael Duane (c.) as Ted Lewis, with Larry Parks (l.) in IS EVERYBODY HAPPY? (1943). Photo courtesy Wisconsin Center for Film and Theater Research.

big city. At the conclusion of the flashback narrative, Lewis reveals that the one-armed musician and girl singer in the story were the young man's parents. When asked who the clarinet player (called "Tom") in the story was, Lewis extends his hand and says, "Meet Tom." Asked why he changed all the names in his account of the band's rise to success, Lewis coyly explains: "A story always sounds better through the eyes of another man."

IS EVERYBODY HAPPY? stands apart from the body of work analyzed for this study in that it is structured in such a way as to question its own primary assertions via a wealth of contradictory aural and visual information. Lewis himself appears as the Lewis of 1943, but another actor appears as Tom/Ted in the flashback drama of the young musicians' struggle for acceptance of their new brand of jazz. Yet the actor who plays the band's cofounder also portrays (at a concluding wedding sequence and with appropriate age makeup) the father of the young couple to whom the older Lewis relates his story. Various events and locations in the flashback, such as the band's debut at Rector's New York restaurant, where the historical Ted Lewis got his start, coincide with the actual history of the Lewis band as well, thus casting serious doubt on the film's printed disclaimer. The apparent contradiction can be resolved if one accepts the notice as an extra-diegetical extension of the older Lewis character's practiced deception in telling the myth-infused story of his band's quest for acceptance and of his friends' lost-and-found love. Curious and duplicitous as its narrative structure may be, IS EVERYBODY HAPPY? marked the beginning of the sub-generic cycle of filmed biographies of popular musicians.

The next film in this category appeared in 1947, and again it employed its real-life hero (in this case--heroes) in a self-depicting performance, certainly the ultimate congruent invocation of the familiar. THE FABULOUS DORSEYS designed its imagery around the motif of a scrapbook of memories, compiled and doted over by an admiring mother. Yet the challenge in bringing this story to the screen was a considerable one for the film makers involved. The widely reported feuds between the Dorsey brothers had long been a matter of public record. The crucial element of audience sympathy could easily be jeopardized if the pair were merely depicted as two maladjusted sibling rivals, grown to manhood without ever having overcome one of childhood's major emotional dilemmas. By choosing to employ the mythic infrastructure of separation and reunion, the screenwriters therefore obviated the potential pitfall of audience alienation and actually made use of pre-existing public knowledge (about the brothers' bitter disagreements) to invoke the familiar in a dramatically profitable manner.

The archetypal elements of the characteristically American rags-to-riches story populate the narrative at the opening, with young Tommy and Jimmy (portrayed at first by child actors) as two rambunctious Irish kids in a small Pennsylvania coal town. Their father, who works in the mines by day and gives music lessons in the evening, wants his boys to become great musicians and escape the drudgery of the coal pits. Although Pa Dorsey is amused by the boys' early involvement in barroom brawls ("Ya gotta fight for things in life ... I want 'em full o' scrap!"), Ma Dorsey speaks the "lesson" the boys will not fully learn until the story's conclusion: "If they just stick together, they can lick the world."

The boys' coming-of-age, signalled by the appearance of their real-life selves portraying their screen characters, is followed by their decision to start a jazz band. Later they pick up a replacement for their recently departed piano player by convincing the accompanist at a small-town silent movie theatre to join them on their road to eventual success in New York City. The Dorseys' girl singer is a young lady from back home, and her attraction to the new pianist forms the basis for the narrative's love story sub-plot, conveniently eschewing the depiction of romantic liaisons for either Tommy or Jimmy, and the legal complications that might have ensued had any real-life ex-flames been inclined to sue.

Echoing several songwriter biographies, the new pianist has classical aspirations. It is the triumphant performance of his concerto which concludes the narrative and re-unites the by-then long-estranged brothers. Bandleader Paul Whiteman, who appeared as himself in RHAPSODY IN BLUE, performs similar invocational duties in THE FABULOUS DORSEYS when the boys temporarily join his aggregation prior to re-forming their own orchestra. When their spiteful wrangling causes them to split up and form two separate orchestras, the girl vocalist goes off with Tommy's band, and the pianist stays for a while with Jimmy. Thus the reunion of the bandleader-brothers, prompted by a bedside plea from their dying father, is also an archetypal

reunion of parted lovers, aided by the familiar plot device/
motif of advertising the concerto under a false name so that
the recalcitrant composer can be temporarily deceived in
furtherance of the romantic sub-plot.

The film's concluding shot, of Tommy and Jimmy
playing their respective trombone and saxophone side by side
at the concert, fulfills the mythic need for stasis and closure via reunion. The real-life Dorseys, despite their collaboration in making the picture, continued the separate careers of their earlier days, so aptly outlined by the film's
central "dual success" montage, which counters each Variety
or Billboard notice of one of Tommy's achievements with a
similarly impressive one of Jimmy's.

The "Big Band Era," which exists as a time conception in the nostalgia realm of American popular culture, is
generally considered to have been in its final phase about the
time THE FABULOUS DORSEYS was released. The jazz
style known as "swing" was being superseded by "be-bop,"
and the large, generally white dance orchestras which had
been influenced by the earlier style were breaking up or cutting back on personnel. Although THE FABULOUS DORSEYS
can be classified as a contemporaneous invocation of the familiar, the next musician biography, also of a bandleader and
the beginning of a closely interrelated series of bandleader
films, was definitely a nostalgia item.

The 1954 release of THE GLEN MILLER STORY exploited the attractional factor of nostalgia not for an era that
was a full generation or two in the past, but for a time that
perhaps seemed just as distant, because of the cultural upheaval brought on by the Second World War. Miller himself
had been dead for ten years, a casualty of wartime service.
The news of his being lost in a plane that supposedly crashed
at sea, but was never found, had made headlines at the time,
surrounded by the aura of mystery that accompanies most
stories of "lost flights." The music of his orchestra had
been immensely popular from the late 1930s through the early war years, and many other musical groups of the time
had adopted the characteristic "sound" of his instrumental
arrangements. The mere mention of his name was, in the
popular culture of the 1950s, sufficient to summon up wide-
ranging memories of the recent, but forever lost, past.

When the Dorsey brothers appeared as themselves in
THE FABULOUS DORSEYS, the film's title appropriately

advertised exactly what it delivered, and the film's numerous performance segments were filled with Dorsey hit songs, members of the real Dorsey orchestras, and even some of the star vocalists who had appeared with the bands in earlier years. THE GLENN MILLER STORY, released seven years later, lacked the congruency and immediacy of the Dorsey film, and instead was a re-creation, an impersonation, an invocation of the familiar via facsimile. Both films' narratives made use of historical lives as the outward material, covering and supported by mythic constructions of a more recondite nature, but when the bandleader cycle started in earnest with GLENN MILLER, the only thing approaching the genuine was the sound, and even that was altered in the film making process.

The cycle spanned five years (American popular music tastes were rapidly changing at the time) and included the release of THE GLENN MILLER STORY (1954), THE BENNY GOODMAN STORY (1955), THE EDDY DUCHIN STORY (1956), THE FIVE PENNIES (1959), and THE GENE KRUPA STORY (1960). Miller, who as noted above was something of a key figure for the era depicted, understandably was the first of the bandleaders to serve as subject material for re-creation. The intense public memory of his death was a factor the film makers chose to confront directly in the narrative. Thus denied the possibility of a happy ending, they constructed a story infused with the myths of quest and sacrifice. Dispensing with the complications of lost-and-found love, Miller is quickly married off to his college sweetheart in the early stages of the plot and remains faithful to her, except for the suggestion that music is possibly the greatest passion in his life. The balance of the drama revolves around the hero's idealistic quest for the perfect means of personal/instrumental expression. Young Miller declares his deep desire to "express" himself in the "best way," with a band that has a "sound all its own ... a personality."

When he is drafted and becomes Commander of the Army Air Force Band, Miller imposes his unique personal vision on that organization and devotes himself entirely to perfecting its sound and pleasing the troops and war-ravaged civilians who listen to his nightly BBC broadcasts. The mythic overlay of sacrifice interfaces with the quest when Miller is reported missing while flying across storm-tossed waters in the English Channel. He was on a dangerous flight, undertaken to do needed advance work in preparation

Sig Ruman and James Stewart in THE GLENN MILLER STORY (1954). Photo courtesy Wisconsin Center for Film and Theater Research.

for his band's arrival in France, where it was to provide morale support for the soon-to-be-victorious Allied forces. News of Miller's presumed death is dramatized in a personal manner, as it is received by his wife and children while they prepare for Christmas Eve festivities. The firmly established Hollywood "tear-jerker" formula, causing audience members to identify strongly with a family structure, then tearing that configuration asunder so as to summon up the most painful of childhood fears (familial separation and death) is operant in THE GLENN MILLER STORY's conclusion, concurrent with the mythic act of sacrifice. This doubly effective combination of dramatic device and plot construction greatly assisted the film in becoming an outstanding commercial success, but it is not the purpose here to explain the pleasure-from-pain phenomenon which enables skillfully crafted tear-jerkers to evoke such positive audience response. Rather, this narrative maneuver is noted as a significant accessory component of the show-business biographical film, employed partially in several previous entries (THE STORY OF VERNON AND IRENE CASTLE, SWANEE RIVER, RHAPSODY IN BLUE, etc.) but rarely to such an extreme and archetypal borrowing from tragic melodrama (the father of young children dies on Christmas Eve).

The prime attractional factor of hearing "that Miller sound" carried over directly into subsequent bandleader biographies. Just as the original Miller band arrangements were used in recording the sound track for THE GLENN MILLER STORY, vintage orchestrations written by and for Benny Goodman, Eddy Duchin, Red Nichols' Five Pennies, and Gene Krupa were dusted off and employed in scoring the later pictures. Yet certain subtle changes were made (whether at the whim of each film's musical director or soloists is unimportant) in the tempo, relative volume levels of instruments, and ad lib solos. Jazz purists can pick out these variations easily, but to the general public the effect was a much closer approximation of the originals than was ever attempted in the cycle of songwriter biographies, where numerous well-remembered songs were depicted (in performance segments) in the vehicles (stage shows and musical films) in which they were introduced, but with gross inaccuracies concerning performer identity and style of rendition.

While THE GLENN MILLER STORY invoked the auditorially familiar to the extent of employing many of the surviving Miller band members in Henry Mancini's sound track orchestra when the recording sessions took place at Universal Studios, THE BENNY GOODMAN STORY, shot on the same lot the following year, advertised itself as featuring Goodman himself, doing the solos mimed on camera by actor Steve Allen. Just as NIGHT AND DAY followed RHAPSODY IN BLUE and WORDS AND MUSIC followed TILL THE CLOUDS ROLL BY as near-mirror-image followups, crafted by many of the same people and re-working similar historical material into differing mythic patterns, THE BENNY GOODMAN STORY is THE GLENN MILLER STORY's direct genre-descendant. The historical time period, locations, and style of entertainment depicted are roughly identical. What sharply separates the films is the alteration in operant myths. Bandleader Goodman had not sacrificed himself for a noble cause, indeed was alive and well, and was still a successful entertainer in 1955. Even though the period of his greatest popularity had passed, he had survived the

Steve Allen as Benny Goodman in THE BENNY GOODMAN STORY (1955). Photo courtesy Wisconsin Center for Film and Theater Research.

repeated dissolution and re-formation of his aggregation (sometimes it was only a trio or quartet) and continued to make records, appear at concerts, and perform on television programs. Clearly a different mythic structure was needed.

  THE BENNY GOODMAN STORY, rife with lengthy and authentic-sounding performance segments, and concluding with his archetypal "swing concert" at Carnegie Hall, relied on a duality of quest (for the ideal musical self-expression) and lost-and-found love. A shy Jewish boy from Chicago, little Benny (like so many show-business biographical characters before him) is raised by his culture-loving but working-class parents to love, respect, and perform the masterworks of classical music. When the lad turns to Negro-style jazz as a more viable means of expressing his innermost emotions (he has trouble verbalizing), his parents plead with him: "Benny, Benny ... don't be that way!" Indeed, this phrase becomes the litany of the film, spoken to Goodman so often that he finally uses it as the title for a hit tune.

  Conflicts and setbacks dog his upward progression, and even when he is an established bandleader, he believes that he will never achieve the ultimate success of making it big in, of course, New York City. A tour of the western states, where Goodman's late-night, East-Coast-originated radio show is heard much earlier in the evening, is greeted with such wild enthusiasm that he finally summons the courage to conquer his "jinx town." First with a series of standing-room-only morning concerts for teenagers at the Paramount Theatre, and ultimately with an enormously successful black-tie performance for the elite at Carnegie Hall, Goodman takes the town by storm and fulfills his quest, not only for recognition, but for self-expression.

  The film's concluding sequence features his lost-and-found shikse, to whom his mother has long objected, sitting happily beside the older woman in the concert hall audience. Mrs. Goodman, who by the narrative's end has come to realize that the feared shikse is "really a nice girl," asks the young woman if Benny is ever going to get the courage to propose marriage. The girl listens to Goodman's solo for a moment, notices that he is looking directly at her, and replies, "He's asking me now." In OH, YOU BEAUTIFUL DOLL, Alfred Breitenbach concluded the narrative by surrendering his old-world values to those of the new, only in a secular sense. THE BENNY GOODMAN STORY gives no quarter at all. The acceptance of jazz by a representative of the old world is now reinforced by an abandonment of the deepest values of all.

THE EDDY DUCHIN STORY, despite its hero's specialization in a type of lush "dinner music" that could hardly be termed jazz, relates directly to both the Goodman and Miller stories, combining their themes and plot material in a tale of suffering and death that, while clearly in the tearjerker tradition, is curiously devoid of any overt act of sacrifice. The film's dramatic mode is tragic; its mythic structure, seasonal. The narrative incorporates the essential historical facts that Eddy Duchin, after a quick rise to popularity as a star cafe entertainer and bandleader, lost his wife to childbirth complications and died himself a few

Tyrone Power and Rex Thompson as Eddy Duchin and his son Peter, in THE EDDY DUCHIN STORY (1956). Photo courtesy Audio Brandon/Films Incorporated.

years later, suffering from an exotic and incurable disease and leaving his young son an orphan. Duchin's season-keyed life-on-film begins when the narrative introduces him as a recently graduated pharmacy student who has rejected his parents' plans for his career as a druggist. Instead, he has followed his dream of success as a piano player to New York City, arriving in the spring of 1927 on the very day that the personification of youthful American ambition, Charles Lindbergh, completes his historic trans-Atlantic flight. A convenient newspaper headline, caught by the camera, sets the date, and the locale, which becomes the centerpiece of the diegesis, is Manhattan's Central Park, where the vegetation and the elements reinforce the imagery of seasonal change.

Duchin's romance with wealthy designer Marjorie Oelrichs, a warm-hearted shikse whom the young man's old-world parents find impossible to reject (as was the case with Benny Goodman) is played out in a series of pastoral tableaux-in-motion, surrounded by the natural beauty of the park in scenes of sunshine and shower. The class tension in their budding relationship is less between contrasting forms of music than between the girl's society-oriented friends and family and Duchin's clearly evident working-class origins. Even his supposed acceptance into her "crowd" is marred when he accepts a party invitation without realizing he is expected to perform, not attend as a guest.

The summer phase of the narrative arrives when Duchin achieves his sought-after success in cafe society, playing to capacity crowds at the chic Central Park Casino, marrying Marjorie, and eventually debuting as the leader of his own orchestra. On their wedding night, a cold gust of wind startles the couple just as they are entering their new home. "I hate the wind," says Marjorie, "I have dreams ... that the wind blows between us." Foreshadowing the tragic events to come, the frightened woman tells her new husband: "Your talent is the important thing. If everything else were to disappear--even me--it really wouldn't matter." Thus the stage is set for the onset of the trials of autumn while dialogue underlines the heroic nature of Duchin's special gift of music.

Marjorie's death, like that of Glenn Miller, occurs at Christmastime, with Central Park's autumn leaves covered by the first snows of winter. The embittered new father rejects his young son, a Variety headline announces the tearing down of the Central Park Casino, and the onset of World War II prompts Duchin to enlist in the navy. An encounter in the South Pacific with a native boy, whom Duchin teaches to play "Chopsticks" on a piano which has survived a recent Japanese bombing, reminds Duchin of his estranged son. The repentant man writes the boy (who is now in grade school and living with relatives) a letter of apology, and the coincident myth of separation and reunion is thereby allowed to run its own course within the larger drama.

Reunion with young Peter Duchin is difficult for the returning ex-musician. His understanding new girl friend assists in temporarily forming a loving family unit, with plans for a second marriage and a new life together, but the mythic cycle of seasons has entered the winter phase. Eddy Duchin laments the impossibility of turning back the clock as he explains to his would-be second wife that the happiness he knew with Marjorie is gone forever: "We were kids together. How often can you be kids together? Only once. No one gets the big jackpots of life more than once ... like having a child ... or watching your parents grow old." Then Duchin reveals the cause of the pain in his hands that has plagued his attempted comeback as a pianist: "I'm going to die. I've only a year to live. It's hematosecosis. So much for love ... or whatever future we might have had."

The borrowing from tragic melodrama which moved so many viewers of THE GLENN MILLER STORY to purgative tears repeats itself, possibly to even greater effect in THE EDDY DUCHIN STORY, because of the larger amount of screen time devoted to the ripping asunder of the family unit. Duchin cries out to his God: "Why do you have to destroy a man twice?" Then the distraught musician ponders how to break the news to his son: "Oh God, give me the proper words to say to him!" Young Peter Duchin and his father are next seen at a deserted playground in Central Park, on the very spot where the Casino once stood. Under a gloomy sky the elder Duchin tries to tell his boy that they will soon have to part company again--this time forever. The narrative's final sequence symbolically depicts the parting in a manner which brings the seasonal myth full circle. Peter and his father are practicing a duet version of one of Eddy's most popular numbers. Seated at two separate pianos, the elder Duchin remarks encouragingly, "You're getting awfully good, son. It's hard to tell where I leave off and you begin." The camera pans over to show only the lad at

146 / Star Myths

his own keyboard. A pan back to the other piano reveals it to be deserted. Eddy Duchin is gone, but his talent, which Marjorie had said was the most important thing of all, lives on--re-born in their son, who went on in real life to equal his father's success in the world of popular music. Winter's death is followed, true to the archetype, by the wonder of re-birth.

The myth of separation and reunion appears again as the foundation of the 1959 biography of bandleader Red Nichols, THE FIVE PENNIES. With the diegesis including the world of black-influenced white jazz of the 1920s and 1930s, the linkage phenomenon with earlier entries in the cycle is rather pronounced. Like Eddy Duchin, Nichols is initially seen as an "innocent" entering New York City for the first time with high ambitions for a musical career. After meeting

Danny Kaye and Barbara Bel Geddes in THE FIVE PENNIES (1959). Photo courtesy Wisconsin Center for Film and Theater Research.

and marrying his "one love" early in the narrative, linkage begins to function as he teams up with several other aspiring musicians, including Jimmy Dorsey and Glenn Miller. Possessed of the familiar personal vision of an ideal musical form (in this case, dixieland-style jazz with a strong lead trumpet), Nichols does enact a career-establishing quest within the preparatory stage of the separation drama to come, working at confining jobs in "hack" and novelty orchestras until he is able to establish his own band, cut a hit record, and begin a successful first tour. The central dramatic conflict, however, is enacted not as an impediment to Nichols' achieving success, but as the consequence of his subordinating familial obligations to the expansion of his initial career success. From the point at which his good fortune as a bandleader prompts him to tell his wife, "If things keep going like they are, we can start a corny, old fashioned family in a couple of years," the main conflict begins. Her reply: "I'm three months corny."

Nichols' attempts to bring his wife and infant daughter along on his seemingly endless series of tour engagements works as a career/family compromise for a few years, but eventually the girl is placed in a boarding school. Red blames himself when the child contracts infantile paralysis following some unsupervised play in the rain, and in a bitter rejection of his established life pattern, he drops his beloved trumpet off the Golden Gate Bridge. Thus the lost-and-found love of this particular enactment of the separation/reunion myth is actually Nichols' love for his music, symbolized by the battered and trusty horn (a survivor of many pawn shop visits in leaner days) that he now rejects in a moment of personal crisis.

Just as the narrative of YANKEE DOODLE DANDY pretends that its hero retired from performing for so many years as to be forgotten by a new generation of youthful consumers of popular culture, THE FIVE PENNIES creates a diegesis in which Red Nichols quits music entirely, supplementing his savings with employment as a shipyard worker while seeing his crippled daughter through more than a decade of medical treatments. At a house party attended by the teenaged girl's classmates, Nichols is confronted by a blunt-spoken lad who quotes his own father: "Mr. Nichols, my dad says you were smart to get out of the business when you did ... before the parade passed you by." The young Nichols girl is incredulous when she is told by her chagrined father that as a toddler she traveled with the likes of latter-day music heroes Miller, Dorsey, and trombonist Jack Teagarden.

The joyous reunion that concludes the narrative and completes the mythic structure, although it does not take place in Carnegie Hall, where earlier in the film Nichols had predicted that one day he would play, takes place in a fashionable nightclub. Many of Nichols' old friends (including the by-then historically dead, but diegetically very much alive Glenn Miller) attend the comeback festivities, billed as the "Return of Red Nichols and the Five Pennies."

A triumphant return also concludes the last in the cycle of bandleader biographies, 1960's THE GENE KRUPA STORY. Released at a time when the strict censorship of the Hollywood Production Code was beginning to abate under the competitive onslaught of commercial television, this film's attractional factors went beyond nostalgia to include scandal, adopting aspects of the "confessional" cycle of performer biographies to be dealt with in later chapters. Krupa had risen to stardom as a featured performer in name bands of the 1930s (including Benny Goodman's) before striking out on his own as the leader of an orchestra bearing the Krupa name. His widely reported arrest for marijuana possession, an event which seriously interrupted and threatened to destroy his career, was therefore chosen as the dramatic centerpiece/crisis of his bio-film's narrative, easily facilitating the story's assumption of a rise-and-fall mythic pattern.

The air of controversy which still surrounded his name as late as the filming of THE BENNY GOODMAN STORY may have been responsible for Krupa being portrayed anonymously in that film by a drummer/actor who is never referred to by name, but who performs at the Carnegie Hall concert in a fair approximation of the style that Krupa made famous. By 1960, however, the Krupa name was deemed an attractional, not detrimental, factor in fashioning an entertainment aimed less (as was the case with earlier bandleader films) at the family trade and more at the growing and commercially important youth market. The actor chosen to portray Krupa was 20-year-old Sal Mineo, a popular youth star of the 1950s whose career had already included portraying a number of troubled young men, juvenile delinquents, and "rebels." Thus the public images of both the historical Krupa and the star of THE GENE KRUPA STORY served to reinforce each other.

Yet despite the film's avoiding the more noble image of previously bio-filmed bandleaders, the bulk of the narrative continues the established generic formula and relates directly to what went before. Once again, the hero is an ambitious young man with a vision. "There's music in drums," he exclaims, and his aim is to discover that music and bring it to the world. Parental opposition (Papa Krupa wants his boy to enter the priesthood) is as vehement as ever. "Drums are from the Devil," says the enraged father, and young Gene relents for a time, entering a Catholic seminary.

Summer vacations and extended weekends allow the boy to renew his participation in a local Chicago jazz band. The exhilaration he feels in "beating those drums" (an enthralled female fan asks him, "Are you beating the Devil?") eventually frees Krupa from his spiritual bonds and leads him back to jazz as a lifetime vocation. The familiar pull of New York City soon prompts Gene to leave home in search of greater fame and fortune, with his arrival fixed historically in the same year as Eddy Duchin's entry into Manhattan. Instead of a newspaper headline, however, a theatre marquee announces Al Jolson's talkie debut in a film erroneously titled YOU AIN'T HEARD NOTHIN' YET!

Krupa and a fellow musician from back home subsist in a cold-water flat for a time, searching for jobs while living on the charity of Gene's hometown girlfriend, Ethel. The romantic triangle of ST. LOUIS BLUES, polarized by a good woman and a bad woman vying for the heart of an easily-led-astray musician, relates directly to the plot formation of THE GENE KRUPA STORY, with the rise-and-fall narrative in the latter film substituting the handicap of public disgrace (the marijuana arrest) for W. C. Handy's bout with temporary blindness. Instead of only one bad girl tempting him, Krupa is set upon by several in the course of the story, and the implication is definite, but never overtly declared, that his drug possession arrest was the result of a frame-up engineered by a rejected lady friend.

Krupa's years of success as a star soloist with other bands are de-emphasized, despite the linkage appearances of Red Nichols (in person) and actors portraying the Dorsey Brothers. Instead, the narrative gives greatest importance to Krupa's achieving his stated ambition of leading his own orchestra. The requisite character defect which precedes the hero's "fall" is presented as stemming from his supposedly premature achievement of his goals. "Success is when you can handle it," warns Ethel just before Gene's disastrous arrest. The inflated ego syndrome, which in show-business biographies dates all the way back to THE MIGHTY BARNUM, claims another victim in Gene Krupa. A significant alteration is that a new auxiliary factor, illicit drug consumption, acts as a dramatic catalyst in this situation. The crucial task of maintaining audience sympathy, circa 1960, would not allow a film to plead its hero simply guilty, however. Krupa is shown to have successfully weaned himself off drugs, with the help of the watchful Ethel, just before the police pounce on him and find the wrong kind of cigarettes in his coat pocket. Earlier, Krupa had defended his transformation from a humble-kid-with-music-in-his-soul to a swaggering, decadent star of the jazz world: "What good is making good if you can't have everything that goes with it--parties, girls, kicks!" After his release from jail (the charges were dropped) Krupa finds himself blacklisted as a bad risk, and Ethel explains: "Success to you is like whiskey to an alcoholic. You were not big enough to handle it."

As if to prove Krupa worthy of a personal renaissance, of another chance at the big time, the narrative assigns him a figurative act of penance--learning to read music. With this key step in his maturation process completed, Krupa gets his crucial shot at a comeback from a benevolent Tommy Dorsey, who promotes a concert appearance of his own band as "The Return of Gene Krupa." Hecklers in the audience threaten to disrupt Krupa's first number and force him off the stage, but he endures shouts of "Hey, jailbird!" and "Got a reefer?" while banging out a performance that wins over the crowd to the sound of cheers and applause. The image of the disgraced artist taking to the stage in front of an angry crowd and transforming their hostility into wild approval is, of course, not new. It is the archetypal image of the prophet, the seer, the leader, the disguised god, the ageless hero, confronting and captivating the multitude with a message they cannot resist. It is a mythic construct eminently adaptable to the field of show-business biography.

Just as SCOTT JOPLIN marked the 1977 reappearance in television drama of the long-dormant motion picture subgenre of composer biography, LOUIS ARMSTRONG--CHICAGO STYLE became a 1975 revival of the bandleader biography cycle which had ended with THE GENE KRUPA STORY fifteen years earlier. Until these television productions of the mid-1970s,* the only show-business biographical film with a black hero had been the 1958 ST. LOUIS BLUES, a picture specially tailored to exploit the contemporary popularity with white audiences of singer Nat "King" Cole. Black celebrities from the world of American show business, despite the considerable success many of them had enjoyed in entertaining the white majority, were consistently bypassed in film biographies for more than four decades.

LOUIS ARMSTRONG--CHICAGO STYLE took as its central character an extremely popular black trumpet player/ bandleader (and linkage figure) who himself had appeared, as himself, in two previous bandleader biographies (THE GLENN MILLER STORY, THE FIVE PENNIES).** Armstrong had been dead only four years before his biography was filmed, and he had continued to make television and personal appearances until just a few months before his passing, at the age of 71. His career spanned a full half-century of American jazz, and his profound influence on the idiom was universally acknowledged. Building a motion picture around events from his life was therefore an overall invocation of exceptionally familiar images and subject matter. Yet his bio-film's narrative limited its span of chronological delineation only to Armstrong's early years in the prohibition-era, mob-owned nightclubs of Chicago. The fact that the film was created as a 78-minute television drama destined to debut in a 90-minute time slot may have obviated the possibility of depicting more of the man's long and colorful career, but the film makers' decision to concentrate on but a brief span of time may also be significant in that it suggests a willingness on the part of certain film makers to experiment with a basically anecdotal narrative dressed out with the iconography of a show-business biography.

Louis Armstrong is depicted as a gifted musician who escapes his unenviable beginnings (playing for beer and tips in New Orleans whorehouses) with the help of a manipulative

---

*The 1970s theatrical films LADY SINGS THE BLUES and LEADBELLY will be dealt with in later chapters.
**In addition to his numerous "guest star" appearances in fictional musical films, he also appeared as himself in the historical drama NEW ORLEANS which, though not a biography of a particular show-business personality, was an alleged re-enactment of the birth of jazz in the red-light district known as Storyville.

white agent. Despite the parallel with Scott Joplin's origins, the character of the white advisor is portrayed here as more malevolent than benign. Armstrong's agent stoops to framing his client on a marijuana charge (fifteen years after THE GENE KRUPA STORY, innocence is still important) in order to make the musician more beholden to him. When the agent decides to "sell" Armstrong to a corrupt nightclub owner who is a rival of the more sympathetic club owner for whom Armstrong has been performing, Louis finally rebels against being a white man's "private nigger," leaves Chicago, and accepts another promoter's offer to tour the jazz-hungry capitals of Europe.

Even in the essentially anecdotal, non-career-spanning structure of the film's narrative, a mythic pattern remains operant beneath the surface dramatic transactions, for the story being played out is that of Armstrong's quest for self-determination, the right to be "his own man." In a larger, parallel sense, the narrative is but a partial myth, the figurative ritual of birth--the birth of what Louis Armstrong's fans perceived as his image--that of a great entertainer. His long and successful career as a bandleader, following his triumphant return from Europe, is omitted from the narrative at hand. Public knowledge of the heights still to be scaled by the hero completes the understood line of the mythic pattern only begun in the television drama.

The last bandleader biography to date, although radically different in the historical period covered and the style of the performing sequences presented, echoes the birth motif of the Armstrong biography, even to the employment of a specifically time-limited title. THE BIRTH OF THE BEATLES, a 1979 television film, appears to be the first motion picture devoted to telling the supposed "story" of a band from the so-called rock-and-roll era, a time popularly perceived to stem from the late 1950s through the present. THE BUDDY HOLLY STORY, to be dealt with in a later chapter about singers, actually preceded the release of THE BIRTH OF THE BEATLES but dealt with the process of a star vocalist's emergence from what he found to be the confines of a group/band relationship. Such predecessor films as ROCK AROUND THE CLOCK (1956), DON'T KNOCK THE ROCK (1957), CATCH US IF YOU CAN (1965), FERRY CROSS THE MERSEY (1965), and the Beatles' own starring movies did indeed lace their fictional stories with episodes of a contemporary, semi-biographical nature, but it was not until THE BIRTH OF THE BEATLES that a film devoted its narrative exclusively to dramatizing the historical achievement of success by a big-time rock-and-roll band under the guidance of its visionary leader.

Again the confines of limited television time (even in a two-hour slot the narrative cannot exceed 98 minutes) may have played a role in setting chronological boundaries, but the myth-infused birth motif (shared with the Louis Armstrong TV-film) might also represent acknowledgment by film makers that the attractional factors of a commercial biographical drama are not necessarily reduced by omitting the customary promise to display a "whole life" in the span of a single film. Realization by the target audience of the practical impossibility of doing so might actually serve as an ameliorating factor in dealing with the always risky (for theatrical films) factor of possible spectator disappointment, which leads to the cycle of initial rejection, bad word-of-mouth, low attendance, and financial disaster. However, since this cycle itself is obviated by the economics of pre-selling films to television (even if they open in American theatres first), no facile conclusions can be drawn about the as yet infrequent practice of severely restricting the span of biographical/chronological coverage. In the sub-generic specialization categories of singers (Grace Moore's early years in SO THIS IS LOVE) and comedians (THE EDDIE CANTOR STORY), examples of beginnings-only biographies appear as early as 1953-54, a full decade before the appearance of made-for-television movies.

Considered as a self-contained drama, despite its unfolding on the nation's television screens under the shadow of the shared public memory of the group's unprecedented later world successes, THE BIRTH OF THE BEATLES comfortably fits the familiar generic formula/myth of quest-for-popular-success. An oft-repeated question-and-group-response chant punctuates the dialogue as Beatle John Lennon queries his mates, "Where we goin'?" and they reply, "To the top!" Then John asks, "What top?" Their answer: "To the very top!" Whereas previous bandleader biographies allowed for only the most rudimentary character delineation of all but the leader and a couple of his closest associate musicians (plus manager and family members or sweethearts), THE BIRTH OF THE BEATLES has narrative space (because of the much smaller group of musicians) to establish character traits of each member and to involve the entire ensemble in the central plot. Nevertheless, the film is far from an equal depiction of each Beatle's contribution to the group's ascendency. Considerably more screen time is spent with the Lennon character than with any one of the others, and the boys repeatedly defer to his ideas, desires and judgment as their de facto leader. When pressed for a reason, one of them explains impishly, "it's 'cause you're older." Thus THE BIRTH OF THE BEATLES, despite its invocation of the familiar 1960s image of the group, is in its generic relationships yet another show-business biography of a leader and his band. The size of the aggregation is no longer "big," but the group is still a band, and its leader has a vision.

While the "birth" of Louis Armstrong was a struggle to free himself of his scheming manager, followed by Armstrong's "coming of age" as the toast of European cabarets, the struggle and maturation process endured by the Beatles center on some painful personnel changes (the sudden death of one guitarist and the firing of their first drummer) and on their triumph in winning over audiences of jaded German youth in some of Europe's most tawdry night spots. A break with generic convention, possibly indicative of the times, occurs in the narrative's depiction of the Beatles' highly ambitious manager. Agents and managers, from the earliest business associates of P. T. Barnum and Florenz Ziegfeld, had always been presented as strong characters, wise in the ways of the world and attuned to the contemporary desires of the public. Brian Epstein, a local Liverpool record-store operator who approaches the Beatles with an offer of his services in guiding their career, is a relatively weak and naive young man. Only his extreme sincerity has any effect in convincing the boys (and later the executives at Britain's largest recording company) that he is the right "outsider" to assist them and that the boys have the talent to merit a recording contract and a marketing campaign. Epstein's homosexuality, the sort of historically accurate character trait that had previously been either omitted or only obliquely suggested in show-business biographical films, is presented without question in this 1979 production, but never as a source of amusement or deserved shame. Rather, it functions as an integral plot element in a sequence set up to demonstrate the compassion and tolerance of John Lennon. When Epstein attempts to hide himself from his clients until the bruises he has received from a night of "rough trade" have disappeared, Lennon locates his distraught manager and consoles him. "It's all right, Eppie," says John. "We knew about you from the first time we met. Any loving between people is okay. There's not enough love in the world as it is."

The Bandleaders / 155

Rod Culbertson, Jon Altman, Ray Ashcroft and Steve McKenna as Paul, George, Ringo and John, in THE BIRTH OF THE BEATLES (1979). Photo courtesy Capitol Communications.

Despite this significant concession to changing American popular values of the last third of the century, THE BIRTH OF THE BEATLES still echoes many of the conceptions about the entertainment business and the insatiable audience which surfaced in earlier films covered here. Making no pretentions to "art," Lennon is shown telling an EMI producer that every song the group records is going to be aimed at making number one on the hit parade. When Lennon's aunt, who has raised him since his mother died, pays an untimely visit to the boys in the midst of a wild party (with plenty of liquor, smoke, and girls in various stages of inebriation and undress), she asks her boy, "Is this what you really want, John?" Echoing Gene Krupa, Lennon replies, "Of course it is ... it's success." On the eve of the Beatles' first American concert tour, which is where the narrative (and its mythic quest) concludes, Epstein warns them that success will make addicts of them, requiring bigger and bigger doses of popularity to stave off madness. Although this open-ended exchange might seem to deny the possibility of satisfactory narrative closure, Epstein is given a foreshadowing dialogue passage which invokes the familiar yet to come--the band's widely publicized dissolution, still some eight years in the future. Calling George the "soul," John the "mind," Paul the "heart," and Ringo the "flesh and blood," Epstein declares that the band will exist and thrive only so long as all four parts of the "body" continue to work together. The narrative makes the assumption that the audience already knows when and how the dream will end.

As mentioned earlier, the aural invocation of the familiar was, because of publicly remembered individual styles of performance, a far more exacting task in bandleader biographies than in those of songwriters. The employment of authentic arrangements and musicians on the soundtrack, whenever possible, facilitated the invocational process. Benny Goodman, Red Nichols, and Gene Krupa recorded their own solos off-camera, the Dorsey Brothers mimed to their own custom film recordings, but Glenn Miller, of course, had to be doubly impersonated, as did Louis Armstrong. (The use of old phonograph records, perhaps because of the limitations of earlier technology, has been consistently avoided.) It would seem that the only limiting factor in auditory authenticity was the living-or-dead status of the star soloist in question. The lack of a living Eddy Duchin actually led the makers of his bio-film to add an additional attraction to the project--advertising "music performed by Carmen Cavellero."

Re-creating in 1979 the sound of the early Beatles, who had long before sold their "life stories" to a film producer, involved a more complex situation. Since they were in no way involved with the latter-day film project and had repeatedly refused all offers to record with each other again, the options to the film makers were but two: use the old records or make new ones with other performers. Pitting early 1960s recording technology versus the sound track capabilities of network television circa 1979 revealed no great differences, but either legal and financial problems in clearing reproduction rights to the records, or the aesthetic decisions of the film makers, caused the latter option to be selected. The familiar sounds of the early Beatle hits were therefore note-for-note impersonations of the originals, but performed by entirely different personnel. In essence, this served as an undeniable distancing factor, underlined by a highly visible (and spoken) disclaimer at the end of the opening credits: "The following is a dramatization, using actors, of the early career of the Beatles. It is based on factual accounts including the recollections of former Beatle Pete Best, as well as other sources. The music sung during this period by the Beatles was recorded for this dramatization by the group Rain." Whereas previous bandleader biographies invoked the familiar sounds of their heroes with an authenticity hampered only by the inexorable imposition of death, THE BIRTH OF THE BEATLES broke with this practice in what might be considered a most blatant way--unless the viewer perceives the 1979 state of the group as exactly what the Brian Epstein character implied it would someday be if its four "body parts" ceased to function together. Seen this way, the film conforms to yet another firmly established genre convention. The actual sound of the Beatles can not be heard because the group is as dead as Glenn Miller.

CHAPTER VIII

THE SINGERS

Earlier the relationship was noted between the emergence of the show-business biography and the rise of the talkie musical. Films based on the lives of singers Jenny Lind and Lillian Russell were shown to have roles in establishing the conventions of the overall category of motion picture narratives here being analyzed. During this same period, the great bulk of overtly fictional 1930s dramas with professional singers as their lead characters (and sporting plot situations which easily lent themselves to the insertion of songs aimed by the studios' publishing subsidiaries at the hit parade) built up a much more extensive tradition of narrative conventions and interrelated diegetic material which reappeared a few years later in film narratives which function as overt and specific biographical texts.

During the initial period of rapid proliferation of show-business biographical films, which followed the American entrance into World War II, singer biographies continued to appear, but with considerably less frequency than composer biographies. Yet by the early 1950s, filmed biographies of singers easily matched those of songwriters in terms of annual frequency and accumulated numbers. Even when the songwriter biography went into eclipse, with the segmenting of American popular music, singer biographies continued to appear, well into the 1960s and 1970s. This would suggest that while the songs of a period may be the prime attractional factor in dramatizing the life of a composer, this is much less the case in filming the lives of singers, whose dramatized, myth-infused careers can hold the interest even of viewers who are not at all attuned to a specific style of musical material.

Unlike songwriter biographies, films about the lives

of singers have consistently employed both male and female
performers as their central characters from the very beginning, even to the point of statistically favoring females.
(The only other professional specialty where this distribution
can be found is in filmed biographies of actors and actresses.)
Women's historically verifiable lack of success in composing,
regardless of the possible societal or sexual causes, is
thus reflected in the overall category of films under study,
just as feminine achievement in certain of the performing
arts (on a much more equitable ratio with men) is acknowledged by a fairly large number of other biographical films,
those about female singers and actresses.

The world of vaudeville, threatened by the silent
cinema, weakened by radio, laid low by the Depression, and
finally destroyed by the talkies, was already a potential nostalgia period by the time of World War II. This ethos contributed to the success of YANKEE DOODLE DANDY, with
many of its song-and-dance segments set in the vaudeville
houses that once dotted the American landscape. SHINE ON
HARVEST MOON, the third show-business biography to be
released in the wake of DANDY, restricted its characters'
specialties to that of performing on vaudeville bills of fare.
No previous biographical film, not even THE STAR MAKER,
had told the life story of a performer whose aspirations and
accomplishments were limited to the world of vaudeville.
Overtly fictional films, such as the 1940 Shirley Temple
vehicle, YOUNG PEOPLE, had paved the way for this type
of musical motion picture, but SHINE ON HARVEST MOON
marked the initial combination of backstage vaudeville drama
(heavy with stage-framed musical numbers) with specific biographical delineation of a career.* Lillian Russell moved
on to leading roles in Broadway plays, as did George M.
Cohan, and the Castles spent much of their career dancing
in cabarets. The song-and-dance team of Nora Bayes and
Jack Norworth, even when they appeared on the bill in
Florenz Ziegfeld's "glorified" multi-act revues on Broadway,
were still doing vaudeville-style turns, only in a grander
showcase than usual.

---

*The ill-fated MARCH OF TIME (1930), a panoramic, would-be nostalgia trip through the history of vaudeville, was abandoned by MGM after extensive shooting and never released.
BROADWAY TO HOLLYWOOD (1933), which borrowed some
footage from the earlier film, was a strictly fictional drama
of a vaudeville family act's rise to success.

Mention is made in the narrative, however, of Jack's ability to write music. In one sequence he is shown making plans to convince publisher Jerome Remick to buy the film's title song, which (although not identified as such in the dialogue) eventually became the team's theme song, after their discovery by Ziegfeld. Such an invocation of the familiar thus functions by means of the implicit assumption that the target audience of 1944 still remembered the names of Bayes and Norworth with sufficient clarity to associate them with their theme. This song, which early attained the status of a "standard," was for obvious reasons selected as the film's title, echoing the contemporaneous practice employed in titling songwriter biographies.

Yet SHINE ON HARVEST MOON is classified here as the first singer biography of show-business biography's second phase of development. Were it to be viewed as a songwriter biography, SHINE ON's narrative would have to place its emphasis on the crucial task of Jack Norworth's getting his own song(s) published, performed, and accepted by the public. Instead, the critical and painfully delayed event on which the drama hinges is the elusive chance at stage success long hoped for by the team of Bayes and Norworth.

The operant myth in the narrative is one of separation and reunion, complicated by the interposition of a romantic triangle. Jack's rival for the affections of Nora is a big-time booker/entrepreneur, said by Variety to control most of vaudeville of the time (1905) by his power to withhold the services of the most important performers. To stay employed, Bayes and Norworth have to split up. Ego-wounded Jack quickly descends into a boozy haze, working in low-class burlesque houses while Nora believes he has left her for a new (professional and romantic) partner.

When Nora at last discovers Jack's misfortune and comes down from the audience to rescue a failing performance by him as a single, a Ziegfeld talent scout in the theatre mistakes their fortuitous reunion as a brilliantly conceived act. The narrative concludes (in a surprise Technicolor production number with numerous chorus girls dressed as vegetables) on the eve of the team's greatest success, as featured artists in the Follies, singing the title song.

SHINE ON HARVEST MOON's linkage with previous show-business biographies is strongest, by means of reciprocity, with THE GREAT ZIEGFELD. In terms of an

The Singers / 161

Ann Sheridan (center) in SHINE ON HARVEST MOON (1944). Photo courtesy Wisconsin Center for Film and Theater Research.

extra-diegetic time continuum, SHINE ON is but one of several parallel historical event progressions (later portrayed via film narrative) which intersect on the stage of New York's New Amsterdam Theatre. As will be demonstrated, a surprising number of Ziegfeld's top-billed performers eventually had their individual careers dramatized/mythologized for the popular cinema audience. Particularly curious is the fact that Bayes and Norworth, whose fame was definitely more fleeting than, for instance, that of Will Rogers or Fanny Brice, were the first Ziegfeld stars to have their careers transformed into film/myth. In THE GREAT ZIEGFELD they do not even rate an attempt at impersonation. Only their names and a piece of their theme are heard as part of the Follies' backstage cacophony. The historical condensation/distortion of depicting all of Ziegfeld's biggest attractions as appearing in a single Follies show adds to the confusion, but a likely answer can be found in noting that historically Bayes and Norworth graced Ziegfeld's earliest bills of fare, thus placing them in an era more distant (1907) from 1944 than the Follies of the 1910s and 1920s, which sported several stars who were still very active performers in the mid-1940s, and thus not as likely candidates to be "brought back" from the fond-but-fading regions of popular memory.

The next singer biography offered to American film audiences was a British import of 1944, CHAMPAGNE CHARLIE. Directed by the multi-national documentary specialist Alberto Cavalcanti, it was an expensively mounted re-creation of the early days (circa 1860) of American vaudeville's antecedent, the British music hall. Borrowing from the Hollywood practice of invoking maximum familiarity via a popular song title, the picture was named after the song that became the theme of entertainer George Leybourne. The narrative depicts Leybourne's rise to fame, complicated by his heated skirmishes with rival singer Alf Vance.* A romantic sub-plot of lost-and-found love between subsidiary characters hews to the previously noted convention of denying romantic lead parts to older or eccentric performers (the actor playing Leybourne is far from handsome), but the narrative's dramatic emphasis clearly favors the subterfuge-filled adventures of Leybourne and Vance as they seek to outdo each other in gaining popularity with London's music hall fans. (Both performers specialize in satirizing the gentry and popularizing outrageously worded drinking songs.)

A relatively unusual mythic structure underpins this biography, for it embodies a quest variation akin to the prince setting out to slay the usurper, only to compromise at the close and share the throne with the former rival. After a long and pitched competition between them, Vance and Leybourne unite in a mutual effort to prevent the London authorities from closing down all music halls in the name of eliminating a public nuisance. The film's final performance segment is a semi-bawdy duet featuring both Vance and Leybourne, uniting in a special show aimed at saving the music-hall business from ruin. With the threat

---

*Indicative of the even more legally cautious nature of the British cinema at this time is an introductory disclaimer which denies the historical existence of the real George Leybourne: "All events and characters are fictitious." Unlike the American-made IS EVERYBODY HAPPY? of a year earlier, no clever excuse for this deception is ever supplied.

of disruption from an external source removed, a new
stasis/compromise ushers in a supposedly satisfactory
closure.

Separation and reunion is again the operant myth in
1945's THE DOLLY SISTERS, based on the career of another
famous vaudeville team which ultimately succeeded in becoming a Ziegfeld headline act. Once more the ever-present
conflict potential of professional division (will the team split
up?) is exploited for dramatic effect by the interposition of
a romantically inclined interloper. A key difference in the
structure of the threatened partnership (sisterhood, not heterosexual attraction) changes only the surface identities, not
the basic elements of the myth. One of the sisters is courted by a fellow vaudeville artist, a song-and-dance man who
wants her to break with her sister and form a new partnership (romantic and professional) with him. For dramatic
symmetry, the other sister also has a beau, but he is a department store owner, not an entertainer, and therefore not
a direct threat to the successful stasis of the sister act, despite his equally insistent offers of marriage. Jennie Dolly's
eventual marriage to vaudevillian Harry Fox does not result
in her teaming with him professionally, however, and she
even cancels out on their honeymoon to avoid missing a crucial booking with her sister at the Folies Bérgère in Paris.
The despondent husband, cuckolded by the sisters' success,
not by a sexual rival, nevertheless seeks solace in alcohol
and in salvaging his own, small-time career. The threatened partnership of the sisters (reinforced by the bulk of
the film's performance segments) is never broken; only Jennie and Harry's marriage splits asunder.

Reunion for the estranged couple, true to the accumulating narrative pattern, is a public event. In this case it
is enacted on the stage of New York City's Metropolitan Opera House, where an all-star benefit, heavily populated by
Ziegfeld headliners, even includes the recently risen-in-the-world Harry Fox, a last-minute fill-in for Eddie Cantor.
Prevented from using her divorcée's freedom to marry "the
wrong man" by a providential auto accident, Jennie recovers
from her injuries just in time to join Rosie at the benefit.
Jennie's emotional reunion duet with Harry expands to a trio
when Rosie joins them in the final chorus. As in SHINE ON
HARVEST MOON, what the diegetical theatre audience perceives as an act, the extra-diegetical film audience sees as
a climatic return to stasis and closure of the central myth.

THE JOLSON STORY, released in 1946 and very likely the most successful (in terms of the number of tickets sold) show-business biography of all time, severed the anticipated reunion from the separation myth, and thus transformed the career-related domestic crisis of the hero and heroine into a supreme act of sacrifice. Al Jolson, the consummate entertainer, the man who excelled in pleasing audiences more than anyone else in the business, is shown giving up the "great love of his life" rather than accept the confines of domesticity and conjugal devotion. It is as if the film makers were telling the audience, "Al Jolson loved <u>you</u> more than anything or anyone else. He sacrificed his own happiness just to make <u>you</u> happy."

With the exceptions of the semi-disguised heroes of THE STAR MAKER and IS EVERYBODY HAPPY?, THE JOLSON STORY marked the first time a show-business biographical film confronted the challenge of depicting a living, recently active performer as its lead character. No sizable expanse of time had elapsed to allow the public's memories of the real-life hero to fade, and Jolson himself was still around, open to easy, possibly unfavorable comparisons with his screen imitator. George M. Cohan never lived to see James Cagney enact the Cohan part, and Cohan's last active years (ending within five years of the picture's release) had been spent on Broadway, not on film and radio, before the critical eyes and ears of the nation. Jolson, on the other hand, had a face and voice with which only the very youngest movie-goers of 1946 were unfamiliar. Credibly invoking the familiar was a task of considerable difficulty.

The solution to this dilemma (prefiguring the music dubbing of the bandleader biographies of the 1950s) was to have Jolson himself record the songs and coach the leading actor in all the appropriate Jolson gestures, facial expressions and stage movements. The fictionalized narrative, based on Jolson's own reminiscences of his career, invoked the familiar in a whole host of ancillary ways. Performance segments borrowed extensively from actual Jolson vaudeville routines, Broadway shows, radio broadcasts and motion pictures. The auditory parade of "standards" was every bit as equipped to exploit the nostalgia phenomenon as had been the score of ALEXANDER'S RAGTIME BAND. Names of celebrities with whom Jolson had been associated virtually peppered the screenplay, and montage sequences overflowed with marquee shots, lobby posters and title cards from Jolson's long string of successful stage and screen vehicles. Yet at the center of the diegesis was a legally necessitated deception which unavoidably stood at odds with all the film's extensive attempts at verisimilitude. Jolson's widely publicized courtship, marriage and divorce from musical star Ruby Keeler, although depicted in the drama, featured a thin disguise. The historical Keeler character was concealed under the pseudonym of "Julie Benson." (At the time of the film's production, Jolson's still bitter ex-wife would not sign a release for the use of her name.) This collision of public knowledge with filmic practice is most apparent when Julie Benson's own career is summarized in a montage of film posters advertising her starring roles in 42ND STREET, SHIPMATES FOREVER, DAMES, and GO INTO YOUR DANCE, all genuine Ruby Keeler vehicles from the previous decade, and the last a film in which she co-starred (as does Julie Benson) with Al Jolson.

THE JOLSON STORY also prefigures the conflict between old and new world values which infuses many subsequent songwriter and bandleader biographies. Yet this conflict (specifically between a performer's Orthodox Jewish beginnings and the culturally heterogeneous world of show business) had already been a staple of overtly fictional dramas, most pointedly functional in the narrative of Jolson's own 1927 film debut, THE JAZZ SINGER. Far from innovative as well was the domestic crisis precipitated by Julie's insistence that Al give up his endless round of performances in order to take up the lifestyle of domestic retirement she so intensely desires. The seeming incompatibility of home life with the limelight, one of the most recurrent motifs in all show business drama, is the crux of THE JOLSON STORY's dramatic structure. What makes the film truly unusual, in terms of audience expectations and gratifications of the period, is the manner in which the conflict is resolved. Coerced into early retirement by his wife, the veteran performer resigns himself to his fate but continues to be restless for a chance to return to the activity that has been his life--performing for a wildly appreciative audience. A similar narrative situation in YANKEE DOODLE DANDY righted itself with George M. Cohan's successful comeback on the Broadway stage, following his encounter with a group of teenagers who, he discovered, had never heard of him. The triumphant return to performing by an equally forgotten Red Nichols in THE FIVE PENNIES was also spurred on by an encounter with youthful ignorance. Al Jolson's return to the spotlight, while both a dramatic act of closure to the narrative and a fulfilling of the underlying

Larry Parks (r.) as Al Jolson, with Ludwig Donath and Tamara Shayne as his parents in THE JOLSON STORY (1946). Photo courtesy Wisconsin Center for Film and Theater Research.

mythic pattern, is not so much a symbolic re-assertion of a man's professional life as it is an act of sacrifice for the public's benefit. While Jolson and his wife are entertaining his visiting elderly parents, the group dines at a cabaret. Jolson is soon recognized and implored to perform, but he refuses at first, aware that the main reason he has been able to preserve the happiness of his marriage is his retirement from carrying on his "love affair with the audience." When he finally yields to the request and begins a medley of hit songs he once introduced, the crowd responds ecstatically and the Jolson marriage dissolves. Quietly, his wife slips away from the table. A shot of her empty chair reinforces the action as a final separation. The narrative concludes with Jolson energetically performing for an intensely appreciative crowd. His loss is our gain.

The impersonation of Al Jolson by actor Larry Parks took the cameo performer impersonations of THE GREAT ZIEGFELD a giant step further in demanding audience acceptance. The veil of time which had protected screen portrayals of singers Jenny Lind, Lillian Russell, Bayes and Norworth, and The Dolly Sisters offered actor Parks little protection from invidious comparisons. Cagney as Cohan risked rejection by the New York theatre crowd, but Parks as Jolson stood the chance of near-universal opprobrium, so widely well-remembered was the real-life singer. The film's general acclaim and financial success alleviated such fears on the part of film makers and paved the way for a host of more contemporaneous biographies, no longer limited in subject to behind-the-scenes personnel or the faintly remembered performers of an earlier era. THE JOLSON STORY proved that with sufficient pre-conditioning of the target audience (attendant publicity announced and explained the vocal substitution), the familiar could be invoked via film at will, regardless of the recognizability of the biographical subject-person.

In other respects, however, THE JOLSON STORY was much less innovative and quite in keeping with the established patterns of filmed show-business biographies. Jolson's screen character was presented with the same softening, myth-infused distortions of history that had been deemed essential to gain audience sympathy for the likes of P. T. Barnum and Florenz Ziegfeld. Jolson's notorious ego, both the driving force behind his stellar career and the cause of much acrimony in his personal and professional relationships, was subsumed into the textual camouflage of his obsessive need to satisfy an audience's hunger for entertainment. The oft-repeated anecdote about Jolson's habit of running the water in his dressing room so he would not have to hear the applause given other performers is absent from the narrative, just as is the famous and controversial quote about "suckers" missing from THE MIGHTY BARNUM.

The next singer biography to appear on the nation's theatre screens was a 1947 release titled after a once-popular song, MY WILD IRISH ROSE. Essentially a star vehicle for Warner Brothers' then highest-paid actor, singer Dennis Morgan, it was a supposed depiction of turn-of-the-century tenor Chauncey Olcott's rise to fame. Possessed of a voice of such clarity and power that it had become a popular standard of excellence akin to that of Jenny Lind, the historical Olcott was long dead by 1947, his vocalizing fame having been surpassed by that of the songs he introduced. It was a situation far different from that which attended the christening of THE JOLSON STORY. Thus the film makers opted to employ one of the best-known songs in the prime attractional position of film title, again following the practice of the parallel songwriter biographies of the 1940s.

The narrative's operant myth is similarly that of the quest for fame and success, almost in a regal sense, and in this instance greater weight than usual is given to the element of intuitive destiny, functioning at odds with the traditional parental interdiction. The young Chauncey Olcott is warned not to waste his "heaven-sent" voice on the "sinful stage," but because he "just knows" he will someday become "another William Scanlan" (the preeminent Irish tenor of the day), Olcott leaves his steady job as a tugboat sailor to pursue a singing career in vaudeville. In a variation on the show business biographies in which the leading character changes his name in order to go on the stage, Olcott adopts the pseudonym of "John Chancellor" only on a temporary basis. His reluctant mother, who has decided to let her son try show business only to "get it out of his system," advises, "Don't use your real name until you're a success."

Linkage factors populate the film from the opening sequence, in which Olcott is smitten with the charms of touring Lillian Russell, who is appearing on the same bill with comedians Weber and Fields. Although impoverished, Olcott assumes the role of "stage door Johnny" so as to escort her to an expensive restaurant. Before the bill comes due and he is ejected by the manager, Olcott proclaims to the visiting celebrity his intention to go on the stage. "I hear that every night," says the aloof Russell, adding, "Don't you people realize the world of the stage is totally foreign to you?" This reinforcement of the parental interdiction only makes the ambitious Olcott all the more resolved to climb to the top of the entertainment ladder, and by the middle of the narrative he has parlayed his talent (by way of minstrel shows and singing in a New York saloon) into a leading role opposite the great Russell herself in a hit Broadway show.

Olcott's love affair with a proper girl from a "good family" is threatened by published rumors of an offstage romance with his leading lady. His attempts to assuage the girl's suspicions are unsuccessful, and eventually Russell feels constrained to deliver one of the more significant speeches in the entire category of films under study. Em-

The Singers / 169

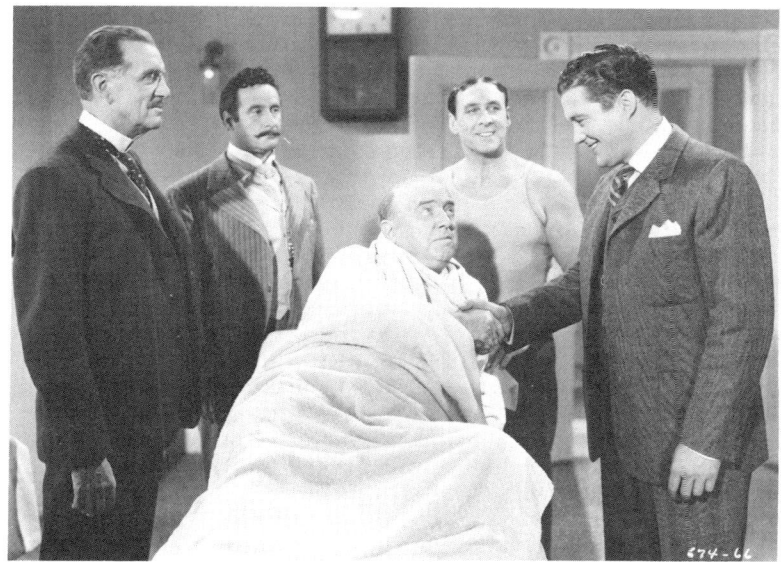

Dennis Morgan (r.) and William Frawley (center) as Chauncey Olcott and William Scanlan in MY WILD IRISH ROSE (1947). Photo courtesy Wisconsin Center for Film and Theater Research.

phasizing the supposed "apartness" of entertainers, Lillian Russell explains to Olcott's fearful girl friend that stage romances are chimerical and basically unreal: "Don't pay the slightest bit of attention to a word he says [to me]. We in the theatre live apart from the outside world. We don't say a word but to further our career. We can't hurt each other because we are in love with the same love--the theatre."

Not only does the film's narrative emphasize the duplicity and ingenuousness attendant to pursuing stage success; the element of self-degradation is also given the spotlight. Fired from his first Broadway job and still relatively an unknown, Olcott/Chancellor next finds employment in a stage equivalent of the task the real Al Jolson performed during the filming of THE JOLSON STORY. The eminent William Scanlan, the hero of Olcott's youth, has allowed a drinking habit to distort and weaken what was once the most prized voice on the American stage. Chauncey Olcott is subsequently hired as Scanlan's "ghost singer," anonymously belting out a series of Irish-tinged ballads from behind a curtain, while the decrepit Scanlan mouths the words before cheering audiences and receives all the glory. When the imperious star is finally afflicted by drink to the point that he can no longer even stand up straight before an audience, Olcott is required to go on in the dying man's place and perform for an eager crowd of Scanlan fans. The assemblage quickly sinks to mob status when they suspect they will be disappointed. True to the generic archetype of the hero-perfomer's extraordinary power to calm and satisfy the angriest of crowds, Olcott's rendition of "A Little Bit of Heaven" (penned by IRISH EYES ARE SMILING's Ernest W. Ball) quiets the mob and turns its jeers to cheers. In mythic terms, the old king has been displaced by the new monarch. The ailing Scanlan staggers to the stage, presents the scepter-like token of his prized pocket watch ("Given to me by the Prince of Wales") to the surprised Chauncey Olcott, and proclaims to the crowd, "A new star is born." A success montage and a happy marriage conclude the narrative, but it is this act of symbolic coronation which fulfils the myth.

No singer/vaudevillian biographies were released in 1948, but early 1949 saw the arrival of an entry in this subgenre which introduced into show-business biography the heretofore untried element of self-reflexivity. JOLSON SINGS AGAIN was an unusual effort not only in its singularity as a functional and overt sequel to an earlier bio-film, but also in choosing to deal with the act of bio-filming as an appropriate career-culmination ritual. Over a myth-infused structure of rise-and-fall the narrative of the second Jolson film picks up exactly where the first one concluded, with the singer losing his wife as the direct result of his yielding to requests that he perform once again. Although the historical Jolson career does not divide so conveniently into periods of temporary retirement and sacrificial comeback, such a dichotomy facilitates the mythic task at hand, as the figuratively "revived" Jolson supposedly resumes his spectacular career, going right back to starring in a series of new (and apocryphal) Broadway shows. (No mention is made of Jolson's post-Julie/Ruby, post-Warner Brothers career as a character actor in biographies and pseudo-biographies at Twentieth Century-Fox.) Jolson's supposed "Broadway renaissance" is cut short by his failing health, and he seeks recuperation on a leisurely around-the-world cruise, while his faithful manager and elderly but still-devoted parents await his return and assemble press clippings and travel photos in a scrapbook. Thus the initial rise of the new Jolson career is abated by its first setback, exacerbated by the unexpected death of his mother and his personal agony at discovering the widespread persecution of the Jews, which is beginning in Europe. Against the background of the chanting of the <u>kaddish</u> at his father's synagogue (Al has returned from traveling too late to bid his mother farewell) the older man tells his middle-aged son that the prayers are for all the Jewish people who are suffering at the hands of the Nazis.

The fluctuating curvature of rise-and-fall ascends when Jolson, too old to enlist for combat, finds an unexpected measure of success in entertaining World War II troops as part of a USO traveling show. At an isolated air base in Alaska, Jolson apologetically introduces his act by telling the young men, "I sing. If you don't believe me, ask your grandmas." Since the heyday of Jolson's popularity was barely more than twenty years before the period depicted in the narrative at this point, the calculated exaggeration of the Jolson remark serves to make the renewal of his career seem even more surprising and unlikely, in terms of changing popular taste. Yet win the boys over he does, to the sound of cheering and a personal testimonial from one of the officers, who remembers seeing Jolson when the national touring company of "Robinson Crusoe" played the remote spot of Duluth, Minnesota.

As the exceptionally gifted hero of a myth-infused drama, Jolson appears repeatedly as a man possessed of a vocal talent capable of charming the masses, regardless of the state of contemporary taste, and subject only to the personal and circumstantial constraints which occasionally prevent him from employing that talent to maximum effect. In the first of the two Jolson films the major impediment to his singing arises from the emotional commitment of his marriage. In the second film his professional career is hindered by the even more personal element of his state of health. The sacrificial dissolution of the first Jolson marriage facilitates the revival of his career in the earlier narrative, but since he cannot divorce himself from the infirmities of his aging body--an infected lung cuts short his USO tour--only benevolent outside intervention (in the form of a devoted nurse who becomes his second wife) can lead the way to yet another ascendant phase of the latter film's rise-and-fall structure.

The narrative's nadir is actually not reached during Jolson's heroic battle for life and his loss of one lung, but rather when the boredom of enforced rest gives way to the realization that a "whole new crop of singers has pushed [him] right off the map." The "all-star benefit" which made possible the joyous reunion of Bayes and Norworth in SHINE ON HARVEST MOON invokes maximum familiarity again in JOLSON SINGS AGAIN, this time updated to the mid-1940s and boasting a long celebrity roster which includes Jack Benny, Fred Astaire, Humphrey Bogart, and Eddie Cantor among its highly recognizable names. Indicative of Jolson's slide into relative obscurity, his slot has been relegated to the end of what promises to be a long evening, and he has been denied billing, being lumped in with other lesser lights in the category advertised as "and many others." By the time of his scheduled appearance, many audience members have left, but fortuitously a curious film producer is among those remaining who are enthusiastically impressed with the warmth and deepened texture of the recovered Jolson voice. So favorable is the crowd response that influential Hollywood columnist Sidney Skolsky muses in print the next day about finding a new vehicle that would allow the American public to rediscover the wonders of the Jolson voice. An Army Air Force colonel, the one who earlier recalled a Jolson performance in Duluth, pays a visit to the singer the following day and comes up with the suggestion of filming a Jolson biography as the perfect tribute to "the biggest man in entertainment for thirty years, [who sang] the biggest songs."

Thus the show-business biographical film, nearly twenty years after its debut, begins to feed upon itself in the narrative of JOLSON SINGS AGAIN, introducing an element of self-reflexivity specifically referential to the act of biographication.*

Following an invocationally ambiguous sequence in which the aging Jolson character is introduced to the young actor who is to play the lead in THE JOLSON STORY (Larry

---

*Five years earlier, in 1944, an overtly fictional film titled SOUTH OF DIXIE took notice of both the increasing popularity of show-business biographies and a certain degree of public skepticism about their accuracy. The film's plot concerned a New York-based composer of popular "Southern songs" who fabricates a sentimental life story of himself in hopes of selling it to a Hollywood studio.

Parks plays both parts via makeup and trick photography), the Jolson character is seen in conference with "the writers." Here Jolson delivers a speech which possibly encapsulates the myth-based, familiar-invocational rationale behind the entire category of films analyzed here:

> I don't think anybody cares about the facts of my life. Names, dates, places--I'll give you a bunch of them and you can juggle 'em around any way you want. What really matters is the singing-- and the story of a kid who ran away from home at fifteen.

A montage of the making of THE JOLSON STORY follows, leading up to a comic sequence depicting Jolson's extreme anxiety at the first sneak preview. The curve of rise-and-fall ascends to its last peak when the film becomes a huge success, radio stations begin playing Jolson records "all day long," and a crowd of "squealing bobby-soxers" attends the first broadcast of his new network radio show. As visual reinforcement of Jolson's spectacular comeback (historically, Jolson did replace Bing Crosby as the host of "The Kraft Music Hall" some months after the release of THE JOLSON STORY) the narrative concludes with the following year's Hollywood Community Chest all-star benefit show. No longer banished by lobby posters to the category of "and many others," the Jolson name shines out in the midst of a list of other headline stars of the day. The iconographic value of "billing order," long a part of the show-business bio-film formula and tradition, certifies the hero's rise to stellar prominence once again.

This supplementary vindication of a career, something of an anti-climax to the tumultuous success shown greeting the depicted release of THE JOLSON STORY, demonstrates that although the act of bio-filming a performer's life now ranks with the archetypal "Carnegie Hall concert" as an appropriate life-culmination ritual, live contact with a prestigious and approving audience is still essential to the ultimate affirmation.

It should be remembered that only Jolson's voice appeared in the film (although he can be glimpsed standing in for Larry Parks in some of the extreme long shots of his stage routine). The second Jolson bio-film goes further than just showing how Jolson's synthetic (impersonated) presence retains the heroic ability to enthrall a crowd. He can still "wow 'em" in person, too. Yet in stripping back the layers of pseudo-reality, the fact remains that the in-person Jolson, who concludes the narrative of JOLSON SINGS AGAIN by thrilling the benefit show audience with his rendition of "Rockabye Your Baby," is still an impersonation.

The risky business of synthesizing a currently active and highly recognizable celebrity for the screen was avoided to a great extent by the next singer biography to reach America's movie theatres, an expensively mounted 1951 release which became one of that year's most successful films, THE GREAT CARUSO. Its mythic structure encompassed another act of sacrifice, but on a more self-oriented level than that of THE JOLSON STORY. The Enrico Caruso of the narrative is depicted as being so devoted to his pursuit of fame and success as a turn-of-the-century opera star and concert artist that he attempts to postpone culminating a promising romance (marrying the girl who loves him) until his career is firmly established. When he returns home to collect his delayed bride, he discovers that she has married another. The promise of greater fame leads him to leave his native Italy for a contract with New York's Metropolitan Opera, where the by-now middle-aged singing star enters into a new romance with a girl much younger than himself. Dramatic conflict supplied by her father's opposition to the match and by a depicted professional rivalry with another singer fills out the story to feature length (with many insertions of lengthy performance segments). By the time Caruso has solidified his preeminent position in the opera world, married the girl, and fathered a child, his health begins to fail. He collapses in the midst of a concert performance of "The Last Rose of Summer" (the use of musical numbers to comment on the action continues apace) and dies, with the penultimate shot of the film dissolving into that of a bust of the late singer, stone statuary being the visual signifier of a legend firmly established despite the passage of time.

The film's generic overlap with "tear-jerker" drama (the ripping asunder of the family unit) is thoroughly in keeping with the narrative's sacrificial, mythic underpinnings, but the implication is clear that if the historical Caruso had not postponed personal and family happiness in furtherance of his career, the world might never have heard from him. Al Jolson's act of sacrifice was based on the sure knowledge that the crowds loved him and wanted him back in the spotlight, whereas Enrico Caruso knows little of the music-hungry crowds that will someday await him when he postpones, and ultimately shortens, his own happiness. Once he achieves stardom, however, the narrative ennobles his efforts by having him raise the volume of his singing in order to delight the "common people," who adore him from the cheapest third balcony seats or in the alley just off the stage door. Another significant difference which excludes the earlier film from this type of generic overlap is that the diegetic Jolson marriage produces no children. Julie/Ruby is free to walk away without obligations or tears. Caruso (as was the case with Stephen Foster, Glenn Miller, and Eddy Duchin) leaves a grieving widow and child.

The surviving Caruso recordings, much more so than even those of the early Al Jolson, could not have been used for the film because of the technological gap of an intervening half-century. Caruso was, however, a name like Jenny Lind or Chauncey Olcott--a name that had survived in popular memory as an easy invocation of superlative vocal performance. Combined with well-known arias and period ballads, it fitted appropriately into the total attractional package of the film. Yet in some ways the extreme success of THE GREAT CARUSO was unexpected by the Hollywood powers. Not since the mid-1930s, when a series of opera/operetta films starring such performers as Grace Moore, Jeanette MacDonald, Lily Pons, and Gladys Swarthout were released, had there been such middle-brow acceptance of "high art."*

The difference was that this time the performing star was the young and relatively inexperienced Mario Lanza, a minor RCA Red Seal Recording artist who had been signed to an MGM contract three years earlier and had appeared in two flop films. Just as non-star Larry Parks became Al Jolson for the camera, Lanza became Caruso, only Lanza enacted the role entirely with his own voice. This was apparently the first case of a singer biography being filmed with both the face and voice of the leading player a relatively unfamiliar commodity. The act of invocation was only in the character names, settings, and melodies.

Vocal dubbing by a still-living star again became

---

*The fact that this "art" (performance segments of operatic music) was heavily commingled with ample doses of familiar and accessible popular myths goes a long way toward negating this seeming paradox.

part of the pro-filmic event in the production of WITH A SONG IN MY HEART, a 1952 release which, despite its change in central character from male to female, closely paralleled the narrative construction of the combined JOLSON STORY and JOLSON SINGS AGAIN. The real-life heroine was the once-popular radio singer Jane Froman, whose career, though certainly lacking the spectacular successes of Al Jolson, had sufficient triumph and tragedy to lend itself to the biographic process and emerge in appropriately myth-infused fashion. Froman's rise to fame was depicted to emphasize both her intense ambition and love of performing, but the euphoria of ascendancy again was only prelude to the vicissitudes of staying at the top and overcoming serious health problems. Froman's fervent devotion to her craft leads her to become a stalwart on the USO camp circuit during World War II (as was Jolson), but an injury sustained in a plane crash (Jolson lost a lung) causes her to lose the use of one leg.

Her comeback, aided by a crusty nurse from Flatbush (Jolson had the moral support of his Brooklynese-speaking ex-vaudeville partner) thus becomes both a physical and spiritual triumph as she overcomes her handicap and resumes her singing career. As was also the case in the Jolson narratives, the sympathy-jeopardizing problem of divorce and remarriage is confronted rather than avoided, with the first liaison's dissolution ameliorated sufficiently to generate audience support for the second union with a younger and more ideally matched spouse who ably assists the performer in the arduous process of rehabilitation. (Jolson married his nurse; Jane Froman takes up with the young soldier who rescued her from the plane crash.)

While WITH A SONG IN MY HEART prompted no direct sequel akin to the duality of the Jolson films, it did trade on a similar attractional premise--promoting the voice of the real Jane Froman on the sound track as a special inducement for her many fans to attend the picture. Yet the title choice eschewed her name in favor of a song she had popularized years earlier. In the American film industry's hierarchy of attractions, Froman herself ranked below the best of her own material.

WITH A SONG IN MY HEART was the first female singer biography of the post-World War II era. Seven years had passed since THE DOLLY SISTERS graced the screen, but the considerable success of the Froman picture forecast that the careers of a number of other women vocalists would soon be mythologized on film. Between the release of WITH A SONG in early 1952 and the autumn of 1957, the lives of singers Blossom Seeley, Grace Moore, Marjorie Lawrence, Ruth Etting, Lillian Roth, and Helen Morgan were each exploited as source material for biographical films. This was, of course, during the mid-1950s, when an economically troubled, in-transition Hollywood was combating the television challenge in part by recycling the past on a massive scale, producing more show-business biographies of all types of entertainers than at any other period in the history of the film industry. While no causal relationship can be proved, it is significant to observe that as the financial situation of the studios worsened, so did the general outlook with which the films approached their subject matter. Prior to the mid-1950s, most show business biographical films emphasized success, rather than failure. Even when the leading figures in the narratives suffered painful setbacks or premature death, the message to the audience was a variant on "... but his music lives on forever!" The change to a more pessimistic approach, while certainly not characteristic of all show-business biographies from this point on, is most sharply visible in the above-mentioned string of closely-spaced songstress films.

SOMEBODY LOVES ME, a late 1952 vehicle for the maturing Betty Hutton, claimed to depict the career of vaudeville headliner Blossom Seeley, centering on her stormy romance and partnership with musician Benny Fields. The mythic infrastructure is a rather uncluttered rendition of separation and reunion, wherein she and her partner split (romantically and professionally) for a time and emotionally reunite in the last sequence. Much is made of the A STAR IS BORN-style sexual/professional jealousy caused by uniting a spectacularly successful female performer with a decidedly less successful spouse. Also, a note of bleakness is introduced in the film in that Benny Fields, when he becomes enraged by charges of "living off his wife's talent," soon learns that he simply can not succeed on his own. The fault is not a run of "bad breaks" or a change in public taste (as happened to the fictional Norman Maine prior to his taking to the bottle). Fields is clearly not a very deft performer. In essence, the charges leveled against him by show-business cynics are represented in the narrative as correct. The subjugation of his own raging, wounded ego dominates the second half of the story, and while this allows Blossom Seeley to condescend from her unchallenged position of vaudeville and cabaret eminence to rescue her man from despair (she even threatens to quit performing in order to save her marriage), this foray into the nether regions of show business, where performers grapple with the demon of talentlessness, marks a hitherto unexperienced darkening of the show-business biography's diegesis.

SO THIS IS LOVE, the 1953 biography of Grace Moore, broke with convention in a more subtle but no less significant manner. While there had been a number of previous films which adopted an anecdotal rather than a life-spanning form for their narratives, this film depicted the career of a singer whom most of America had come to know through her motion picture performances, but limited the dramatization of that career to her earliest stage work. The operant myth is therefore that of birth, but the attractional factor of the title suggests romance, an element which the narrative ultimately denies.

The plot structure employs a lengthy flashback, launched by Moore's thoughts in the last minutes backstage, before her celebrated 1928 debut at New York's Metropolitan Opera House. Her voice-over narration recalls her first visit to the Met, ten years earlier, when she was a dream-filled teenager, "clutching an SRO." "Tonight," she tells the film's viewers, "I enter by a different door." The drama that follows is the true-to-formula story of an aspiring performer who proclaims, "I have a dream," defies parental opposition, and leaves home in search of a stage career. Confronting the sexual barriers of the time, Moore exclaims, "I wish I'd been a boy," and her response to a relative's advice that she find a husband and have babies is: "That would be all right, if we were all the same ... [but] I want to express myself!" In the course of the narrative Moore does become involved with two suitors, both of whose proposals of marriage she rejects in favor of concentrating on her career. When the introductory framing sequence comes full circle at the end of the flashback, her reward is a record number of curtain calls (for her enactment of Mimi in "La Boheme") but no clinch with the lover of her choice. SO THIS IS LOVE (a title that could almost make use of a question mark) ends with a voice-over line which makes the implicit functioning of the birth myth explicit: "I received twenty-seven curtain calls. One for every year of my life ... and one to grow on."

The film's total omission of Moore's subsequent film career is therefore necessitated by the given time frame, but her pre-opera career as a popular ingenue in Broadway musicals of the early 1920s does receive ample depiction in expanding the narrative's base of familiarity invocation. The linkage phenomenon is equally active, with the young Moore idolizing star vocalist Mary Garden (as Chauncey Olcott did William Scanlan), being introduced at an early recital by John McCormack, auditioning for Ziegfeld colleague Abe Erlanger, and receiving personal advice from George Gershwin. Thus SO THIS IS LOVE can not be classified as a major deviation from established generic practice, but the narrative's negation of all romantic relationships does mark another act of formulaic transition.

INTERRUPTED MELODY, released in 1955, combined key elements of the three previous films as it told the story of operatic singer Marjorie Lawrence, who is first seen as a child, sneaking away from home before dawn (risking paternal wrath) to travel to an open audition in a distant city. Like that of Grace Moore, Lawrence's talent so impresses the influential people who hear her sing that she is given her first big break early in life, studies with teachers who are eager to train her voice, and becomes a continental stage star without pausing for marriage. When she does enter into a romance and subsequent marriage with an American doctor who is studying at a European medical institute, the narrative relates most closely to the troubled relationship of Seeley and Fields, with the doctor coming to resent bitterly his de facto status as "Mr. Marjorie Lawrence." The crisis (paralleling the crippling of Jane Froman) which saves the marriage by uniting the couple against adversity comes in the form of Lawrence's battle with infantile paralysis. Only after her physician husband has guided (and driven) her through long and painful months of physical therapy does she regain her courage to perform in a specially restaged opera at New York's Met. Prior to her official "come-back" she also builds up her poise and confidence with a practice identical to Jane Froman's specialty, singing to cheer up wounded soldiers at a military hospital. The narrative concludes on a note of transcendence which even exceeds its direct filmic predecessors. At the conclusion of her final aria at the Met, Lawrence rises from her supposedly necessary chair and miraculously walks across the stage, to the tearful surprise of her anxious husband, who has been watching from the wings. The

Eleanor Parker as Marjorie Lawrence in INTERRUPTED MELODY (1955). Photo courtesy Wisconsin Center for Film and Theater Research.

operative myth of rise-and-fall finishes with a renaissance phase which enters the realm of the marvelous, with no rational explanation offered for the surprise ending.

Unlike the previous female-singer biographies of the mid-1950s, INTERRUPTED MELODY offered neither the attractional factor of the real-life heroine's voice on the track nor the expected performance of a familiar star who was also known for her vocal ability (Betty Hutton as Blossom Seeley; Kathryn Grayson as Grace Moore). Instead, opera star Eileen Farrell was quietly called upon to provide the offscreen voice for actress Eleanor Parker. The fact that Lawrence was a native Australian who gained much of her fame performing in Europe may have lent something of an alien quality to this American (MGM) production, but the film's concluding invocation of the familiar (signifying the apotheosis of comeback success as a triumphant return to the stage of New York's Met) registers most of the proceedings as safely within established generic categorical limits.

Coming as it did, in the midst of a spate of increasingly pessimistic bio-films of female singers, INTERRUPTED MELODY marked the last note of clear optimism in such a film for twenty-three years. Three more films were to close the cycle by 1957, which would not resume until the late 1970s. These films relate less to their aforementioned generic predecessors than to the mid-1950s' cross-genre cycle of scandal/confession films, fighting the encroachment of television by giving the target audience more drinking, decadence, debauchery, and desperation than the home screen was allowed to offer. The show-business biography was at a turning point, abandoning in part the practice of glorifying the entertainers of the past, of giving nostalgic endorsement to their struggle to reach the top. Desolate portraits of fictional entertainers had already been tried and proved commercially viable in numerous non-biographical dramas, and a relatively recent one (YOUNG MAN WITH A HORN) had gone out to the public with an effective word-of-mouth campaign that it was the disguised story of jazz great Bix Beiderbecke's downfall.

LOVE ME OR LEAVE ME, the 1955 biography of Ruth Etting, made overt the filmic practice of covert exposé. Etting, a Chicago cabaret singer whose 1920s and 1930s career expanded to include network radio shows, headlining for Ziegfeld on Broadway, and appearing in Hollywood movies, was long known in the industry as having been the unwilling protégé of gangster Marty "The Gimp" Snyder, who was not averse to using his "influence" to get her "the breaks." Neither was he the least bit hesitant about "slapping her around" to "keep her in line," and their brief marriage was widely regarded as a stormy and brutal one. The facts of Etting's personal life were far from glamorous, and not the sort of material which would previously have been deemed suitable for a show-business bio-film according to the standard formulae. With both her and her ex-husband still living at the time of the film's production, their necessary approval of the script also seemed likely to make any accurate representation of their relationship quite impossible. Yet the producers and writers of the film, suspecting that the time was right for such an exposé, prevailed (with adequate cash) upon the former couple for permission, and even advice as to the authenticity of detail. The only real point of dispute to arise out of the agreement was reportedly over Snyder's insistence that actor James Cagney walk with the correct type of limp.

LOVE ME OR LEAVE ME, despite its dwelling on the sordid aspects of a marriage that begins with a rape and a career based on coercion, did not abandon the generic formula entirely. Mingled with the dirty business of the Etting-Snyder partnership (he builds up her career in hopes of possessing her; she acquiesces out of a numb sense of debt) is the familiar separation and reunion myth. A piano accompanist who befriends Etting during her early nightclub days re-enters her life years later as the musical director of her films, resumes their friendship (although he is shot by the jealous "Gimp"), and ultimately survives to become her salvation from a nightmare marriage. Particularly notable, as a continuation of tradition, is the film's invoking familiar ballads of the period as a direct comment on the narrative, with star vocalist Doris Day, who uses her own voice to approximate the Etting style, singing such appropriate numbers as "You Made Me Love You" and "Mean To Me." Hollywood rewarded the narrative's intentional de-glamorization and perceived frankness. LOVE ME OR LEAVE ME won the Academy Award for Best Original Story. Paradoxically, the same year's Oscar for Best Story and Screenplay went to the much more "uplifting" INTERRUPTED MELODY.

The final two female singer biographies of the 1950s increased the darkening of outlook found in the earlier films and emerged squarely in the category of the scandal-exposé pictures which were enjoying a new wave of popularity, facilitated and enhanced by the contemporaneous weakening of the production code. I'LL CRY TOMORROW (1955) and THE HELEN MORGAN STORY (1957) offered the public closely related expansions of the rise-and-fall myth depicting the heroine as victim--victim of the destructive undertow of the glamour world of show business. Both films cover the same historical period, starting in the "Roaring Twenties" and following the heroine's rise to early stardom and long descent into the pit of alcoholic despair. I'LL CRY TOMORROW purports to tell the story of "jazz baby" Lillian Roth, whose career, when she was barely out of her teens, included singing in a string of late 1920s Broadway musicals and early 1930s Hollywood films. The element of fate is also blamed for the heroine's misery, starting with an introductory voice-over: "My life was never my own ... it was charted before I was born."

In keeping with the theme of external forces propelling her on the road to ruin, Roth's initial rise is not prompted by her own desires for fame and success. From the time she is eight years old she is compelled by her "stage mother" to attend a continuing string of auditions, taking time out only for minimal schooling and a heavy dose of practicing to become vaudeville's youngest singing star. Roth's mother is the one with the giant ambitions, and she silences her daughter's sobs of protest with promises of "Broadway and Hollywood." "You can cry tomorrow," the woman tells the distraught little girl.

Roth's fall from stardom and sanity is prompted by the sudden (and fateful) death of her "solid citizen" fiancé, a young lawyer who had offered her the chance to forsake show business for quiet domesticity. She seeks solace instead in drink, beginning what her narration describes as a terrifying exploration of "the darkness in me." Waking from a drunken stupor, she discovers she has married an alcoholic timber merchant from Pittsburgh. Their marriage, a continual round of bar-hopping and fighting, eventually dissolves in 86-proof solvent. She goes on to marry yet another alcoholic, leaving her ruined career behind her while suffering from his savage beatings and her continuing case of gradual alcoholic poisoning.

The last stop on Roth's figurative descent into Hell is a skid-row flophouse, where she plans a suicide leap from an upper floor, then cries out "Dear God help me!"

and collapses back into her room. Roth's renaissance, following the enactment of the rise-and-fall myth, is coupled with the narrative's endorsement of the commendable volunteer work of Alcoholics Anonymous. A kindly AA member comes to her aid, convinces her to "take the pledge," and even becomes her new romantic interest, rescuing her from her personal Hell just as Ruth Etting's musician friend performed an analogous task in LOVE ME OR LEAVE ME.

The narrative concludes, however, not with any sort of professional comeback for the performer (her voice, damaged by alcohol, was not used on the film's sound track) but with an act of public career culmination/vindication which relates most directly to the ending of JOLSON SINGS AGAIN. Lillian Roth, after years of absence from public appearances, is the special guest on the live network television program whose contemporaneous success and impact dovetails precisely with the peak years of show-business bio-film production. Following the successful publication of her "confessional" autobiography (which is the film's story source), she is introduced by Ralph Edwards as the subject of a broadcast of "This Is Your Life."

THE HELEN MORGAN STORY, repeating I'LL CRY TOMORROW's focus on a 1920s singing star whose success and personal life crumble during the following decade, casts the pall of initial villainy not on a desperately ambitious mother but on a ruthlessly exploitive manager/lover/dominator. Fictitiously named Larry Maddox and enacted in the style of a young confidence man by Paul Newman, he enters, exits, and re-enters her life at crucial times, sometimes helping to boost her career, but always exacting an emotional toll on her psyche. From her deflowering and desertion by Maddox in the narrative's first sequence to her final torment in a hospital's alcoholic ward, when he shows up to comfort her, only to be led away to prison for his role in a hijacking, Helen Morgan is portrayed as Maddox' victim, suffering, as did Lillian Roth and Ruth Etting, because of her painful relationship with a flawed and destructive man who was not worthy of her. Morgan's alternate love in the narrative, a "respectable" lawyer, turns out to be a married man, and at various points in the story she utters such self-pitying lines of dialogue as: "I always get involved with men who are bad for me," and "Everything I touch turns bad." Her false refuge is the same as that resorted to by a distraught Lillian Roth--perpetual intoxication. "You're five feet high; you can't hide in a one-foot bottle," a character warns her, but to no avail.

Ann Blyth, star of THE HELEN MORGAN STORY (1957).
Photo courtesy Wisconsin Center for Film and Theater
Research.

Morgan's career on stage (apart from her casting by Ziegfeld in the original "Show Boat") is but briefly acknowledged by the narrative, and her film work is ignored. THE HELEN MORGAN STORY accentuates her balladry in smoky nightclubs, where her quavery-voiced delivery of sad songs of lost love earned the real-life singer the near-definitive title of "torch singer," a specialty she authentically shared with few others, but quite directly with her contemporary, Ruth Etting, whose own bio-film reciprocates the generic relationship. As in LOVE ME OR LEAVE ME, the familiar-invocational songs selected for the heroine to perform meld seamlessly into the imagery of the performing woman as victim. As Helen Morgan, actress Ann Blyth (voiced by then-popular 1950s recording star Gogi Grant) is seen at the appropriate times singing "The One I Love Belongs to Somebody Else," "Why Was I Born," and "Can't Help Lovin' That Man of Mine."

Although this is primarily a study of the interrelatedness of various motion picture elements across a chronological expanse/continuum, and not a critique of individual visual styles, it should be noted that THE HELEN MORGAN STORY, unlike most show-business bio-films, makes extensive use of the compositional and lighting codes which are generally associated with the critical term film noir. The criminal activities of her romantic nemesis become all the more familiarly appropriate to these framing devices, but the ultimate invocational act comes in the authenticity-tinged narration by the actual voice of newsman Walter Winchell, who appears on camera as himself, emceeing the story's apocryphal, all-star-attended comeback celebration, paying tribute to a recovered Helen Morgan at the reopening of her own, long-shuttered New York nightclub. Employing the same verbal dynamics which enlivened his actual columns and broadcasts of the period, Winchell lauds the girl who

> made us forget the bad booze, bamboozlers, and tinsel ... the tarnished years of the '20s. Those were years of mistakes, and Helen made some of the biggest of 'em. But the thunder of the '20s will rumble down through history. And somewhere, above it all, will be the sad, sweet notes of a grand gal with a grand voice, sitting atop a grand piano....

This tribute-that-never-was, which Helen Morgan never lived to hear or see, becomes genuine via the em-

ployment and fulfilling of myth. To complete the pattern of
rise, fall, and renaissance, it had to occur, if only through
the latter-day artifice of cinema. This is not to say that a
sentimental act of closure can expunge the narrative's diegetic expanse of approximately a decade's worth of misery
and mental decay. Rather, the significance of the inclusion
of the fictional festivities in the film lies in the demonstrated
cohesive power of the operant mythic pattern. Even when
covered over with the sordid trappings of an exposé, via an
anti-nostalgic overview of "the tarnished years," the archetypal drive towards renaissance/closure will not be denied.

In the invented finale to LOVE ME OR LEAVE ME,
Ruth Etting forgives her ex-husband and agrees to save his
financially threatened nightclub from "closing before it
opens," with a plan to perform at opening night festivities
and draw a large and happy crowd. In I'LL CRY TOMOR-
ROW, Lillian Roth courageously appears on live television
in a celebration of her personal triumph, which becomes
part of a weekly life-affirmation ritual of 1950s popular culture. The price of fame, particularly for female singers,
may have risen to excruciatingly painful heights in this cycle
of films, but a reward is still granted, to both audience and
heroine, in the last reel.

THE HELEN MORGAN STORY concluded this cycle of
female-singer biographies, a cycle which was echoed by certain of the late 1950s actress biographies to be dealt with in
the next chapter. During the years these films appeared, it
should be noted, there were no further bio-films of male
singers at all. The success of THE GREAT CARUSO did
lead the way for a cross-generic cycle of films employing
operatic music as an attractional factor (including two of
the earlier entries in the female singer cycle plus the previously mentioned DEEP IN MY HEART), but Mario Lanza
finished out his career in overtly fictional musical dramas.
It may also be worthy of note that Gordon MacRae and Howard Keel, two additional "great voices" of the cinema at this
time, were never called upon to impersonate other famous
male singers of the past.*

There appears, in retrospect, to have been a sex-
limited uniqueness about the mythologized lives of female

---

*However, MacRae did appear as a songwriter (who sings) in
the bio-film THE BEST THINGS IN LIFE ARE FREE.

singers which synchronized with or reinforced certain mid-1950s attitudes prevalent in popular culture. The contemporaneous cycle of bandleader bio-films centered on men with dreams and visions of an ideal "sound." Their dramatized lives were spent in pursuit of an aesthetic goal. The female singers, while sometimes mouthing the genre's basic phrases about wanting to "make it to the top," were much more passive in their ascents, ultimately functioning as victims to the surrounding men and intervening disasters.

By 1957, the upheaval and segmentation of American popular music firmly displaced from the hit parade the broad-based singing styles to which most adults previously had responded. Country/western, rhythm-and-blues, and rock-and-roll made their primary divisions of the most financially active portion of the popular music trade, and no further singer biographies of any kind appeared on America's movie screens for eight years. The film industry was temporarily abandoning old formulae in its losing battle with television. The days of the songwriter bio-film had ended, and bandleader biographies were soon to begin a long hiatus, as noted in earlier chapters. By the time the next singer bio-film appeared, it was 1965.

YOUR CHEATIN' HEART, produced on what for MGM was a very low budget, neither reflected a trend nor inaugurated a new cycle. It could almost be classified as an anomaly, a film "out of its time," except for its subject-hero's identity as the original author and performer of several songs which had enjoyed a second round of "top ten" popularity in the early 1960s, via new recordings by younger artists. Based on the life of the unchallenged "King of Modern Country Music," Hank Williams, it was yet another story of rise-and-fall, with a talented and popular singer unable to cope with "everybody wantin' a little piece of [me]," and ultimately seeking refuge inside the bottle. "Nobody ever asked me if I wanted to be king," the anguished singer exclaims when his career is at its peak and his spirits are lower than ever. Although the subject-hero is once again male (fourteen years have passed since the release of THE GREAT CARUSO), the agonies that engulf him relate more directly to the suffering of Lillian Roth and Helen Morgan.

This time, however, the narrative, hewing surprisingly close to the basic details of the man's real-life career, allows no room for an actual comeback. The mythic concession to audience expectations and established narrative

practice comes in the depiction of Williams' death in an
automobile crash as having occurred after he had experienced
a personal spiritual revival and weaned himself off "the
booze." En route to an appearance at the Carnegie Hall of
country music, Nashville's Grand Ol' Opry House, Williams
stops his car at a roadside general store and renews his
"roots," talking with an elderly black man who reminds the
singer of the Negro blues guitarist who first inspired Hank
as a boy. At the store Williams performs for the locals
with a prescient rendition of his next-to-best-known song
(the best-known is the film's title), "I'm So Lonesome I
Could Cry." The cue for the audience is the last word in
the song's title.

Back at the Opry House, the emcee tells the shocked
audience that police have just informed him that "Sometime
between six and seven this evening, Hank Williams passed
away. The doctors say his heart just stopped." The brutal historical details of the crash, and of the illegal drugs
police found in the wrecked car, are not mentioned. Viewers lacking prior knowledge might easily assume that Williams' death was from natural causes, while others are
spared an unpleasant reminder of the unheroic facts.

YOUR CHEATIN' HEART, despite its decade-later
revival of the road-to-ruin/singer bio-film formula, still
limits the degradation of its hero to alcoholism and the inability to handle fame. Being male, he does not have to
submit to the sexual domination/exploitation of his filmic
predecessors Etting, Roth, and Morgan; indeed, he is actually given time in the narrative to marry a highly supportive woman and father a son. (Hank Jr., following in
his father's footsteps as a successful country singer, dubs
the songs for actor George Hamilton.) Thus Williams'
death at age forty-nine also relates to the tear-jerker construction of some of the bandleader biographies. The significant difference is that few, if any, outside forces, other
than the continuing influence of the so-called "tremendous
price of fame," can be blamed for the severing of the family unit. Williams simply becomes a raging, destructive
drunk on several occasions, then repents, but dies anyway.
Another divergence from the previous pattern of character
relationships can be observed in the subsidiary figures.
Instead of the usual agent, accompanist, fellow musician,
or lover/spouse acting as closest confidant to the hero,
Hank Williams receives his most important guidance and
counsel from his music publisher, Fred Rose, of the

George Hamilton as Hank Williams in YOUR CHEATIN' HEART (1965). Photo courtesy Wisconsin Center for Film and Theater Research.

powerful Acuff-Rose Company. "You're like a father to [Hank]," Williams' wife tells the older man. Yet even the sage advice of one of country music's kingmakers has little effect on Williams as the singer continues to deaden his senses with alcohol. "What's he trying to do, kill himself?" Rose asks in dismay when he learns that Williams has been spending a large amount of money on a new collection of fast cars. The implication of a "death wish," though seemingly negated by Williams' supposed reformation, does tie in to the extra-diegetic public knowledge of his death.

To conform to the rise-and-fall structure, the narrative clearly shows Williams' career as being temporarily damaged by his excessive drinking. His scheduled return to the Grand Ol' Opry stage even functions as something of a promised comeback, since earlier dialogue refers to his having been "kicked out" by the Opry. It is only after he has been "on the wagon" for eight weeks that he is invited back to Nashville. His irrevocable absence is signified by the film's closing shot, of a lone microphone stand on a dark stage, lit by a single spotlight. The Opry audience has risen to its feet and is singing Hank's famous gospel song, "I Found the Light." Williams' renaissance is not of this world.

Seven more years passed before another singer biofilm appeared.* The release in 1972 of LADY SINGS THE BLUES (echoing the earlier release of ST. LOUIS BLUES, and several years after the applicable cycle had ended) functions as a cultural avatar, re-working an inactive generic formula within an alternative racial context. Crossover singer Diana Ross (popular with bi-racial audiences, as was Nat "King" Cole) starred in the role of 1930s blues singer Billie Holiday, who gained particular notoriety at the time as the first black vocalist to travel and sing with a white band. The rise-and-fall pattern of her life story became yet another tale of road-to-ruin despair, but it shared no firm position in a contemporary cycle of bio-films, relating instead to the female singer portrayals of nearly two decades earlier. Holiday's character fits the 1950s pattern with considerable consistency: A passive pursuer of fame and fortune, pushed up the ladder of success by those who profit from her

---

*The Fanny Brice films will be dealt with in the chapter on comedians.

talents, is exploited by parasites in human form and crushed by her unwise recourse to narcotizing herself as an escape from the unbearable pressure.

With official censorship ended, Holiday's real-life drug addiction problems could be depicted by the film makers in harrowing detail. Societal self-criticism permitted by changed American values also added to the aura of undeserved doom which envelops her in the diegesis. All around her is the stench of white racism, an integral part of the film's re-creation of the period. How much of the self-destructive flaw in her depicted character is attributable to American society in general is the narrative's open question. Didacticism aside, the most appropriate mythic counterpart to this destructive force would have to be fate--the ill-fortune of having been born in a time and place where every step forward ascended a sharp and treacherous slope. Holiday's fall, after she had achieved a wholly unexpected measure of fame and success, is shown to be swift and final.

Just out of her grasp as the narrative draws to a close is the archetypal symbol of attainment and acceptance so familiar from previous bio-films, a concert appearance at Carnegie Hall. Having become unwillingly involved in the drug-related California murder of her devoted piano accompanist, she receives a bitterly ironic phone call from her agent in New York City, telling her that she has finally been accepted for a Carnegie Hall date. Resolving to "go on living," despite the tragedy, she returns to the city whose cabaret licensing commission has long refused her permission to sing in its nightclubs because of her record of narcotics arrests. She had hoped that a prestigious Carnegie appearance would soften the commissioners' opposition and allow her to continue her singing career in her home city, without having to suffer the temptations and pressures of touring, which have included the heartbreak of being separated from the man she loves. A newspaper headline fills the screen following Holiday's triumphant concert: "Billie Smash at C. Hall; Flop at License Commission." A montage of subsequent newspaper stories fades into view as the last notes of her final concert song die away: "Appeal Denied ... Singer Re-Arrested on Drug Charges ... Billie Holiday Dead at 44." In the concluding shot she bows to the audience and accepts her applause. A freeze-frame dissolves into a faded, black-and-white photo.

The mythic infrastructure of LADY SINGS THE BLUES

can be analyzed as both denying its heroine a renaissance
(she dies in disgrace) and transcending that ultimate ignominy. The tragedy of the early, self-destructive death which
lies ahead is not concealed, as was the case with Helen
Morgan, who (without a gracious comeback-tribute) died at
forty-one. Neither is the narcotics-connected cause of her
early death hidden from view (as it was for Hank Williams).
Yet the film's closing images are also of victory, albeit
temporary, with the dingy photo a signifier of a joyous
memory fixed in time.

The attractional factor of exposed scandal, which underlay the invocation of the familiar in the later singer biofilms of the 1950s, had been muted considerably by the 1972
release date of LADY SINGS THE BLUES. Films about
drug addiction, once forbidden from the screen by the Production Code, had become commonplace. The novelty of
major Hollywood films with black performers in starring
roles had turned into a temporary phenomenon, and LADY
SINGS in retrospect can be classified as a specific instance
of applying a formula from an earlier era to the early
1970s "black star" cycle. Diana Ross' follow-up picture,
MAHOGANY, revived in contemporary black terms another
long-dormant sub-genre, the career-woman-in-crisis romantic melodrama. LADY SINGS THE BLUES, while it drew
viewers from one target audience, that of 1930s' jazz fans,
and thus functioned as a nostalgia piece, also aimed its attractions at another, younger, minority segment of the populace, lacking in the tendency to react to the nostalgia factors but likely to respond to the racial subject matter and/
or the star presences of Diana Ross, Richard Pryor, and
Billy Dee Williams. Such split targeting had long been the
practice in show-business bio-film production (c.f. the vehicles constructed for Bing Crosby or Fred Astaire), but in
LADY SINGS THE BLUES the re-activation of a dormant
sub-generic formula had never before followed so many
years of inactivity. The width in the angle of audience approach had finally switched from acute to oblique.

Two 1976 releases, LEADBELLY and BOUND FOR
GLORY, aimed at equally wide targets of audience diffusion
(relatively small groups of stylistic musical adherents and
the socially concerned, politically liberal, "activist" elite
who had come to media prominence in the just-concluded
years of domestic turbulence). No coalition of viewers
emerged at the box-office window, however, and both films
were financial failures, receiving scant exhibition of any

sort because they fell into the soon-to-be-modified category of Hollywood "flops" from the last years before the rise of pay-TV. Although this study does not attempt the herculean task of explaining all hits and excusing all failures, neither can it ignore the resounding, trend-establishing financial successes of THE GREAT ZIEGFELD, THE JOLSON STORY, or THE GREAT CARUSO. In like manner, the quick disappearance from theatre marquees of LEADBELLY and BOUND FOR GLORY calls for investigation.

LEADBELLY, the bio-film of Huddie Ledbetter (better known by his nickname, the film's title), might have attracted more of a younger, black audience had it starred a "name" actor or singer, but in creating the illusion of realism the film makers cast an unknown lookalike (Roger E. Mosley) as the 1930s Southern blues singer and used a far-from-famous contemporary blues artist (HiTide Harris) to dub the authentic-sounding vocals. The narrative, however, did invoke, via performance segments, the hero's many familiar songs ("Good-night Irene," "The Midnight Special," "Cotton Fields") and even culminated in an archetypal, career-vindicating concert for the "black tie crowd" at Carnegie Hall. The racism that bedeviled Billie Holiday is shown to dog Leadbelly's heels even more menacingly, but the character flaw that proves his undoing is much more threatening to the viewer than Holiday's passive escape into drugs. A giant of a man with a hair-trigger temper, Huddie Ledbetter is depicted as being never more than one angry remark away from a fistfight. His involvement in the murder case which sends him to a Southern chain gang is staged with equivocation, however (audience sympathy is not totally ignored), and the raw brilliance of his talent is a given in the diegesis. The man's musical ability actually proves a detriment when the governor of the state where Ledbetter is imprisoned repeatedly refuses requests for clemency because the official enjoys having the singer perform for private parties at the executive mansion.

The stepson of a Louisiana sharecropper, Ledbetter leaves the family farm in 1923 to take up the life of a drifter, singing in various low-life "dives" for free drinks and a night's lodging. Prior to the young man's leaving home (to escape the consequences of impregnating a neighbor girl), his stepfather utters an aphorism which serves both to foreshadow and explain the harsh road down which his boy will soon travel: "If you give a dog a bad name, folks gonna chuck rocks at him. Bye and bye ... he gonna bite somebody." Many fights, "cathouse" nights and scrapes with the law later, Ledbetter is tracked down during one of his multiple prison terms by Professor John Lomax, a folk music researcher working for the Library of Congress. Although Ledbetter at first rejects Lomax's requests to record the singer's music for posterity ("You gonna kill 'em--stick pins in 'em and kill 'em. Songs gotta fly free like birds fly ..."), he eventually agrees to make a series of recordings. When he is released, Ledbetter goes on, as a closing title informs the viewer, to "sing his way across America," performing his songs of poverty, oppression and suffering for delighted white liberal audiences all the way to the stage of Carnegie Hall. Unlike the tragic postscript to LADY SINGS THE BLUES, no mention is made of Ledbetter's subsequent brushes with the law and his return to prison a few years later. Rather than utilize the mythic pattern of rise-and-fall, LEADBELLY functions as a drama of struggle and delayed discovery, a quest by the hero for self-expression through his music. His inner demon of violence joins forces with the obstacles set in his path by white society to oppose his quest, but the narrative presents his eventual triumph as a just reward for his talents.

BOUND FOR GLORY, released a few months later during America's Bicentennial Year, is also the story of a drifter who seeks self-expression rather than fame. Again, the latter quality does not catch up with him until a final printed title closes the film. The narrative tells the story of Woody Guthrie, whose songs, like those of Huddie Ledbetter, were revived as an integral part of the early 1960s folk renaissance in American popular music, a phenomenon which paralleled and echoed youth involvement in the civil rights movement. Yet Guthrie too was a man of an earlier era, an itinerant entertainer who found his calling in life when he took up the cause of unionizing unskilled laborers driven by the 1930s "dust bowl" to the orchards of California.

The film's mythic structure is that of birth--the birth of one of labor's most gifted spokesmen, eloquent not in the explosive power of his rhetoric from some lofty podium, but in the persuasively subversive qualities of his music. "Oh, You Can't Scare Me--I'm Stickin' to the Union," sings Guthrie, and frightened workers find new courage to stand up to the bosses. "This Land Is Your Land," proclaims Guthrie, with the backing of only his guitar, and the dispossessed resolve to reclaim the America stolen from them by the "robber barons."

David Carradine as Woody Guthrie in BOUND FOR GLORY (1976). Photo courtesy Wisconsin Center for Film and Theater Research.

The film offers a story of personal transition, in essence, from show business to politics. The narrative begins with Guthrie leaving his sign painter's job in a small, impoverished Texas town and hopping a freight to the West Coast. His new life as a hobo is brief, for all it takes is a borrowed guitar and a song to pass an audition and get his own radio show in California. The narrative concludes when his popularity earns him the chance to sing to the nation via a contract with CBS in New York. While Guthrie's career as a folk singer prospers, he also becomes deeply involved in labor agitation, bickering with sponsors and radio executives who oppose his politicizing the airwaves. Whereas this may be perceived as an admirable, heroic struggle by the target audience, the narrative simultaneously depicts Guthrie's abject failure as a family man. He appears to feel no compunction about repeatedly abandoning his wife and children. At one point the distraught woman exclaims, "You're always tryin' to fix the world, but you don't care nothin' 'bout your family." His reply: "I can't sit still. I always feel like I should be somewhere else." Perhaps not as deadly a fault as the angry violence which made impossible any truly heroic portrait of Huddie Ledbetter, this insensitive wanderlust undermines in like manner the ideal of Woody Guthrie as the gallant troubador of the oppressed. The images of the two singers, continuing their quests, converge in the closing titles, with BOUND FOR GLORY also referring to its hero's travels across America, "visiting farms and factories, singing his songs."

Another biographical show-business narrative functioning as a birth myth can be seen in RAINBOW, a 1978 television movie about the early Hollywood years of singer Judy Garland. This time the familiar doom that awaits female vocalists is kept off the screen, but only by the arbitrary limit to the chronology depicted. The pitiful fate of the historical Garland, the subject of intense coverage in the other media of popular culture, is only vaguely suggested by the narrative's tangential inclusion of the girl's first use of prescription drugs to combat a sleeping problem. Audience members who know "the rest of the story" can congratulate themselves on their perspicacity. Others need not be distracted or concerned.

Invocation of the familiar is intense and frequent throughout the film, although the child performer (Andrea McArdle, Broadway's original "Annie") selected to play young Garland is more of an attractional factor in herself, and never approaches anything resembling a close impersonation of the Garland voice or appearance. The acts of invocation occur via the inclusion of many appropriate songs from the period (the mid-1930s) and via the settings--the last vaudeville shows, the star-populated MGM studios. Linkage with the actor biographies to be dealt with later is extensive.

The vicariously ambitious Mrs. Gumm, who pushes her reluctant three daughters into show business as a trio, relates directly to the "stage mother" of Lillian Roth in I'LL CRY TOMORROW. The Gumm (later changed to Garland during an appearance in the Chicago World's Fair) Sisters' early auditions share a painful similarity with Roth's first tryout. The parallel with the opening scenes of GYPSY (to be dealt with in the chapter on dancers) is even more precise.

When her two older sisters break up the act, young Judy becomes her mother's last hope for family stardom and is sent on an extensive round of lessons and auditions in Hollywood, where the girl makes friends with an aspiring child actor named Mickey Rooney, who encourages her to make a name for herself. During a later encounter with Rooney, he actually invites her to "Come join me on the silver screen," now that he has been signed by MGM.

The archetypal death of a loved one, coincident with a moment of triumph, occurs when Garland, fresh from signing her own Metro contract, appears on a live radio broadcast sponsored by and originating from one of the studio's sound stages. Her beloved father, with whom she had maintained a warm and close relationship despite her parents' divorce, listens to the show from his hospital bed and passes away. His replacement, in the structure of character relationships, comes in the form of one of the studio's musical arrangers, Roger Edens, who takes the girl under his wing and guides her to the mastery of style, delivery, and poise which enable her to win the leading role in THE WIZARD OF OZ. Thus the narrative concludes with the birth of a new star, whose eventual self-destruction, via drugs and alcohol, is omitted from the diegetic time frame and does not interfere with the structure of the birth myth. Her concluding line of dialogue emphasizes the process of birth/metamorphosis: "Baby Gumm is dead. I'm Judy Garland!"

Since THE BIRTH OF THE BEATLES has been classified here as a latter-day successor to the 1950s cycle of bandleader biographies (the images of "group" and "leader" having taken precedence over any solo singing star), it will not be covered in this chapter. Three other television films and a theatrical feature do, however, concentrate on singers from the rock-and-roll era and constitute a cycle of their own.

The successful release of THE BUDDY HOLLY STORY in 1978 demonstrated that the early years of rock-and-roll, by then a full generation in the past, had become ripe for the same sort of cinematic nostalgia mining that the American film industry had applied during the 1940s to the legacy of vaudeville. Scrupulous re-creation of detail and ambience was never the intent or the effect in those films. The task at hand had not been documentary, but mythic.

The central character of THE BUDDY HOLLY STORY is a noble hero on a quest, seeking, like many of the songwriters and bandleaders of earlier films, the perfect means to express and perform the music in his head. Unlike those other heroes, however, Holly himself becomes a star, the object of teen adulation via media and audience response to his performances. Previous singer bio-films usually concentrated on the personal ordeals of the performer, rather than on his ideals. (However, the unsuccessful LEADBELLY and BOUND FOR GLORY did cross the line between music as a given and music as a message.) Holly's ideals, though not ostensibly political, are very strongly held in terms of style of performance and overall sound. The fictionalized (and legally evasive, because certain clearances could not be obtained) narrative would have the viewer believe that Holly struggled to the top virtually by himself. His back-up band, the "Crickets," is reduced in the film from three to two members, both small-town, Texas homebodies, remarkably devoid of any burning drive for success. The real-life Holly's well-known personal manager/producer, Norman Petty, is never seen or mentioned. Even the arranger of Holly's last recording sessions, who introduced string arrangements and transformed Holly from a rock to a pop vocalist, is replaced in the narrative by Holly himself, mastering the art of scoring with violins and cellos to "sweeten" the sound of "Raining in My Heart."

The Buddy Holly portrayed on screen is as strongwilled as any military hero, always insisting on his own way and always proved right. His quest follows the established mythic pattern from the very beginning. Holly is first portrayed as a nineteen-year-old Texan who had long planned to study for the ministry, but the call of show business becomes too strong for him to resist. The pronouncement of interdiction comes straight from the pulpit, when in 1956 the minister of his church preaches against "what happened at the roller rink last night." (Holly and his band, who had been entertaining there with country-style songs, switched to a black-sounding "boogie beat" and the teenage audience erupted into a frenzy of jitterbug-type dancing on skates.) The uproar convinces Holly that his future lies in the newly emerging rock-and-roll music, a white blend of black and country styles, and he leaves home with his back-up musicians

to seek fame and fortune, encouraged by his success on a
local radio station and the promise of a recording contract.

The quest eventually takes him to New York City and
the stage of Harlem's famous palace of black vaudeville, the
Apollo Theatre, where the eager crowd, who know Holly and
the Crickets only through their records, is astonished to discover the performers are white. In the fictionalized/mythic
nature of this shock confrontation, the suddenly hostile audience is quickly won over in archetypal fashion when the
group's infectious rhythms start the crowd clapping in time
and dancing in the aisles to the music of "Oh Boy," "It's So
Easy," and "Rave On." Invocation of the familiar functions
at high intensity particularly during this sequence, generically akin to the appearance of earlier bio-filmed stars in the
Ziegfeld Follies. Appearing on the same bill with Holly are
Chuck Berry, Fats Domino, The Drifters, and Sam Cooke,
each depicted in the diegesis in resemblant impersonation.

To endear him to the film's target audience, Holly is
portrayed as a young man totally devoid of racial prejudice,
in one instance more amused than upset when, on a 1957
"Caravan of Stars" personal appearance tour, he is forced
to pose as a white valet for saxophonist King Curtis in order to obtain lodging at an all-black hotel. The great love
of his life is a Puerto Rican, Maria Elena, whom Holly must
court in verbal disguise because her strict aunt/guardian
forbids the girl to become involved with musicians. The
story's conclusion, following the fistfight-spurred breakup
of the Crickets in conjunction with an appearance on "The
Ed Sullivan Show," has Holly marrying Maria Elena and pursuing a career as a solo pop artist. The narrative would
have the audience believe that the group's dissolution was extremely amicable, and that Holly's loss of a front tooth, just
prior to his live television performance, was the result of
too much drinking by one of the musicians, not the result of
any long-standing resentment toward an egotistical star who
had come to overshadow the group. True to form, audience
sympathy is not jeopardized.

The narrative relates directly to the "tear-jerker"
formula employed in several other show-business bio-films,
when Holly's final personal appearance tour begins just following the news that he is about to become a father. Prior
to his departure from their New York home, Holly spends a
few sentimental moments with his wife and a neighbor child,
who had come to ask Holly for advice on mastering the guitar.

He plays and sings, teaches the child a few chords, and then departs. It is the last moment of solace before disaster, as was Hank Williams' pastoral stop at a country store before his death. One of Holly's biggest hits as a solo artist, "True Love Ways," is employed instrumentally on the sound track to underscore the pain of departure and separation.

At a concert stop in Clear Lake, Iowa, the familiar is invoked one last time, as the stars of the "1959 Winter Party" appear on stage. Their names are sure to have a deadly ring to them in the minds of film viewers who share previous information or memories of the events about to be related. J. P. "Big Bopper" Richardson sings "Chantilly Lace"; Richie Valens shakes his famous maracas. Buddy Holly takes the spotlight with a medley of his hits, sung in very close approximation by the actor who has been portraying him all through the picture, Gary Busey (who had previously played and sung with a rock band under the name of Teddy Jack Eddy). As Buddy Holly he now belts out "That'll Be the Day," "Oh Boy," "Peggy Sue," "Maybe Baby" (reprising their earlier appearance in performance segments), and concludes with the (once again, presciently titled) "Not Fade Away."

As happened in the films of Hank Williams and Glenn Miller, graphic depiction of the violent end of the artist is spared the audience. Although the other vocalists and musicians in the caravan will make it to Moorhead, Minnesota, their next stop, dialogue (a final phone call by Holly to his wife) has explained that these three stars will be traveling by air, to avoid the delay caused by a snowbound bus. While Holly is savoring his final moment of triumph, performing "Not Fade Away" for a crowd of cheering fans, a printed title is superimposed on the screen, unmistakably underscoring the fact that myth (whether one calls it pop history or legend) is the real matter at hand: "Buddy Holly died later that night, along with J. P. Richardson and Richie Valens, in the crash of a private plane. And the rest is rock and roll...."

DEAD MAN'S CURVE, a 1978 television film, its ironic title taken from a hit song, attracted viewers by offering the story of rock singer Jan Berry's battle with aphasia, an affliction characterized by a severe speaking disability and brought on in Berry's case by an automobile accident. The narrative's structure and theme relate most closely to the triumph-over-infirmity ordeals of the female

singers in WITH A SONG IN MY HEART and INTERRUPTED
MELODY. As in those films, the pattern of rise-and-fall
does not pivot about a character flaw, but rather around a
medical/physical hurdle which must be surmounted in order
to regain the life-affirming ability to perform.

The historical Berry was half of the singing team of
Jan and Dean, who, although far less influential in the evolution of rock music than Buddy Holly (they followed him in
popularity by about four years), did succeed with a number
of "top ten" records in the early 1960s. The narrative follows the boys, as was the case with Holly and his friends,
from their first, tentative recording sessions with amateur
equipment to their achieving stardom. Dean Torrence is
portrayed as the passive member of the duo, often standing
in awe of his partner's drive for success and his extreme
perfectionism in creating exactly the right sound on record,
an obsession certainly shared with the portrayal of Buddy
Holly.

Berry, as the central character of the drama, is allowed two romances in the course of the narrative, but both
are tangential to the primary mythic structure. Although the
members of the boys' back-up band are never introduced or
commented upon, and Berry's own family receives minimal
attention, the film shows him being treated almost as a second son by Torrence's parents, reinforcing the character relationship of fraternal closeness between the two singers.
Overlaid with the rise-and-fall pattern, therefore, is a congruent one of the separation and reunion of two friends.
The disabling auto crash which ends their singing career
also parts them emotionally, as the increasingly bitter,
speech-impaired Berry retreats into a world of self-pity
with the passing of the years. When the pair were at the
height of their popularity, Jan had commented to Dean on
how their success had been built on selling the "California
myth"--bikini-clad girls, surfing, and fast cars--to America's teenagers. "I don't want to be a thirty-year-old rock
star," says Berry, adding that the chances of it are slight,
because "The minute you slip ... these kids'll turn their
back on you." The fickle nature of the audience, postulated
in the earliest show-business bio-films, is as operative as
ever.

Just as George M. Cohan, Al Jolson, and Red Nichols
were disturbed to find that the intervention of time had made
them nonentities to a new generation, a 1970 sequence depicts

Berry's encounter with some "hippies" who have never heard of him or his music. An old high-school girlfriend then becomes his live-in, volunteer therapist, echoing the therapy-into-romance situations of JOLSON SINGS AGAIN and INTERRUPTED MELODY. A while later he is visited by his former partner, and Berry eventually overcomes his reluctance to try his hand at composing music once more. Despite his continuing difficulty in coordinating his speech, Berry even agrees to appear with Torrence at a nostalgia concert for fans of early 1960s music. To hide the effects of Berry's aphasia, they attempt a lip-sync performance of "Surf City," but the playing of their old recording is interrupted, and the audience, realizing the fakery, becomes surly and abusive. The boys try it again, this time with their own voices, and archetypally win over the angry crowd, miraculously (as in INTERRUPTED MELODY's "walking sequence") discovering that Berry has regained the ability to sing.

Just as Buddy Holly was shown to be unreceptive to comparisons of himself with Elvis Presley, Jan and Dean react negatively when told that they are reminiscent of The Everly Brothers and The Beach Boys. The sequence in which one of Jan's girlfriends refers to a Beach Boys song as her "favorite Jan and Dean record" particularly emphasizes the gap between unfocused audience perceptions and the not-always-successful striving for individuality by the performers of popular culture.

The subject-hero of the next singer bio-film, which was also made for American television but was successfully released theatrically in other countries, had much less to fear from confused perceptions and comparisons. ELVIS!, a 1979 release, was a modified reversion to the archetype of the singer as despondent sufferer, watching his/her own talent and future slip away down the sewer of time. In production while sensational media revelations about Presley's multiple-drug dependency were circulating, the film skirts the issue of whether he hastened the approach of his early death chemically, and concentrates instead on the doom factor first seen, in the films under study, in RHAPSODY IN BLUE. In the narrative of ELVIS! the formerly vague sense of impending premature death becomes overt, specified, and obsessive.

The film covers Presley's life from his first childhood encounter with a guitar to his triumphant comeback as a concert performer, following nine years of hiding from the fearsome crowds either behind the lens of a Hollywood movie camera or behind the fortress-like gates of his Memphis mansion. Told in flashback as he waits offstage for his entrance (a device paralleling the openings of SO THIS IS LOVE, LOOK FOR THE SILVER LINING, and TILL THE CLOUDS ROLL BY), Presley's life is portrayed as that of an outsider, a loner, who by dint of perseverance and a shockingly unique talent, gathered around him the wealth, fame, possessions, and entourage of a modern-day potentate, but who still could not fill the mysterious, aching void in his heart. Whether this is an accurate assessment of the Presley malaise is of less concern here than the functioning of this image in terms of a bio-film tradition and the audience expectations and responses which have shaped that tradition. Presley as the lonely king is a hero to be pitied, whereas Presley as a drug-gorging satyr, stuffing his mind and body with all forms of self-indulgence until they burst (an alternate picture of the man, provided in several print accounts), would be a figure ripe for audience revulsion. (Had Ziegfeld and Jolson been portrayed on screen as monsters, the history of the bio-film could have been quite different.) Even with the passing of the years, and the perennial raising of the threshold of public outrage, the makers of ELVIS! opted for a limited exposé, suffused with sympathy and convenient omission.

The doom that haunts the man is indeed mystical, bound up in his ESP relationship with his early-dying mother and in his telepathetic conversations with the twin brother he lost at birth. "I'm afraid of losing it," cries the anguished singer when he has scaled heights never even approached by any popular vocalist before him, filling his mansion walls with gold records, amassing a personal fortune, becoming the androgynous sex idol of untold millions from all corners of the earth. After he watches the Kennedy and Oswald shootings on television, Presley becomes unshakably certain that he will meet a violent death while he is still a young man. His defensive fondness for guns becomes a dangerous mania, and in a sequence strewn with the iconography of popular culture's view of our "angry, modern era," Presley draws a bead and fires at a hotel television set which has been spewing out troubling news, dissolving the image of the reporter in a loud, smoky implosion of shattering glass and flying sparks.

Much of the early part of the narrative relates directly to the previous year's BUDDY HOLLY STORY, with

Kurt Russell and Season Hubley in ELVIS! (1979). Photo courtesy Capitol Communications.

the early Elvis recordings mistaken for those of a black
singer, and a spectacular string of hits leading to a key
linkage phenomenon, the 1950s act of temporal/cultural
sanctification known as an appearance on "The Ed Sullivan
Show." (Functioning as one of the avatars of the Ziegfeld
Follies, the Sullivan program also figured as a worthy
plateau to be scaled in THE BIRTH OF THE BEATLES.)
Just as Holly was condemned by moralists for inducing
animalistic gyrations among his followers, Presley, who
historically preceded Holly, is chastised in the press for
his own "undignified" behavior while performing, which
earns him the journalists' nickname, "Elvis the Pelvis."
When Presley asks his mother if she thinks he is vulgar
on stage, her only reply is: "I'm just afraid you'll wear
yourself out." The predictive nature of this remark is
soon demonstrated.

Presley's innumerable sexual liaisons are skimmed
over so lightly as to create the impression that he failed
for years to recognize fully or exploit on a carnal level the
magnetism and license afforded by his position in the hierarchy of popular culture. When he manages to obtain a
date with actress Natalie Wood, he is shown as much more
the desperate fan than the arrogant star, going so far as to
dye his brown hair the exact shade of black worn by actor
Tony Curtis. Only late in his life, following his decision
to return to the concert stage, does he appear the master
of his own image, reacting against the Las Vegas "tyranny
of the tuxedo" to create a flamboyant new look for himself
in a bejeweled karate jacket, topped by an intricate coiffure
worthy of a Japanese geisha.

Presley's marriage to the daughter of an army officer is given as sentimental a treatment as possible, considering the dramatized fact that he virtually bought the
teenager from her parents (who were stationed in Germany
at the same time the singer served his two-year hitch) and
set her up as a kept woman-child in his mansion when she
was only sixteen. The infidelity which eventually destroys
the Presley marriage is also never specified, only hinted at
by the well-established generic practice of inserting appropriate songs in the sound track. "Suspicious Minds" signals
the approach of domestic trouble. "Until It's Time for You
to Go" blends with Priscilla Presley's farewell speech, in
which she describes parting from Elvis as if she were a
finally grown girl who is about to leave her father and
mother: "You raised me ... but now I can make it without you."

Presley's retreat into self-doubt and fatalism intensifies following his divorce. In a subsequent sequence he tells a shadow on the wall (signifying his dead twin): "I'm gonna be with you and Mama before too long. It's gonna be like the Kennedys and King. I ain't gonna go on much past forty. But if I can make it in Las Vegas one more time ..." Presley's fear of growing older parallels a line in DEAD MAN'S CURVE. In anticipation of the birth of his first (and only) child, he rhetorically asks, "What's wrong with me? ... I'm thirty-two ... but I don't wanna be forty, and still up on stage singing 'Heartbreak Hotel.'" Thus the audience is emotionally bolstered for the approach of Presley's early passing at forty-three, with the narrative of the film strongly suggesting that the pain of his existence is becoming too much to bear. Death, the story suggests, would be a merciful and welcome relief.

The singer's climactic return to the Las Vegas spotlight is also the narrative's climax. Just as LADY SINGS THE BLUES and THE HELEN MORGAN STORY end with their singing stars basking in the glory of the appreciative crowd one more time, ELVIS! concludes on a note of triumph. Since Presley was a singer, rather than a composer, it is dramatically necessary for him to appear at and participate in this ritual of honor, unlike the doomed Stephen Foster or George Gershwin, who both meet death at just the precise moment for their tribute concerts to become instant memorials. Unlike Billie Holiday, who has her final splash of glory visually welded to her obituary, Presley is allowed to depart the screen without even the briefest superimposed epitaph. The target audience's shared prior knowledge of his fate has been judged sufficient. His heroic stature is subsequently not challenged, but reinforced. The film's fade-out is set to the tune of "The Battle Hymn of the Republic." If music, in the lexicon of popular culture, is truth, then there can be no doubt that Presley's does "go marching on."

ELVIS!, despite its second-class status as a television film, achieved such high ratings (and outstanding foreign box-office receipts) that it prompted a direct sequel by a different production company, something unique in the category of films under study, even with the inclusion of the Al Jolson and Fanny Brice pictures. ELVIS AND THE BEAUTY QUEEN, first shown in 1981, filled in the details of the singer's "last serious love affair," which had been omitted entirely from the previous narrative. Such had also been the case with JOLSON SINGS AGAIN, and in both sequels the story of a star vocalist's romance with a girl half his age is treated with considerable sympathy in a bid for audience acceptance. The narratives differ principally in that the Jolson film unfolds from the man's point of view, while the Presley film is constructed from the viewpoint of the ultimately wronged female. The difference in outcome is the difference between triumph and tragedy.

Far from a career-spanning drama, ELVIS AND THE BEAUTY QUEEN is essentially anecdotal, the story of an inexperienced girl's devoted and sincere efforts to make her love affair with a troubled man succeed. Her failure is depicted not as a cause for recrimination, but as the inevitable result of irreconcilable differences. The Presley she encounters is not the doom-haunted mystic of the earlier bio-film. Instead, he is a drug-decayed, nearly burned-out shell of his former self, too far gone on the road to oblivion for redemption in this world. The mythic infrastructure of the plot differs greatly from the bio-film tradition, employing the hitherto unused myth of the prodigal, who wanders into an alien country, drawn by a glittering city only to be beaten down by insurmountable odds and to crawl back home, having learned a valuable lesson.

The prodigal is virginal Linda Thompson, a recent winner of the Miss Tennessee contest, who is picked up by one of Presley's hired "girl getters" to be the singer's date at a private movie screening in a near-empty, rented theatre. Her playing "hard to get" fascinates Presley as a challenge he has rarely encountered, and she parlays his refusal to accept erotic defeat into a standing offer to be his constant companion during his next series of Las Vegas concerts. Her acceptance of the trip, with all its attendant luxuries, but without sexual reciprocation on her part, prompts the frustrated superstar to offer the girl a permanent residence at his Memphis mansion (where he can wear down her resistance). Despite parental interdiction, she accepts. Eventually Presley succeeds in his attempts, without granting Thompson's wish for marriage, and the pair become what she believes is an exclusive couple, with her ministering to his fragile ego and helping him in wifely fashion through some very rough bouts with drugs. When Presley's drug abuse becomes a horrendous part of her daily life, she comments to a girl friend, "If the press found out, they'd crucify him!" Coincident with the enacting of the myth, the narrative obviously also functions as the sensationalist, topical exposé which the previous Presley film could not be. Rather than a doomed hero, this Presley is a mere ruined mortal.

Linda Thompson, the actual heroine, is about to learn her lesson.

After five years of unsuccessful attempts to rescue her lover from a web of pharmaceuticals and suspected promiscuity, Thompson transfers her affections to a piano player in Presley's back-up group and moves out of Graceland Mansion. The lesson she learned from her sojourn is summed up in her description of the tabloid and fan magazine accounts of her "dream romance" with Elvis Presley: "It's all a bunch of romantic nonsense!"

Both Presley films invoke the familiar extensively, each employing different, little-known actors who are made up in the "Elvis look," and who lip-sync during performance segments of Presley songs to sound tracks cut by two of the more convincing Elvis impersonators active on the nightclub circuit in the late 1970s. While the first film, which began production plans not long after the singer's death, catered to audience expectations and heroic beliefs about him which helped assuage the pain of his loss, the second picture (with the benefit of greater hindsight and anti-romantic media revelations) concerned itself less with the man's plight and much more with the ordeal of the young woman, who significantly is listed in the credits as the production's program consultant.

The last two singer bio-films to date form another closely related pair, employing the primary attractional factor of country music, which phenomenally increased its popularity with urban audiences in the 1970s. COAL MINER'S DAUGHTER (1980) and the television film STAND BY YOUR MAN (1981) were both advertised as telling the life story of a well-known and successful female country vocalist, and both employed actresses who did their own singing after being coached in their impersonations by their real-life counterparts. COAL MINER'S DAUGHTER depicts the rise-and-fall of Loretta Lynn, who, after achieving an astounding twenty-one "number one" country records, finds the pressures of success unbearable and attempts to shut out the world with drugs. The parallels with the 1950s cycle of troubled female singer bio-films transcend the changed locale, since a mythic pattern unfolds with equal facility whether the setting is a Manhattan "speakeasy" or a Nashville "honky-tonk."

Lynn's ascendence to stardom is traced from her childhood marriage (at fourteen, to an ex-soldier boyfriend) to the present. Her career, boosted at first by her encouraging spouse, eventually becomes a threat to her marriage, with her ego-wounded husband archetypally shrinking from the shame of "living off his wife," yet rallying to her support when her drug-induced nervous breakdown calls a halt to her performing. True to form, she concludes the narrative with a professional renaissance, a glorious comeback concert in which she sings the film's career-affirming title song.

Motifs from generic predecessors abound, such as Lynn's idolizing an established performer (Patsy Cline) only to become friends with her and to serve eventually, after Cline's death in a plane crash, as her replacement. Invocation of the familiar and linkage instances are, of course, from the world of country music, and as in YOUR CHEATIN' HEART (as well as in the first portion of ELVIS!), appearances at Nashville's Grand Ol' Opry function as a signifier of having "made it," having achieved the coveted status of an accepted country singer.*

STAND BY YOUR MAN, based on the career of Tammy Wynette, one of Lynn's closest rivals for the non-official title of "First Lady of Country Music," traverses much of the same territory, but with a significantly different mythic underpinning, one of quest-and-ordeal, rather than rise-and-fall, with a curious sexual reversal in one of the central motifs. Wynette is first seen in socio-economic straits not much above the poverty which Loretta Lynn barely escaped by marriage at fourteen. Young Tammy begins the story married to an unreliable, bad-tempered drifter, who loses one job after another and moves his "poor white trash" family from one upaid-for furnished apartment to another, all across the South. An untrained, amateur vocalist, Wynette is fond of singing along with the radio, particularly when the songs of her hero, recording star George Jones, are being played. Her dream, like that of Loretta Lynn, is to move to the country music capital of Nashville some day and appear on the Grand Ol' Opry. Violent, painful domestic battles with her husband lead to a divorce and custody fights over their child. Finally on her own, she wins a TV singing audition, and then a recording contract. Her debut at the

---

*Presley, as that film explains, transcended his country music origins when he gained wider acceptance as a rock-and-roll singer.

The Singers / 211

Opry culminates in an unexpected duet with her hero, and soon they become a singing (and romantic) team, paralleling the duality of the heterosexual vaudeville partnerships in earlier bio-films.

Wynette's ordeals on the road to stardom are compounded, however, by her discovery that her charming new husband has a dual personality and becomes a raging fiend whenever he drowns his own self-doubts in liquor. More domestic battles ensue, including one in which the seemingly demonic Jones attempts to destroy by his own hand all the expensive furnishings in the couple's Southern mansion and has to be carried away by the proverbial "men in the white coats." Such is the price of fame for Tammy Wynette, who subsequently becomes terrified of trying as a solo performer to face an audience of devoted Jones-Wynette fans. Archetypally, the crowd is hostile to her first attempts, and catcalls fill the air, mingled with shouts of "Where's George?" True to form, she wins them over with her impassioned introduction to the song that serves as the film's title: "I don't know where he is. Even George doesn't know where he is. But I still believe in [this song]. And I think that's the way it should be." Thus the narrative, when it cannot conform to audience expectations, persists in catering to audience beliefs.

The many lax court judgments in libel law during the 1970s apparently prompted the film's producers to proceed without obtaining legal clearance from the ex-husband depicted in the story, relying instead on divorce court transcripts as the necessary, protective "public record" source material. Should this trend continue, bio-films of the future may someday abandon the convenient re-structuring of history into dramatically effective myth for a more accurate mode of depiction. Yet this seems less than likely, if only for the sake of time limits and budget. Following the CBS broadcast of STAND BY YOUR MAN, the ex-husband in question told the press that he was considering a lawsuit for defamation of character. In the course of his announcement, he also revealed that the film completely omitted three more of Wynette's husbands.

CHAPTER IX

THE ACTORS

Biographical films about songwriters, bandleaders, and singers have each offered easy opportunities for the exploitation of a prime attractional factor--the music--often employed in a manner and selected from a period which will evoke the positive audience response commonly referred to as nostalgia. Performance segments dot the narratives of these films, sometimes to such an extent that the actual amount of dramatic dialogue is significantly less than in a similar, non-musical picture of equal length. As demonstrated in earlier chapters, music was the popular culture catalyst which helped initiate the generic practice of filming show-business biographies, shortly after the successful introduction of sound films. Motion pictures based on the lives of non-singing, non-composing, non-instrument-playing or non-conducting performers got off to a much slower start. With the exception of 1940's THE LADY WITH RED HAIR, actor biographies do not even appear in this chronology of entertainer bio-films until late in the second decade.

THE PERILS OF PAULINE, a 1947 release supposedly about the life of pioneer movie actress Pearl White, appears, upon closer analysis, to be a hybrid of sorts, employing multiple musical performance segments to display the comic vocal talents of former band singer Betty Hutton, even though such material is far from germane to the career of an actress who specialized in silent films. Hutton, it should be noted, was the film's prime attractional factor, and the narrative constructed for the purpose of showcasing her abilities is most aptly described as a star vehicle, akin to many of the songwriter biographies of the 1940s. The premise of telling the story of Pearl White functions on one level as a device to justify the insertion of an extended series of seemingly dangerous stunts, which are subsequently burlesqued ("laughing in the face of danger") for maximum comic effect.

The historical Pearl White became world-famous for her performances in early motion picture serial adventures. In each weekly chapter she would find herself frustrated in the pursuit of some noble goal by the machinations of a menacing male villain, which would frequently result in the young woman becoming entrapped in a position of extreme danger, facing great risk to life and limb--locked in a burning boxcar, plunging down an elevator shaft, tied to a ticking time bomb, thrown from a plane without a parachute, bound, gagged, and about to be decapitated by a whirring buzz saw, etc. These "cliffhanger" situations, borrowed from Victorian stage melodrama and cinematically exaggerated beyond the bounds of adult credulity, have long since worked their way into the legacy of popular culture imagery passed down through successive generations.

In 1947, however, such images were not quite as universally unsurprising as they are today, and their invocation in THE PERILS OF PAULINE (its title identical with White's best-remembered serial), in addition to furnishing the above-mentioned comedic premise, also operated on the level of nostalgia-prompting familiarity: the Pearl White serials flourished less than two generations before the film in question. Meanwhile, contemporary serials of the 1940s played mainly to Saturday matinee children's audiences. Therefore, re-creating the style (albeit burlesqued) of the original thrill-chapters, for adults who had not experienced them since their youth, was an analagous process to the "revival of the old songs" which achieved favorable audience response during the cycle of composer bio-films.

The operant myth beneath the plot is one of separation-and-reunion, with White's true love being a haughty "ham" actor from the second-rate theatrical stock company she joins to escape the drudgery she first endures as a seamstress in a sweatshop. Her subsequent stardom in the early movie serials enables him to follow her onto the nation's movie screens as the hero who saves her from each peril, but he disdains the crudity of early film acting: "It's like playing for ... the feeble-minded!" After their archetypal separation due to the intervention of the first World War, he becomes a Broadway "matinee idol." Dismayed by the news--conveyed via an iconographically consistent Variety headline--that the public has lost its taste for serials, White sails for Europe, discovers that her popularity is undiminished there, and begins a new career as an acrobatically inclined cabaret headliner at the famed Casino de Paris. The narrative concludes with a variation on a standard tearjerker

214 / Star Myths

formula involving not the dissolution of a family unit, but
the noble self-sacrifice of a newly-afflicted invalid. White
acts totally unresponsive during a planned reunion/rendez-
vous with her long-estranged lover after she is crippled in
a stage fall during her act. Concealing her inability to walk
(the conversation takes place in the back seat of an automobile), she rejects the actor's offer of marriage, and he sadly departs. Their ultimately successful reunion, within a
career-affirming tribute ritual, takes place at a Paris revival theatre's festival of White's old movies, where the re-
jected-but-still-devoted actor discovers her infirmity, tearfully sweeps her up in his arms, and carries her away.

THE PERILS OF PAULINE, along with the earlier-
mentioned HOLLYWOOD CAVALCADE, marked the first
stirrings of nostalgia invocation/exploitation in regard to the
early days of the motion picture. Re-creations of the departed world of vaudeville, so frequent in the musical films
of the 1940s, whether biographical or not, were in later
years to give way to an increasing number of period pieces
about the motion picture segment of show-business history.
Many of these pictures, as will be seen, were actor and
actress biographies.

Of the three films to date which have offered the public highly contradictory accounts of the life of silent film
star Rudolph Valentino, the 1951 version, ostensibly based
on an original screenplay prepared as early as 1938 (when
music-scored re-issues of two Valentino-starring pictures
did excellent business), ranks above possibly all other films
in this book in terms of total distortion of not arcane, but
widely known and reported facts. The historical private
lives of songwriters, which may have suffered the most
overall in terms of dramatic invention for the screen, were
made up of many facts hidden, by lack of reportage, from
public view. Valentino, however, had almost no private life
during his years of stardom, his marriages and career problems being continuous grist for the media mill during the
1920s. The 1951 VALENTINO blatantly disregards nearly
every publicly remembered or press-reported fact of his
life and career, with the exception of his name, the titles
of the films in which he starred, and the date of his death.
These skeletal bits of information comprise the only specific
means of invoking the familiar. All else is mythic fabrication without the disguise of interspersed historical detail or
linkage figures.

The Actors / 215

Anthony Dexter in the lead role in VALENTINO (1951).
Photo courtesy Wisconsin Center for Film and Theater Research.

The myth itself is one of rise-and-fall, stemming from the unsuccessful course of a parallel pattern, the myth of separation-and-reunion. While crossing to America on an ocean liner, Valentino neglects the romantic needs of his employer (the female director of a dance troupe) in favor of a shipboard romance with a mysterious American lady. A few years later, when he begins to work in films, he discovers that she is the actress-wife of the director who gives Valentino his "big break" and begins to guide his career. Fearful of their on-screen love scenes revealing too much remembered passion from their earlier brief affair, the two performers resist the director's requests that they act together in more than one film. When they are finally compelled to do so, their secret leaks out, scandal threatens, and Valentino eventually "defends the lady's honor" in a deadly fistfight with members of the press. The actor suffers an attack of peritonitis and dies, but the grieving actress goes on to pay yearly visits to his tomb, concealing her identity behind a veil. Thus is supposedly solved the historical mystery of the "lady in black," long reported by the press as a perennial figure in the Hollywood landscape.

VALENTINO's generic relationship with THE PERILS OF PAULINE arises not so much out of mythic parallels as out of the iconographic overlap and the extreme degree of composite characterization. Both films include the exotic locale of the silent picture studio, until the time of their release a familiar part of the past usually considered by film makers as too recent for nostalgic invocation. Both narratives also give the impression that a single director took command of the star's career and was in charge of all of his/her vehicles. While the correct titles of these films are invoked, no other authentic proper nouns are spoken or displayed in titles or advertising material.*

As portrayed by exact lookalike Anthony Dexter, who allegedly spent three years training for the part by studying the old films to master the exact movements, gestures and expressions, Rudolph Valentino is a debonaire, self-assured heartbreaker, brought down by the fearful power of true love and the fear of public scandal. The visual congruency of the actor with public memories of the real-life hero is, however, thoroughly contradicted by the paths taken by the narrative: the fictionalized Rudy never marries, is never legally barred from film making for a year, never has his masculinity challenged, speaks with no trace of an Italian accent, has no petty criminal background, does not die of a stomach ulcer, and is not memorialized by a street riot in New York City. Apart from the most rudimentary details, fact and fiction converge on only one plane, that of mythic reality. The real Valentino literally worried himself to death, unsure of how to reach a mental accord between his own venereal-disease-impaired bisexuality and his frequently attacked public image of robust, heterosexual aggressiveness. The Valentino portrayed in the film, whose fall is triggered by propriety's impediment to reunion with his one true love, suffers fatal internal injuries in physical combat with the era's hypocritical guardians of public morals, the press. Yet in mythic terms, both men die for, and of, love. It is in this way that popular culture again assuages the potential envy of

---

*Nevertheless, Agnes Ayres, the historical Valentino's actual leading lady in THE SHEIK, did bring legal action against Columbia Pictures for constructing a supposedly defamatory story around the female star of that picture.

the crowd by reminding all who will look and listen of the non-negotiable price of fame.

The next actor bio-film to appear, 1954's aptly titled THE ACTRESS, is difficult to classify as indicative of any larger cycle, since it was the first filmed stage-actress biography in fourteen years and came at a time when the parallel female singer cycle was shifting from obstacle-overcoming optimism to the depths of desperation and degradation. Anomalous as it was for its time, THE ACTRESS does function mythically as a fundamentally archetypal "birth" story. Closely adapted from Ruth Gordon's autobiographical stage play of a decade earlier, it depicts her teenage success in overcoming parental opposition in order to leave her New England home and pursue a theatrical career in New York City. As the film emerged from the MGM production line, its attractional factors were centered on its status as another star vehicle for actor Spencer Tracy, this time reworking prime elements of his characterization as the lovable, flustered FATHER OF THE BRIDE. Actress Jean Simmons, portraying the title character of the 1954 film, functions as the embodiment of youthful, idealized ambition and unsophisticated pretension. Archetypally idolizing an established stage star, Hazel "The Pink Lady" Dawn, the girl eventually meets her heroine and redoubles her efforts to emulate and possibly someday replace the woman in the hearts of the Broadway theatre crowd. The teenager's powers of parental manipulation are sorely tested (the drama's central conflict, therefore the mythic counterpart of the birth ordeal) until a public humiliation of her proud father (his pants fall down during a calisthenics exhibition) breaks his haughty spirit and he relents. Whereas a frequent motivation for parental opposition in songwriter biographies was the parental hope of the child's entering a religious vocation, the generic variation in THE ACTRESS transforms the ministry into the more secular, but still beloved by the father, vocation of physical culture instructor. Nevertheless, young Ruth Jones gently defies her father's wishes and ends the narrative by leaving for New York and a term of residence at the famous Three Arts Club. Invocation of the familiar is quite limited during these proceedings, even to the point of never explaining to the viewer that the heroine's real-life counterpart dropped her surname (when success beckoned) and substituted her middle name, thus becoming Ruth Gordon. The fact that the historical Gordon had at the time of the film's release done little film work helps to explain this omission, which runs counter to the widely employed generic practice of identifying a character from his earliest youth by the stage name he actually assumed several years later.

The "birth" of another, less prestigious stage actress, Evelyn Nesbit, was actually tangential to the plot of THE GIRL IN THE RED VELVET SWING, a 1955 release which opulently re-enacted the headline-grabbing, turn-of-the-century murder of celebrated architect Stanford White by deranged playboy Harry K. Thaw. Nesbit was the girl over whom they quarreled, a modestly talented chorus girl/model who was, in effect, bought and raised to sexual maturity by White in a manner akin to the cultivation by Elvis Presley of his future bride. In the scandalous aftermath of the New York murder trial, when the details of her private life have been made public, Nesbit is offered a ready-made acting career by an agent who believes he can thereby exploit the public's inherent curiosity. Nesbit, portrayed as the quasi-innocent victim of fate, agrees to his plans, and "a new star is born."

PRINCE OF PLAYERS, released the same year, reached all the way back to the middle of the previous century for its familiarity-invoking hero, although his ill-fated brother, a subsidiary character in the narrative, was by far the better-known of the pair to the film's contemporary audience. One of the two men had become, with the passing of the intervening halves of two centuries, a name synonymous with an historical achievement best known to aficionados and students of theatrical lore. He was the first American stage actor to achieve a favorable reputation from coast-to-coast and across the capitals of Europe. The tastemakers of the day hailed him as "America's greatest actor." His brother was also an actor, but one whose ill-fame stemmed from but a single night's performance of a play in which he was not even scheduled to appear. They were the Booth brothers, Edwin and John, and PRINCE OF PLAYERS is the story of Edwin's quest to achieve greatness in the profession of acting. Counterpointed against his struggles to build his career and to entertain the public is his brother's descent into madness and ignominy, summarized by his wild-eyed declaration that "to destroy greatness is to partake of greatness."

The structural pattern is not of two men working at cross purposes, so much as it is of a dual set of quests, one sane and noble, the other demented and perhaps pre-

John Derek (l.) as John Wilkes Booth and Richard Burton (r.) as Edwin Booth in PRINCE OF PLAYERS (1955). Photo courtesy Films Incorporated.

destined for disaster. The men's father, also an actor, had gone insane with drink, and talk of the heritage of "the mad Booths" suggests that the personality defect had been passed down through several generations. In the strictest formal sense, both quests succeed in a form of lasting fame, but it is Edwin, the hero of the myth, who must archetypally face the hostile crowd and win their approval by means of his oratorical powers. Enraged with the knowledge of President Lincoln's assassination by an actor named Booth, the crowd is so abusive and threatening that any continuance of Edwin's career seems sorely jeopardized. The prior loss of his wife to illness had already weakened his spirit and tempted him to drink away the pain, but the mob's threats to tear down the theatre snap him out of his depression and give him the courage to face their wrath. "All actors should not be blamed for what Johnny did," says the re-inspired performer; and he adds, "I owe my profession a debt, and I intend to

repay it." He starts his scheduled performance as Hamlet
with the second scene, so that he will already be on stage
and ready for the hostile crowd when the curtain rises.
Amid a shower of rotten vegetables and screaming voices
Edwin Booth relentlessly delivers his Shakespearian speech,
and the combined brilliance of the author's lines and the actor's delivery, true to form, transforms the avalanche of
anger into a floodtide of approval. From the deserted box
seat where his devoted wife would have been sitting, comes
what he imagines is her voice, joining in the chorus of support. Edwin Booth has paid the painfully high price of fame
and succeeded in his quest.

A third 1955 actor biography qualifies for the generic
designation only in a marginal sense. TO HELL AND BACK
is actually the biography of a war hero, World War II's most
decorated serviceman, Audie Murphy. The film functions as
the pivot point in Murphy's career, for it was his performance as himself in this picture which transformed him into a
genuine movie star. His subsequent years of acting, most
often in Hollywood-produced westerns, are by chronological
stricture, necessarily absent from the narrative of this film.

As outlined in an earlier chapter, the mid-1950s saw
the release of a number of singer biographies which differed
sharply in emotional tone from the songwriter biographies of
a few years earlier. Gone was the optimism and high spirits which prompted the nation's tunesmiths to write its hit
songs. These singers, primarily female, were a much sorrier lot, beset first by physical handicaps and later by mental despair. The price of fame seemed to be their sobriety
and sanity; the exploitative men who managed their affairs
had other demands as well. By 1957, when MAN OF A
THOUSAND FACES appeared, the world of show business
displayed in these films had become a much more harrowing
place than it had ever been for the likes of Victor Herbert,
The Dolly Sisters, Lillian Russell or Al Jolson. Silent film
actor Lon Chaney, whose studio-devised nickname became
the title of his film biography, was another performer whose
time had come for nostalgic re-invocation. Like Pearl
White, whose film career had flourished a decade before
his, and whose bio-film preceded his by an equal span of
time, Chaney was a name that easily conjured up many
icons of a bygone period of popular culture. Through ironic coincidence he died at the end of the silent era, succumbing to cancer of the larynx. The bare facts of his personal
history, structured only by the undramatic hand of an obitu-

The Actors / 221

arist, assumed the shape of a tragedy. The makers of MAN OF A THOUSAND FACES seized upon those facts at a time when show-business nostalgia had turned bleak, and what they produced was an archetypal drama of yet another season-keyed life, ending in symbolic re-birth.

The narrative contains some significant parallels with THE EDDY DUCHIN STORY, a considerable box-office success of two years earlier which tackled the same key dilemma --how to make palatable the hero's premature death from an incurable disease. The solution, in mythic terms, was to have the artistic spirit re-born in a son, who, in the concluding sequence, is handed the equivalent of a dying king's crown and scepter. From Duchin to son it is musical talent and a style of performing. From Chaney to son it is the skill of pantomime and the art of disguise. The two Duchins play a duet at twin pianos; the two Chaneys share a makeup kit.

Chaney's life, like Duchin's, is structured according to the myth of rise-and-fall, although in both cases the fall is not one of character flaws, but of destiny's allotment of life being a relatively short one. Both men arrive in their cities of future greatness with high hopes and empty pockets, and success arises out of a combination of personal drive, talent, and propitious opportunity. Chaney's story, however, is a much bleaker one, relating directly as well to the gloom of the aforementioned singer bio-films. The figure of the self-destructive female alcoholic recurs in the form of his wife and former vaudeville partner. Terrified upon learning the long-hidden fact that both of her husband's parents are congenital deaf-mutes, she erodes psychologically into a quivering purveyor of meanness and vituperation, first out of fear that their child will be similarly afflicted, and later in a continuing revulsion fueled by alcohol. Her attempted suicide by drinking poison during one of Chaney's vaudeville sketches succeeds only in destroying her voice, thus grimly tying together the affliction of his parents with the terminal disease which will eventually still his own voice--and his heart.

Chaney's career as a film actor is depicted as a rapidly ascending progression of triumphs, with invocation of the familiar functioning continuously in an extended series of montages and re-creation sequences very accurately depicting his numerous character roles, often of grotesquely deformed and mentally unbalanced villains or anti-heroes. The extreme

222 / Star Myths

Dorothy Malone and James Cagney in MAN OF A THOUSAND FACES (1957). Photo courtesy Wisconsin Center for Film and Theater Research.

care taken in these re-creations does not, however, extend to the arcane details of which studio released the films or who directed them. As was the case with the 1951 VALENTINO, accuracy of title, setting, and costume (what the target audience was expected to remember best) was deemed of greatest invocational importance. Yet in a significant departure from that film, MAN OF A THOUSAND FACES did offer the public a personal history remarkably close to the actual sufferings of the real-life subject-hero. Perhaps the facts conveniently fitted the chosen myths: Chaney's diegetic life exhibits a familiar pattern of rise-and-fall in a tragic mode, and it is also a quest via trial by ordeal. The dominant emotion in the drama is neither love nor ambition. It is pain, and the viewing audience is in effect asked to sit in awe of a man who endured intense pain in order to thrill and amuse his public. Certainly other bio-filmed performers suffered for the sake of the audience, but never until MAN OF A THOUSAND FACES did the pain of performance (rather than interminable offstage sufferings) come to the foreground to such a degree. Even in the 1953 HOUDINI (to be analyzed in the chapter on miscellaneous specialists) the hero's ordeals were endured with a smile and a wisecrack. It should be noted that paternel oblige also plays a role in motivating Chaney to twist and contort his face and body from film to film. Denied custody of his young son because of his unsteady income, the actor appears in a continuous stream of pictures to earn the money to "get my kid out of hock."

The narrative's hewing to the facts makes an apocryphal celebration/testimonial impossible as a concluding note of triumph, but the framing of the story within a flashback performs the same archetypal function via a dramatized historical incident. An opening title informs the viewer that "On August 27, 1930, the entire motion picture industry stopped work to pay tribute to one man. This is his story." At Chaney's funeral, the young and famous production executive Irving Thalberg (portrayed by lookalike future producer Robert Evans) delivers the eulogy--which becomes the film's narrative. Chaney's show-business "sainthood" is thus established by the narrative's invocational inclusion of a tribute paid by the one studio chieftan whose own early death (in the service of entertaining the public) has been mythically memorialized for the masses in the form of a namesake Oscar for consistent, creative excellence.

An actress bio-film which relates with exceptional directness to the chronologically parallel cycle of self-destructive female singers is 1957's JEANNE EAGELS. Her dramatized introduction to show business is twin to that of the diegetic Helen Morgan--a "fixed" beauty contest. Eagels' supposed first professional (and sexual) encounters are similarly under the exploitative guidance of a "sleazy hustler," in this case a carnival spieler who oversees her "bumping and grinding" in a "cooch show." Eagels does demonstrate greater ambition than her generic sisters, however. Her pronouncements of burning ambition more closely resemble those spoken by the male heroes of numerous other show-business bio-films: "Maybe I come from nowhere ... but I'm goin' somewhere!" After Eagels begins her climb to the top as a 1920s actress in New York City, the turning point of her career occurs when she deviously wrests the chance to star in a new Somerset Maugham play away from a fictionalized rival actress. Rationalizing her lies and unfair tactics, Eagels declares, "Even if I step on her neck ... I'll do anything to get the part." Like the diegetic Helen Morgan, Eagels is the focus of a romantic triangle, positioned between her aristocratic, Princeton-educated new husband and the sideshow grifter who launched her on the road to stardom. Her husband, before their inevitable break-up, experiences the archetypal self-loathing of so many previous men married to celebrity wives in bio-films. The increasingly cruel Eagels, succumbing to alcohol in yet another futile escape from the pressures of fame, taunts him by asking, "How do you like being Mr. Eagels?"

JEANNE EAGELS' invocation of the familiar centers, by means of a performance segment, on her most famous stage success, her portrayal of prostitute Sadie Thompson in Maugham's "Rain." Her other stage work receives only scant attention, and her concurrent career as an actress in feature films made during the daytime at Paramount's Long Island studio is invoked not so much to authenticate the pro-

Kim Novak in JEANNE EAGELS (1957). Photo courtesy Wisconsin Center for Film and Theater Research.

ceedings as to assist in explaining her swift decline. Just
as Helen Morgan's decline was given an explicatory poem,
mouthed by Morgan in the words of Edna St. Vincent Millay
("... my brief candle burns ..."), Eagels' descent into the
pit of emotional and professional desolation (supposedly an
equally disastrous case of "burning the candle at both ends")
is exacerbated by overwork. Reflecting on her continuous
round of acting in movies by day and in the theatre by night,
the anguished performer excuses her search for escape via
intoxication: "Sometimes it gets dark and you get scared."
Although her excessive drinking is extensively depicted, narrative dialogue also suggests her increasing reliance on illegal drugs, a motif which was to become far more explicit
in the post-censorship bio-films of later years.

An odd, counter-invocational sequence occurs in the
depiction of Eagels' film work. During a performance segment in which she is seen portraying a Southern belle in a
Civil War drama, the man directing the production is clearly
visible as real-life film director Frank Borzage, who is
diegetically identified as himself by the name emblazoned
on his chair. Not only did the real-life Eagels never appear in any such film, she in fact never worked for Borzage
at all. Similar grossly inaccurate performance segments in
musical bio-films abound, often in concession to changed
contemporary tastes in performing styles, the availability of
"guest star" performers, or the facile exploitation of widely
held but erroneous audience perceptions/memories. This
sequence, however, defies plausible analysis.

The bleakness of JEANNE EAGELS, so exemplary of
the circa 1957 attitude of popular (movie) culture to show
business history, is encapsulated in Eagels' response to a
star-struck youngster's request for counsel on entering the
acting profession. World-weary and having temporarily re-
covered from near-suicidal dependence on liquor, and from
blacklisting by the Actors' Equity union, the haggard actress
turns to the young girl who has entered the woman's dressing room. "Take my advice, kid," Eagels growls, "Don't!"
Just as the comparably blacklisted Billie Holiday would later
find a brief moment of renaissance to be only the jumping-
off point to the depths, Eagels returns to her addiction. In
her character's last appearance on screen, she sinks out of
the shot and below the frame. The carnival hustler who
first loved and used her reappears in the closing sequence,
emphasizing the motif established in the words of the famed
acting teacher who once molded Eagels' raw talent into the

skill of a dazzling Broadway star. Madame Neilson had later likened her protégé to a swift-burning, celestial body: "She's like a comet, without a background--sick with that awful self-destruction that comes with great talent." Subsequent to Eagels' early death, the narrative archetypally grants her a familiar form of immortality. The ex-pitchman is seen recapturing memories of the fascinating woman he and the public have now lost, by attending a theatrical screening of one of her starring films. Its apocryphal but generically appropriate title: FOREVER YOUNG.

The attractional factor of exposed scandal which accompanied the release of JEANNE EAGELS was employed again the following year in the judgmentally titled TOO MUCH, TOO SOON. Appearing on the nation's theatre screens in 1958, at the end of the cycle of doomed songstresses, this actress biography grimly extended the cross-professional switch of the Eagels film with two significant variations. Diana Barrymore, the subject-heroine, was still alive at the time, necessitating a diegetic "recovery" which would more closely parallel that of the bio-film of similarly troubled Lillian Roth, I'LL CRY TOMORROW. In addition, Diana's life story, in like manner adapted from her own recent, best-selling autobiography, bore witness to the alcohol-assisted destruction of a far more famous acting career, that of her father, John Barrymore. The two life stories not only overlap, but echo each other, and Diana's fear that she would repeat her father's addiction to alcohol even functions as a motivational factor in her dramatized distress. The senior Barrymore's life is nearly over when the narrative begins, and it concentrates on his brief contact with, but lasting effect on, the life and career of his actress daughter.

Growing up apart from her famous father, young Diana has come to know him primarily through his motion picture appearances and the accounts of his private life published in the fan magazines, one of which (with his picture on the cover) serves as the film's opening image. Her divorced mother, a famous and successful lady author, has forbidden the girl to communicate with her father for ten years, but when Diana finishes her education and decides to move to Hollywood, the mother is powerless to stop the girl. The structure of this opening sequence, responding to the anticipated biographical curiosity of the viewing audience with a depiction of the subject-heroine's own biographical curiosity about a famous actor who is also her father, sets up a duality of informational quests. Diana's arrival in the movie capital and her encounters with her father reveal him to be a far different individual than the studios' publicity machines have presented to the girl on paper. The man's interest in his long-unseen daughter is (contrary to what her mother had predicted) genuine, but it eventually palls, falling victim to the boredom induced by her girlish, fan-like prattle. When he suddenly deserts her in favor of a spur-of-the-moment yachting excursion to Rio with his drinking buddies, she directs the power of her envy of his success into a personal campaign to become an actress and to "follow in his footsteps."

The exploitational nature of show business is keenly emphasized in her discovery of how eager producers are to give her leading roles--not because of her talent, but in order to "cash in" on her family name. TOO MUCH, TOO SOON is in no way a celebration of its heroine's talents. Rather, in the generic tradition of its time, it is an exposé of her brief rise and steep downfall, the story of how she became yet another victim of the process which has been defined in American popular culture as "the rocky road to fame." During the time she shares her father's nearly empty (the furniture has been repossessed) Hollywood mansion, she--and the audience--first witness the final stages

Dorothy Malone, Errol Flynn and Murray Hamilton in TOO MUCH, TOO SOON (1958). Photo courtesy Wisconsin Center for Film and Theater Research.

of John Barrymore's own self-destruction by drink. Following his demise, the remainder of the narrative repeats the process, in greater detail and through a succession of three husbands, as Diana herself becomes a slave to self-doubt and continuous intoxication.

The film's invocational factors avoid the name-identified depiction of other celebrities contemporary with the historical period of the diegesis. Even Diana's famous uncle Lionel receives but a brief mention, and her aunt Ethel (whose film work was far less extensive) is ignored. The actual studio where Diana was under contract, Universal, is referred to as "Imperial Pictures," just as the identity of her unfortunate string of husbands is also partially disguised. Yet invocation does function via a singular, ironic duality of screen and historical identity. The actor portraying her alcoholic, ex-matinee-idol father is the similarly dissipated, close-to-death Errol Flynn, a former drinking partner of the late Barrymore and a man widely identified in the popular press of the time as a "fallen star" who was subject to the same weaknesses which killed the man whom Flynn is impersonating.

Diana Barrymore's first "grab for the bottle" occurs literally as the grief-stricken girl, believing herself guilty of her father's death because she could not halt his drinking, becomes mesmerized by an unfinished liquor bottle sticking out of the pocket of his coat, which is hanging on a rack in the empty mansion. Only when her rapidly acquired habit has destroyed her career and finally transported her to the gutter does she discover the means of re-claiming control over her smashed life, one which generically parallels the rise-and-fall of Lillian Roth throughout much of the narrative. The final parallel (acknowledging her alcoholism and seeking a cure) reaches to extra-diegetic lengths, however, when she is depicted as meeting and agreeing to collaborate with author Gerold Frank on her confessional autobiography. Frank, as the popular audience of 1958 was likely to recall, was the same man who assisted Lillian Roth in the writing of *her* own story.

While Roth was supplied by the narrative with a concluding romantic interest in the person of the kindly AA volunteer who rescues her, Barrymore enjoys a romantic renaissance which draws upon the congruent myth of separation and reunion, tinged with the mild irony sometimes referred to as "poetic justice." The handsome suitor she rejected

back when she was an attractive debutante re-enters her life
by dramatic coincidence as the narrative closes. Her final
bout of delirium tremens (a store-window-smashing spree
triggered by the sight of her aged and alcohol-ravaged facial
reflection) had emphasized the emotional shock resulting
from her loss of the beauty deemed so essential for show-
business success. The no-longer young man shares with
her his own loss of youthful comeliness by lifting his hat
and revealing a shiny, bald head. Thus the beauty ethic,
maintained by popular culture as concomitant with the quest
for show-business success, is both acknowledged one final
time and simultaneously obviated. The heroine has survived the mythic ordeal of rise-and-fall, prematurely aging,
but escaping (within the diegetic time frame) the early death
to which so many of her generic sisters had been prone. In
real life, however, the public had its myth-infused impression of Diana Barrymore's "recovery" negated by the widely
reported news of her death, little more than a year after the
film's release, at age thirty-nine. It was as if the archetype
of a performer's self-destruction had extended (following in
the wake of Errol Flynn's death the previous year) past the
boundaries of the frame and into the future.

Since a pure archetype is by definition timeless, an
idée fixe out of the collective unconscious, unbound by clock
and calendar, this extension should not seem surprising. Its
power (and therefore validity) is attested to by the public's
continuing, cyclical hunger for tales of scandal and doom
concerning the admired (and envied) elite. During the mid-
1950s this hunger surfaced for a time in the form of the
female singer/actress show business bio-film exposé. TOO
MUCH, TOO SOON marked the end of this specific cycle.
Other exposés would continue to appear, of course, but from
the vantage point of a quarter-century later, the frequency
and proximity of this individual cycle has yet to be matched
in the medium of film. Popular culture's other, less costly
and much more voluminous outlets demonstrate cycles of
their own, which sometimes reinforce the emphasis of films
in a given historical period. The successful rise (until the
courts applied the libel statutes) of the scandal-mongering
Confidential magazine should be noted as a companion phenomenon to the appearance of the show-business/exposé
bio-film.

The next filmed biography of an actor was released
in 1961, more than a decade after the first VALENTINO.
THE GEORGE RAFT STORY marked the bio-film's initial

contact with the relatively untested attractional factor of nostalgia not for the lost world of the silent picture, but for the early days of the talkies. Shifting of the target audience, an ongoing process which had already removed the world of vaudeville from the list of nostalgic attractional possibilities, was also distancing the sound film's early years into a category ripe for filmic invocation. To suggest that THE GEORGE RAFT STORY explored entirely new ground would be to overstate the case, however, in light of the fact that the overtly fictional musical SINGIN' IN THE RAIN had succeeded a full decade earlier. It was with THE GEORGE RAFT STORY, however, that the bio-film specifically applied the structure of a career retrospective to a film actor from the sound era.

Closer analysis of the film's text reveals significant cross-generic patterns as well. A brief renaissance of the early 1930s gangster film cycle had occurred on America's theatre screens between 1957 and 1961 (THE RISE AND FALL OF LEGS DIAMOND, PORTRAIT OF A MOBSTER, MURDER INC., MACHINE GUN KELLY, BABY FACE NELSON, AL CAPONE), while television's "The Untouchables" was displaying similar material on the home screen. THE GEORGE RAFT STORY exploited this new wave of interest in the mobsters of old by invoking the familiar name of Raft, a major film star whose reputed close associations with the kingpins of the underworld had been widely reported in the popular press. Yet his bio-film was something of a negation of the exposés which preceded it, if not an outright apologia for its subject-hero. Made with the full cooperation and support of Raft himself, it related more closely to the previous year's exculpatory bio-film of bandleader Gene Krupa, while excusing Raft for his perhaps "unwise and excessive" loyalty to the underworld types who gave him his first opportunities in show business.

THE GEORGE RAFT STORY's mythic infrastructure relies on a career pattern of rise-and-fall, with an ephemeral comeback rooted most tenuously in his winning a bit part in a recent hit film. Employing first-person narration by the actor portraying Raft (Ray Danton, a linkage figure himself to the recent gangster films in which he had starred), the film traces Raft's rise from working as a gigolo/exhibition dancer in the gangster-owned nightclubs of the late 1920s to his achievement of star status, appearing characteristically as a mobster's bodyguard in SCARFACE (1932) and as a dancer in BOLERO (1934). Relying on the familiarity of these two titles to carry the invocational load for the balance of his career, the narrative thereafter makes heavy use of condensation and fictionalization in depicting Raft's fortunes during the intervening decade and a half of his success in films.

Raft's fall from this state of grace is mythically represented as an act of sacrifice for a friend. When Raft appears in a courtroom to testify as a character witness for accused underworld boss Bugsy Siegel, the actor becomes persona non grata in the image-conscious film colony. Impoverished, hounded by the Internal Revenue Service, and on the verge of suicide, he seeks refuge in a distant city, working under the protection of the crime syndicate as an official "greeter" in a Havana casino until the Castro revolution forces Raft to flee back to America. In a sequence which functions as negation of audience suspicions of Raft's possibly criminal character, a shady fight promoter visits the unemployed performer and asks advice in arranging a "hit." "You got connections ... you can fix it," the promoter declares, just before the graying and middle-aged Raft stirs with enraged decency and punches out his visitor, knocking him down a flight of rickety rooming-house stairs.

"Inside, you're just a pushover," his ex-agent tells Raft. He goes on to lecture the actor (and the audience) about the "lesson" his misfortunes should have taught him: "You've repaid all your friends who've taken advantage of you. Quit them." Raft's reward, a comeback to popular acclaim, completes the archetypal pattern. He is cast in a new hit movie, playing a comic version of the impeccably tailored, coin-flipping gangster that once was his most familiar screen image. The picture is SOME LIKE IT HOT (1960), and its success leads Raft, in the bio-film's concluding sequence, to anticipate a full-scale comeback.

Invocationally, THE GEORGE RAFT STORY is sparse in its depiction of celebrities from the past, fictitiously labeling or ignoring the famous actresses with whom he was romantically involved, the studios where he worked, and the titles of nearly all of his films. Nightclub operator Texas Guinan (herself bio-filmed in 1945) does rate an identified portrayal, but the key invocations are not of Raft's fellow entertainers, but of the mobsters of his era. An exemplary sequence depicts Raft's visit with Al Capone, who offers the actor an inside critique of SCARFACE, apparently having enjoyed all of it except the ending. Raft's excuse (in this excuse-laden bio-film) to "Big Al" is that the censors required an alteration of history. Reflexively, an extradiegetic question of the bio-film's own accuracy is therefore also raised.

Two actress biographies appeared on film in 1965, and both were about the same woman. Released only a few months apart, their markedly different approaches to a common subject demonstrated to the public in a unique manner how secondary the historical events are to the myth-infused dramatic material which makes up the bulk of a bio-film narrative. Since both films employed the same title, they will be referred to here in terms of their chronological appearance: HARLOW I and HARLOW II. The first of these, inexpensively staged as if it were a live television show and hurriedly released to theatres as a black-and-white kinescope, was rushed into production to capitalize on the wave of latter-day popular-culture interest in Jean Harlow which was triggered by the surprise best-seller status of a scandal-tinged biographical book. HARLOW II, which claimed the book as its "authorized source," was a lavishly mounted color production, started before HARLOW I but completed sometime after. The fact that both films reached American theatres without legal impediments, despite the machinations of the opposing producers, is in itself convincing testimony to the judicially established principle that a deceased person's dramatic likeness is in the public domain.

HARLOW I fits basic details of the life of the actress into a tragedy of rise-and-fall, archetypally suggesting that the price of early success is early death, and therefore relating the proceedings to the show-business bio-film's doomed females of a decade earlier. Invocation of the familiar functions at its most intense in an early sequence, set in a Hollywood studio commissary, peopled by exact lookalikes of several highly recognizable celebrities from the past, including Al Jolson, Stan Laurel, Oliver Hardy, and Marie Dressler. The customary mis-naming of two of the men who played key roles in the real Harlow's life (William Powell and Howard Hughes) suggests, on the other hand, lack of clearance from the still-living pair.

Much irony is generated from the contrasting of Harlow's sexually active/combative parents and her own failure to find romantic fulfillment. Her disastrous marriage to cultured and cynically philosophical ("Sex is the opiate of the people") producer Paul Bern, which ends with his suicide, emphasizes the image of the woman as fate's victim, cheated out of her right to happiness. The nightclub bouncer who offers himself to the actress as a surrogate for her impotent husband delivers a line of dialogue which epitomizes this archetypal narrative attitude: "Most of the guys and gals come out here to break into the movies. Instead, the movies break them."

Character actress Marie Dressler, certainly the opposite of Harlow by virtue of being a screen veteran who has "paid her dues," futilely advises the distraught young woman: "You don't believe in anything ... success came too fast.... Go away and soak up the wisdom of the ages. Throw out the leeches. All the big things in life have to be done alone." Harlow's search for instant maturity leads her to study with acting coach and Moscow Art Theatre actress Maria Ouspenskaya, who offers the contradictory counsel, "You are Oak. Woman should be Willow." Harlow's desperate response is to flee Hollywood for a time, and upon her return she begins what promises to be a wholly satisfactory romance with an older, sensitive actor named William (Powell) Mansfield. Her sudden death from an unspecified illness causes the Mansfield character to re-emphasize the fated nature of her brief life by comparing her passing to the demise of poet John Keats, also at age twenty-six.

The one Harlow picture given any invocational emphasis is her breakthrough film, HELL'S ANGELS (1930). The balance of her career is glossed over, with the narrative invoking celebrity names in preference to film titles. Louis B. Mayer, a linkage figure to numerous other bio-films, is one of those who rate an impersonation in the diegesis, and his response to news of Harlow's death conforms to the popular image of his paternalistic concern with the lives of his contract players: "Terrible, terrible ... I'm losing a daughter." The film's final shot, suggesting the inexorability of an allotted span of time having expired, is of a music box running down and stopping.

HARLOW II rejected any sentimental view of the actress as a fated flower of youth who blossomed too soon. The mythic structure in the second film was one of sacrifice, of a girl who was victimized by the archetypally cruel show business system and ultimately destroyed by falling into the "meat grinder" of filmic exploitation. HARLOW II is an angry film, a bill of particulars against the Hollywood machine (although all its film titles and studio names are false) and an indictment of the way in which the industry supposedly wronged an innocent. Generically it presages the accusational tone of LADY SINGS THE BLUES, but the demons of HARLOW II are less external to the entertainment process than is the racism depicted in the Billie Holiday film. The heroine of HARLOW II is a willing participant in the exploitation of her bodily charms. To accuse the film industry of evil intent in its marketing of images of sexual attraction, and to do this within the contemporary framework of just such a latter-day exploitational project (the production and promotion of HARLOW II) is a reflexive narrative maneuver which essentially functions at cross purposes to itself.

The story is told from the point of view of an individual who was invisible in the earlier film, Harlow's agent. His view of the way in which his client was supposedly savaged by her chosen profession colors the tone of all that is presented in the diegesis. The actor portraying him, Red Buttons, is, however, a linkage figure to other bio-films of a markedly different approach. He also appears as the hero's agent in YOUR CHEATIN' HEART and in LOUIS ARMSTRONG--CHICAGO STYLE, in addition to serving as an icon of similar show business "types" in numerous overtly fictional dramas.

The assembly-line nature of 1930s film production is established by the film's documentary-style opening sequence, and Hollywood's alleged dehumanizing of its performers/victims is emphasized repeatedly. Early in her career Harlow bemoans, "Oh Mama, all they want is my body. I'm not a person to them, I'm just a thing." Harlow's agent evaluates the ethics of the industry: "This movie business is a crap game with loaded dice." Yet he himself excuses his ruthless attempts to make his client a star: "I'm a nobody to them until I have a somebody. I've used every promotional trick and committed every social crime to keep her working...." After Harlow gains a measure of success by appearing in a series of sexy and scantily-clad roles, she suspects an unpleasant change is occurring in her offscreen personality: "You can't play to a half a million peeping Toms without it doing something to you." The William Powell character, here named Jack Harrison, who offers her the chance at true love and happiness, describes her career in perhaps the most vitriolic terms of all: "You're a piece of meat. They'll throw you in the meat grinder and make meatballs out of you, then throw them to the public a little at a time."

The Actors / 235

Harlow's marriage to the suicidal Paul Bern is also treated with considerably more rage and disgust than in the previous picture. Instead of escaping from her wedding night to flirt with a bouncer/stud at a speakeasy, she flees to her agent's home, where he and his wife administer first aid and sympathy to the bleeding bride, who has been severely beaten by her impotent and cynical husband. Just prior to his death, Bern utters a line which, taken extra-diegetically, attempts to sum up the attractional factors of this type of bio-film exposé, which began as a cycle in the mid-1950s but returned with a vengeance in this decade-later avatar: "The public feeds more on our shortcomings than it does on our virtues."

The unspecified cause of Harlow's death in the first film becomes self-inflicted pneumonia in the second, brought on by sleeping off a drinking binge on a cold, damp beach. Her agent, however, supplies a myth-consistent moral, emphasizing Harlow's act of sacrifice: "She died of life. She gave it all to everybody else, so there wasn't any left for herself." Both films ignore the persistent rumors of her death from a botched abortion, and in doing so even avoid the published clinical diagnosis of kidney failure and uremic poisoning. To "die of life" is much more appropriate to a mythic figure.

Bio-films of stage stars, despite their lower invocational potential in the minds of the target audience, continued to be produced in the years following the mid-1950s flurry of bio-film activity. One of the highest-budgeted productions of the more sparsely film-populated 1960s was a picture which came to be known by at least three titles: GERTIE WAS A LADY, THOSE WERE THE HAPPY TIMES, and STAR! (1968). Re-edited several times, sometimes exhibited with all of its lavish performance segments intact, and at other times chopped down to a much briefer running time, STAR! was a latter-day return to the star vehicles of old, an expensively mounted showcase for the singing and dancing talents of Julie Andrews, who had two years earlier won the box-office confidence of Hollywood's understandably nervous bankrollers by playing the lead in one of the post-TV-saturation era's biggest commercial successes, THE SOUND OF MUSIC. Andrews was the prime attractional factor; her vehicle was a musical bio-film whose subject-heroine had been a leading light of the New York and London stage world of some three decades earlier: Gertrude Lawrence.

Lawrence's career had been closely intertwined through the years with another stage luminary whose film appearances had been similarly few, playwright and actor Sir Noel Coward. Their relationship, however, had been based on professional compatibility, not sexual attraction. The screenwriters faced the same dilemma raised by the 1940s challenges of the lives of George Gershwin, Cole Porter and Lorenz Hart: how to mask the homosexuality of a central character within a heterosexual romantic myth. The solution was to de-emphasize the Coward character while at the same time bringing to the foreground the equivocal nature of the heroine's quest. Coward's role, however, was by no means eliminated. Instead he is portrayed as a peripatetic father confessor/advisor to the amiably scatterbrained Lawrence, popping up to assist and inspire her whenever her fortunes lead her down another blind alley on the road to success. In the narrative of STAR!, the quest myth is actually partitioned, in accordance with Lawrence's dramatized attempts to live out a series of multiple identities. "I want to be lots of different people," she says to Coward, explaining how she refuses to be typed as only one kind of performer or only one man's romantic partner. His characteristically barbed reply: "You'll never decide what you want to be until you decide who you are. You can't take a whole auditorium home to bed with you without being accused of immorality on a grand scale."

Her career and her succession of romances are traced from her earliest performing days in music halls, through her string of major stage successes, to her starring role in "Lady in the Dark," one of the Broadway musicals written for her. A key performance segment has her singing the most reflexive song from that show, "Poor Jenny-- Who Would Make Up Her Mind." Archetypally learning her "lesson," not to continue her acting when she is offstage and to become more definite in her personal and professional goals (she does at last embark upon a happy marriage), Lawrence can be heard in voice-over comments while the end credits roll: "I know that the most important things are understanding, happiness, and being absolutely genuine all the bloody time." Just as HARLOW II revived the scandal/exposé formula of a decade earlier, STAR! was a reversion to the optimistic bio-films of the 1940s.

STAR! (as suggested by its series of title changes and revisions) was a sizable box-office failure. Eight years passed before the film industry attempted another actor or

Julie Andrews as Gertrude Lawrence in STAR! (1968).
Photo courtesy Films Incorporated.

actress biography, and when it appeared, in 1975, the subject-heroes were once more the film colony's own folk and the approach was again a cynical one. GABLE AND LOMBARD employed the myth of separation and reunion to a famous offscreen love affair which had been extensively reported in the fan magazines of forty years earlier. While sentimentalizing (in contemporary terms) the personal relationship of the ill-fated lovers, the narrative simultaneously blasted the old Hollywood establishment for its alleged state of vicious, life-denying sexual hypocrisy. The narrative of GABLE AND LOMBARD depicts the courtship and marriage of film stars Clark Gable and Carole Lombard during the 1930s and into the early World War II years, a period which partially overlaps the settings of the two Harlow bio-films, released a decade earlier. The attractional factor of nostalgia (for a target audience which remembered the depicted stars from initial contact with their first-run films) had by 1975 become decidedly widened in its angle of accessibility. The reason: the continuous revival of old theatrical films on television (a process well underway at the time of the Harlow films) had served to extend the life of a star's popularity to encompass two or even three generations. Thus the subject-heroes of GABLE AND LOMBARD were candidates for familiarity invocation for film viewers of all ages.

The two performers are presented as "secret" lovers, at odds with the moral strictures of their world, and caught up in a time-limited relationship which will end in tragedy. The story is framed as a flashback, introduced by a radio bulletin describing Lombard's death in an airplane crash. The ensuing narrative is visually identified as Gable's reminiscences of their relationship, beginning with their antagonistic meeting at a 1936 Hollywood party. Their courtship is dramatized in a style that attempts to imitate the "screwball" romantic comedies of that period, which often featured aggressive, uninhibited females verbally and physically sparring with passive, confused males. A significant alteration in approach, however, is the overlay of post-censorship crudity on the value system which the narrative champions. Instead of re-creating a typical romantic liaison such as would be depicted in a 1930s "screwball comedy," the film offers the audience a relationship characterized by frequent acts of obvious fornication and much sexually explicit dialogue. The institutionally enforced sexual denial, which supplied a base of unspoken tension to the comedy style being imitated, is removed in GABLE AND LOMBARD, as the film pitches its appeal to a film-going audience of a different era. Yet the underlying reliance upon timeless myths continues.

The lovers are separated by the intervention of studio discipline and contemporary moral standards. Linkage figure Louis B. Mayer, who runs the MGM studio where the married Gable is a contract actor, insists upon their parting before a public scandal breaks and threatens the economic safety of the studio empire. (The power of "promorality" lobbies is a recurring theme.) An apocryphal segment which serves to emphasize the polarization of the public and its stars is a "Ladies' Wholesomeness and Patriotism" rally where Clark Gable, under studio orders, is to be the guest speaker. Carole Lombard disrupts his speech and causes an uproar when she enters the hall and begins to scream obscenities from the convention floor while acting as if she were a drunken whore. The distraught Mayer provides additional linkage when he likens Lombard to some tragic predecessors, explaining that she is "no different than all the other blighted actresses--Eagels and [Mabel] Normand. [It's] drugs, booze, suicide. [You should] never let them be alone." The lovers' separation is exacerbated when Gable becomes the object of a waitress's paternity suit. His acquittal seems unlikely until the estranged Lombard makes a surprise courtroom appearance and testifies that Gable could not be guilty because he had been in bed with her on the night in question. The anticipated firestorm of public outrage is prevented, however, when the pair finally marry (Gable's wife has agreed to a settlement) and face their fans at a gala premiere. A hush falls over the crowd when the pair emerge from their limousine, but their subsisting popularity quickly proves too strong for the anger of the moralists. Archetypally winning over the mob, Gable and Lombard are greeted with cheers of wild approval sealing their reunion.

All that is left is to bring the narrative full circle, with the closing of the flashback framework. The year is again 1942, and Gable, in uniform and riding in an Army staff car, is being driven away from the site of the fatal crash. To emphasize the loss of his beloved wife, he tells a fellow officer of her charming sense of vulgarity, and relates a dirty story she once told him. This sequence and certain others, also bearing upon the supposedly enchanting foul-mouthedness of Lombard, are extensively altered in the version of the film prepared for television exhibition. The crudity of the Lombard character, presented as an asset in gaining the sympathy of the target theatrical audience, is deemphasized in the video version. Many lines of dialogue are stripped of their sexual explicitness, and a key sequence change is the re-shooting of her presenting a Christmas gift to Gable. In the television version she gives him a pair of hand-knit mittens. The supposedly younger, more sexually active and uninhibited theatrical audience saw her present him with a knit muffler specially shaped and fitted to warm his genitals.

As has been demonstrated, GABLE AND LOMBARD offered essentially no new form for the show-business biofilm, nor did it discard the reliance upon mythic formulae. Its invocation of the familiar was limited to only a few central characters. (Lombard's real ex-husband, William Powell, a disguised character in the two Harlow films, was still living and no more cooperative a decade later, but in the diegesis of GABLE AND LOMBARD he ceased to exist.) Even the use of well-remembered film titles did not venture much beyond the inclusion of GONE WITH THE WIND. Where GABLE AND LOMBARD did undertake innovation was in the narrative's approach to the attractional factor of scandal, excusing rather than exploiting its subject-heroes' violations of the historical moral code and reuniting them in triumph. The canard uttered by Louis B. Mayer about doomed actresses (a point of view previously reinforced by numerous biofilms) is in this case forcefully denied. Lombard's subsequent death, in the service of her country while traveling on a war bond sales drive, is an act of sacrifice wholly unrelated to any hint of vice.

Also in 1975 came the release, directly to television, of another biography of Rudolph Valentino. THE LEGEND OF VALENTINO was sub-titled "A Romantic Fiction," yet it hewed substantially closer to the historic record than either the 1951 version or the 1977 theatrical film which was just starting production. This difference was, of course, of no importance in mythic terms, for all three bio-films display a similar pattern of rise-and-fall. The 1975 LEGEND opted not to solve a mystery (the woman in black) or to exploit the sexual magnetism of the Valentino mystique. LEGEND instead imparted a lesson, linked to the man's downfall, regarding just where he went wrong in his quest for success. The fault lay in his rejection of the Jewish mother figure, screenwriter June Mathis, who discovered him and fully understood his talents.

Except for the re-naming of Pola Negri and Valentino's first wife (Negri and Jean Acker Valentino were still alive in 1975), the narrative accurately identifies his second wife (Natacha Rambova) and her strong-willed mentor (Alla Nazimova), depicting how the pair took over the hapless actor, both personally and professionally, as if he were a business. The issue of the two women's lesbianism versus Valentino's tortured bisexuality is more suggested than stated, but that is not the point of greatest importance. What is central to the myth is Valentino's forced rejection of June Mathis, who at one point supposedly leaves Hollywood, dejected over the loss of her discovery, to return to Brooklyn, "where most other girls look like me." The fact that she was from Leadville, Colorado, is ignored in deference to working out the myth-infused tragedy. Valentino's own trip to New York, during which he attempts an unsuccessful reunion with Mathis, is climaxed by his confessional speech on stage at the premiere of SON OF THE SHEIK, where he tells the crowd that he is really just another Italian immigrant who came to America by way of Ellis Island, but who has been transformed by the magic of film into a creature of the public's child-like imagination. Mathis' refusal to "take him back," supposedly because of his relationships with too many other women, apparently breaks him, both emotionally and physically, and his apocryphal speech ends with his being rushed to the hospital while hemorrhaging internally. The embittered woman who had offered to fix the ailing star some chicken soup but not to renew their friendship speaks her last words to the dying man: "I'm not your mother ... I hate happy endings." A sepulchral narrator intones that "The fairy tale was over," and that only in the act of death did Valentino "finally [do] something by himself."

The flashback framework for THE LEGEND OF VALENTINO uses his empty, unfinished mansion as a point of departure and return, and the image of the actor as an empty, hollow man, filled only with the fanciful notions of a screenwriter, runs throughout the narrative, highlighted by a sequence in which the actor is distressed to find a young and willing female fan curled up in his bed and waiting for her big chance. When he declines her offer, the bewildered girl exclaims, "I thought you were Rudolph Valentino!" "For a while, so did I," he responds.

Just as the Harlow films of a decade earlier attempted

an air of historical placement by emphasizing the supposed
novelty of the star's aggressive sexuality in the films of the
period, so too does THE LEGEND OF VALENTINO purport
to depict an epiphanic moment in film history, albeit some
ten years prior to the Harlow explosion. Studio head/
father-figure Jesse Lasky, displaying the same heartless
paternal concern of the diegetic Louis B. Mayer, is shown
in LEGEND to be delighted with the public's novel response
to the Valentino image, but equally confident that he could
be replaced by any other "bum" (such as Ramon Novarro)
with the proper publicity build-up. Even the fictitious depiction of Valentino's first meeting with Mathis (he is caught
by her while burglarizing her bungalow) has a mythic accuracy in revealing the man as having been but a nonentity (a
petty criminal) until his assumption of a new identity, manufactured out of the public's dreams, set him on his course
of rise-and-fall. When he rejected the source of his new
being (June Mathis), he lost the only thing that made him
seem real, even to himself. He lost his inspired artificiality.

The 1977 theatrical release, which for clarity will be
referred to here as VALENTINO II, employs a flashback
structure far more fragmented than that of LEGEND. This
third Valentino bio-film, again embodying the myth of rise-
and-fall, also functions as a tragedy, and it spins many of
the same historic facts into necessary dramatic distortions,
but what is significantly different is that the concluding emphasis is on neither mystery (the woman in black) nor the
interpersonal mechanics of spoiled relationships. VALENTINO II stresses erotic spectacle and historical pageantry,
re-creating at great expense the exact look of high living in
the 1920s as a backdrop to a series of near-ritualized exercises in sexual tension. This is not to say that there is no
narrative, for indeed one exists in the structuring/ordering
of sequences, fragmented as they are in the form of flashbacks to various events in the actor's career, each triggered
by the central spectacle of the New York City riot which accompanied his lying in state at a Manhattan funeral chapel.
As in LEGEND, Valentino's strange relationship with Nazimova and Rambova is central to the drama, but his dependence upon June Mathis ceases to be crucial to his downfall.
Instead of her discovering him as a housebreaker, his early
years in America are briefly outlined in a sequence which
in like manner establishes his starting out in the depths of
society: he escapes to California as a fugitive from a murder investigation involving his shady New York friends.

The Actors / 243

Michelle Phillips and Rudolf Nureyev in VALENTINO II (1977).
Photo courtesy Wisconsin Center for Film and Theater Research.

The familiar is invoked considerably less in VALENTINO II, with fewer of his films mentioned and no footage from any of the actual features included, as they were repeatedly in LEGEND. In a major departure from established generic practice, however, VALENTINO II does show the actor as working with a variety of directors, some of whom are correctly identified by name, even though those names likely mean nothing to the target audience. As in LEGEND, Valentino's masculinity is ridiculed by others but never directly questioned by the narrative's depiction of events in his personal life. Even in 1977, the homosexual or bisexual hero of a show-business bio-film was still absent from the screen. On the contrary, the actor's supposed heterosexual seductiveness, emphasized in a sequence which takes place on the set of THE SHEIK, but not during filming. In full costume, Valentino plays the real-life sexual predator and, in tableaux-like fashion, eventually undresses both himself and his lady. A sequence set in a jailhouse "holding tank" cell goes so far as to allege that the man suffers an actual horror of the carnal approach of other men, exemplified by his cringing in terror as his sadistic cellmates torment him.

One invocational figure who appears in the narrative, as the future sorry example of a lesson Valentino needs to learn, is film comedian Fatty Arbuckle, who is seen getting roaring drunk in a speakeasy, carousing with would-be starlets and shocking people by means of a hand buzzer. Just as Arbuckle is spotted, a friend warns Valentino, "God help you if you ever have anything worth taking. Some broad is going to give you the ride of your life." Although the allusion is a bit shy of the mark (Arbuckle's career was destroyed by the press' defense of a dead girl who could no longer benefit from his being picked clean), the danger of achieving stardom is nevertheless archetypally underlined in strong terms. Once again, not only is it a world of high pressure at the top, it is the peak of a slippery slope. Valentino describes his unhappiness as stemming neither from his marital troubles nor from his difficulties in pursuing an independent acting-producing career, free of studio domination. He explains his tragedy as having been "born into a time when a machine can turn a man who wants to be a farmer [meaning his peasant self] into a god."

Valentino's fall from the grace of stardom barely has a chance to begin when he dies suddenly from a beating, inflicted again (as in VALENTINO I) by a representative of the press, but this time, instead of defending a lady's honor, he is standing up for his own. (A Chicago newspaperman has called him a "pink powderpuff.") United Artists chief Joe Schenck displays a fatherly interest in trying to stop the fight, but to no avail. As the nude body of the dead actor lies on a mortuary slab, the film concludes with a reference to the Valentino mystique's effect on popular culture. On the sound track can be heard a phonograph record of a popular song specially composed to exploit the man's passing: "There's a New Star in Heaven Tonight."

Sexual ambiguity also figures in the 1976 made-for-television bio-film of another early-dying actor whose shocked fans formed something of a "death cult." JAMES DEAN was dramatized for the video screen as a personal memoir by his friend and former roommate, writer-producer William Bast. Working out some deep-seated psychological complex of guilt and attraction, Bast's story (which he wrote and produced) never clearly settles on a familiar mythic formulation with which to encase and structure the selected events of Dean's life. This avoidance marks a significant break with generic practice up to this point. VALENTINO II came close to doing so with its fragmented reminiscences keyed to visitors at a funeral parlor, but the overall shape of rise-and-fall can still be visible from a distance, once the film is analytically related in retrospect to its predecessors. JAMES DEAN, perhaps because of its deliberate tone of ambiguity in regard to the basic identity of its subject matter, makes mythic classification even more difficult.

The young actor and the pattern of his short life are presented as overlapping enigmas. The success he enjoys is related, not depicted, in conversations with friend Bast. From the enforced point of view of Bast, who was absent from Dean's life for significant stretches, many of Dean's activities, particularly his acts of coldness and cruelty, are inexplicable contradictions of the heroic image Bast, as an unofficial "death cult" member, strives desperately to maintain. Complicating easy classification even further is the narrative's commingling of dream and memory. Bast's nightmares interlock with the depicted events. In an opening sequence, Dean's death in an automobile crash is denied, with the man instead functioning as an inmate in an asylum. When he receives a visit from Bast, their meeting is interrupted by the arrival of a limousine, chartered to return Dean to his rightful place, in his grave. A closing sequence re-posits the fantastic situation, with the frantic actor struggling with the attendants who wish to re-bury him. "I trusted you!" he screams as the astonished Bast tells the audience in voice-over narration, "I never let him know how much I loved him."

If the text of JAMES DEAN is read as the testament of a man whose unfulfilled, possibly unconscious sexual attraction to his college roommate results in a lingering sense of guilt over the actor's early death, then the classificatory task eases into shifting the central figure of the drama from Dean to his obsessed, writer-producer friend. A sequence in which Dean tricks Bast into accepting a blind date with a strange, middle-aged gentleman in a bar indicates that Dean may have been fully aware of Bast's emotional state. Dean's non-explanation of the trick is to give Bast a copy of the book The Little Prince, whose hero Bast subsequently identifies as a Dean-like figure. Bast sums up his enigmatic view of Dean by referring to him in the narrative's close as "the laughing man with golden hair, who refused to ask questions." If William Bast is the real subject-hero of JAMES DEAN, then a mythic pattern emerges after all. The drama is one of guilt and expiation, with the central character working out his atonement for having failed (by withholding love) to save the object of his affection from a possibly self-inflicted death.

Two biographical dramas depicting the life of actress Sarah Bernhardt appeared in the late 1970s. Both based their attractional factors on the apparent star quality of the performers essaying the role more than on any significant nostalgia phenomenon, other than the continuing use of the character name as a matchless standard for performance-- like Lind, Booth or Caruso. The era of Bernhardt was primarily of the last century, much more removed from popular memory than the mid-1950s of James Dean, or even the 1920s of Rudolph Valentino. The 1976 film, released first

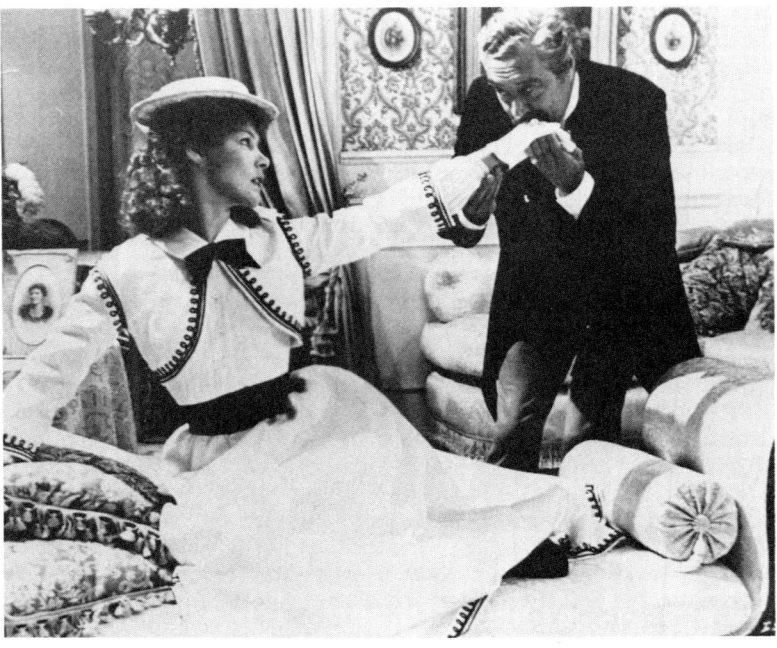

Glenda Jackson as Sarah Bernhardt in THE INCREDIBLE SARAH (1976). Photo courtesy Films Incorporated.

to theatres, was titled THE INCREDIBLE SARAH, while the
1979 direct-to-video version billed itself, more modestly, as
simply SARAH. THE INCREDIBLE SARAH is clearly an employment of the rise-and-fall myth, with a triumphant comeback providing a concluding renaissance/climax. SARAH is
much more of a personal and professional quest, a lifelong
attempt to prove one's superiority in all categories. Since
both narratives are based upon common source material, including some of the original written material about the famous French actress, published long ago, many similarities
between the two films are to be expected and do occur. It
is where the narratives diverge, with altogether different
emphases, that their mutually exclusive terrains begin to
take shape, as was the case with the Valentino films. Even
though THE INCREDIBLE SARAH employs a pattern of rise-
and-fall, the diegetical time frame selects but a few years
from her long career. Her audacious audition for the Comédie
Française begins her ascent, performance segments from
"Phaedre" and "Camille" signify her artistic zenith, the publication of her outrageously false "memoirs" triggers her
temporary fall from public approval, and her staring down
and winning over a jeering crowd, during the opening of her
production of "Joan of Arc," functions as her renaissance.
SARAH, on the other hand, is a series of reminiscences,
depicted in flashbacks, which follow the opening sequence in
which the actress, in her old age, ponders the chance to become "immortal" by accepting an offer to star in a new kind
of theatrical production--a motion picture. The successive
flashbacks illustrate several stages of her ascent to greatness. Although THE INCREDIBLE SARAH takes the performer no further than her first British tour, SARAH also
includes her encounter with America, where the archetypal
inclusion of historical hindsight-inspired dialogue has her
and her colleagues making trenchant comments on the American style of publicity. The late nineteenth-century setting
even overlaps with the era of Jenny Lind and Lillian Russell; Bernhardt attends a party held at one of the prime
linkage locations from other bio-films of the period, Delmonico's Restaurant.

Both films characterize as Bernhardt's major character flaw her habit of making talentless performers into
her leading men, taking them as lovers, and then discarding them. Another shared characteristic is Bernhardt's obsession with death, signified by her carrying a ready-made
coffin with her at all times. Her dialogue in both pictures
is repeatedly punctuated with self-declarations of greatness,

which contrast markedly with her choice of a husband--the inept weakling, Aristelle Danala. In THE INCREDIBLE SARAH he condemns himself as being a mere "lapdog," but only in SARAH (despite the fact that it was made for television) is his debilitating drug habit depicted in the narrative. A hopeless morphine addict ("Half the city of Paris is on it!"), Danala degenerates to near-infantile status and requires the constant nursing care of his haughty wife, who still insists, "We're superior people."

While THE INCREDIBLE SARAH ends on an archetypal note of triumph, SARAH concludes its heroine's quest for superiority with a return to the flashback's framing sequence, in which the old lady, surrounded by the evidence of her success (souvenir programmes, medals, autographed portraits of the great, etc.), is still musing on the passing of the years. One of her legs has had to be amputated because of a circulatory problem, but this trauma does not worry her in the slightest. She is even amused by a final piece of linkage news. An offer has come from an admirer who wants to buy her discarded leg. His name is P. T. Barnum.

The acceleration of the overall bio-film cycle, a prominent feature of America's popular culture in the late 1970s, brought forth still more stories of actors and actresses, but primarily those whose old movies were still a staple of late-night television scheduling. Employment of the nostalgia phenomenon in these instances was again to be applied along a broad front of demographic attack, since the choice of these subject-heroes from the past, as noted earlier, allowed the familiar to be invoked for audience members of all ages. BOGEY, a 1979 made-for-television production, adapted the facts of the actor's film career and later personal life into a race-with-time type of pattern, with an archetypal transcendence-of-death end-title which emphasizes the mythic immortality an actor gains by appearing in a series of popular films which continue to be revived long after his passing: "The man and his films are timeless."

Bogart's early years, as a sailor and as a Broadway stage actor, are omitted, except for the dramatization of his breaking out of a long succession of "juvenile" roles by winning the part of the Dillinger-like gangster in "The Petrified Forest." Bogart's chance to repeat the role in the Hollywood version begins the important part of his screen career (his earlier film work is mentioned, however), and the balance of the narrative concentrates on his stormy adaptation to the film colony lifestyle. A significant trend in the bio-films of later years is epitomized in BOGEY, with a decreasing narrative use of fictitious subsidiary characters, false film titles, and composite studio and director names. The casting of relatively unknown look-alikes (although the practice dates back many years) also increased in the 1970s, even more so in the made-for-television productions, where budgetary considerations may have had an influence. At the time of these films' first showings, none of the performers portraying Clark Gable, Carole Lombard, James Dean, Buddy Holly, Jan and Dean, both Elvises, and Tammy Wynette had achieved star status.

The narrative of BOGEY parallels the ascendency of his career with the depiction of two of his marriages, both to actresses, but of highly differing temperaments. His years spent with Mayo Methot are shown to be one continuous round of violent quarrels and reconciliations, fueled by large quantities of alcohol. Bogart's last marriage, to half-his-age Lauren Bacall, is idyllic, but his race against time is archetypally lost when he dies of throat cancer at age fifty-six, leaving a grieving widow and two small children. An echo of MAN OF A THOUSAND FACES and THE EDDY DUCHIN STORY can be detected in the narrative's opening and closing sequences. Bogart receives a ring from his dying father as the story opens and passes that ring on to the actor's young son when the end is near. Whether Bogart's son carried on in his father's profession is not mentioned, however.

Bogart's character is portrayed as constantly at odds with the enforced propriety of studio discipline; he is thus typed as a rebel against the system, a conflict enacted in more flamboyant terms in the studio-vs.-actor conflicts of GABLE AND LOMBARD. The two films' latter-day view of Production-Code-era Hollywood as a bastion of hypocrisy which pandered to the repressed sentiments of the nation's most conservative sectors marks these films as embodying a new kind of revisionist nostalgia, catering to a latter-day audience which is believed desirous of feeling superior to the re-created milieu and its denizens. Nostalgia's function of reinforcing time-limited prejudices, a specialized form of a practice essential to the success of most forms of popular culture ("making people feel good") is still operative in this type of revisionism--only the prejudices have become inverted. The narratives of the Sarah Bernhardt biographies, although set in the nineteenth century, follow similar lines, with the

actress proudly announcing to her public the birth of her
bastard son, as if she had performed some heroic act.

    THE SILENT LOVERS, one of a series of three 1980
TV-movies exhibited under the umbrella title MOVIEOLA,
reverted to a more traditional retroview of Hollywood's own
mythology. Based on the courtship and career interaction of
silent film stars Greta Garbo and John Gilbert, the mythic
infrastructure was again rise-and-fall, keyed to the oft-told
(in movie lore) "tragedy of John Gilbert." The narrative of
THE SILENT LOVERS parallels Gilbert's own misfortune with
the professional demise of famous Swedish film director
Mauritz Stiller, whose numerous European successes at first
win him a Hollywood contract with MGM, accompanied by a
similar pact offered to his live-in protégé, Greta Garbo.
Following Stiller and Garbo's arrival in America's film capital, they are soon parted by image-conscious linkage figure
Louis B. Mayer. Stiller's inability to work according to
studio regimen eventually makes him unemployable, and he
returns to Sweden a broken man. Garbo's intense love
scenes with Gilbert in FLESH AND THE DEVIL are shown
to be extensions of their budding affair, and it is only her
reticence to be "owned," especially if it means being "someone's third wife" (in light of Gilbert's previous failed marriages), which causes her to refuse Gilbert. When he finally prevails upon her (while she is intoxicated) to consent to
his proposal, she fails to show up at the appointed time.
Gilbert dampens his anxiety with liquor, then gets into a
brawl with studio chief Mayer, who retaliates with a threat
that the actor has committed the unpardonable sin--attacking
Hollywood's most powerful man--and is therefore "finished
in this industry." Mayer subsequently sabotages Gilbert's
talkie debut (through technical tampering to make his voice
sound funny) as an act of revenge. Garbo goes on to a long
string of hit films, and Gilbert's career founders as he
drinks himself into a fatal heart attack. Years later, on
the set of the 1936 CAMILLE, Garbo learns of Gilbert's
death, recalls how much he had feared getting old, and
mentions that "I almost married him once, you know."
Character actress Laura Hope Crews, to whom Garbo has
confided (just as Jean Harlow confided in Marie Dressler),
delivers a line which expresses a rationale of the nostalgia-
based, bio-filmic process: "Remembering is better than
nothing."

    THE SILENT LOVERS, in addition to its re-working
of the exposé formula of the self-destructive star who drinks

himself into oblivion, also sets itself up as presenting the alleged solutions to a series of mysteries which had persisted in popular culture's Hollywood lore for half a century: Did Garbo get her MGM contract only at the insistence of Stiller? Why did she never marry? Was Gilbert's voice really inferior in his first talkie? Just as the first VALENTINO posited the identity of "the woman in black," THE SILENT LOVERS makes difficult-to-prove historical assertions function as the missing pieces of a puzzle. Audience knowledge of the inferred and standing questions, however, is a wholly extra-diegetic function.

Another 1980 made-for-television bio-film, SOPHIA LOREN--HER OWN STORY, also avoided the exploitation of potentially scandalous material in favor of re-working the more supportive approach to biography which had been prevalent prior to the mid-1950s. Employing a cinematically autobiographical narrative device previously used in THE FABULOUS DORSEYS, the leading role in SOPHIA LOREN is played by the actress herself, except in the early sequences in which a younger actress portrays Loren as a girl. The attractional factor of a star of her magnitude appearing in this production is doubled, in effect, by the use of the actress in the narrative's early sequences to play her own mother.

The mythic infrastructure makes use of a dual quest, overlaid with a romantic separation and reunion in the latter half of the story. Historical placement (the 1930s) and linkage with THE SILENT LOVERS is provided as Loren's mother, a small-town Italian girl named Romilda Villadi, wins a "Greta Garbo Look-Alike Contest" sponsored by MGM's European division and hopes to travel to Hollywood in search of success as an actress. Additional linkage occurs in the parental interdiction against doing so because of fear of her meeting with the same kind of Black Hand/Mafia-connected difficulties which local rumor says cost another Italian-born movie star, Rudolph Valentino, his life. Nevertheless, Romilda leaves her rural village to travel to Naples in search of fame and quickly falls prey to an exploitative man who pretends to have important connections in the Italian film industry, but is only intent on seducing the woman. This archetypally recurrent image of the victimized woman whose quest is thwarted gives way in the second part of the narrative, wherein her illegitimate daughter grows up to become the actress who takes the stage name of Sophia Loren, marries established producer Carlo Ponti, and becomes an international film star. Thus the mother's quest aspirations are achieved by her daughter. Although stardom comes relatively early and easily for the daughter, her ultimate quest, to become a mother, proves much more difficult. Only by means of spending an entire pregnancy confined to a hospital bed is she at last able to carry a fetus to term and give birth to a healthy child. This final personal, rather than professional success, ends the drama.

SOPHIA LOREN--HER OWN STORY, in addition to invoking the familiar with ample doses of film titles and celebrity names from her career, centers its separation-and-reunion sub-plot on her highly publicized affair with actor Cary Grant during the filming of THE PRIDE AND THE PASSION (1957). Removed from her future husband Ponti by conflicting professional obligations, she succumbs to Grant's famous charm but eventually leaves him upon learning that Ponti has been granted a Mexican divorce from his first wife. Rather than exploit the sensational aspect of this series of events, the narrative depicts the Grant-Loren affair as, in her words, "a fairy-tale meeting of two different worlds." Illustrative of the legal chances taken by some latter-day TV bio-films (including STAND BY YOUR MAN and the MOVIEOLA productions) no prior approval apparently was sought from the real-life Grant for the (wholly favorable) impersonation of him by an actor who trod the thin line between depiction and caricature, and to date no legal action by Grant has been reported.

Just as THE LEGEND OF VALENTINO attempted a look of authenticity which transcended mere invocation of names and approximate re-creation of iconography by the inclusion of actual film clips featuring the real-life hero, SOPHIA LOREN employs authentic excerpts from her motion picture career, but intercut at later stages with the most congruent of impersonations.

Loren's difficulties with pregnancy were mild indeed, compared with the ordeal of Patricia Neal in THE PATRICIA NEAL STORY, a 1981 TV-movie which harkened back directly to the paralysis of Marjorie Lawrence in INTERRUPTED MELODY. PATRICIA NEAL founds its narrative structure soundly on the myth of rise-and-fall and concludes with a successful quest to overcome an adversity of deadly proportions after tracing the life of the famous actress through only three years of her celebrated career. However, these are the years of her struggle to conquer the results of a massive stroke, which left her crippled and unable to speak.

As the story opens, Neal's rise to fame and success has been duly certified with American popular culture's unique citation of nobility--which is situated midway on the fan-magazine value scale between sainthood and knighthood-- the Academy Award. Suddenly she is stricken with a loss of cerebral blood supply and lies near death. The dedicated ministrations of a brain surgeon (who is also a family friend) rescue her from the greatest danger, but she faces a long and exceedingly difficult road to full recovery of her faculties.

Fortunately, Neal has the strong emotional support of her devoted husband, author Roald Dahl, and her close friend, actress Mildred Dunnock (who re-creates for the film her actual part in Neal's recovery). The intensity of Patricia Neal's suffering is magnified by the narrative's mention of the sad fate of her three children. Two have suffered brain damage; a third has died from the most commonplace of childhood illnesses, measles. Adding to the crisis atmosphere of the story is the fact that at the time of her stroke, Neal is expecting another child. Concern for the baby's health accompanies the family's fear that Neal may never recover from her terrible affliction.

Neal's dim chances of full recovery lead her into the depths of bitterness, exacerbated by a depicted incident in which she and the family watch the 1965 Oscar telecast, on which she had been scheduled to appear to fulfill the tradition of the previous year's winner for best actress giving the coveted statue to the newest recipient. An actual kinescope of the program is included for maximum familiarity invocation. Agonizingly long hours of physical therapy await Neal, but her luck takes a definite turn for the better when she manages to give birth to a perfectly healthy baby daughter. (Dialogue reveals that Neal's state of depression might have caused her to commit suicide, had it not been for the hope of new life inside her.)

THE PATRICIA NEAL STORY contains a self-reflexive point of narrative by virtue of its depiction of her series of interviews (in the halting speech of a stroke victim) with the Life magazine reporter whose subsequent book, Pat and Roald, later functioned as source material for the screenplay. TV-movies about courageous people overcoming disabling adversity have been a staple for many seasons, and the adaptation of author Barry Farrell's book as a show-business bio-film for television therefore relates directly not only to the generic process covered by this study, but to a parallel evolutionary process in many other myth-infused narratives of popular culture.

The archetypal public tribute/reward for a performer whose career has been damaged or halted at the nadir of the rise-and-fall pattern occurs in THE PATRICIA NEAL STORY via a duality of crucial events. Tricked and cajoled by her husband into committing herself to a speaking engagement--a benefit dinner for brain-damaged children, held at New York's Waldorf Astoria Hotel--Neal reluctantly returns to America from the English country estate (of her husband's family) where she has been undergoing her recuperation. Her speech, demonstrating the amazing results of committed personal effort, expert speech therapy, and strong family support, is a resounding success. Introduced by actor Rock Hudson (playing himself), she delivers a thoroughly professional and impassioned message which receives international television news coverage. A theatrical producer in the audience speaks to an associate and mentions Neal in regard to the forthcoming film version of the hit Broadway play "The Subject Was Roses," indicating that she had been sought for the stage version five years earlier and would now be perfect for the motion picture.

Neal's double triumph ends with her and Roald being driven away from the film's gala premiere in a limousine and sharing the joy of reading an exuberant review of her performance, printed in an early edition of the next day's newspaper. In a remarkable diegetic transference to the world of perceived reality, Patricia Neal herself appears at the end of the closing credits in a brief, documentary-style epilogue depicting her work in sponsoring the Patricia Neal Stroke Rehabilitation Center in Knoxville, Tennessee. The opportunity for viewer comparison of actress Glenda Jackson's portrayal of Neal with the stern-but-enthusiastic countenance of the real-life Neal breaks with the long-established practice in show-business bio-films of avoiding consideration of the question of accurate resemblance except from extra-diegetic viewer memory.

THE PATRICIA NEAL STORY, while rooting its subject matter in the Hollywood of less than a generation ago and invoking the familiar image of the noted actress who won the Oscar for her performance opposite Paul Newman in the

1963 production of HUD, sets much of its narrative in rural Britain, filming on location the love-conquers-adversity story of an idealized, definitely non-Hollywood-style couple who are wholly devoted to their family and to each other. The historically accurate tragedies which dogged much of Neal's life are given closure by the narrative. The suffering is over, says the film's mythic message, the heroine has triumphed and, by implication (the emotional power source of these popular, "inspirational" dramas), so can you, the viewer. But some months after the film's premiere network airing, newscasts told of another extra-diegetic coda to the drama. Patricia Neal and Roald Dahl were divorcing.

The exposé bio-film, so popular in the mid-1950s, had several representations in the 1970s as well, and at least three narrative films to date have been released with 1950s actress Marilyn Monroe as their subject, in addition to a compilation/documentary rushed into release shortly after her death in 1962.* Another supposed Monroe bio-film, 1973's THE SEX SYMBOL, premiered on ABC Television with all of its character names fictionalized, despite its consistently close adherence to many major events and personalities from the historical record of the life of the actress. Although the film's wholesale employment of thin disguises prevents its description as an overt bio-film, note should be taken of the extraordinary publicity campaign launched by the network, which invoked the Monroe name in every possible way short of exact identification. Pressure from the Kennedy family reportedly even caused last-minute re-editing of the sequence in which the sexual relationship between the fictional actress and an important political figure precipitates her death. Rarely has the line between overt and covert biography been strained by attractional-factor promotion to such an extent. This incident focuses a strong light on the issue of target audience perceptions, questioning whether even the most explicit disclaimers and ficticious names can counteract the powerful effect of unlimited, advance publicity.

A 1976 Australian import, GOODBYE NORMA JEAN, took the historical Monroe character as the heroine of a

---

*THE JAMES DEAN STORY (1957), JAMES DEAN--THE FIRST AMERICAN TEENAGER (1975), and the numerous Bruce Lee bio-documentaries, similar pastiches of excerpts and interviews, also do not meet the criteria for inclusion here.

vehicle which crossed significant generic borders. So sexually oriented as to be perceived by the public as soft-core pornography, the picture concentrated on the alleged erotic escapades of Monroe's teenage years, before she changed her name and won stardom. This carnal variation on the birth myth, prior to the quest for fame, received only limited distribution, perhaps because of its unclear generic identity.

THIS YEAR'S BLONDE, another of the 1980 MOVIE-OLA TV-movies, re-employed the birth myth, but with an important revision. The narrative is structured to give greatest emphasis to the self-sacrifice performed by talent agent Johnny Hyde, who is depicted as taking the starlet under his wing because he recognizes a special talent in her that others in the Hollywood system have missed, despite her previous screen tests and acting assignments. More a father figure to Monroe than a lover (although he eventually attempts both roles), Hyde resolves to transform his discovery into a luminary of the screen by undertaking a shrewd campaign which will ultimately demand of him all he has to give. "We're gonna make a movie star," he tells his ambitious client, explaining, "It's like a big offensive in war."

Hyde walks out on his secure position with the huge William Morris Agency in order to devote himself full time to the challenge of making Monroe a major star. Plagued with a weak heart, Hyde literally works himself to death, succumbing to cardiac arrest just as she is about to make her first, serious impression on the public and the industry with her sultry/not-so-innocent performance in THE ASPHALT JUNGLE.

Monroe's brief relationship with Hyde figured as only one of a series of episodes in another 1980 TV-movie, MARILYN--THE UNTOLD STORY. Based, as was HARLOW II, on a controversial best-selling book (Norman Mailer's Marilyn), this Monroe bio-film attempted in its three-hour (with commercials) length to encompass crucial incidents from her entire life. The string of episodes unfolds as an extended chronological flashback, introduced at the opening by a tableau of her supposed suicide in June of 1962 and a prior sequence from earlier that day which reveals the depths to which she had sunk mentally and professionally. With her judgment impaired by drugs and liquor, she has been placed on suspension by her studio and appears to be

The Actors / 257

Catherine Hicks as Marilyn Monroe in MARILYN--THE UNTOLD STORY (1980). Photo courtesy Capitol Communications.

unconcerned about her future. "How can I work with people who treat me like some kind of a joke?" she asks as her desperation visibly mounts.

Each of the subsequent flashback segments depicts the actress as being rejected or deserted by every person who plays an important role in her life and on whom she depends for emotional support. Her mentally unstable mother, a single parent, attempts to raise the child Marilyn in the shadow of Hollywood's overpowering glamor and tinsel. Employed as a studio negative cutter, the woman devises a vocationally related solution for her daughter's need for daycare: Marilyn is left in the custody of the ushers at Grauman's Chinese Theater. There the young child (age 10) is obliged to sit through continuous showings of a long stream of Hollywood's mythic fantasies, becoming steeped by this process in the lore and lure of stardom which will subsequently devour her. One day the mother does not arrive after work to retrieve her daughter. The puzzled child returns home to her shabby apartment by herself, only to discover the shocking evidence of impending desertion. Her mother, face frozen in the horror of catatonic schizophrenia, is about to be carted off to a mental hospital on a one-way journey.

Marilyn's adolescent years are spent in a Hollywood orphanage, an institution which significantly overlooks the seductive artificialty of a brighter world down the street: from its windows she can see the backlot of RKO. Eventually the orphanage matrons learn how to manage the troubled child by catering to her deepest longings. A most effective way of assuaging her fits of crying and depression is to let her put on makeup and playact at being a movie star.

In her late teens, Marilyn (still called by her given name of Norma Jean Baker) marries her draft-age sweetheart and manages to secure two whole years of relative emotional security before he is sent overseas for duty in World War II. Still terribly immature and dreading loneliness, she departs her new rural home, files for divorce, and returns to Los Angeles in search of new companionship and a job in the movie capital. While working as a seamstress she is spotted by a commercial photographer and started on a professional modeling career. The lure of show business, dormant in her since childhood, engulfs her, and soon she is making the rounds of casting calls in hopes of landing the archetypal big break. Small parts and walk-ons follow as she learns to perform, both on and off camera, in an enticing manner which appears to promise fulfillment of the standard male sexual fantasies of the day. Yet she is already learning the price she must pay in secret humiliation for conforming to the entertainment industry's image of the desirable but disposable "dumb blonde." "Someday I'm gonna find someone who respects me," she says to a confidant, "I'm tired of being treated like dirt!"

Monroe's encounter with Johnny Hyde occurs at this point, assaying essentially the same narrative territory (in condensed form) as THIS YEAR'S BLONDE, but structured to parallel Monroe's growing dependence as well upon her Russian-immigrant acting coach, Natasha, who strongly advises her pupil to resist Hyde's offer of marriage. The show-business bio-film's recurrent theme of sacrificing one's personal life for professional success comes to the fore with Natasha's pointed statement of the choice Monroe is told she must make: "Decide if you want to be a great actress--or somebody's wife."

Instead of Monroe's appearance in THE ASPHALT JUNGLE functioning as a career victory, MARILYN--THE UNTOLD STORY cites it as a setback, with the MGM studio cancelling her contract following the film's release because she appears to be a performer of very "limited" abilities. Johnny Hyde's heart attack appears to be triggered by this bad news, but he does live long enough in the hospital to speak his deathbed prediction, "You're going to be a star," to his client/lover just after learning that she has signed a new, seven-year contract with Twentieth Century-Fox. This sharp rearranging and reinterpretation of historical events, while unusual, mainly because so few show-business bio-films have been remade, is clearly indicative of the variety of interpretive options available to the creators of all of the supposedly fact-based filmic material covered here.

Invocation of the familiar functions at a remarkably high level throughout this TV-movie, partly because so many details of Marilyn's private life had previously been covered and re-covered in the popular media both of her day and during the years after her death. Yet her first marriage after achieving stardom, to baseball celebrity Joe DiMaggio, is outlined in such a polite and sentimental fashion that something more than mere catering to public memories of the liaison is suggested. That the real-life DiMaggio played some role in the film's creation is also implied by the uncanny way in which the voice of the actor (Jason Miller) portraying DiMaggio sounds like that of a much older man, leaving open the improbable possibility that the film's producers may have borrowed a technique from THE JOLSON STORY and allowed the real DiMaggio to substitute his own voice via the dubbing process.

The narrative pins the blame for the marriage's dissolution on the sensitive and circumspect ballplayer's inability, despite his intense love for the woman, to handle the sometimes crude publicity stunts and incessant public leering to which Monroe's career subjects her. Although their separation is depicted as due to no emotional negligence on either's part, DiMaggio is compelled to walk out of her life. Monroe's subsequent marriage to playwright Arthur Miller, which functions as the culmination of her flight from Hollywood to New York in search of drama, culture, and intellectual respectability, also founders. Her growing habits of self-destructiveness (non-punctuality, reliance on drugs, alcoholism, and promiscuity) torment him until he can take no more. A platonic friendship with actor Clark Gable, whom she has long fantasized to be secretly her father, is ended by his sudden death from heart disease. (An earlier, attempted reunion with her real father had only won her his angry rejection.) Retreating into the mental miasma of a nervous breakdown, Monroe finds herself confined briefly in a hospital's psychiatric ward, more a prisoner of her delusions and drug dependency than of the institution's locked doors.

Neither a visit from the estranged but still-devoted DiMaggio nor a conciliatory phone call from her father does as much to restore her grip on things as her spoken realization that the Norma Jean Baker of her youth is finally dead, replaced entirely by the imaginary, public creature the world knows as Marilyn Monroe. "Who's Norma Jean!" she asks herself, answering, "I had a doll by that name once."

Monroe's futile return to work, on the ill-fated picture (SOMETHING'S GOT TO GIVE) that will never be finished, is terminally interrupted by her suddenly abandoning work at the studio and flying to the East Coast to sing "Happy Birthday" at President John Kennedy's birthday party. The exasperated Twentieth Century-Fox executives watch a news report of this event, her final public performance, on an office television set and then decide to dispense with her services for good, acknowledging that at the age of 36, Marilyn Monroe is finished.

The narrative's flashback structure gives way at this point to a return to the opening sequence, with a drug- and alcohol-besotted Monroe secluded in her Hollywood residence. Whatever the true nature of her relationship with the Kennedy family (something about which author Mailer speculates much more freely in the printed text), the film narrative provides only a scant, disjointed clue. In the opening portion of the framing sequence, Monroe's housekeeper had told her of some telephone messages from DiMaggio and a press agent, adding, "No, Mr. Kennedy didn't call." Now, at the story's conclusion, the disheveled, incoherent actress is seen in closeup, lying on her rumpled bed and saying to no one in particular, "I wish you'd stop bugging me!" She opens her mouth, and a hand, possibly not her own, drops in a pill which she obediently swallows. A still frame of this scene is accompanied by the printed information: "Sunday August 5, 1962. Marilyn Monroe was found dead. Cause of death--probable suicide." Rock star Elton John's elegiac ballad to her memory, "Candle in the Wind," plays behind the end credits but is sung by some other artist.

With the partial exception of THIS YEAR'S BLONDE, each of the Monroe films to date has relied upon the archetype of the female performer as victim, exploited by a variety of ambitious and self-centered individuals, most of them men. Just as happened in the exposé bio-films of the 1950s, the woman comes to a decidedly bad end, choosing self-destruction over a continued painful existence in a world where the demands of stardom have become unbearable. Even in THIS YEAR'S BLONDE, where the paternalistic ministrations of Johnny Hyde are depicted as being as noble as those of Jean Harlow's agent in HARLOW II, the vision of Monroe's place in the Hollywood milieu does not change. Hyde sees himself as attempting to rescue the girl from the exploiters, as a guardian angel who has only her best interests at heart. The implication of his death is that Monroe will once again be at the mercy of the exploiters. Audience general knowledge completes the tragedy offscreen.

Almost a companion piece to the Monroe film is THE JAYNE MANSFIELD STORY (1980), a made-for-television biography of the voluptuous, blonde comic actress who was hired by Monroe's home studio, Twentieth Century-Fox, as a "threat" to keep their established blonde star in line.

Loni Anderson and Arnold Schwarzenegger as Jayne Mansfield and Mickey Hargitay in THE JAYNE MANSFIELD STORY (1980). Photo courtesy Capitol Communications.

"Maybe this'll get Monroe off her duff," a Fox executive is heard to exclaim when news of Mansfield's six-year contract is announced. THE JAYNE MANSFIELD STORY's crucial plot linkage, however, is to the bio-films of Jean Harlow. The long-planned and often-announced Harlow story might have provided the leading role which the narrative of THE JAYNE MANSFIELD STORY identifies as Mansfield's most bitterly unrealized goal. Her failure to be cast as Harlow epitomizes the failure of her career. "I did so not want to be a joke any more," she moans, as she faces the harsh reality of her imminent professional decline, after less than two years of being "the most publicized woman in the world."

A rise-and-fall drama told in flashback as ex-husband/muscle man Mickey Hargitay relates his memories of the actress to a reporter, THE JAYNE MANSFIELD STORY sidesteps the issue of whether the woman had sufficient talent to become a serious performer. The exploitational nature of the Hollywood system also is not overtly blamed for destroying her dreams. Mansfield's loss of one promising role after another is more of a series of fated occurrences, although the "using up" of her contract by casting her in a group of what the narration calls "cheap European pictures" does seem to be a fiscally necessary act of malice by studio chiefs who have lost confidence in her value as an attraction. The grisly details of Mansfield's death by decapitation in an automobile accident are spared the audience. The archetypal early demise which claims her is announced in a brief teletype message which appears on the screen prior to the establishment of the flashback framework. The ironic preparatory sequence which precedes her death, in which she telephones to arrange a meeting with the estranged Hargitay in hopes of rebuilding her career with a new cabaret act, is repeated verbatim at the narrative's conclusion, giving the rise-and-fall tragedy an exceptionally circular closure device, solidly encasing the actress' life in a framework of doomed aspirations.

Both THE JAYNE MANSFIELD STORY and the Monroe films continue the latter-day practice of superficially accurate invocation of familiar data, even though the occasional libel-prevention obfuscation can still be spotted upon close inspection. (The mendacious Fox executive who misleads Mansfield about her options is, of course, a fictitious composite with no legal rights.) The possibility exists that the recurrent critical outcry over gross inaccuracies in bio-films may have even been a stimulus for the increasing inclusion of narrative details whose invocation is familiar only to the cognoscenti. What is visible on the screen, despite the disappearance of the massive factual errors of the past, is still a selecting, shaping, and ordering of actual events into a myth-infused dramatic form whose basic patterns appear few and finite. As long as the operant culture's popular segment allows for celebrity worship, the function of the bio-film (or its media-evolved successors) appears assured.

The position in time of these last productions, roughly twenty years after the peak of their heroines' popularity, repeats the nostalgia phenomenon in yet another generation-delayed incarnation. The Monroe films in particular have been accompanied in the ancillary forms of popular culture by what appears to be the largest number of books, magazine articles, newspaper stories, and television news features ever devoted to the sex life and early death of an individual performer, although the Elvis Presley cult, at the time of this writing, threatens to surpass the Monroe phenomenon in terms of sheer material volume.

Entertainer necrophilia of a much more immediate nature underlies the attractional-factor composition of DEATH OF A CENTERFOLD: THE DOROTHY STRATTON STORY, a 1981 TV-movie enactment of one of the all-time fastest examples of a show-business performer's rise and fall. The narrative concerns the brief journey of a pretty Canadian teenager from working as a waitress in a Vancouver ice cream parlor to starring in a big-budgeted, Hollywood science fiction film. The route she takes to her brief moment of stardom is via the centerfold pages of Playboy magazine, where she first appears nude as a "Playmate of the Month," then reappears unclothed, to much fanfare, as 1980's "Playmate of the Year." As a reward, as well as an act of exploitation, for the sizable amount of public attention paid to her pubic hairs and mammary glands, she is cast in the title role of GALAXINA, a futuristic story about a female robot. Because of her total lack of experience or ability at delivering dramatic dialogue, she plays her character as a mute.

Attempting to reassure Stratton about her capabilities as an actress, a sympathetic film producer tells her, "Jane Fonda you ain't, but you got a presence." "You mean my body," she dejectedly replies. In an act of verbal linkage to the tragedy-infused Monroe films, the producer reminds

Stratton, "That was all Marilyn had at first, too." A grimmer cross-reference to Monroe's fate will occur at the film's conclusion.

While the producer, named David Palmer, acts as a confessor and source of refuge for the troubled girl during her stay in the movie capital, the narrative's true father figure (as opposed to the pimp/pornographer role in which his character might have functioned, had there been no danger of a libel suit) is Playboy publisher Hugh Hefner, shown presiding over his California castle of nudie-cuties with the grace and charisma of a wise old philosopher. DEATH OF A CENTERFOLD posits nude modeling for a men's magazine to be a glamorous, positive, and career-enhancing experience, a far cry from the position taken by a wholly fictionalized 1978 TV-movie, KATIE: PORTRAIT OF A CENTERFOLD, which portrayed the practice as a sleazy enterprise that can permanently damage an aspiring actress's career and sense of self-worth.

The villain in the piece is shown to be Stratton's personal manager, Paul Snider, who literally discovers her behind a lunch counter and who coerces her first into a modeling/acting career, then into becoming his wife. An ex-convict whose previous show-business experience came from promoting male strippers, Snider is portrayed as an inept Svengali, abusive, crude, malevolent, and maniacally possessive of the beautiful innocent who dutifully caters to his every whim. During her extended visit to the modern-day sultan's harem, Hefner's Playboy Mansion, the wide-eyed Stratton is amazed to discover a world of sophistication and genteel behavior which stands in marked contrast to the lifestyle of small-time hustles and crassness she had been sharing with Snider. When he senses that she is slipping out of his grasp, that Playboy has elevated her far above his own two-bit measure of importance, Snider's treatment of his wife becomes increasingly cruel and vicious. Stratton leaves him and seeks a divorce, but her evil mentor will not relent, and pesters her with phone calls, threats, and tears. In the narrative's horrifying conclusion, Snider savagely beats the girl, rapes her, then blows her head off with a shotgun. He excuses his demonic behavior with the line, "Sorry baby--I can't lose no more!" He then turns the gun on himself.

The widespread publicity given this actual event supplies an extra-diegetic attraction factor quite apart from the fleeting fame generated by Stratton's drastically abbreviated career. Indeed, at the time of this writing a much more explicit, lavishly-budgeted theatrical feature, tentatively titled STAR 80, is in production to re-tell the essentially public domain story (extensively reported in the news) to a paying audience. In that subsequent incarnation the tale's narrative shape may be significantly different from the linear progression toward doom displayed in DEATH OF A CENTERFOLD, but it will be difficult to escape the convenient mythic meaning we call tragedy, which human understanding (at least in our western culture) usually assigns to such events as an aid to digesting mentally the ghastly waste of a promising young life. In catering to the sometimes undeniably morbid curiosity of the viewing public, the show-business biographical film had never before traced such a precipitously accelerated pattern of dubious rise and terminal fall.

As a parallel development with the above cycle of bio-films about doomed sex goddesses, the Elvis Presley media memorial continues to ferment in the public mind. THIS IS ELVIS (1981), a generic hybrid of "found footage" (newsreels, concert films, home movies, publicity shots, etc.) and re-constructed, actor-performed bridging segments, strives to push past the drama-shaped limits of the bio-film format in search of a means to allow the target audience to relish the revived presence of their godlike hero without the interface of the extended, impersonational dramatic device. Therefore, in THIS IS ELVIS it is Presley who plays Presley in a quasi-narrative which was not fashioned until nearly four years after his death. The functional myth is that of immortality. Perhaps, if the latest (by Albert Goldman) and most heretical of the published biographies of the man is ever set to film at some later date, the motion picture segment of popular culture will experience its own "religious" war.

The debunking of the medium's demigods has already begun, in the bio-filming of actors and actresses. The fact that neither of the deceased subject-heroines of HAYWIRE (1980) or MOMMIE DEAREST (1981) has sustained in the afterlife anything even approaching the fanatically reverent "death cult" which worships the Presley memory has diffused the reaction to the narratives of these motion pictures, however. Generically they qualify not as hostile challenges to the creed of the faithful, but more precisely as two recent variations on the formula of exposing the unhappy private life of a celebrity. The films' mutually significant alteration of archetype is their narratives' overt acknowledgment of revenge.

Both motion pictures take as their well-publicized source material autobiographical books by their subjects' allegedly mistreated and resentful daughters. As was amply explained to the public in pre-publication publicity, the act of writing these books (for their authors) was one of purgation and possible retribution for a hellish childhood. Lacking this information, a viewer of the films' individual narratives may still decipher the process of revenge, however, and not only from the book titles acknowledged in the opening credits. Both films are inherently antithetical to the myth of the rewarded quest for success, as was the entire antecedent cycle of exposé films, but HAYWIRE and MOMMIE DEAREST are much less concerned with the damaging effects of success on the actresses who quest for it. The seekers are not the primary victims; their innocent children suffer even more. The guilt of an inflated ego may in part justify in the audience's mind the self-inflicted agony which supposedly accompanies stardom; hence the colloquial popular culture phrase, "the price of fame," delivered with all its inherent flippancy. In HAYWIRE and MOMMIE DEAREST there are grievously wounded victims who sought none of the evil which befalls them.

HAYWIRE, a made-for-television film, dramatizes the failed raising of their children by actress Margaret Sullavan and producer Leland Hayward. More concerned with their respective careers in films and stage plays of the 1930s and 1940s, the couple neglect the vital task of communicating with their youngsters until the crucial opportunities have passed, leaving the parents' marriage broken, one daughter a drug-induced suicide, the son a mental patient, and the other daughter overflowing with bitterness. MOMMIE DEAREST, a theatrical bio-film of the middle and last years of actress Joan Crawford (primarily from the late 1930s through the early 1960s), centers on her tempestuous relationship with her adopted daughter Christina, whom the performer supposedly treated with sadistic abandon and unreasoning strictness.

The details of the careers of both actresses are tangentially outlined with a minimum of familiarity-invoking detail. Only two of Crawford's many starring films are referred to by title, and Sullavan's career receives similarly imprecise treatment. Such a lack of historical points of

Lee Remick and Jason Robards, Jr. in HAYWIRE (1980).
Photo courtesy Capitol Communications.

reference (in marked contrast to the plethora of authentic titles offered in the latter-day Marilyn Monroe, Greta Garbo, and Jayne Mansfield bio-films) does not indicate a return to the gross fictionalization of detail found in VALENTINO I or HARLOW II, however. Both of the revenge films are close-up views of a career seen from a child's point of view. Only those details and aspects of the parent's career which impinge on the function of parenting are deemed of great importance. The process of invoking the familiar, while not avoided, does suffer a diminution of intensity in this shift of emphasis from the actress herself to her relationship with her child, as perceived and remembered by the young daughter/victim.

Show business, that seductively attractive, soul-devouring monster which haunts the diegesis of the exposé bio-film, is again on the prowl in these revenge dramas. The significant change is that the beast is now visiting its wrath on the next generation. The parental quest for success

The Actors / 269

Faye Dunaway (r.) with Mara Hobel and Jeremy Scott Reinbolt in MOMMIE DEAREST (1981). Photo courtesy Audio Brandon/Films Incorporated.

exacts a fearful toll on the child, now that the role of victim has been handed down from the adult(s). As the career-weary Margaret Sullavan says in HAYWIRE, "Maybe parents shouldn't be an example--they should be a warning to their children." When Joan Crawford adopts daughter Christina, the new mother promises, "I'm going to make a perfect life for you." After years of beatings, psychological torture, and repressive social confinement, the girl begs, "Why did you adopt me? Why can't you treat me like any stranger on the street would?" Then Christina answers her own question: "Because I'm not one of your fans."

Different motivations are given in the narratives for the mistreatment of Sullavan's children and those of Crawford (who also adopts a son), but the fault is easily traced back to show business in both instances. The voice-over narration of the actress portraying young Brooke Hayward attributes her family's agonizing dissolution to her parents' being so busy with their careers that they became "careless with the best of our resources--each other. It was as if we took for granted the fact that like our talents, interests, and riches, there would always be more where we came from-- another chance, another summer, another Maggie, another Leland, another Brooke, or Bridget, or Bill."

The first-person, voice-over narration of HAYWIRE specifies the film's point of view as being that of daughter Brooke, whose act of revenge (an indictment of parental neglect), more elegiac than vicious, is still a feature-length, post facto, and accusational declaration, fused into the mythic form of an entire family's rise-and-fall. MOMMIE DEAREST's series of horrors perpetrated upon a daughter who functions as a "punching bag" (for an actress-mother whose career frustrations make her violent and cruel) has no continuing, sound-track source of attribution for its diegetic allegations. Yet the lone title credit ("based on the book by Christina Crawford") does receive a powerful reinforcement in the narrative's closing scene. At the reading of her late mother's will, ironically following the reassurance of a loyal family servant that the departed actress "really loved" her children, the fact is revealed that Joan Crawford even managed to continue her torture of Christina beyond the grave, by dictating a cruelly worded last testament. "As usual, she has the last word," says Crawford's son, Christopher. Christina's prescient response: "Does she?"

CHAPTER X

THE DANCERS

Bio-films of actors and actresses, perhaps due to the doubly reflexive nature of situations in which an actor might be seen portraying an actor who is acting (in a dramatic production), usually contain fewer and briefer performance segments than do films about singers, composers, or musicians. If the quality of a subject-hero's emoting ability is being tested during a crucial moment in the narrative, then the heightened level of performance in the acting-acting (versus the naturalistic base level of the preceding and subsequent diegetic events) becomes subject to extraordinary viewer scrutiny which may tend to weaken, rather than support, the overall, consensual illusion of the dramatized, fictional narrative. This is not to say that lengthy performance segments are absent from the films analyzed in the preceding chapter; quite the contrary is true in a few cases, such as PRINCE OF PLAYERS or MAN OF A THOUSAND FACES. On the whole, however, actor bio-films have tended to avoid stressing the spectacle of actors acting, in favor of a concentration on the other standard attractional factors. Conversely, bio-films of singers, composers, and musicians, even when their leading players possess no singing or instrument-playing ability, usually offer the attractional factor of extensive performance segments, dubbed by unseen talent.

Bio-films of dancers pose a casting challenge to the film makers which is not so easily met. Except for the possible substitution of more able performers in certain long shots, performance segments in dancer bio-films require the leading players to dance with convincing skill to match the naturalistic level of the surrounding drama. This extra-diegetic constraint may be responsible in part for the relatively small number of such films (eleven) which could be identified, located, and analyzed for this study.

Dan Dailey and Betty Grable in MOTHER WORE TIGHTS (1947). Photo courtesy Wisconsin Center for Film and Theater Research.

During the establishment phase of the show-business bio-film, only one dancer biography appeared, 1939's THE STORY OF VERNON AND IRENE CASTLE. The other ten films from this specialization populate the expansion phase and start with 1947's MOTHER WORE TIGHTS. Several of the films dealt with in this chapter, including this one, present problems of specialization overlap, due to the multitalented nature of their subject-heroes. A necessarily subjective distinction has been made, therefore, as to which of the performing abilities--comedy, singing, acting, etc.--predominates both in the diegesis and in the historic performer's popular culture-based reputation. As portrayed in the film, the vaudeville team of Burt and McKinley fit the classification of a "flash act," known more for their visual appeal (costumes, props, and dance routines) than for their vocalizing ability. While the iconography of MOTHER WORE TIGHTS relates the film most directly to the 1944 bio-film of the historically parallel vaudeville team of Bayes and Norworth, SHINE ON HARVEST MOON (analyzed in the chapter on singers), MOTHER WORE TIGHTS gives much greater visual emphasis to its performers' use of choreography, in keeping with their characters' depicted specialization.

The mythic infrastructure is one of separation and reunion, but its visible enactment takes an unusual turn. Instead of the drama centering on the courtship and marriage of a man-woman vaudeville team, the duo's professional/romantic interaction is tangentially preparatory to their rejection and ultimate re-acceptance by their two daughters, who develop a distaste for the "low" world of show business while studying at an exclusive boarding school. Based on an autobiographical book by one of the girls, the narrative (with visual reinforcement in the title sequence) functions as a "family album" of reminiscences, opening into a flashback structure which follows the team's career up to the point when their daughters overcome their school-induced prejudice. A concluding sequence reveals the gray-haired parents as living comfortably in retirement, happy to have a family album of memories which they can relive in the favorable, nostalgic fashion in which the preceding drama has been presented to the target audience.

Since Burt and McKinley never reached the "big time" of Bayes and Norworth, invocation of the familiar is stressed only in terms of the narrative's period and style, with some appropriate musical numbers of the era included for an air of authenticity. More than anything else, MOTHER

WORE TIGHTS can be viewed as a star vehicle for Betty Grable, in which she was again provided with ample opportunity to display her famous legs in a wide variety of dance routines.

LOOK FOR THE SILVER LINING offered 1949 audiences the story of multi-talented Marilyn Miller, the Broadway star whose career, which peaked in the 1920s, was greatly assisted by her long association with linkage figure Florenz Ziegfeld. Miller's dancing is central to the film's narrative and is the talent for which she was most highly acclaimed, despite the fact that her singing and acting abilities also contributed to her success in such popular Ziegfeld musical comedies as "Sally" and "Sunny," both of which were filmed at the dawn of sound with Miller repeating her original roles. A linkage figure herself, she had previously been portrayed (under a disguised name) in the 1936 Ziegfeld bio-film and is referred to numerous times in other Ziegfeld-linked dramas covered here, including the 1946 TILL THE CLOUDS ROLL BY, in which she is portrayed (in a supporting role) by Judy Garland. Yet Miller was judged by the film makers as ultimately too unfamiliar to the target audience to justify invoking her name in the picture's title. Instead they opted, in composer bio-film fashion, to use the song with which she had become most identified, having introduced it in the Jerome Kern-scored show, "Sally."

LOOK FOR THE SILVER LINING's underlying myth is the ill-fated quest, the race against time which was previously run and lost by George Gershwin in RHAPSODY IN BLUE, but the historical fact of Marilyn Miller's early demise at age thirty-seven is only suggested in the narrative by her closing remark (after she has experienced chest pains) that "when I make my exit, I want it to be at the end of a tap dance." Audience knowledge is again required to complete the tragedy. Miller's quest for success as a dancer is depicted via the same flashback framework employed three years earlier in the film in which her character had previously appeared. In TILL THE CLOUDS ROLL BY Jerome Kern attends the 1946 Broadway revival of his musical "Show Boat" (although the real-life composer died in 1945) and reminisces about his early years. In LOOK FOR THE SILVER LINING not only does Miller fictitiously attend a revival of one of her early successes, she is shown to be repeating her original role. (Miller had been dead for twelve years when "Sally" was finally revived on Broadway in 1948, just a year prior to the release of her bio-film.)

The Dancers / 275

June Haver (center) as Marilyn Miller, with Rosemary DeCamp and Charles Ruggles in LOOK FOR THE SILVER LINING (1949). Photo courtesy Wisconsin Center for Film and Theater Research.

The narrative of LOOK FOR THE SILVER LINING follows Miller from her stage childhood (performing in her family's vaudeville act, the Columbians) through her starring performances in a succession of hit shows of the 1920s. Always an upward quest for greater success, her life is shown as being more dedicated to the theatre than to personal romantic commitments. After her first husband's death in an automobile accident, she tells a concerned producer, "The only man in my life now is Mr. Show Business." She does marry twice in the narrative, but her romantic relationships remain subordinate to her career. Her pursuit of fame causes one character to describe her as a "beautiful racehorse," hurrying from one success to another. Significantly, no mention is made of her most publicized marriage, her tragic pairing with the alcoholic actor Jack Pickford. In keeping with the message of the title song, the narrative is

essentially optimistic in its approach to the uncompleted
tragedy of Marilyn Miller. This optimism is in full view
in the many performance segments which depict her series
of starring stage roles.

    Linkage with THE GREAT ZIEGFELD occurs on several levels, invoking not only show titles and songs, but
Ziegfeld himself (offscreen) and his stage stars, most of
them mentioned in dialogue or on marquees. Ziegfeld headliner Will Rogers (portrayed by his look-alike son) functions
in the narrative as an advisory figure, giving encouragement
to the young Miller, who becomes a headliner herself while
still in her teens. Vaudeville dancing star Jack Donohue
(played by eccentric dancer Ray Bolger, who had appeared
earlier in THE GREAT ZIEGFELD) is depicted as Miller's
mentor, teaching and coaching her in a wide variety of
crowd-pleasing steps and routines. A curious alteration of
show titles occurs (in contrast to the extensive invocation of
authentic material): the name of the series of pre-Ziegfeld
revues in which the teenage dancer actually appeared is
changed from the "Passing Shows" of various years to the
"Profiles of 1914," the "Big Show of 1915," and the "Hi
Spots of 1916." Catering to the understandably vague 1949
audience memories of the era, the term "Passing Show" is
summarily rejected in favor of apocryphal titles whose intimation of period gaiety more explicitly evokes the nostalgia
reflex. That modern-day dancer Bolger was as much an attractional factor as the public's memories of Marilyn Miller
is indicated by the performance segment in which his Jack
Donohue character is allowed to use one of the biggest hit
songs from all of Miller's Broadway shows, "Who," merely
as background for a major Bolger dance number. This is
the sort of historical performance revisionism which infuses
a large number of the films under study and is no different
in basic function from, for instance, the staging of the Kalmar and Ruby song "I Love You So Much" in THREE LITTLE WORDS as if it were written for a far more glamorous
Hollywood musical rather than the spare Wheeler and Woolsey vehicle in which it actually appeared.

    Mid-twentieth-century audience knowledge of dancers
from the nineteenth century was probably even more marginal than accurate public recollections of the period's actors, singers, and composers. Thus GOLDEN GIRL, the
1951 bio-film of Lotta Crabtree, allowed its producers exceptional leeway in constructing a myth-based drama of the
woman's career. Star of a traveling troupe of players who

Mitzi Gaynor and Dennis Day in GOLDEN GIRL (1951).
Photo courtesy Films Incorporated.

specialized in touring the mining camps and gold rush towns of the latter half of the century, Lotta Crabtree eventually settled in San Francisco, where her popularity with the city fathers was so intense that they erected a monument to her memory. GOLDEN GIRL opens with a few narrated travelogue shots of the city, leading to a sustained shot of the Lotta Crabtree Memorial, which bears the date of 1875 and an inscription heralding her as "The Most Popular Actress of Her Time." (The word is used in its archaic sense, not denoting specialization, but rather being indicative of any woman who performs on stage.) This type of legitimation via statuary had occasionally been employed in biographical and historical films outside the realm of show business, but the marble or bronze invocation usually functioned as a closing visual rather than an introduction. This image of a memorial edifice, standing as a bulwark against time and the elements, then gives way through a dissolve and additional voice-over narration to the reconstructed story of her quest for fame, beginning with her teenage aspiration to emulate a notorious courtesan-turned-stage performer, Europe's Lola Montez, who embarked on her first American tour just prior to the outbreak of the War Between the States.

Archetypal parental interdiction against taking up a dancing career fails to dampen Crabtree's ambitions, and when her father suffers financial reverses and the loss of the family home, Lotta suggests putting together a traveling show as a way of keeping the family together and making a good income. Having just witnessed a performance by the real Lola Montez, Lotta exclaims, "She didn't do a thing I couldn't do. There's no trick to being an actress." Faced with the alternative of penury, her parents agree, although her mother continues to speak out against the evils of the stage and becomes increasingly horrified as her daughter sheds one piece of costume after another during the little troupe's travels from town to town. Each time the girl's outfit becomes briefer, the woman-hungry prospectors, cowhands, and frontiersmen in the audience applaud all the louder and toss more coins on the stage. Even though she eventually ceases shedding garments at the point of costume brevity allowable by the censorship standards in force at the time of the film's release (1951), the narrative's equation of popular success with the selling of exposed sexual attractiveness is most definite. The diegesis may be internally identified as nearly a century away from the extra-diegetic present, but a key merchandising point of show business is shown to transcend time.

Lotta Crabtree's quest for success is overlaid with the myth of separation and reunion, as she begins a romantic relationship with a man she believes to be a professional gambler, only to learn to her dismay that he is actually a Confederate spy, out to steal the shipment of Union gold which her caravan of wagons is secretly carrying to a Yankee destination. Although she later believes him to have been killed in the war, he returns for an emotional reunion with her on the night of her greatest triumph, when she is archetypally asked to sing and dance at New York City's prestigious Niblo Gardens. Linkage occurs when her hard-won fame leads as well to a party invitation from P. T. Barnum and Jenny Lind.

Just as Marilyn Miller was depicted as a dancing goddess, too young and out-of-reach for Jack Donohue, the man who taught her all he knew about show business, so is Lotta Crabtree given the benefit of considerable professional assistance from a man who pines away for her but cannot have her--western impresario Mart Taylor, who first meets the girl while he is posing for hire as a potential suicide, about to "do himself in" publicly because of a fatal fascination for the woman who paid him to put on such an act, Lola Montez. As the narrative of GOLDEN GIRL points out, skillful manipulation of public perceptions (the classic publicity stunt) is part of a time-honored tradition in entertainment history.

Another 1951 release, LITTLE EGYPT, opted to tell the story of a dancer whose entire (and brief) career barely exceeded the definitional limits of a publicity stunt. Her moment in the limelight, during the run of the 1893 Chicago World's Fair (a linkage factor in itself with the professional origins of THE GREAT ZIEGFELD), is told in a dramatic structure which is more anecdotal than mythic, although the concluding dialogue implies that a lasting image of popular culture has been born, quite separate from the inisignificant, fake Egyptian dancer whose real name was quickly forgotten.

The narrative centers on the shady promotions of a confidence man named Nick Cravat, who, while traveling in Cairo, attempting to bilk some wealthy Chicagoans by means of a phony scheme to reclaim Egypt's Nile Delta, becomes the victim of a blackmail plot by a dancer who wants to be introduced to the wealthy Americans as a genuine "princess of the blood." Her "authentic religious dancing" so impresses the well-connected Chicagoans that she is hired to perform

280 / Star Myths

Rhonda Fleming and Mark Stevens (r.) in LITTLE EGYPT
(1951). Photo courtesy Wisconsin Center for Film and
Theater Research.

at the "Streets of Cairo" exhibit (sponsored by a cigarette
company whose logo is a familiar Egyptian scene). Attracted to Cravat, but jealous over his attentions to a society girl, the dancer seeks revenge for his inattention by
changing the demure dance routine into a much more exposed, erotic display which causes a scandal. The uproar,
complete with a police raid for alleged indecency and a well-publicized Cook County Court trial, generates a storm of
publicity and the involvement of the prominent women's
rights advocates of the day, who argue that the dancer was
treated unjustly because of her sex. Following the girl's
acquittal and despite the fact that she had admitted to being
born in New Jersey, she returns to the fair to continue her
dancing for the hordes who subsequently flock to see her.
Credited with saving the exposition from financial ruin by
boosting ticket sales, "Little Egypt," as the press calls her,
has earned her place in history. Marveling at the power of
effective publicity, Cravat remarks to an associate, "They've
forgotten that she's [supposed to be] a princess, but they'll

remember Little Egypt for a long, long time." Although the dialogue is less explicit in regards to her musical accompaniment, the sound track suggests that the familiar "Snake Dance" may have been born into popular culture at this time also.

While the narratives of GOLDEN GIRL and LITTLE EGYPT both carried overtones of the relationship between commercialized exposure of the female body and the attractional powers of show business, the theme became explicit in a film released the very next year. MILLION DOLLAR MERMAID (1952) depicts the career of swimmer Annette Kellerman, whose public appearances in the early years of the Twentieth Century often combined her expertise in the water with professional dancing and showmanship. Kellerman's "water ballets" may never have been as lavish and extensive as those constructed for her character by MGM in this obvious star vehicle for latter-day swimming celebrity Esther Williams, but the reality of Kellerman's show-business career provided a point of departure for a dramatic plot infused with the reliable myth of separation and reunion.

Just as GOLDEN GIRL began with a shot of a time-honored monument to its heroine and LITTLE EGYPT began with a view of the everlasting city of Cairo, so MILLION DOLLAR MERMAID opens with a symbol of the transcendence of time, although the point is less certain since the stately pleasure palace called the New York Hippodrome had already been demolished by the time of the film's production. "Gone, but not forgotten," intones the voice-over narrator, allowing for the realities of urban renewal, but he continues by invoking the familiar names of famous entertainers who have performed there: "Houdini ... Pavlova ... Marceline the Clown." The story about to unfold is to be of one of the Hippodrome's famous stars of the past.

The narrative then depicts young Kellerman in the year 1900, when as the crippled child of a music professor in Sydney, Australia, she manages to shed her leg braces after gaining strength and coordination through swimming. No longer will she have to stand on the sidelines and watch her little friends take dancing lessons. Later, as the teenage swimming champion of New South Wales, she learns she must move with her family to London, where her father hopes to find better employment. On the boat to England she meets the archetypal promoter so prevalent in bio-films, a young man who at first offers to manage only one aspect

Esther Williams in MILLION DOLLAR MERMAID (1952). Photo courtesy Wisconsin Center for Film and Theater Research.

of her life (professional or personal) and soon becomes the master of both. Despite Kellerman's hopes of a career as a ballerina, the promoter, Jimmy Sullivan, sees her as a marketable oddity and devises ways to use her swimming ability to attract attention to his schemes. Although Sullivan is not portrayed as being inherently cruel (as later biofilm promoters would sometimes be), the motif of the exploited female performer does become apparent.

The scandal Kellerman creates by attempting to swim the Thames River with her bare legs exposed (in an era when respectable women wore much more extensive bathing costumes) dwarfs the importance of the boxing kangaroo she was supposed to be promoting. The plans she and Sullivan hatch to stage a water ballet at New York's Hippodrome come to naught until she repeats the bare-legged swimming stunt at Boston's Revere Beach. The resulting public indecency trial, echoing the one in LITTLE EGYPT, brings her to national prominence and makes her a marketable attraction, amid more of the same rhetoric about women's rights. In a self-justificatory sense, the narratives of these films, GOLDEN GIRL included, postulate the commercial exposure of women performers' bodies to be a liberating experience. The fact that the argument is made in so reflexive a vehicle as the show-business biographical film only serves to underscore the overall voyeuristic function of the medium often argued by contemporary feminist-informed film theoreticians. Yet the collapse of censorship which lay ahead of these pictures would eventually press the case for the "liberation of exposure" into far more explicit challenges of cultural taboos without the framing device of courtroom-based dramatic dialogue. What happens in GOLDEN GIRL, MILLION DOLLAR MERMAID, and LITTLE EGYPT is actually not revolutionary at all, but rather a time-distanced negation of assumed audience prejudices which had already been conquered in the evolution of popular culture. This is but another instance of the pleasure-through-shared-hindsight phenomenon identified earlier.

Dubbed by the press as "the one-piece bathing suit girl," Kellerman achieves fame and success with a series of Hippodrome water ballets and a new career turn--starring in motion pictures under the supervision of a director who sports the familiar composite (Griffith/DeMille, etc.) trappings previously identified in HOLLYWOOD CAVALCADE. The separation-and-reunion machinery begins to turn as Sullivan's fortunes plummet and his wounded ego keeps him

away from his beloved Annette. In a dramatic conclusion
which closely relates to the climax of THE PERILS OF
PAULINE, Kellerman is crippled with a spine injury sustained during the bursting of a film studio water tank, and
Sullivan rushes to be at her bedside. With physicians offering the hope of an eventual recovery, the narrative closes
on a note of reunion.

The reflexive process inherent in filming show-business biographies, given its first wholly overt presentation in
1949's JOLSON SINGS AGAIN as a career culmination ritual,
functions as the actual framing structure of a 1953 film
called THE I DON'T CARE GIRL. Although its subject-heroine, Eva Tanguay, became a dancing (and singing) star
for Ziegfeld more than a decade before Marilyn Miller,
their bio-films share a common iconography and flashback
structure. Where THE I DON'T CARE GIRL departs from
all previous practice is in its depiction of the bio-filming
process not as tangential, but as central to the unfolding
narrative.

Singer-comedian George Jessel, a Broadway headliner
from the 1910s and 1920s, switched during the 1940s to the
role of a staff motion-picture producer at Twentieth Century-Fox studios, where he specialized in show business biographies and similar nostalgia-tinged fare (I WONDER WHO'S
KISSING HER NOW, OH, YOU BEAUTIFUL DOLL, TONIGHT
WE SING, etc.). As the producer of THE I DON'T CARE
GIRL, he also took a part in the production as an actor,
playing himself. The premise of the narrative's framing
flashback is that Jessel has become dissatisfied with the
conventional show-business bio-films he and others have
been manufacturing. His latest project, a biography of Eva
Tanguay, distresses him to the point that he suddenly calls
a halt to the filming and complains, "I don't want the story
of a madcap ... I want the story of the real girl!" While
the diegetic Jessel professes a desire to avoid repeating the
archetypal motifs, themes, and plots which he had helped establish and perpetuate, what Jessel himself actually delivers
to the audience is but another variation on the separation-and-reunion myth surrounding a central character who conforms to popular culture's interpretation of the term "madcap"--an excitable, amusing, often irrational adherent of
benign exhibitionism and guileless self-indulgence.

The film's genuine innovation for its generic category
is its unorthodox, CITIZEN KANE-like structure. Jessel

assigns his screenwriters to discover the "truth" about Eva Tanguay by tracking down and interviewing some of the oldtime vaudevillians who actually worked with her in the early years of the century. When they are located, the narrative displays in flashback their sometimes contradictory stories of her rise to fame. The drama centers on Tanguay's alleged love affair with a songwriter-singer, a relationship broken by the familiar intervention of the First World War. Just as Jessel is expressing his belief that "We can't finish a musical comedy picture with the boy and girl apart" (thus indicating Jessel's desire for an archetypal act of reunionclosure), a stranger breaks into the production office and announces that he is the suitor in question, as well as the man with the "real" story of Tanguay. Only the persistence of the studio guard has prevented this intruder, so he says, from entering Jessel's office weeks earlier, when news of the film's production was first announced. The old-timer finishes the story by means of his own flashback, in which he is reunited with Tanguay after the war in a "blaze of glory," with the two of them performing on stage together. At the conclusion of their number, a backstage shot reveals Jessel himself, neither made up to appear younger nor outfitted in an appropriate period costume. Asked by the vaudevillians in the wings, "What are you doing here?" Jessel replies enigmatically, "I just wanted to see how it finished."

Despite its mythic standardization (with a title taken from the popular tune which became closely identified with Tanguay's onstage antics), THE I DON'T CARE GIRL deviated far enough from catering to audience expectations that its internal contradictions of narrative linearity and diegetic integrity may have alienated preview audiences. Whatever the reason, the studio deemed the film of marginal commercial value and gave it only a limited release, without benefit of advance promotion or press previews. Jessel never produced another film, but the failure of THE I DON'T CARE GIRL may not have been the only reason. The vaudeville era, which he had specialized in invoking, was receding further into the background of popular memory as younger people entered the target audience and older ones passed away, or at least became content to stay at home and enjoy the increasing variety of programming on television. The era of the cynical exposé bio-film was beginning, and the supportive, optimistic nostalgia items Jessel had been producing were fading from fashion.

With only six biographies of dancers having been

released during the show-business bio-film's development
phase, the brief cycle ended. The films had not been greatly different in execution from the singer and composer biographies of the time, except for the specialization of the performance segments. Linked as they were to the vaudeville
era, these dancer films dealt with the skill of dancing as if
it were merely a given in each subject-heroine's array of
talents and a basic component of the onstage life. When another dancer film appeared ten years later, the type of dancing it featured was presented more as a fearsome skill which
could be mastered only through intense mental resolve to
master first one's own inhibitions.

Although GYPSY (1963) does begin by reviving the bio-
film's depiction of the lost world of vaudeville, it shifts midway to a setting less familiar to the motion picture screen
(partly because of censorship), the burlesque houses of the
Depression years. Yet the style of dancing associated with
such locations relates directly to the bodily exposure theme
of some of the previous dancer bio-films. In GYPSY the art
of striptease dancing puts in the foreground the voyeuristic
function of commercial entertainment as explicitly as was
possible under the censorship of the early 1960s. At the
same time the basically optimistic tone of the drama (the
hit song was "Everything's Coming Up Roses") shapes the
heroine's choice to become a stripper as a sensible, re-
warding decision. The operant myth is that of birth--the
emergence of a new striptease dancing star who has taken
the stage name of Gypsy Rose Lee.

Prior to Louise Hovick's transformation into a top-
billed burlesque performer, the narrative displays the quest
of her archetypal stage mother for vicarious success through
her offspring. Beginning with a family vaudeville act in
which the younger daughter, "Baby June," is the star, "Mama Rose" Hovick expends an enormous amount of time and
energy to win her child top billing, good notices, and waves
of thunderous applause. When her plans for June are de-
railed by the girl's marriage, the mother's attentions are
then focused on her "second-banana" daughter. Although it
becomes obvious that Louise will never repeat her sister's
success in dying vaudeville, fame beckons in burlesque, the
"low" world which is despised by true vaudevillians in the
same manner as popular music was held in disrepute by
"serious" musicians and composers in the bio-films of those
professions. The "hell hole" of burlesque in which the Ho-
vicks seek shelter from the economic storm is ultimately

Natalie Wood in GYPSY (1963). Photo courtesy Wisconsin Center for Film and Theater Research.

redeemed by a veneer of glamour, with the heroine protected from corruption by her new star status of unattainability and elegance.

GYPSY, although its considerable box-office success inaugurated no generic cycle (it was merely one of a series of popular stage musicals filmed at a time when original screen musicals had become too financially risky), the film did continue the linkage phenomenon with a great deal of invocational name-dropping, including Fanny Brice, Irene Castle, Florenz Ziegfeld, the New York Hippodrome (and its destruction). Congruent invocation occurs as well, with comedian Jack Benny portraying himself at a time in his own career when he was just another vaudeville performer, bound for fame but still an unknown comic.

The fact that GYPSY was based on a stage musical also accounted for its numerous songs often being dramatically integrated with dialogue, rather than their being inserted as performance segments. Throughout its evolution the showbusiness biographical film had rarely experienced this type of stylization, but as the Broadway musical began to adopt the bio-film's topical premise on an increasing number of occasions, the cross-fertilization was to become more evident in later years.

The vaudeville and musical comedy dancers of the past now belong to an era which is currently out of nostalgic fashion. Only three more dancer bio-films have been released to date, and their subject-heroes have each been from the world of "high-brow" culture. This is not to say that Nijinsky and Isadora Duncan were totally removed from performing for paying crowds, suffering the slings and arrows of critics, or dealing with the archetypal psychological pressures of stardom. They too qualify as show-business figures in the same respect as the operatic vocalists portrayed in singer bio-films.*

The two Isadora Duncan films, 1966's THE BIGGEST DANCER IN THE WORLD and 1969's THE LOVES OF ISADORA, were both British imports which received wide dis-

---

*As explained earlier, classical music composers, dependent on royal subsidies and frequently employed in court, academic, or ecclesiastical positions, fall outside the scope of this analysis.

tribution in America, the former on PBS television and the latter as a highly-promoted theatrical release by Universal. Their principal showings in this country were in reverse order to their actual production, but the release dates noted here correspond to when they were completed in England.

BIGGEST DANCER employs the rise-and-fall myth in a tragic mode, depicting Duncan's career as founded on hopes of greatness which were first encouraged, then dashed by a fickle public made up of the so-called intelligentsia. The film's continuing, almost clinical voice-over narration emphasizes Duncan's role as a tragic figure, archetypally possessed of a vision of dance as the liberating spirit of art. Her ultimate rejection by both capitalist and communist audiences (when she tours first Russia and then America with a series of dance concerts) causes her to sustain psychic wounds from which she never recovers. The film portrays Duncan as a gifted young woman who seeks to revive the dance forms of ancient Greece but whose passionate rebellion against the bourgeois values of her native United States drives her to alienate the same audience she had hoped to win over with her forceful, personalized interpretations. After she has been unable to find or continuously please any large group of people, her descent into the rejection-alcoholism syndrome pauses for an aborted comeback, thus adding to the tragic sense of lost opportunity. Duncan's accidental strangulation by a scarf, blown by the wind and tangled in the spokes of a touring car wheel, is set to the tune of the invocationally familiar "Bye Bye Blackbird," a popular tune from the year of her death (1927) and one which serves as an anthem of the period and its values, so at odds with the aesthetic standards championed by the failed dancer.

The various romantic liaisons of Duncan are related cursorily and dispassionately by the narration, whose careful wording is counterpointed by the flamboyant visual style which later became the trademark of the film's director, Ken Russell. This stands in marked contrast to the detailed examination of Duncan's love life provided in the more conventionally shot LOVES OF ISADORA, which softens the blow of her death by using it as an opening flashback point of departure and by emphasizing in the dialogue the "fated" nature of existence, of the appropriateness of dying "at one's own time." Mary Desti, cosmetics executive, mother of comedy specialist Preston Sturges, and the woman who became Duncan's constant companion in her later years, plays a far more important role in LOVES OF ISADORA than in BIGGEST

DANCER. The recurrent flashback framework which ties together the sequences of LOVES consists of shots of Duncan dictating her autobiography (one of the screenplay's sources), but Desti's own book about Duncan, The Untold Story, receives no screen credit.

A key scene in both films which relates to the dancer film cycle of fifteen years earlier is the notorious performance which results in Duncan's deportation by American authorities. After working herself into a frenzy with a routine in which she intends to portray the fury of the Russian workers as they recently freed themselves from their capitalist chains, Duncan rips off the top section of her customary and flowing Greek robe, baring her breasts to the shocked and enraged audience. This act of self-exposure continues the cinematic equation of dancing with the revealing of the female body beyond the historical period's standards of prudery. Duncan bills her performance as "The Dance of Liberation," but unlike the comic optimism of earlier films, the mode has turned tragic; she pays for her social crime. Duncan's call to awaken the primal anarchism supposedly repressed by American society is not heeded, but rebuked. In LOVES OF ISADORA the rage of the mob which repeatedly gathers outside the halls in which she appears is personified in a fire-and-brimstone preacher called "Gospel Billy," who delivers an impromptu sermon against the wickedness which he and his followers believe she represents. Just as the early stage revues in which Marilyn Miller appeared had their odd-but-authentic titles changed to fictional ones which would be less likely to confound or distract the modern viewer, so does the narrative of LOVES OF ISADORA re-name the historical evangelist Billy Sunday with a label less confusing and instantly identifiable to viewers who do not share prior knowledge of the man.

With its title an appropriate suggestion of its dramatic emphasis, LOVES OF ISADORA's intricate recounting of Duncan's marriages and romances consumes considerably more screen time than BIGGEST DANCER, although basically the same lovers and husbands are mentioned in both, including the invocationally familiar sewing-maching tycoon, Paris Singer. The accidental drowning of her two children figures in both narratives, as does her own bizarre death, preceded again in LOVES OF ISADORA by a gramophone rendition of "Bye Bye Blackbird," as it was in BIGGEST DANCER.

The two Duncan films, with their overlapping portraits

of a highly unconventional artist who brazenly defies the morals of her day and tours the world's capitals in the glaring spotlight of intensive publicity, form a generically related counterpart to the two Sarah Bernhardt biographies. Where the contrast with the Duncan films is the sharpest is in the Bernhardt films' identification of the actress as a victor and a survivor, savoring the spotlight into old age (in SARAH) and able to withstand all attacks on her private life by virtue of her buying the support and approval of the crowd with her performing abilities. Bernhardt excels in giving the people a kind of entertainment which they can eagerly accept. Duncan, on the other hand, breaks with convention both on- and offstage, violating not only the public's sense of decency, but also the period's aesthetic standards of balletic dancing. The spoken narration of BIGGEST DANCER partially attributes her failure to a lack of theatrical training, but a line of dialogue given her in LOVES OF ISADORA indicates that the fault lies with the audience, not the artist. "We were wild once," she cries to a crowd of concert-goers who are walking out on her, warning that the loss of America's pioneer spirit has led to a climate of conservative prudery. "Don't let them tame you," she exclaims, but by then the auditorium is empty.

What attractional factors can be identified in the Duncan films appear to center around the sensational elements of the story, rather than on the lasting show-business reputation of the subject-heroine. Until Universal's massive pre-release publicity campaign for the theatrical film, it was likely that few people, other than adherents of modern dance (who say they owe her an artistic debt) and those elderly enough to recall Duncan's original notoriety, knew who she was. Duncan was to America of the 1960s little more than one of the oddities so cherished by cultural historians, a naïve American who desperately tried to challenge our bourgeois standards of art. The process of bio-filming her rise and fall offered to the target audience a cultural heroine to be re-evaluated during a time when the values she opposed were well on their way to crumbling. Thus Isadora Duncan can be viewed as the direct generic successor to Lotta Crabtree, Annette Kellerman, "Little Egypt," and Gypsy Rose Lee.

While the popular dance culture of recent years has offered the audience only overtly fictional films such as SATURDAY NIGHT FEVER, ALL THAT JAZZ, and

FAME,* the only other dancer biography to date again chose to reach across the century and revive interest in a celebrity performer from an era beyond the generation-bound borders of nostalgia. NIJINSKY (1979) also employed rise-and-fall in the tragic mode, keyed to a flashback structure which opens in an insane asylum where the subject-hero spends his days staring blankly into space, snug in his straitjacket. The narrative then depicts, essentially, what drove him there. The tragedy of the historical Nijinsky, according to the film which bears his name, was that he violated the homely maxim vainly quoted to him in the narrative by his mentor/lover, Ballet Russe master Serge Diaghilev: "We are what we are --and we should never forget it." Once he had been transformed into a world-famous ballet star by Diaghilev, Nijinsky tried to jettison his homosexual ties to the man who made success possible, according to the story, and in a foolish attempt to prove his independence, married a woman more in love with his fame than with him. The falsity of his denying his sexual identity then drove him mad and wrecked both his career and his life.

The cultural taboo which previously had restricted bio-films from acknowledging onscreen the homosexuality of various show-business celebrities ceases to function from the very first flashback sequence of NIJINSKY, a sequence which includes a bedroom scene with kissing between master and pupil. The danger of losing audience sympathy, always a pitfall to be avoided in the process of commercial bio-filming, is not overlooked even at this late date, however. Young Nijinsky and middle-aged Diaghilev are portrayed by attractive, conservatively mannered actors. Their lack of overtly effeminate mannerisms is bluntly counterpointed with the behavior of some of the drama's "swishier" characters.

Diaghilev's artistic and personal domination of Nijinsky is first threatened by the latter's desire to choreograph a production by himself. Diaghilev taunts Nijinsky with the threat of replacing him in a prize part with a more compliant youth, and this stokes the fires of independence in the young dancer, with ultimately disastrous results. Nijinsky's break with his mentor, signified by his ill-advised marriage

---

*The recent CAN'T STOP THE MUSIC is hardly a career-retrospective biography, but rather a fact-fiction exploitation of instant fame along the lines established by ROCK AROUND THE CLOCK and A HARD DAY'S NIGHT.

The Dancers / 293

to a fanatical admirer who has gone to the excruciating length of training to become a ballerina just to be near her idol, brings on the tragic conclusion. The rejected ballet master fires his ex-protégé from the company and Nijinsky's mind snaps. Even his wife's pleas that Diaghilev take the dancer back as both lover and employee fail to work a reconciliation. Suffering a form of religious mania, Nijinsky is confined to a mental institution. Ending titles reveal that following his final performance in 1917, the deranged dancer spent the next thirty-three years of his life in an asylum. His last words in the narrative, taken from his diary: "I am a clown of God."

Filled with elaborate performance segments from famous ballets, attractional factors in themselves, NIJINSKY also offered the public the star performance of a talented dancer from the contemporary world of ballet, George de la Pena. Yet these "high-culture" attributes, combined with a taboo-breaking screenplay, did little to attract an audience for this expensively mounted production. This is not to say that it stands as a generic oddity, however. Within its diegetic bounds the film easily yields to an analysis which reveals it to be functioning directly in the bio-film tradition and in some ways (starring a real-life ballet dancer, centering a plot on a cross-preferential, disastrous marriage) directly relating to VALENTINO II, which starred dancer Rudolph Nureyev and which contains a sequence depicting the actor's copying Nijinsky's physical appearance in "Afternoon of a Faun." Invocation of the familiar and the illusion of historical accuracy abound in NIJINSKY, with dates and places of each ballet production appearing as superimposed titles, other celebrities from the era freely mentioned, and even a theme-establishing admonishment delivered by composer Igor Stravinsky, who proclaims, "Loving someone doesn't automatically turn them into something they're not."

CHAPTER XI

THE COMEDIANS

As the popular culture representative of the age-old figure of the court jester, the professional comedian came relatively late to the show-business biographical film. Even fictional representations of him were few, except in subsidiary roles, until more than thirty years of entertainer biofilming had passed. The turn-of-the-century comedy team of Weber and Fields, as noted previously, reappeared (both congruently and via impersonation) as invocational figures in some of the earliest biographies set in the vaudeville era. The comedian as a central character in overtly fictional drama can be seen in such films as LADY OF BURLESQUE (1943) and ALWAYS LEAVE 'EM LAUGHING (1949).

This last film is one of those marginal cases which assume a biographical construct without the guise of authenticity with which to cover a myth-infused plot and dramatic fictionalization. Filmed at the time when comedian Milton Berle was just beginning to enjoy a new wave of popularity as the star of a phenomenally popular program shown weekly on the fledgling medium of commercial television, ALWAYS LEAVE 'EM LAUGHING told a fictionalized story of his rise to video prominence. However, in the style of many late silent and early sound pictures which sought to capitalize on the popularity of rising radio and stage performers of the period, all the names in the story were fictitious. Berle portrayed comedian Kip Cooper, who, after years of mediocre success on stage, becomes a huge success as a television star. In keeping with the illusion of a parallel fiction, Cooper's vaudeville-style variety show is sponsored by Pelican Cigarettes (rather than Berle's sponsor, whose logo was a penguin). Another comedian, suffering from inexperience and lack of success, visits backstage with Cooper's producer. During a live telecast, which can be seen through the control-room window, the studio visitor asks about the chances for his own success as a TV star. The producer pontificates about how difficult it is to "become good" at comedy and then regales the novice with the Cooper success story, which follows in flashback and bears only a few passing points of resemblance to the historical record of Berle's own career. ALWAYS LEAVE 'EM LAUGHING approached the biographical form with the story of a comedian, but it made no overt claims on the audience's ever-assumed desire for personal knowledge of celebrity entertainers. The claims were all covertly indirect, by means of a narrative of fame quest and ego deflation constructed to be only superficially similar to actual persons, places, and events. Three years later, THE STORY OF WILL ROGERS (1952) made the claims overt and brought the profession of comedian into the generic fold, stamping the specialization as acceptable for bio-filming.

Throughout the history of comedy a paradoxical question has plagued authors who chose to include clowns and jesters among their dramatis personae: Is the funny man equally amusing when he is not performing? Does his private life echo his humorous approach to problems, or is he the saddest of persons when he is offstage, one who uses laughter as a mask for the agony of his soul? The archetype of the sad clown, so memorably embodied in "I, Pagliacci," has continued through generations of fiction, and more recently even has the backing of some schools of psychoanalysis. Yet the target audience for commercial motion pictures, particularly show-business bio-films, was assumed (prior to the exposé era) to be desirous of "life stories" which would be an extension of the pleasure-giving process primarily associated with the specific celebrity being impersonationally showcased.

THE STORY OF WILL ROGERS reached the screen just before the arrival of the cynical exposés, and it fully reflects the optimistic, supportive values of the earlier bio-film tradition. Since Rogers' nation-shocking death in a plane crash at age fifty-five did not fit with the archetype of a tragic artist felled by fate while still in his youth, the mythic imagery of a losing race with time was deemed inappropriate to his story. Rogers' career, however, was at its peak when he died in 1935, thus excluding the implementation of a rise-and-fall structure. Since each of his accomplishments supposedly resulted less from his own drive to succeed than from others urging him to master new

Eddie Cantor and Will Rogers, Jr. in THE STORY OF WILL ROGERS (1952). Photo courtesy Wisconsin Center for Film and Theater Research.

challenges, emphasizing the quest myth was ruled out as
well. Heavy fictionalization might have allowed for one of
these approaches, but the source material chosen was his
wife's memoirs, and the production was undertaken with the
full cooperation of the Rogers family. What emerged was a
season-keyed narrative, embodying the myth of a full life
lived to the utmost. Just prior to his fatal flight with aviator friend Wylie Post (to check on Alaskan defense installations at government request), a dialogue passage has Rogers commenting on his being blessed with "a wonderful life,
wife, and family." "I've been an awfully lucky boy," he
tells his wife, adding presciently, "I've always wanted to
quit while I'm ahead."

The spring of Rogers' life is spent as a cowhand and
a drifter. Overawed by his father's success as "the senator
from the Indian Nation," (Will is part Oklahoma Cherokee),
the young man avoids setting down roots or taking up responsibilities. Archetypal summer arrives when he courts (in a
shy, backward fashion) and marries his wife Betty, who
agrees to travel with him in his new, still drifting, vocation
--riding and roping in the "wild west shows" which entertained America at the turn of the century. Autumn finds
Rogers at last taking his career more seriously, when a
temporary substitution for a vaudeville performer reveals
the cowboy to have a natural gift for ad-lib humor as well
as rope tricks. Agents ply him with offers to perform as
a philosopher-comic, and soon Ziegfeld is starring him in
the Follies of 1916 and many subsequent shows. Invocation
of the familiar functions at a very high level in these sequences, with Rogers' famous Follies contemporaries costarring on marquees and he himself being invited to the
White House, where Woodrow Wilson commends him for his
daring political humor and urges him to take up serious
writing as a "voice of the people," so that he may assume
his "rightful place in the community." Rogers demurs at
first, but newspaper and radio executives eventually convince
him to become a columnist and commentator in his spare
time. Winter sets in after Rogers moves to Hollywood at
the insistence of eager movie producers who find his folksy
humor in a long string of starring pictures to be pure gold
at the box-office. The season's chill is the terror of economic calamity which blows across the nation out of Wall
Street in 1929. With discontent seething among the nation's
unemployed and dispossessed, Rogers is urged by the rich
and powerful (he is invocationally seen conferring, for example, with Ford and Rockefeller) to beat down the threat

of revolution by using his columns and broadcasts to instill public confidence in the basic soundness of America. "Don't sell this country short," is his battle cry. The dark spectre passes, according to the narrative, partly because the wit and warmth of Will Rogers were able to teach people to "laugh at themselves again." Rogers' aging father, never impressed with his boy's success on stage or in film, finally appears pleased when the state of Oklahoma nominates the beloved comedian as its "favorite son" candidate for the U.S. Presidency.

With Will Rogers' life having run through the fullness of the archetypal seasons, there remains only his physical exit from the world's stage. The shared knowledge of the target audience makes detailing the passing of this nostalgia figure, who perhaps ranked closer to sainthood than any other entertainer in the popular culture of his day, unnecessary. His airplane flies off into a darkening sky, storm clouds gather, and then the sun breaks through to the sound of musical rejoicing. The final shot grants Rogers one of the archetypal, earthly measures of immortality--a noble statue in his likeness, towering over a plaque bearing his famous motto: "I never met a man I didn't like."

The portrayal of Will Rogers by his lookalike and soundalike son, Will Jr., as close to congruence as possible without the presence of the departed star, was quite different in effect from what transpired in the making of the next comedian bio-film, THE EDDIE CANTOR STORY (1954). Although it forms something of a companion piece to the Rogers film, being produced on the same studio lot just a year after the previous picture and sharing numerous instances of linkage, the Cantor film offered viewers a leading role performed less as an impersonation than as a caricatured impression. Actor Keefe Brasselle, much taller than the diminutive Cantor and possessing a facial structure with little resemblance to the singer-comedian, was nevertheless meticulously made up at all times to resemble Cantor's stage makeup, thereby undermining the surrounding diegetic illusion of naturalism in each of the offstage sequences. Repeating the practice of the singer bio-films of the time, the film makers did succeed in obtaining near-congruent musical numbers, since the real-life performer dubbed each of them for Brasselle and coached him in the unique Cantor mannerisms and dance steps.

The omnipresent question of whether a comedian's private life is happy or sad, whether he is amusing or

The Comedians / 299

Keefe Brasselle as Eddie Cantor and Jackie Barnett as Jimmy Durante in THE EDDIE CANTOR STORY (1954). Photo courtesy Wisconsin Center for Film and Theater Research.

morose offstage, was answered in the double affirmative by
THE STORY OF WILL ROGERS, where the entertainer's
gentle humor was shown to warm all of those with whom he
came in contact. THE EDDIE CANTOR STORY, despite its
positive initial portrayal of the hero as a youngster (by a
child actor) and as a young man embarking upon marriage
and a new career as a Ziegfeld star, also reveals the dark
side of a comic's success. "Working to stay on top is
harder than getting there," he says to his exasperated wife,
who complains that he is seriously neglecting his growing
family by devoting all of his time to the theatre. A concerned physician friend, witnessing the destruction of the
Cantor marriage and the performer's maniacal self-absorption
in his work, finally dresses him down with a Freud-style
lecture: "You need applause like other men need air. You
got appreciation from other kids for your clowning around,
in order to make up for the love you never got from a mom
and dad. [Now] something's got to give."

Although Cantor survives the Wall Street crash (he
had invested heavily) by writing a best-selling humor book
and by beginning a second career as a radio comic, he is
unable to withstand the pressure of devoting his every waking moment to the business of making people laugh. He
suffers a heart attack, becomes bitter at the possibility of
a forced early retirement, and broods about his inability to
live up to his popular image as America's "apostle of pep."

The mythic infrastructure imposed upon Cantor's life
is clearly one of rise-and-fall, with his comedown triggered
by an inflated ego. His renaissance takes place when he
reluctantly agrees to appear at a benefit show for the charity-supported summer camp which years earlier had offered him
a childhood escape from a sweltering summer in Manhattan's
Lower East Side ghetto. The new sense of joy he experiences
in performing for the benefit of others works wonders. His
doctor observes, "He's alive again ... a man who's forgotten
all about himself." The "new" Cantor resolves to become a
dedicated family man and atone for his years of neglect.
From that point on he restricts his performing to charity
functions, and a montage of his work for such groups as the
Red Cross, the Veterans' Hospitals, and the March of Dimes
dissolves into a Thanksgiving holiday scene, with President
Roosevelt giving a seasonal speech on the radio and reading
a note of holiday greetings from his "friend," Eddie Cantor.

Despite the film's intense diegetic linkage and invocation of the familiar, including Cantor's childhood career as a member of Gus Edwards' Singing Newsboys, his friendships with George Jessel and Jimmy Durante, his star-studded years in the Ziegfeld Follies (with Will Rogers, Jr. portraying Will Sr. again) and his radio and stage renditions of many of the songs he made popular, THE EDDIE CANTOR STORY curiously bypasses his extensive film career entirely. A sensitive topic with the real-life comedian, who believed that he was cheated out of his just financial rewards during his long association with producer Sam Goldwyn, Cantor's work in film may have been omitted from the diegesis at his own insistence, in the same manner that Al Jolson's original vaudeville partner, his older brother Harry, ceased to exist in THE JOLSON STORY. The revenge bio-film was still sixteen years in the future, and personal grudges were not believed to mix well with movie myths.

The doubly reflexive process which functions in JOLSON SINGS AGAIN as the Jolson character (played by Larry Parks) is introduced to the actor who is to portray him in the Jolson bio-film (Larry Parks again) is revised to facilitate an equivocal impression of authenticity in THE EDDIE CANTOR STORY. The narrative's framing sequence opens with shots of a major film preview being held in a screening room on the Warner Brothers lot. The picture which the guests view is the Cantor bio-film. At its conclusion, the end title is framed as an image on the studio's preview screen, and a cut to the audience reveals the real Mr. and Mrs. Eddie Cantor in attendance. As if fully cognizant of the visual discrepancy between himself and the made-up Keefe Brasselle, Cantor facetiously remarks, "I never looked so good."

Comedians Rogers and Cantor, despite their disparate styles of performing (one a countrified, wry social critic, the other an antic, often put-upon little "wise guy"), had both broadened their careers beyond the Broadway stage (and the occasional road tour) to include extensive work in radio and films. Thus they had become well-known to the entire U.S. population. Twenty years after both comics' prime, the audience could easily recall and react to their names as nostalgic attractional factors. (Cantor, the film's narrative to the contrary, was still an occasional performer on radio and television as late as the picture's release date.) Eddie Foy, the subject of the next comedian bio-film, was strictly a comic out of the lost world of vaudeville, an era whose prominence in the nostalgia process had essentially passed

out of fashion by 1955. The actor who portrayed him in
THE SEVEN LITTLE FOYS, released that same year, was
however, still an attractional factor in himself--Bob Hope.
The picture can therefore be identified as one of his own
star vehicles.

This is not to say that Foy was an unknown figure;
he was only a considerably more obscure one to the target
audience than were the two comics who preceded him in bio-
films. Yet THE SEVEN LITTLE FOYS relates directly to
THE EDDIE CANTOR STORY in that its depiction is of a
performer who manages to raise a large family only to sorely neglect them while devoting all his energies to pleasing
the paying customers beyond the footlights. In Foy's case
the neglect may be more excusable than Cantor's, since the
narrative presents Foy as spending little time playing theatres in the vicinity of his family's New Rochelle, New York,
home. Montage after montage shows him traveling the length
and breadth of the country, following the various vaudeville
circuits on which his hard-working agent (and family friend/

Bob Hope (r.) as Eddie Foy in THE SEVEN LITTLE FOYS
(1954). Photo courtesy Wisconsin Center for Film and
Theater Research.

confessor) has been able to get the comedian bookings. The death of his wife leaves Foy devastated, facing a hostile group of youngsters who resent his lengthy absences. Then the agent/friend posits the ideal solution: make the children part of their father's act. The suggestion is supposedly inspired by the successful family act of the Four Cohans, and linkage figure George M. Cohan even appears in a celebrity banquet sequence in which he does a dance-and-insult-patter routine with his friendly rival, Eddie Foy. Adding to the linkage is the fact that Cohan is portrayed by the same actor who starred in the Cohan bio-film of fourteen years earlier: James Cagney. In YANKEE DOODLE DANDY Cohan and Foy (the latter impersonated by his son Eddie Jr.) also were depicted as friendly rivals.

To underline the lesson learned by the children's repentant father, Foy has to testify at a custody hearing, called to determine if they should be sent to an orphanage. "I laid a pretty big egg in the father business," he confesses, adding, "but [this] is what their mother wanted." (Foy's late wife had also been a "trouper" before she retired from the stage to raise a family.) While THE SEVEN LITTLE FOYS does impose a mythic pattern of rise-and-fall on Foy's own career as a "single," the film's narrative also enacts the ritual of birth, depicting the emergence of one of the most beloved and famous vaudeville acts of all time. The visible tension between the father and his children (which sets up the insult-based humor both onstage and off) is never directly confronted by the narrative, although the implication is present, especially in the voice-over narration by one of Foy's grown children, that they may have sometimes resented being used as "props" by an exploitative parent. Be that as it may, the Eddie Foy character attempts to dispel such notions with his cheery sarcasm in the production number in which he sings, "I'm the Greatest Father of Them All."

Commercial exploitation of public nostalgia for the silent film era, which reached its peak as nostalgic views of the vaudeville era were fading from the screen, combined with the 1950s bio-film exposé cycle in 1957's THE BUSTER KEATON STORY.* Here the question of a comic's inner joy

---

* MAN OF A THOUSAND FACES, released that same year, also contains some exposé elements. It is covered in the chapter on actor biographies.

or gloom was answered in pessimistic fashion. The celebrated film clown had much to cry about, according to this narrative, and in his escape from the Hollywood pressure cooker he followed the same alcoholic trail as did Lillian Roth, John and Diana Barrymore, Jeanne Eagels, and Helen Morgan. Nevertheless, the depiction of Keaton's private life was true only in its mythic formulation. His romantic and career difficulties did drive him to drink, but the details of how this happened were presented no more accurately than were the affairs of his contemporary, Rudolph Valentino, in his first bio-film.

Keaton's rise-and-fall begins with his childhood as part of his parents' knockabout vaudeville act. By the time he has grown to manhood, the business is supposedly dying. An apocryphal Variety headline, some ten years ahead of its time, announces "Movies Killing Vaudeville," and Keaton

Donald O'Connor and Ann Blyth in THE BUSTER KEATON STORY (1957). Photo courtesy Wisconsin Center for Film and Theater Research.

The Comedians / 305

takes his comedic/acrobatic skills with him to search for a
new job in film. At first he lands only bit parts, but his
ability to draw laughs and favorable audience comments in
even the smallest roles leads to a studio contract and starring performances in his own comedy features. His affections for a glamorous actress at the studio are in vain, as
are those of the lady casting director who loves him from
afar. By the time he realizes that she is the only woman
worth pursuing, she has announced her engagement to another man, so Keaton begins to drink to numb his sorrow.
When talkies arrive, his inability to adapt to them depresses
him so severely that he becomes a helpless alcoholic. The
lady casting director rescues him from one of his binges
and he thanks her by marrying her, although he remembers
nothing of it the next day. She remains devoted to him, trying to wean him off liquor, but to no avail, and one day she
resolves to leave him for good. A therapeutic baseball game
with some neighborhood children causes Keaton to snap back
into sobriety. His realization: he needs to entertain for live
audiences, not just in front of a motion picture camera. Reunited with his wife, Keaton happily returns to what remains
of vaudeville and to the cheers of appreciative crowds.

    This gross fictionalization, omitting Keaton's appren-
ticeship with Fatty Arbuckle, his unhappy marriage to Natalie
Talmadge, his personal contract with brother-in-law Joe Schenck,
his problems with MGM executives when they bought out his
contract, and his uneasy teaming with Jimmy Durante, cava-
lierly interweaves actual titles from some of his productions
with false ones, and strings them together in a seemingly
random order. Yet the underlying myth of the cyclical curvature of his life and career could just as easily be applied
to the historical facts which the screenwriters (perhaps out of
fear of lawsuits) so scrupulously avoided.

    The narrative's factual weakness is paired at every
turn by a wealth of invocational strengths. Celebrity names
from the silent era are freely tossed about in the dialogue,
and a multitude of comic moments from actual Keaton pictures are re-created with precise accuracy. Following in
the tradition of the musical bio-films which employed congruent dubbing by the surviving singers and musicians whenever
possible, THE BUSTER KEATON STORY employed Keaton
himself as technical consultant, making sure that every per-
formance-segment gag executed by Keaton-coached actor Donald O'Connor functioned exactly as its original designer had
intended, from the lap-dive sequence in COPS to the soda-

fountain sequence in COLLEGE, the ice-fishing sequence in THE FROZEN NORTH, the canoe gag in BALLOONATICS and the sinking of THE BOAT.

Certain elements of condensation and simplification (such as keeping Keaton at the same fictitious studio for his entire career) also relate directly to VALENTINO I, as well as to THE PERILS OF PAULINE. Like MAN OF A THOUSAND FACES, THE BUSTER KEATON STORY features a subject-hero whose life away from the cameras has more than its share of grief, but the significant difference is that most of Lon Chaney's characters suffered a great deal on-screen as well. He lived the pain of many of his parts, but Keaton's sorrow is a secret from his public. His impassionate face is that of the clown who must cry alone until he gives up drink, returns to his stage roots, and remembers a maxim his father taught him back in vaudeville: "It's a wonderful thing to make people laugh, for there are so many people and they have so many troubles."

Keaton's real-life renaissance was a more protracted affair than the narrative depicts, but the mythic element of recovery from personal and professional disaster does echo reality, just as it did in the bio-films of previous performers who managed to escape from alcoholism. Nightclub comedian Joe E. Lewis, the subject-hero of another 1957 bio-film, battles with the bottle in THE JOKER IS WILD, but instead of showing it destroying his career, the narrative actually presents liquor as a key ingredient in Lewis' successful style of humor. The myth of rise and fall occurs twice in the course of the drama, and during the second cycle it is alcohol consumption which both rescues and threatens to destroy the comedian.

THE JOKER IS WILD, a star vehicle for actor-singer Frank Sinatra based on the life of a close friend who was well-known only to the patrons of certain major city cabarets, begins its narrative in prohibition-era Chicago. A promising young singer, Joe E. Lewis, finds himself caught between two rival speakeasy proprietors, one of whom has connections in the Chicago underworld. The situation presages that of THE GEORGE RAFT STORY and LOUIS ARMSTRONG--CHICAGO STYLE, but in this instance Lewis' brash manner and lack of deference to the mobsters carry a high price. In retaliation for his agreeing to sing in a club other than the one in which he has been appearing, hoodlums beat him severely and slash his throat. He survives, but with his vocal chords so badly mangled that his singing career is ended. With his professional aspirations smashed, he sinks into relative obscurity, working as a small-time burlesque stooge.

Several years later, at the urging of singer Sophie Tucker, and a former accompanist, Lewis shakily attempts a comeback at an all-star charity function similar to the one which started Al Jolson's comeback. However, Lewis is still unable to sing with his former clarity and range. Embarrassed at his vocal fumbling, he starts to joke with the audience and, like Will Rogers, discovers that he is a natural comic, able to ad-lib humorous remarks and please a crowd even more effectively than he had with his original specialty. Lewis's professional re-birth as a comic (whose routine includes a few non-demanding song parodies) does not come easily; he believes he can be funny only when he has been drinking. "If I couldn't drink, I couldn't get the courage to go out on that floor," he tells his doctor, after being warned that continued drinking may be fatal.

The comic's second fall (following his second rise) stems from the pressure of his and his wife's conflicting careers. After entertaining on a grueling USO tour (similar to the one which exhausted Al Jolson), Lewis marries a former chorus girl from his old nightclub act, only to discover her career taking off with a Hollywood acting contract. While they live in Los Angeles, she works days and he works nights. Eventually his drinking and gambling become so excessive that both his marriage and career are threatened. Some time later in Chicago, Lewis takes a late-night stroll past the boarded-up club where the narrative began and engages in a soul-searching conversation between himself and the reflections (of himself and others from his life) he sees in neighboring store windows. Observing that he has just been released from three months of hospitalization for alcohol detoxification, Lewis challenges his mirror image: "Now how about making me laugh for a change!" Whether an act of renaissance has actually transpired remains an open question, for without liquor Lewis may no longer be funny.

The motif of the comedian whose jokes conceal an inner agony was extended to a female character in 1968, with the release of the first of two bio-films about yet another Ziegfeld headliner, Fanny Brice. Fictitiously disguised as the central character of 1938's ROSE OF WASHINGTON SQUARE (filmed while she was still a contemporary star of stage, records, and radio), Fanny Brice was publicly remembered in the late 1960s as only a minor nostalgia figure. Her film appearances had been few, and except for THE GREAT ZIEGFELD (in which she made a brief congruent appearance), they had been rarely revived. The prime attractional factor of FUNNY GIRL was neither its subject-heroine nor its star (a newcomer to film, Barbra Streisand). As was the case with the bio-film of Gypsy Rose Lee, FUNNY GIRL was a film adaptation of an immensely successful stage musical, one that had toured the country via road companies and boasted a score filled with numbers which had gained wide exposure on radio and television. Yet in transferring the stage property to the screen a diegesis was created which extensively overlapped with the whole body of previous bio-films about Florenz Ziegfeld, his many star performers, and the composers who wrote for his shows. Once again, this time on a Columbia Studios sound stage, a set was built to represent Ziegfeld's home base, the New Amsterdam Theatre. Researchers, art directors, set designers, and costume designers embarked on still another mission to re-create the iconography of the bio-film's most-depicted era and locale.

The theme of the comic who hides his grief while playing the fool so that others may laugh is central to the narrative of FUNNY GIRL, which relies on a myth-infused plot of separation and reunion between comedienne Fanny Brice and her first husband, gambler/embezzler Nicky Arnstein. An open-ended flashback structure begins the drama, with a mythic star-birth overlay infusing the narrative's early sequences. As an established Ziegfeld headliner, Brice is first seen leaving her dressing room and striding about the New Amsterdam stage. Savoring her status, she climbs down into the empty auditorium, looks up at the runway and proscenium, and muses about what it must be like to view herself from the audience. Her personal maid brings a message that Mr. Ziegfeld wants to confer with his top female comic ... but only when she is ready. The idea of such a powerful man waiting for Brice to appear, not upon his instant command but at her leisure, delights her. As she recalls the road she traveled to become a star, the flashback which will grow into the main story begins. The framing sequence does not return, its point in the diegetic time frame (when her stardom was a brand new event) being subsequently passed by while the narrative unfolds.

Brice's initially low self-esteem is keyed to her

realization that she is far from beautiful, but she bravely
seeks employment in the chorus of a Manhattan burlesque
show. Although the manager soon wants to fire her because
of her skinny legs, he later agrees to keep her in the show
after hearing her perform a vocal number. Just as the
comedic talents of Will Rogers and Joe E. Lewis were shown
to be discovered in a semi-accidental manner, Brice's humorous way with a song prompts the burlesque operator to
exclaim, "You're no chorus girl--you're a comic singer."
Her early success in burlesque leads to a job offer from
Ziegfeld, who finds her antics to be a bit too vulgar for his
own taste, but a genuine hit with the audience.

Despite her stardom Brice still carries with her the
mental picture of herself as an ugly girl who must work
hard at being amusing to others in order to gain their attention and acceptance. When professional gambler Nicky
Arnstein, whose reputation as a ladies' man is well-known,
begins to pay court to Brice, his unexpected attentions overwhelm her, and she is his for the asking. Her constant
clowning pleases him as a welcome contrast with the many
bland and beautiful women he has known. Eventually they
marry, but he archetypally comes to resent being called
"Mr. Brice" and being overshadowed by her success. A
run of bad luck lands him deeply in debt, and rather than
accept bail-out money from his wife, Arnstein becomes involved in an embezzlement scheme. Its exposure, despite
the best lawyer Brice can buy, sends Arnstein to prison.
According to the true-to-formula emotional logic of the situation, the price of Brice's success has been the loss of the
only man who ever loved her. Although he is gone, she
must continue her clowning and hide her sorrow from the
crowd. "When you're on that stage," he tells her from his
prison cell, "you're the strongest woman in the world."

The separation-and-reunion myth runs its course when
Arnstein finishes serving his sentence and is released. His
homecoming to wife and family supplies the necessary, tearful conclusion. Looking at their baby son, Brice tells her
husband, "You've given him long legs ... and made me feel
beautiful." In an onstage performance segment epilogue,
Brice sums up her emotional sacrifice for her irresponsible
mate. She sings the "torch song" which she made famous,
"My Man."

In addition to its invocation of the familiar aspects of
the Ziegfeld era, FUNNY GIRL also dwells heavily on a show-

business bio-film theme which, although prevalent throughout most of the pre-exposé films, had become either muted or absent from many of the subsequent dramas of entertainers as passive victims of fate or of the determined exploitation of others. Brice's ambition to become a star is an all-powerful, driving force when she begins her life's journey on Henry Street, in the same Lower East Side Manhattan neighborhood which gave birth to numerous other famous entertainers. Of all the songs dramatically integrated with dialogue in the film's score, this theme is most aptly summed up in her aspirational rendition of "I Am the Greatest Star."

Just as THE JOLSON STORY's tremendous profits prompted a sequel, so did the financial success of FUNNY GIRL lead to a follow-up, only FUNNY LADY (1975) did not reach the screen until seven years had passed and its star had completed the many other show-business commitments she had accepted by virtue of becoming the "most bankable star" of the early 1970s. While FUNNY GIRL's creators had not bothered to include much precise historical detail concerning Brice's long professional association with Ziegfeld (and therefore avoided the carping of nit-picking critics), the makers of FUNNY LADY, which depicts Brice's subsequent relationship with producer Billy Rose, invoked the familiar not with generalities, but with specifics. Many of them were dead wrong (such as having Brice marry Rose only after personally salvaging his 1931 "Crazy Quilt" revue, or resurrecting ten-years-dead Bert Williams and altering his name), but the archetypal image of Brice as the unhappy clown was still true to form.

FUNNY LADY begins just after the point at which the previous narrative concluded. The couple's marriage has soured, and they are headed for divorce. As she receives the summons, she jokes, "Easy come, easy go," trying to conceal the pain of losing the only man who has ever loved her, and vice versa. The narrative of FUNNY LADY relies less on integrated songs to reveal Brice's thoughts and more on straight dialogue. To give her character an alter ego with which to discuss her plans and feelings, she is supplied with a sympathetic, effeminate male secretary who listens well and provides emotional support.

The time period portrayed is the beginning of the Depression, and Ziegfeld's financial ruin forces Brice to seek employment elsewhere. A brash, often crude young songwriter-turned-producer, Billy Rose, catches her attention during a round of "shopping for new songs" at Manhattan's speakeasy nightclubs. After dickering with him over the rights to record one of his compositions, "More Than You Know," she confides to her secretary, "This is a shrewd kid ... I think I'll marry him." The Rose-Brice relationship is a case of love at first spite, but their undeniable attraction, after they collaborate furiously to save his newest show (starring Brice) during an out-of-town tryout, leads them to the altar. Later she tells a friend that she only "fell in like with him." As the 1930s pass, Fanny Brice, famous singer of torch songs, still carries one for her first husband. An attempted reunion with him in 1939 fails, and upon her return home she discovers her current husband has been cheating on her with one of the swimmers from his new "Aquacade." "See you in court, kid," she flippantly tells him and departs.

Brice's last years of making people laugh are then depicted via an invocation of what is probably her most familiar, best-remembered vehicle, her "Baby Snooks" radio program, on which she played the part of an exceedingly cunning and mischievous child. On the occasion of her program's tenth anniversary (1947) she receives a visit from her ex-husband Rose. Their meeting is a bittersweet exchange of excuses as to why their partnership failed. "Being married to you was like being married to a parade," says Rose. Brice compares their relationship to an unsuccessful comedy routine: "My timing was always off with us." Following Rose's departure, Brice sits alone with her memories, displayed in a flashback montage ending in an ironic recap of her opening song in the film, "How Lucky Can You Get?"

FUNNY LADY, despite its many moments of humor and its energetic musical numbers, embodies the tragic myth of a failed quest. Fanny Brice, the self-deprecating ugly duckling who disguises her sorrows with verbal and musical slapstick, fails to obtain any lasting happiness in her own life; yet all the time this sad clown has been supplying the crowd with joy and laughter.

The 1976 release of W. C. FIELDS AND ME signified the last of the elite group of Ziegfeld superstars to be bio-filmed, with the lone exception of black comedian Bert Williams. Ziegfeld, of course, had many headliners in his long career, but only a select handful continued with him over a number of years and gained a genuine measure of

Rod Steiger and Valerie Perrine as W. C. Fields and Carlotta Monti in W. C. FIELDS AND ME (1976). Photo courtesy Capitol Communications.

The Comedians / 313

national prominence. One by one, in the thirty years which followed his own bio-film tribute, they came to the screen and were given the full mythic treatment, always in a sympathetic vein. The fact that W. C. Fields took the longest to arrive may be significant, for his offstage manner was reportedly even more unsympathetic than that of champion egotist Al Jolson. Plans for doing a Fields bio-film were discussed in Hollywood as early as the publication in 1949 of the first Fields biography, only three years after his death. The insurmountable problem, barring wholesale falsification along the lines of VALENTINO I or THE BUSTER KEATON STORY, was that the misanthrope that Fields worked so hard at being while offscreen was not susceptible to the character-softening happy endings which enabled him to be irascible but lovable onscreen. A man haunted by phobias and associated mental quirks of many varieties, Fields was a believable candidate neither for sainthood nor reformation. No other option appeared open in the bio-film tradition.

Then in the early 1970s came the publication and best-seller status of a new Fields biography, written from the first-person point of view of his live-in mistress. The book provided an innovative way to approach the film biography of a comic whose archetypal "secret sorrow" had made him a mass of personality contradictions, suspicions, and inventive vindictiveness. If Fields could not be made the sympathetic hero of a quest for fame or the tragic, early-dying victim of the unbearable pressures of show-business success, his loyal mistress, Carlotta Monti, could function as a central character. She would be the system's archetypal victim, sacrificing her own hopes of stardom while devoting herself to the man she loves. Fields' character would then become the narrative's omnipresent and strongest invocational figure, intensely familiar to the target audience of 1976 through a recent wave of film revivals and his recurrent image and caricature in ancillary media.

Even the finished film's title (taken from the book) suggests this duality of focus. W. C. FIELDS AND ME depicts Fields' career from Monti's point of view. Since she did not enter his life until his arrival in Hollywood in the early 1930s, the narrative covers his previous career in vaudeville and as a Ziegfeld star only briefly and with the kind of gross inaccuracies which are actually appropriate to a second-hand retelling of events originally related by someone with a penchant for malevolent fabrication.

Fields' extensive New York-based silent film career (ten films) does not exist in the narrative. His relationship with Ziegfeld is cut short not by the comic's accepting an offer to appear in "Earl Carroll's Vanities," but by a quarrel with Ziegfeld over Fields' use of burlesque-level vulgarities in a Follies sketch. Apocryphally "wiped out" in a real estate swindle, Fields and a dwarf-sized friend then leave for Hollywood, where the former Follies star literally begs a Paramount studio executive for a small part in a film. The dramatized mythic pattern of Fields' rise-and-fall is therefore isolated from the broader scope of his lengthy historical career. From Carlotta Monti's vantage point, Fields' Hollywood years function as the only frame of reference from which she can view and relate to him.

An extra on the set of one of his early Hollywood films, she catches his eye and later is sent for by an underling to "audition" for Fields at a private, weekend party attended by his close circle of drinking buddies: director Gregory La Cava, writer Gene Fowler, actor John Barrymore, and restaurateur Dave Chasen. Fields humiliates Monti by requiring her to take the place of a kitchen maid, then lectures her on the foolishness of wanting to be an actress. When all the drunken guests have departed, he invites her to move in with him. She accepts, so the narrative explains, out of a mixed sense of admiration for Fields' talent, the need of a father figure, and standard Hollywood opportunism, believing he will arrange a screen test for her.

The next sequences depict Fields' universally iconoclastic behavior, defying all forms of authority and standards of propriety, while Monti caters to his whims and cruelty with a form of devotion which gradually turns from masochism to loving concern. After six weeks of his falsely displaying her to friends as if she were not only his housekeeper but his mistress, she tells him he is free to justify appearances, and he does.

While Fields' Hollywood career unfolds in a rise-and-fall pattern, Monti's relationship with the comedian follows the mythic overlay of separation and reunion. Her toleration, even fondness, for Fields' rudeness and blatant selfishness is stretched to the breaking point when she learns that he deliberately sabotaged her screen test in order to prevent her from enjoying a career of her own, thus keeping her dependent on his support. Outraged at his trickery, Monti leaves Fields and travels to New York, where she hopes to find a career as a stage actress. Her lack of New York success combines with her unshakable attraction to Fields, and she returns to find him increasingly dependent on alcohol and in failing health.

Just as THE JOKER IS WILD presented liquor as a necessary component of Joe E. Lewis' style of comedy, W. C. FIELDS AND ME portrays Fields as having a similar need. Although haunted by terrifying childhood memories of poverty and suffering, he has discovered that he can blot them out by drinking. Only when he has imbibed a sufficient quantity of alcohol is he then able to attack through his films what he sees as the falsity, pomposity, and pettiness of "proper" society. "If there are ever any changes in this world, it's because of the s.o.b.'s [like me]," he tells Monti, adding, "Sweet guys never change anything, [but] I like to stick pins in balloons and let the air out of [all the] self-satisfied bastards." Other Fields lines of dialogue which attempt to justify his boorish behavior include: "I am petty, cheap, and possessive, but as my father once said, 'Anything worth having is worth cheating for,'" and "When one has been misused by life, he will misuse others."

Fields' misuse of his own body, via the alcohol he needs to free his malicious wit, takes its toll when he becomes too debilitated to work, but before he drinks himself to death, he experiences an archetypal act of career-vindication mythically equivalent to the most auspicious of testimonial dinners. A surprise visit from the grown son Fields has not seen since the age of three unsettles him at first, until he discovers that the fellow has become one of the comic's most devoted fans. "You're the funniest man alive," says the young man, and adds, "including Chaplin." "I've succeeded with my own son and didn't even try," replies Fields, who for many years had nursed an envy of the "little tramp" so severe that it made Fields physically ill just to lay eyes on Chaplin or his screen image. "I've been an s.o.b. to your mother," says Fields, but his son counters with a line which sums up the narrative's viewpoint in terms of a popular culture image of the comic who is in no way obligated by mere personal standards of comity: "Who'd expect W. C. Fields to be anything else!"

Invocationally loaded with familiar names and iconography of 1930s Hollywood, W. C. FIELDS AND ME pushed the archetype of the sad comic past the point of easy sympathy, brought in his ill-treated mistress as a figure of more conventional audience identification, and then proceeded to draw its viewers into agreement with Fields' patently misanthropic outlook by emphasizing the anti-establishment rage which supposedly fueled his acerbic fire.

Another mid-1970s comedian bio-film depicted a latter-day professional cynic whose public image never benefited from the softened happy endings that occurred in Fields' motion pictures. LENNY (1974) was about subject-hero Lenny Bruce, a nightclub comedian of the 1950s and 1960s whose reputation for controversy spread much farther than the mere sound of his strident, accusing voice. While the Fields bio-film limited its performance segments to brief, re-created excerpts of Fields' juggling, fast-talking, and double-take routines, visually framed to show him performing on movie sets, LENNY's performance segments were much more lengthy, including several verbatim performances of his propriety-challenging monologues.

The CITIZEN KANE-like structure of THE I DON'T CARE GIRL becomes in LENNY not just the introduction for a few flashbacks, but a mechanistically recurrent motif of the entire film. Adopting the visual style of what is popularly known as a "cinema verité documentary," the narrative of LENNY intercuts dramatized interview footage (of Bruce's friends and relatives recalling incidents in his life) with segments of more naturalistically staged events depicting those incidents. The same actors play Bruce's associates and family in both types of sequences.

In LENNY the archetype of the sad comic is transformed into that of the mad comic, ultimately in both senses of the word. While W. C. Fields would be shown, two years later, to be an eccentric, often angry satirist of society's standards, Bruce had already been depicted in his bio-film as a comic artist whose profound displeasure with American mores drove him into an insanely self-destructive, downward spiral of obscenity and addiction. "My whole act is based on the existence of injustice," he tells his nightclub audiences as he taunts the authorities to arrest him for using four-letter words in a public performance. According to Bruce, "It's the suppression of a word that gives it the power of violence." When he gets his day in court, he proclaims, "Your honor, I do so want your respect. I'm not up there to shock the audience. I'm trying to show them that America is a very hypocritical society.... You need the deviate to tell you when you're blowing it."

The Comedians / 317

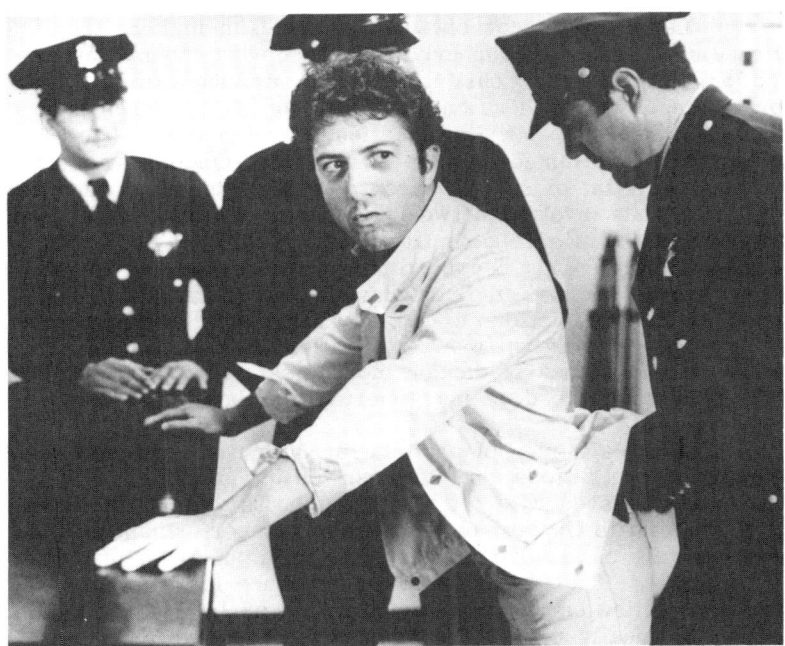

Dustin Hoffman (center) as Lenny Bruce in LENNY (1974). Photo courtesy Wisconsin Center for Film and Theater Research.

Prior to his court appearances, the narrative presents Bruce as a mediocre cabaret comic whose career suddenly "catches fire" when he drops the tired routines of his early years and begins putting into words the repressed sentiments of his audience in regard to sex, religion, political authority and self-worth. Dangerously infatuated with the self-indulgent, anti-establishment "hip" culture espoused by the often heroin-addicted, marijuana-smoking jazz musicians and "beat" writers of the 1950s (at least as portrayed in the popular culture of the time), Bruce and his stripper-wife Honey engage in a variety of society's forbidden activities, including group sex and narcotics consumption. Less enthusiastic than her husband about breaking the taboos, Honey pleads with him, following an all-night orgy: "You talked me into this freak scene ... why do you have to be so fucking hip?" Eventually she turns to lesbianism and divorces him.

Legal clearances obtained by the film makers from Bruce's wife and mother may have precluded the narrative's exploring their own possible roles in driving him off the precipice of rationality, but the suffering he is shown to endure at the hands of the authorities provides more than enough justification for viewing the film's representation of him as a victim of society's repression. Furthermore, with the time-shift involved between the years of Bruce's persecution and the film's release, much of the mid-1970s target audience had already become inured to the presence of four-letter words and sexual frankness in the media and felt no repugnance to depictions of erotic and narcotic experimentation. The challenging of already-fallen inhibitions which functioned in the early dancer bio-films is repeated in LENNY on a much broader, but generically related, scale.

Bruce's series of arrests for both narcotics and obscenity law violations wreaks havoc on his sanity, and he becomes obsessed with his unceasing bouts with the authorities. Towards the end of his career his performances consist entirely of his droning on, reading aloud from his trial transcripts. The "cult" following of Bruce loyalists who pack his every engagement at first amazes him, and when an invocationally placed *Time* magazine reporter asks him to comment on his "social impact," he replies, "I'm just a comic." The magazine labels him "sick." Later, when the threat of a long jail term begins to terrify him, Bruce envisions himself as a doomed champion of the First Amendment. His death, from a heroin overdose, is presented ambiguously, with the denied suggestion that his fear of prison may have prompted suicide. In a reflexive finale, the film's producer is diegetically presented as being in the process of negotiating for the rights to make the film which has just concluded.

Despite its structural complexity, interweaving film footage of highly differing visual codes and borrowing heavily from actual trial testimony and nightclub routines, LENNY maintains a direct relationship to the show-business biofilm's continuing reliance on mythic infrastructure. The implied insistence of the narrative that the film's 110 minutes of dramatized events represent a man's life and career unavoidably requires a perceived mythic pattern for human comprehension, or else the events would remain shapeless and therefore meaningless. The objective here is not only to identify such patterns, but to analyze how they (and their concomitant iconography) interrelate among the dramatic works offered to the American public as qualifying biographies. No amount of chronological fragmentation or interfaced divergent coding can obviate the presence of an operative mythic structure without negating the original biographical purpose. Although the pieces of the rise-and-fall curvature of Lenny Bruce's life may be non-syntagmatically scattered throughout those 110 minutes and represented by random-sequence events with multiple visual codes, the gestalt is of a human life. Such an entity will always be linearly viewable only through myth, which has the power to reconstruct a perceptible, if not accurate, whole out of even the smallest part.

Following the mid-1970s release of LENNY and W. C. FIELDS AND ME, the cycle of sad-comic bio-films moved from theatrical productions to those made for television. To date, four such comedian biographies have been filmed, each presenting the face of the funnyman as archetypally being but the misleading exterior of an individual whose internal griefs and anxieties grant him little mirth of his own. FEAR ON TRIAL, a 1975 self-indictment by CBS Television, recounted the destruction of the career of a storyteller-humorist who had once been a star of the network's radio division in the early 1950s. John Henry Faulk, whose "Johnny's Front Porch" program had once been heard by millions of Americans each week, is depicted in the narrative as becoming a victim of one of the anti-communist "blacklists" being circulated at the time by certain self-styled, social vigilantes. First one sponsor cancels, then another, and eventually the network executives bend to the pressure of the blacklisters and deprive Faulk of his job. Because the "word is out" about his alleged communist sympathies, he finds further employment in his chosen field difficult to obtain. Although he lands a new job as a member of an NBC Television panel show, the producers withdraw their offer. His unemployability as an entertainer painfully leads him to adapt to a much lower standard of living, and the emotional pressures he endures eventually wreck his marriage. Reduced to driving a taxi and selling encyclopedias door-to-door, Faulk has only one hope--to win the lawsuit he has filed against the political entrepreneurs who actually published and sold to producers the blacklist which destroyed his career.

Faulk's lawyer, the famous Louis Nizer, warns his client that the risky suit will probably take more than five years to settle, but the distraught humorist resolves that any chance of obtaining justice would make the ordeal

George C. Scott and William Devane as Louis Nizer and John Henry Faulk in FEAR ON TRIAL (1975). Photo courtesy Capitol Communications.

worthwhile. Following a lengthy trial in which several producers and performers reveal the workings of the blacklist and its financial gain for its authors, a jury finds that Faulk indeed has been wronged and awards him damages totaling three and a half million dollars. The death of one of the two key defendants reduces the actual cash award substantially, but Faulk is nevertheless hailed as the "man who broke the blacklist."

This drama of one man's battle for justice amid a paralyzing atmosphere of the cowardice of others embodies the quest myth in a very linear form. The narrative's invocation of the familiar extends from diegetic locales (the major network headquarters) to the names of other blacklist victims (Philip Loeb, Mady Christians), names of Faulk's sympathetic associates (producer John Houseman, newsman Ed Murrow), and the congruent portrayals of trial witnesses (producers David Susskind and Mark Goodson). A false identity, however, is provided for a famous stage actress who testifies as to how she cleared her own name by agreeing to endorse the work of blacklist publisher Vincent Hartnett. A curious disclaimer, necessitated by the bio-film makers' inability to obtain clearance from Faulk's ex-wife, reads: "In this presentation the character of Mrs. John Henry Faulk has been fictionalized for dramatic effect." This is as if to say that diegetically, the character is Faulk's wife, but extra-diegetically, the real Faulk was married to a different sort of woman. Such a minute differentiation between the real and the represented (within a visual text which, according to generic custom, includes extensive dramatic invention and condensation) establishes a heretofore untried additional level in the filmic hierarchy of perceived authenticity. Besides the entities of the entirely fictitious subsidiary character, the composite character, the disguised character, the authentically identified non-celebrity character, and the authentically invoked famous character, there is now the authentically identified-but-fictitious character, something of an inversion of the fictitiously identified-but-revealed-to-be-authentic characters first seen in IS EVERYBODY HAPPY?

While the agony of John Henry Faulk was portrayed as being chiefly associated with his long years of being unable to perform, BUD AND LOU (1978) returned to the theme of the comic's misery haunting him at the very same time that he is making others laugh with joy. Ostensibly a dual biography of two comedians who spent most of their careers as a team, this story of the pairing of Abbott and Costello (as was also the case in WORDS AND MUSIC and THE BIRTH OF THE BEATLES) avoids devoting equal narrative time to each of the members and concentrates on the private life of only one. The depiction of Bud Abbott as a bachelor may have been necessitated by clearance problems with his widow, but it also allows his personal life to be glossed over in favor of concentrating on the family tragedy which turns partner Lou Costello into an embittered, petty egotist whose character is quite at odds with the likable, good-natured "fall guy" he portrays on the screen.

The two comics' rise and fall begins with their separate careers in burlesque. Both dissatisfied with their current partners, Abbott and Costello join forces and find that they complement each other perfectly. "You guys work together like lovers," says their perceptive agent Eddie Sherman, who convinces them that their extraordinary success in burlesque has taken them as far as they can go in that medium. Even though it means a salary cut, they agree to try for national exposure on radio and land a weekly spot on the "Kate Smith Show," which soon leads to a Broadway revue ("Streets of Paris") and a Hollywood contract with Universal Studios.

A string of hit pictures and their own radio program continue their rise, but the accidental drowning of Costello's year-old son causes his father to undergo an unpleasant personality change. Already suffering from the inflated ego shown in earlier bio-films to be an occupational disease of the newly successful, Costello compounds his problem by becoming abusive to his partner, family and associates. The strain between the partners begins to show in their work, and old, unspoken resentments (such as their original 60-40 income split, won by Abbott on a coin flip years earlier) surface to exacerbate the situation. Audits by the Internal Revenue Service and suits to recover back taxes destroy the team's financial security, forcing them to auction off their household goods in order to escape jail.

Never really accepted by Hollywood society, perhaps because of their crude manners and burlesque backgrounds, Abbott and Costello find themselves figuratively alone in a hostile environment. Their bickering (often over Abbott's drinking, which he has used for years to lessen his susceptibility to epileptic fits) leads to a breakup, precipitated by Abbott's being too drunk to complete one of their Las Vegas bookings. Costello tries working alone for a while, but his history of coronary problems continues to worsen and he has a fatal heart attack. On his deathbed, Costello recants his formerly espoused position that he was primarily responsible for the success he and his ex-partner once enjoyed. "We was the best," says Costello; "I was part of a team--me and Abbott." Alone in retirement, surrounded by memorabilia from past days of glory, Abbott receives the news of Costello's death from Eddie Sherman. A concluding montage of moments from the team's career follows Abbott's closing remark: "More than anyone ... I tried to make him laugh."

The rise and fall of Abbott and Costello is equated in the narrative with a fraternal love affair between two men. Their success, their agent tells them at one point, occurred because "the audience knew that you loved each other." When that love is poisoned by Costello's sorrow turned to bitterness and by Abbott's progressive dependency on alcohol, the cycle runs its tragic course to the finish.

With the exception of disguising the identities of a few Universal Studio employees (such as a director and a producer whose names would not be invocational to the target audience anyway), BUD AND LOU is rife with celebrity references in the dialogue but short on visual impersonations. Linkage, however, occurs in the film's opening sequence, where the team is sharing the bill with Gypsy Rose Lee. CAN YOU HEAR THE LAUGHTER? THE STORY OF FREDDIE PRINZE (1979) is also filled with famous name invocations, but not those of the nostalgic 1940s and 1950s. The Prinze bio-film both begins and ends in the very recent past, for it presents the story of a young Puerto Rican-American nightclub comedian whose rapid ascendence and archetypal self-destruction were both contained well within the single decade of the 1970s.

Accepted in 1971 by New York City's High School of the Performing Arts, young Prinze begins by studying music, but in an act of diegetic linkage, is portrayed as becoming enthralled with the idea of becoming "another Lenny Bruce," just as numerous performers in previous bio-films have set out to emulate some other show-business hero.* The short

---

Even subsidiary characters, such as Bruce's wife Honey, in LENNY, can have linkage impressions of themselves. In one of that film's dramatized interview segments she compares herself to Lillian Roth in I'LL CRY TOMORROW.

324 / Star Myths

Ira Augustain, Ken Sylk and Kevin Hooks in CAN YOU HEAR THE LAUGHTER? THE STORY OF FREDDIE PRINZE (1979). Photo courtesy Capitol Communications.

but spectacular rise and fall of Prinze takes off with his being booked to entertain in nightclubs, becoming the protégé of established comic David Steinberg (via an impersonational invocation) and getting booked to appear on the revived "Jack Paar Show" as well as on the "Tonight Show." Prinze's series of successful national television appearances win him an audition for a proposed NBC situation comedy, "Chico and the Man," and soon he is co-starring in the series with an impersonationally invoked Jack Albertson.

Prinze "trades up" in terms of his girl friends as he climbs the ladder of success, but he still continues his association with a close male friend from school, a black musician named Nat. A later linkage sequence has Prinze wanting to become "another James Dean" and to be known for acting, as well as comedic, ability. Then the archetypal pressures of stardom overcome the comic, and he

The Comedians / 325

escapes into the consumption of cocaine and other illicit drugs. Paranoia seizes him with a fear of losing his identity, and he repeatedly threatens to kill his stand-in. Appearing on stage at Ceasar's Palace in Las Vegas, Prinze panics when he "can't hear the laughter any more." Back in Hollywood, Prinze's insane fascination with guns frightens both his friends and his new wife. In a concluding scene, Nat receives a telephone call informing him that his friend has killed himself by means of a bullet through the brain. The saddened and dazed musician speaks, as if he were addressing the dead comic: "You finally made it, Fred ... you finally made it."

The image of the comedian as a man whose troubles can be temporarily suppressed with humor but not cured is reinforced by the narrative of CAN YOU HEAR THE LAUGHTER? with a terminal certainty. The subject-hero of LENNY was presented as a desperately unhappy man whose drug-induced death could not definitely be identified as self-inflicted. Freddie Prinze, who so wanted to be like Bruce, makes, only ten years later, an exit about which there are far fewer questions. It stands as the first clearly overt act of suicide, rather than the various protracted or equivocal forms of self-destruction practiced by his many generic predecessors, in the history of the show-business biographical film. The archetypal theme that the road to success as an entertainer is a dangerous one, a road which need not be traversed at all, is given voice in CAN YOU HEAR THE LAUGHTER? by the recurrent use of a popular song from the early 1970s as a key part of the musical score. Its title: "You Don't Have to Be a Star."

Truly minor stardom was the focus of a 1981 CBS Television production called LEAVE 'EM LAUGHING. Not to be confused with the 1949 Milton Berle pseudo-biography, the newer film was subtitled THE STORY OF JACK THUM. The show-business milieu of this very recent portrayal of a purveyor of laughs is a far cry from the lights of Broadway or the cameras of Hollywood. Show business to the subject-hero of LEAVE 'EM LAUGHING is centered on the north and west sides of Chicago, not in the city's theatres or nightclubs, but at youngsters' birthday parties in middle-class family homes, at group picnics, on the stage of a grade school assembly program, or in the ward of a children's hospital. The narrative's title character is a professional clown, not one who performs with a big-time traveling circus, but one who wears a clown's makeup and costume for

Mickey Rooney (r.) as Jack Thum, with William Windom in LEAVE 'EM LAUGHING (1981). Photo courtesy Capitol Communications.

The Comedians / 327

a special kind of personal performance designed just for the very young. Well into middle age and in failing health, Jack Thum has been working at his specialty since he was a teenager. Expository dialogue at a neighborhood bar run by an ex-circus performer reveals that Thum was "too soft a guy" to fight for a position in the rough-and-tumble circus world. Thum's softness is his amazing generosity. An orphan himself, Thum and his wife have spent all of their adult lives raising other orphans as foster children, without accepting any governmental aid.

While Thum has supposedly been a genuinely happy individual in the years prior to the start of the narrative, a sense of doom enters his life with a doctor's diagnosis that Thum has lung cancer and that his chances for survival are slim. The last months of Thum's life are chronicled in LEAVE 'EM LAUGHING as he continues to entertain at what jobs he can get, until he is hospitalized for the last time. Of all the people he has encountered, young and old, there are two to whom he has failed to bring a smile or a chuckle. One is his newest foster child, an autistic boy of about ten, who has been abandoned. The other is Thum's elderly hospital roommate, a lonely, dying grouch. Thum himself becomes profoundly depressed as he feels the approach of death, and he begins to question the value of his life and his mediocre career. A surprise testimonial party for him, featuring a reunion of every one of the thirty-seven foster children he has raised, cheers Thum immensely in his last days, and he even succeeds in coaxing happy responses from his two hold-outs, the boy and the old man. The mayor of Chicago proclaims the day of the party "Jack Thum Day," October 31, 1979. A concluding title announces Thum's death, only two months later.

This ritual vindication of an entertainer's career, no matter how humble in scale, is one of the strongest archetypes in the bio-film tradition. Although the public act of vindication has been displaced from its position of centrality and sometimes negated entirely by the adoption in many narratives of the exposé approach, career vindication nevertheless remains an eminently viable means of evoking positive audience response. Essential to its functioning, however, is the shared perception, between target audience and film maker, that professional integrity is possible within the subject-hero's chosen field.

Challenges to this sense of integrity have often come,

in bio-film narratives, from the antinomial representations of the adherents of high and low culture, most notably in musician and songwriter biographies. LENNY transposed the dialectic from an aesthetic to a moral field of contention, and that is the same terrain traversed by one of the most recent bio-films covered by this study, the 1982 TV-movie, MAE WEST. Its heroine is the notorious vaudeville star whose outrageous burlesquing of feminine seductiveness, the courtship ritual, and contemporary moral standards, when transferred to the Broadway stage and the Hollywood screen, won her the cheers of the sexually tolerant and the condemnation of society's moral watchdogs.

Heavily simplifying her stage work (a matter of arcane history) but outlining her film career (still very visible to the public) in roughly accurate detail, the narrative of MAE WEST caters to the prior knowledge of the target audience via some of the same historical priorities operant in the bio-film of her contemporary, W. C. Fields. Although other biographical sources indicate that the young West was pushed into show business by her professional boxer father when she was less than ten years of age, MAE WEST casts the child's father as a crude prude, fearful that his wife's encouragement of their daughter's performing talent will turn the girl into something so disreputable that "No man will want her." This shift in parental sympathy is in accordance with the ambivalently pop-feminist theme of the story--that West realized early the primacy of her own self-interest and self-protection, taking the advice of her maritally embittered mother to treat all men as disposable items. After a row with her brute of a husband, Mrs. West angrily instructs her impressionable daughter: "It's a man's world, they tell us, and I hate it ... and you hate it too. Don't stick yourself with one man. It's going to be your world!" The closest bio-filmic reference at this point is to the Isadora Duncan films, which detail the life of another talented girl who resolved as a child to avoid the snares of the male. Yet, as was the case with Duncan, West's track record of female supremacy is not without its painful setbacks and hard-learned lessons.

While still a teenager, she manages to obtain her father's grudging permission to tour in vaudeville as half of a song-and-dance team called "The Happy Feet: Wallace and West." Her partner, who has scrupulously promised to respect and protect her, eventually marries the girl while the pair are out of town. Disillusionment sets in quickly, however, when she discovers him to be unfaithful. Despite the advice of another female entertainer, "Ya gotta love somebody," West decides to split with her partner/husband and seek booking as a single act, although she never bothers to file for a legal divorce.

West achieves a modicum of success as a comic performer, dressed in a leopard skin and cavorting about the stage as "The Cave Girl," but her career receives its first real boost toward the big time when a kind-hearted female impersonator (modeled on Julian Eltinge and performing a drag act on the same bill as West) takes her aside for some important professional advice. After he tells her how easy it is to spot the bits of stage business and comic technique she has "borrowed" from famous performers of the day, including Minsky's Burlesque headliner Lew Rock, she excuses her pilfering from other acts with the most oft-heard statement of ambition in all bio-films, "I wanna be a star!" Her new advisor's response: "Stars aren't pieced together. They're one of a kind. Look inside yourself. Nobody can steal from a star. The best they can do is imitate 'em." From this point on, in keeping with the archetypal image of stardom, Mae West will be unlike any other stage performer.

With sage advice from Val, the drag artist, and from West's new lover/manager, a Chicago lawyer named Jim Timmany, West creates a unique stage character for herself, emphasizing her sexuality (what Timmany calls "the real you") and an ultra-glamorous, playfully teasing approach (via double entendres) encouraged by Val, who reminds her, "never drop the seventh veil. Suggest the world--but withold the prize."

MAE WEST's narrative has so far been framed as a flashback, introduced by an opening sequence in a police night court where she has been arraigned on a charge of public indecency, as a result of her suggestive performance in a Broadway play of her own devising, called "Sex." The flashback ends with West receiving a ten-day jail sentence for "corrupting the morals of youth," but even behind bars her fame as a sexy stage star continues to grow. A montage of newspaper stories reveals her flirtation with the warden and her invitation to his house for dinner.

West's public success, in accordance with the archetype of the clown with a secret sorrow, is compared in the narrative to her stormy relationship with Timmany, whom

she loves but cannot allow herself to marry. His pleadings
that she become his wife only result in bitter arguments,
since her feminist view that women should be allowed the
same sexual liberties as men clashes with his refusal to
give up the male supremacist "double standard." Although
Timmany abandons his lucrative Chicago law practice to devote himself entirely to her career, she deliberately rebuffs
his ingrained sexist attitudes by flaunting her casual affairs
with other men. Nevertheless, he stills feels protective
toward his client, and at her mother's funeral he punches
out a stranger who merely dares to try to speak with the
grieving actress.

    The concern for audience sympathy, which kept the
kinkier historical elements out of the narratives of bio-films
made more than a generation earlier, still functions, in
some instances, in today's television-tailored biographies.
MAE WEST's narrative makes no mention of the overtly
homosexual themes, characters, and performers which per-
vaded West's Broadway productions in the 1920s, and which
functioned as the exaggeratedly contrastive background for
her personal burlesquing of feminine seductiveness and
glamor. Instead, the film opts symbolically for a single
effeminate character, the professional drag queen (played
with great seriousness and sensitivity by Roddy McDowall)
who acts as father confessor and behind-the-scenes mentor
to the rising star. The casting of actress Ann Jillian in
the role of West even signifies a bit more than the standard
TV-movie attractional factor of employing a contemporary
weekly series star to widen the appeal of a nostalgic, historical curiosity-based story, as was the case in the casting of video siren Loni Anderson as Jayne Mansfield. A
long-distance form of performer linkage is present as well,
for it was Jillian who appeared in the role of Gypsy Rose
Lee's sister June (Havoc) in GYPSY, nearly twenty years
earlier, and the vaudeville-era setting of both narratives
overlaps historically as well.

    West's arrival in Hollywood, following her scandalous
triumphs on Broadway, moves the narrative along its mythic
rise-and-fall curvature to an even higher point of success.
Although she nearly misses the chance to transfer her
sexually based humor to the world's movie screens because
of a contract dispute with Paramount Pictures (she demands
the unheard-of right to compose her own dialogue), a fictionalized studio executive finally agrees to her wishes. Her
co-star in her film debut (George Raft, who actually received

The Comedians / 331

top billing) cynically observes at the conclusion of the picture's Hollywood premiere, "She stole everything but the cameras!"

West's film career is subsequently telescoped with behind-the-scenes dialogue sequences indicating the following points: 1) Her screen debut in NIGHT AFTER NIGHT (1932) is so successful that the studio allows her to film her controversial stage hit, "Diamond Lil," with a young leading man she has "discovered," Cary Grant; 2) Her early films make so much money that they save the studio from going bankrupt; 3) The official Hollywood censors eventually crack down on the sexual suggestiveness of her motion pictures because of complaints of moral outrage from religious leaders and other easily offended citizens; 4) West's randy performance in a nationally broadcast radio skit with ventriloquist's dummy Charlie McCarthy causes such an overnight scandal that the studio executives dispense with her services.

The exact historical role played by the enforcement of the Hollywood Production Code of 1934 is obscured by the narrative, which includes a sequence in which West is warned in 1932 that her style of humor might run afoul of the "Hays Office." The arrival of a stricter code, two years later and in the midst of her blossoming film career, is, however, not acknowledged. Instead, the narrative suggests that the censors' restrictions on West's humor are prompted primarily by personal complaints lodged against her by sexually repressed male members of the clergy. This slight but significant shift in emphasis is thus more in keeping with one of the underlying feminist themes of MAE WEST.

The film's invocation of the familiar, as indicated, extends to the impersonational representation of West's best-remembered co-stars, including George Raft, Cary Grant, and W. C. Fields, but the dialogue given to the still-living and prone-to-litigation Grant is strictly limited to lines (filmed in extreme long shot) historically spoken by the actor in the film version of "Diamond Lil," SHE DONE HIM WRONG. The presence of the Raft and Fields characters also functions as linkage to their own respective bio-films.

West's appearance with Fields in MY LITTLE CHICK-ADEE, made as a one-shot at Universal following her humiliating departure from Paramount, is shown to be an unhappy experience for her, due to constant distress over her reduced star status and the boisterous, scene-stealing tactics of Fields. An omnipresent reporter figure, who has followed West's career for several years, finally secures an interview with her, and the expository dialogue in this sequence reveals her to have become severely depressed during her three years of unemployment after the Fields picture. West's 15-year affair with Timmany had ended during her Paramount tenure, and her futile attempt to seek solace in spiritualism and seances is mentioned by the reporter in connection with a later West male companion named Jack Kelly. West's attempt at a comeback in a minor Columbia musical, THE HEAT'S ON, is shown to be a flop in the same cinematic shorthand employed in THE GREAT ZIEGFELD--the lights on a theater marquee are seen going out. A gray-haired Jim Timmany re-enters West's life at this point, but before the couple manages to re-kindle the embers of their lost love, he suffers a heart attack and becomes an invalid.

The mythic cycle of rise-and-fall has brought Mae West to the depths of despair, but her archetypal comeback finally occurs when she stars in a spectacularly successful Broadway revival of "Diamond Lil." The historical fact that she actually appeared in this revival following a very profitable run in a stage version of her never-filmed screenplay, "Catherine Was Great," a biographical send-up of the Russian empress, is conveniently omitted, just as were certain stage performances by George M. Cohan and Al Jolson which would have contradicted the mythic symmetry and emotional balance of their own bio-films.

Yet there is another generic convention to be observed before the narrative closes. Mae West, perhaps the best-known of all female comedians, is ultimately made to conform, in the narrative's closing sequence, with the archetype of the sad clown. Her earthy, witty, glamorous challenge to the sexually repressive attitudes of her day is, however, shown to be vindicated (and even prefigurative of the collapse of the movies' sexual censorship in 1968-69) by means of a late-night, melancholy long-distance phone conversation between West and her erstwhile, now bed-ridden lover. Reacting to the news that the New York critics are cheering West's comeback, a weary-but-enthusiastic Jim Timmany speaks from California: "You opened the door, Mae--You kicked it in! If only Hollywood could see it!" Her reply: "They will, honey, in another twenty years or so." Realizing how much has changed in both their lives, Timmany adds, "It's too late for this, but I love you dearly."

West sadly responds, "You said one day the curtain would come down and I'd have no one to come home to. Well, tonight the curtain came down."

The comedian bio-film, by means of its intense concentration on the supposedly inherent contradictions between a laugh-maker's public and private lives, between his covert causes and overt effects, has over the years cast doubt on the authenticity of the image projected by the professional funnyman, possibly as a reflection in popular culture of a lingering, unspoken uncertainty on the part of the audience. Confronted with a performer whose high spirits, rapier wit, or graceful ability to surprise far exceeds the ordinary, the viewer, while temporarily delighted, may also experience a cognitive dissonance, best expressed in the statement: "Nobody can be that funny all the time." Comedian bio-films have specialized in confirming just such an underlying suspicion, and can therefore be identified as functioning in popular culture in accordance with the same rationale which explains the envy-assuaging function of exposés in general.

Tony Curtis in HOUDINI (1953). Photo courtesy Wisconsin Center for Film and Theater Research.

CHAPTER XII

CELEBRITY MISCELLANY

Throughout the evolution of the show-business biographical film no discernible cycles have emerged in regard to certain vocational specialties. Magicians, script writers, stunt men and impresarios have all had at least one or two bio-films devoted to their professions, however, and in most cases their generic relationships with the specialization cycles analyzed in previous chapters of this study are apparent.

Two biographies of magician Harry Houndid, HOUDINI (1953) and the made-for-TV THE GREAT HOUDINIS (1976) both diegetically overlap the vaudeville era of several of the singer and composer films. The earlier production is a sentimental tragedy of a "perfect couple" parted by the man's dabbling in the ancient, alchemical art of dematerialization. "It'll kill you," a veteran magician warns, but Houdini proceeds to build a water-immersed torture chamber for himself from uncompleted plans handed down to him by a deceased European master illusionist. Houdini's death is accompanied by his promise to "come back" with a message "from beyond" for his devoted wife. His initial quest fails, but the narrative holds out hope that as a result of his impassioned search for the truth about the afterlife, he will later succeed in a more profound quest. In the more cynical 1976 film he succeeds in sending his wife a message, but the press reports the event as if it were a fraud.

THE GREAT HOUDINIS covers the same historical career with a marked disregard for the sentiment of the production released twenty-three years earlier. Instead of an idealized marriage and partnership (his wife is also his stage assistant), the couple in this narrative face harmony-threatening opposition to their union from the young man's

old-world mother, whose reaction to the feared shikse is
much more bitter and intense than the orthodox parental displeasure
it echoes from the mid-1950s cycle of bandleader
biographies. The subject-hero of the later film also has a
magician brother, missing from the 1953 production just as
Al Jolson's brother ceased to exist in THE JOLSON STORY.
The Houdini of the earlier film is not even ethnically identified
by his offstage name, Erich Weiss. Allowing for the extreme
change in audience sensitivity to sexual matters which
occurred in the years between the two productions, the franker
dialogue and adulterous activity contained in the 1976 film is
not surprising, since the same value-shift is detectable in
other 1970s bio-films which re-work material and situations
treated in earlier biographies. This occurs most notably in
the Valentino films.

A near-mirror image of this time-distanced relationship
occurs between the two bio-films of author F. Scott
Fitzgerald which center on his unhappy years as a Hollywood
screenwriter. (A third film, F. SCOTT FITZGERALD AND
"THE LAST OF THE BELLES" excludes his contact with
show business.) While BELOVED INFIDEL (1959) constitutes
a continuance of the bio-exposés of the 1950s, in comparison
to its 1976 remake (F. SCOTT FITZGERALD IN HOLLYWOOD),
it is equally representative of the sentimentality and
sexual timidity the earlier Houdini film displays in contrast
to its remake. Both Fitzgerald motion pictures invoke the
familiar milieu of 1930s Hollywood, which diegetically overlaps
with such actor biographies as GABLE AND LOMBARD,
W. C. FIELDS AND ME, HARLOW I & II, and THE GEORGE
RAFT STORY. BELOVED INFIDEL invokes fewer celebrity
names, however, and chooses to disguise its impersonations
of Alice Faye and Robert Benchley. F. SCOTT FITZGERALD
IN HOLLYWOOD invokes many more names, but limits its
celebrity impersonations to Fitzgerald's fellow writers,
Dorothy Parker and Alan Campbell. Fitzgerald's mentally
unbalanced wife Zelda, referred to but unseen in the earlier
picture, appears in the later film's recurrent, intercut flashbacks,
some of which are set during Fitzgerald's previous
visit to the Hollywood of the 1920s, in a diegesis which overlaps
with the Valentino, Chaney, Garbo, and Keaton biographies.

BELOVED INFIDEL and F. SCOTT FITZGERALD IN
HOLLYWOOD employ only a section of the myth of rise-and-fall,
with Fitzgerald's rise to prominence as an author of
celebrated novels referred to by dialogue only in the past

Gregory Peck (as Scott Fitzgerald) and Deborah Kerr in BELOVED INFIDEL (1959). Photo courtesy Films Incorporated.

tense. Although he is presented as having mastered the art
of fiction while still a young man, both narratives show him
in middle age as being unable to adapt his skills to the popular motion picture values, techniques, and subjects which the
Hollywood hierarchy champions and exploits. BELOVED INFIDEL's narrative depicts the artistic conflict much more
resignedly than FITZGERALD IN HOLLYWOOD, which has
its subject-hero deliver scathing dialogue passages which
rail against the cinema aesthetics of the time. Fitzgerald's
sole hope of escape from the alcoholic trap he has been setting for himself is, in both cases, shown to be his love affair with gossip columnist Shielah Graham, whom he courts
with dogged determination in BELOVED INFIDEL and receives instant sexual gratification from in FITZGERALD IN
HOLLYWOOD.

Fitzgerald's death, while he was working towards a
literary comeback by begnning a new novel about the studio
executives he has encountered, is presented in both films as
an alcohol-induced waste of talent. The archetype of a gifted
individual being unable to survive the pressures of the showbusiness environment was previously identified as being a
shared feature of the exposé bio-films of both actors and
singers, but in those instances it was success which functioned as the precipitating factor. With Fitzgerald the culprit is not success, but security, the weekly check which
arrives whether his material is used or not.

The only other bio-film to date which centers on a
screen writer is the 1957 service comedy-cum-inspirational
drama, THE WINGS OF EAGLES, based on the life of U.S.
Navy Commander Frank "Spig" Wead. Much of the early
part of the narrative depicts Wead's devotion to the craft of
military flying, with his show-business career beginning
while he recuperates from a crippling accident which has
rendered him unfit for military service. Paralyzed from
the waist down, the naval officer is urged by a friend to
take up fiction writing. Wead's first stories of exotic adventure (echoing the pulp fiction he has read) are summarily rejected, but when he turns to "wrapping lies in pretty
paper," his phrase for writing popular fiction, about the
life he knows best (tales of military adventure on the sea
and in the air), his successful scripts for Broadway and
Hollywood make him a wealthy and happy man. The outbreak of World War II finds him called back for "special
duty" at sea, and his show-business interlude is over.

THE WINGS OF EAGLES, despite its brief depiction of Wead's experiences in Hollywood and in New York, does invoke its share of familiar names and locations. One sequence depicts Wead on the set of his HELL DIVERS (1931), and hindsight-influenced dialogue suggests that a "newcomer" named Clark Gable seems likely to become a star. WINGS OF EAGLES' rise-and-fall plot is more concerned with his military rise, his temporary fall from active duty, and his renaissance as a valuable and beloved officer in the subsequent war. Wead's excursion into show business is really only therapy.

ACT ONE (1963) employs the birth myth present in such films as THE ACTRESS, SO THIS IS LOVE, RAINBOW, and THE BIRTH OF THE BEATLES, as it depicts the emergence of Moss Hart as a promising Broadway playwright. The only show business bio-film devoted to an author known best for his stage work (Frank Wead wrote only one successful play), ACT ONE is also about the birth of a team. Young Hart, aspiring writer and director of amateur theatricals, wants desperately to become a successful author, but all of his scripts are rejected by producers. The problem, he is told, is that he is too serious, is trying too hard to be "another Eugene O'Neill." The year is 1929, and the trade papers are filled with news of the panic in Hollywood caused by the arrival of sound. Sensing a unique situation with comic potential, Hart pens a satire on the talkie crisis and titles it "Once in a Lifetime." When he finds a producer willing to stage it, the veteran showman insists that the eccentric "play doctor," George S. Kaufman, assist Hart with a re-write to improve the dramatic construction.

Thus begins Hart's series of humorous confrontations with the old master of wit and pacing. In being taken under the wing of Kaufman, Hart also finds himself introduced to the cream of 1929's New York-based literati and entertainment elite. A cocktail party attended by Hart is packed with invocational impersonations of Alexander Woollcott, Katharine Cornell, Robert Sherwood, Haywood Broun, Robert Benchley, Helen Hayes, Franklin P. Adams, Fanny Brice, George Gershwin, Edna Ferber, Leslie Howard, Dorothy Parker, John Barrymore (visiting) and George Jean Nathan, many of them linkage figures to other bio-films as well. After a series of false starts, frustrations and additional re-writes, Kaufman and Hart's first collaboration is a resounding success.

Professional daredevil Evel Knievel was chosen as
the subject-hero of a 1971 bio-film which dramatized incidents from his years of defying death for pay. A borderline figure between the worlds of sports and show business,
the Knievel character describes himself in the narrative as
essentially an all-around athlete who dislikes conventional,
rule-bound sports because, "If you lose, you don't lose
much." Yet he also compares himself to Elvis Presley,
Frank Sinatra, and John Wayne, explaining that each of them
"have a responsibility to the rest of the people, whose jobs
mean nothin' to 'em."

Following the linear structure of a basic quest, in
this case for increasingly greater dangers to overcome, the
narration of EVEL KNIEVEL also joins portions of the parallel story of his courtship and "kidnap marriage" with a unique
type of performance segment, spectacles of his car and motorcycle jumps which function as attractional factors akin to the
vocal or dance numbers in a musical bio-film. The stunts
are performed not by the actor portraying him, but by Knievel himself in long shot (possibly newsreel footage) after the
manner of having a genuine singer or instrumentalist dub a
sound track for the star of a musical biography. VIVA
KNIEVEL, a 1977 sequel throughout which Knievel congruently plays himself, crosses the border into overt fiction,
with its hero battling drug smugglers and syndicate hit men.

THE GREAT WALLENDAS, a 1978 television film, depicts the quest of the leader of a famous family of circus
wire-walkers. Karl Wallenda, acrobat and patriarch, is depicted in the opening sequence as being intensely proud of
his profession. "We are superstars and will always be," he
proclaims, "The high wire is the only place we feel at
home." Wallenda's dream is to perfect and perform a
seven-man pyramid, using cross bars but no net. To him
it is the ideal, untried balancing act, a supreme artistic
achievement generically akin to the "perfect sound" sought
by Glenn Miller or the total facial and body transformations
attempted by Lon Chaney. An early attempt fails when one
of the boys "throws the bar," resulting in the death of two
performers and the crippling of a third. Yet Karl Wallenda
will not forsake his vision during years of practice, performing lesser stunts, and arbitrating family disagreements. Just
when his seven-member team is about to attempt another
public performance, they decide to make one more practice
run in a deserted circus tent. Their ability to survive an
accidental power blackout, which leaves them in momentary

darkness, convinces their leader that they now can withstand any danger perfectly. On a note of triumph, they present their new act to the public. The archetypal quest succeeds.

Although there is little celebrity linkage or diegetic overlap with other show business bio-films, THE GREAT WALLENDAS does contain the basic elements for its generic classification. The attractional factor of the nearness of death, important as it is to drawing in the crowds, disturbs Wallenda after his earlier mishap. His reading of press accounts causes him to decry the public's flocking to see the Wallenda "freak show" out of a sense of wonder as to "who'll die next?" Extra-diegetically, his real-life counterpart went on to discover the answer first-hand.

The only bio-film of a motion picture stunt man, SILENT VICTORY (1979) is actually about a woman, as indicated by the sub-title: THE KITTY O'NEIL STORY. One of

Stockard Channing as Kitty O'Neil, with James Farentino in SILENT VICTORY (1979). Photo courtesy Capitol Communications.

a large sub-genre of supposedly inspirational television dramas about handicapped or illness-ridden individuals who make heroic strides to conquer their respective ailments, SILENT VICTORY spends most of its screen time doing just that. Its subject-heroine, deaf from birth, struggles, as she grows up, to be accepted as if she were perfectly normal, and in the process sets one athletic record after another. The large sum of money she inherits from her father is bilked away from her through a poor show-business investment in a tone-deaf singer, but her attraction to racing cars brings her back into the entertainment world when she convinces a motion picture stunt coordinator that she can survive crashes with ease and expertise. Her crowning achievement, however, is in racing, where she sets a new world record for speed on land--and breaks the sound barrier.

Bio-films of impresarios cover a wider range than most entries in the miscellaneous category, although one group of them, the numerous Buffalo Bill films, deals mainly with his alleged exploits as a buffalo hunter and Indian fighter. The 1944 BUFFALO BILL, begun as a cynical debunking of the popular culture image of the title figure but altered soon after to conform to the widely-held belief in his alleged acts of heroism, concludes with an epilogue which covers in montage fashion the career of his old age, staging rodeo-like western pageants for the entertainment of Easterners.

Two other films, ANNIE OAKLEY (1935) and ANNIE GET YOUR GUN (1950) perform acts of linkage with the Buffalo Bill "Wild West Show" by relating separation-and-reunion romances about a female hillbilly sharpshooter whose expert marksmanship eventually wins her a featured position in the Buffalo Bill entourage.

It was not until the occasion of the American Bicentennial, in 1976, that a film appeared which offered a direct challenge to the many Buffalo Bill legends first manufactured in the popular press of the late nineteenth century. These apocryphal adventures of derring-do in the American West, which later found their way into films, had served as long-term advance publicity for the traveling show operated by and starring William F. Cody, otherwise known as Buffalo Bill.

BUFFALO BILL AND THE INDIANS, OR SITTING

BULL'S HISTORY LESSONS, as the full title read, is a show business biography which departs from the standard myths, functioning instead as an exposé not of just one show business practitioner, but of the entire popular culture process of biographication, of the commercial construction of heroes. The film's dramatic mode is satire, its target is the heroic Indian fighter of the dime novels and newspaper serials. The film's narrative reveals Cody to be a total fraud, an imposter of his own image. Turned into a publicly perceived hero by crafty writers and publicists, the man runs a theatrical stock company of sorts which regularly enacts his dubious long-ago exploits in freeing pioneers and settlers from the dreaded menace of the savage red man. Offstage, however, Cody is a rambling charlatan, so besotted with liquor and equally intoxicated with his own legends that he can no longer distinguish fact from fiction.

Sitting Bull, the famous Indian chief who once battled the U.S. Cavalry and then lived to hear his battles turned into popular legend, agrees to join the show and play himself, in order to await his chance to speak about Indian problems to President Grover Cleveland when the chief executive pays his scheduled visit to the members of America's favorite "historical" pageant. The presence of the real Sitting Bull addles the brain of Cody even more severely than it was before, and he begins to slide into madness.

The theme of BUFFALO BILL AND THE INDIANS is that the presentation of American history through the medium of show business has resulted in a form of fakery so seductive that both its producers and consumers willingly enlarge the deception into a patently false way of thinking and living. In attacking a key representative of the embellished myths of American history, BUFFALO BILL AND THE INDIANS moves directly against the grain of traditional heroic/historical drama and attempts to obviate the inherently artificial naturalistic style of the biographical exposé. Implying that all myths kill truth, the film actually turns upon itself, for it, too, is a selective, dramatized series of real and imagined events, fashioned by professional entertainers and flung before a crowd of viewers accustomed to the visual and aural codes of the narrative, myth-infused film. BUFFALO BILL AND THE INDIANS' vehement rejection by the target audience (who were being portrayed in the popular media of the time as alienated from their patriotic heritage and eager for disillusioning experiences) therefore stands as testimony to a continuing public need to perceive events in one mythic shape

344 / Star Myths

or another, regardless of whatever topical prejudices are
being reinforced or attacked at a given moment.

The profession of cabaret operator has had only one
incarnation in a show-business bio-film, the 1945 Betty Hutton star vehicle, INCENDIARY BLONDE. Although its title
was derived from Hutton's own wartime Paramount publicity
campaign, the subject-heroine was a different famous blonde,
one from the nostalgically distanced past. She was Texas
Guinan, a trick-riding graduate of the "wild west shows"
spawned in imitation of Buffalo Bill's success. Guinan went
on to star in stage productions from the turn of the century
and in some of the early, two-reel westerns filmed in California before the Great War. Her hour of brightest glory,
according to the film's narrative, was when she returned to
New York during the prohibition-plagued 1920s to manage
some of the city's gaudiest and most popular speakeasies,
the kind which featured big-time musical entertainment and
a constant string of customers from society's elite.

Each phase of Guinan's varied career is depicted in
its own episode of INCENDIARY BLONDE's narrative, and
musical performance segments are inserted for Hutton in
each, with the exception of her silent film work, where a
non-dramatically integrated song would have been difficult to
rationalize diegetically. The operant myth is of the fatal
race with time, and Guinan's character enjoys the benefit of
a strong premonition that she will die "before I get old
enough to lose my figure." Ambiguously referring to her
pre-ordained early doom as "the black curse of the Irish,"
Guinan works hard at fulfilling the adage, "live fast--die
young." In what might be a bid for audience sympathy, a
libel-prevention necessity, or a narrative avoidance of having
her leave behind a grieving husband, none of her romantic
involvements proves successful.

Although invocation is not particularly high in terms
of the names of celebrities and linkage figures (many disguised identities are employed), the familiar film locales of
Manhattan and Hollywood provide a degree of general linkage
which turns specific in the flashback narrative's framing sequence. Prefiguring the Valentino films, the opening locale
is the same Campbell's Funeral Chapel where the dead actor
lay in state while a riot raged outside in the street. IN-
CENDIARY BLONDE begins with the memorial service for
Guinan, who has just died of a heart attack. Her famous
greeting to the Manhattan socialites who frequented her

bistros (and were charged exorbitantly high prices) was "Hello, suckers!" but she had always managed to "trim 'em and make 'em like it." Her grieving father, looking out over the crowd, assesses her popularity in appropriate show-business parlance: "Even her funeral's a sellout."

Other master showmen depicted by bio-films include Manhattan's turn-of-the-century "Family Vaudeville" theatre operator, Tony Pastor, whose establishment became one of show-business drama's most referred-to and represented locales. In addition to his being impersonated as a minor figure in various singer and songwriter biographies (and in a host of overtly fictional films as well), Pastor functions as a main character in THE DAUGHTER OF ROSIE O'GRADY (1950), an otherwise wholly fictitious, nostalgia-imbued musical about his alleged romance with the girl singer for whom he supposedly composed the title song.

Sol Hurok, the booking agent and concert promoter who made his name synonymous with the American tours of Europe's most highly-esteemed operatic vocalists, balletic dancers, and virtuoso musicians, is the subject-hero of TONIGHT WE SING (1953). A quest comedy-drama about Hurok's rise to prominence in his chosen field, its narrative follows Hurok from his childhood in Russia, where he masters every aspect of music except the ability to compose, conduct, or perform, to his establishing himself as America's number one source for high-culture music, "bringing to you and me," as an opening statement says, "more entertainment than any other living person." Determined to offer the world's finest music to the American masses, Hurok is depicted as favoring large concert halls (such as the New York Hippodrome) in order to keep ticket prices low, thus paralleling the concern for the common people expressed by the subject-hero of THE GREAT CARUSO.

A great deal of TONIGHT WE SING's screen time is devoted to performance segments by artists who are playing the parts of Hurok's early clients, who include dancer Anna Pavlova, violinist Eugene Ysaye, and baritone Feodor Chaliapin. Other celebrity names from the early-twentieth-century world of concert music and dance are also invoked and provide linkage; in one scene Hurok engages in a telephone conversation with Isadora Duncan. Much of the film's comedy comes from Hurok's bumbling campaign first to sign Chaliapin to an American contract, and then to get the playful, recalcitrant, seemingly dense but jovial Russian singing star to fulfill his obligation.

346 / Star Myths

David Wayne and Isaac Stern in TONIGHT WE SING (1953).
Photo courtesy Films Incorporated.

A brief separation-and-reunion sub-plot involves the desertion of Hurok by his exasperated wife, who justly and archetypally complains of being neglected by a husband who has become so obsessed with show business that he has no time to function as a family man. Although Hurok's chosen specialty is the marketing of "serious" music, the ex-hardware store operator goes about it with all the drive and cunning of a songplugger from Tin Pan Alley or a Ziegfeld planning a new Follies. Montages of Hurok's ultimate success reinforce the generic similarity in shared visual terms as well.

Two television bio-films have been made to date about motion picture producers, one a life-spanning chronicle, the other highly anecdotal and limited in diegetic time. THE AMAZING HOWARD HUGHES (1977) spends its three hours and twenty minutes (not counting commercials) depicting

Celebrity Miscellany / 347

Tommy Lee Jones in THE AMAZING HOWARD HUGHES (1977). Photo courtesy Capitol Communications.

nearly every widely reported incident from the tycoon's years in the public eye. His inheritance, at age twenty-five, of his millionaire father's tool business provides him a lifetime income with which to pursue a wide variety of vocations and avocations in the hope of mastering each one. "I intend to be the best at whatever I do," announces the young Hughes, many years before a psychiatric report is shown to label him as a classic example of the obsessive-compulsive personality.

The over-arching myth of this lengthy drama is clearly rise-and-fall, but within each of Hughes' specialized fields of endeavor his assumption of a separate quest for perfection comes to the fore. Hughes' adventures in the motion picture business, which qualify the film for inclusion in this analysis, divide into three phases, each depicted in the highly episodic narrative. His first run of activity as an independent film producer brings him to Hollywood in the late 1920s, where playing the role of film maker provides the basically shy man with a formal excuse to socialize with glamorous actresses. Invocation of the familiar is quite high at this point, with extensive use of celebrity names and impersonations of stars of the era. Even director Lewis Milestone rates a portrayal in a sequence in which he complains that producer Hughes is neglecting the filming of TWO ARABIAN KNIGHTS in favor of devoting more of his time to his experimentation with airplanes.

Hughes' three successful and best-remembered sound films, HELL'S ANGELS, SCARFACE, and THE FRONT PAGE, are also invoked, as are his series of publicized romances with Billie Dove, Ginger Rogers, and Katharine Hepburn. The last of these is dramatized at length, with Hughes and Hepburn going horseback riding and strolling along a beach while he explains his ambitions, and she questions his awesome ability to "arrange things" by amassing and spending large amounts of money. "It's necessary for me to be rich," he tells her, "I have plans...." However, her plans do not include him. (In authorizing this sequence, the real-life Hepburn adds to her own legend, as the unattainable Hollywood goddess who turned down the great Hughes.)

Hughes' brief return to film making, after spending the middle and late 1930s building experimental aircraft and setting world's flight records, is dramatized more briefly, centering on his production of a version of the Billy the Kid legend, THE OUTLAW, which angers the censors. In production before Pearl Harbor, its release without extensive cutting appears doubtful because of its sexual content. Hughes' decision to keep it off the market, however, is shown to be a marketing strategy, rather than an unavoidable suppression because of the Hays Office. "Shelve it a couple of years, say it's too hot ... then release it," he tells an assistant.

Hughes' heavy involvement in wartime aircraft production keeps him away from show business until the late 1940s. (His 1945 association with Preston Sturges and Harold Lloyd is not depicted.) He then returns to film production on a massive scale, buying control of RKO Studios and still pursuing actresses as a sideline. A shot of Hughes in his office, surrounded by portraits of all the beautiful women he has signed to personal or studio contracts, visually sums up the sultan-in-his-harem image conveyed by the dialogue. Noah Dietrich, Hughes' veteran personal accountant and aide, refers in one sequence to the man's "lifelong compulsion to possess the 'great American beauty.'" Acknowledging his employer's growing phobia about cleanliness, Dietrich rhetorically asks, "Even beautiful girls have germs--or do they go to bed with their gloves on?"

Embroiled with other concerns, including the financial difficulties of his airline, Hughes sells RKO in 1956 and moves on to other challenges, taking on the mob in Las Vegas and contracting with the U.S. government to conduct undersea espionage. His last years of decline and delusions conclude the drama.

While THE AMAZING HOWARD HUGHES went to considerable lengths to avoid obvious fabrication in its depiction of the man's show-business career, invoking many names, portraying other celebrities on camera, and never letting disguised but recognizable celebrities spoil the naturalistic illusion, the ultimate employment of the invocational process occurred three years later, in the only other movie producer bio-film to date.

Another of NBC's MOVIEOLA dramas, THE SCARLETT O'HARA WAR (1980) functions on the invocational level of a Hollywood wax museum in motion. A large number of little-known actors and actresses were auditioned and given makeup tests in order to cast the production with look-alikes for nearly every celebrity involved with the famous "search

for Scarlett O'Hara" which preceded the filming of 1939's
GONE WITH THE WIND. The subject-hero of this anecdotal
narrative is independent producer David O. Selznick. Less
recognizable to the target audience than the many celebrities
with whom he becomes involved in the narrative, Selznick is
portrayed by an actual star, Tony Curtis.

Selznick's quest is no lifelong ambition for greatness,
only his attempt to solve a production problem of the moment
--finding the right actress to play the lead in his next film.
Because of the prestigeful nature of the production, based on
one of the decade's best-selling novels, the role of Scarlett
O'Hara is a coveted prize in the eyes of the film colony's
resident leading ladies. The narrative of THE SCARLETT
O'HARA WAR is made up to a great extent by brief scenes
of various celebrities' intensely emotional, often humorous
reactions to the news and rumors of Selznick's talent hunt.
In effect, the target audience, supposedly well-versed in
old-movie viewing, is asked to play "spot the star" as the
drama unfolds.

Since most of the famous people depicted in this film
were deceased at the time of its production and airing, legal
clearances would have been a minor matter, but apparently
the film makers resolved to go ahead without any clearances
whatsoever, as if to proclaim that the whole enterprise of
this unusual bio-film was "all in good fun," a reflexive, joking, backward look by the film industry at a harmless moment of panic during its period of relative innocence. Of
the few characters who had survived to the program's air
date (Paulette Goddard, Lana Turner, Lucille Ball, Bette
Davis, Jean Arthur, Joan Bennett, and George Cukor),
only Goddard reportedly had plans to sue, and nothing has
come of that in terms of press reports at the time of this
writing. A proposed TV bio-film of the life of Elizabeth
Taylor, however, was met in 1982 with threats by the actress to sue the producers for massive invasion of privacy.
Former film star Grace Kelly, long retired to her palace
in Monaco as Princess Grace, was also reported as opposed
to a television filming of her life story, but soon after her
1982 death the network executives who had proposed the project
announced that she had "changed her mind" just prior to her
sudden passing.

Two famous radio performers had their broadcasting
careers highlighted (as differentiated from the many other
heroes of bio-films who excelled in several media) in a pair

Celebrity Miscellany / 351

of anecdotally based dramas. THE NIGHT THAT PANICKED AMERICA (1975) was a TV-movie which concentrated on a single evening in the career of actor-director Orson Welles: the night his Halloween eve, 1938, network dramatization of H. G. Wells' "The War of the Worlds" caused massive panic and confusion across the nation as listeners mistook its realistic, news-bulletin format for an actual invasion from Mars. Hardly a biography in the conventional sense, the film's narrative revealed almost nothing of the character and motivation of Welles and divided its screen time between a recreation of the actual studio performance of the notorious program and a series of fictional vignettes alleged to depict how a cross-section of the populace had their own personal dramas interrupted and altered by the sudden scare of an alien invasion. Welles' extensive career on stage and in film, in addition to the balance of his remarkable work in broadcasting, finds no room for inclusion in this narrowly focused invocation of the sounds of a unique event which was unquestionably familiar to the target audience, either by direct reminiscence or by the power of an oft-told story.

AMERICAN HOT WAX (1978) concentrated on a nationally known radio performer from a generation later. Still an anecdotally based drama, but covering more than a single evening in its hero's life, the narrative depicts the difficulties encountered by pioneer rock-and-roll disc jockey Alan Freed during a week of his 1959 preparations to stage an all-star musical revue at a large metropolitan auditorium, an audacious enterprise which would be against the wishes of both civic authorities and self-appointed guardians of the morality of youth. The real-life Freed had appeared in the mid-1950s in a few quasi-biographical films purporting to illustrate the struggles of rock-and-roll artists to reach the top, and the plot of AMERICAN HOT WAX echoes the antinomies of those earlier cinematic attempts at providing a target audience of teenagers with ritual vindication of their contemporary musical tastes.

Invocation of the familiar functions extensively through the sound track, which includes a mixture of authentic 1950s rock-and-roll records, "cover" versions done by unknown artists hired by the film makers to impersonate the performers of other hit songs of the period, and new versions of popular songs performed on camera by the same recording stars who actually introduced the tunes a generation earlier and are thus impersonating their former selves (Chuck Berry, Jerry Lee Lewis, Screamin' Jay Hawkins, Frankie Ford).

The film makers' difficulties in obtaining additional mechanical reproduction rights, authentic personal appearances, or legal clearances for character-name usage causes the film to display a widely varying level of historical accuracy, even to the point of supplying an alias for the story's leading lady, as was the case in THE JOLSON STORY. While actor Tim McIntyre is clearly identified as the late Alan Freed, actress Laraine Newman's character (obviously based on the still-living songwriter Carol King) calls herself "Teenage Louise" in the narrative. A composite musical group, "The Planetones," is portrayed as one of the star attractions of Freed's extravaganza and performs several hit songs which were actually popularized by others.

Despite its simple plot line (Freed plans to stage a major rock-and-roll show at Brooklyn's huge Paramount Theatre; the local authorities plot to cancel it by searching for incriminating evidence against him. Finding none, they send in police to close the show in mid-performance due to an allegedly "unruly crowd"), the narrative of AMERICAN HOT WAX does merit closer analysis in view of its peculiar hero. However much of a fast-buck, media-manipulator the historical Freed may have been, the myth-infused film portrays him as totally unspoiled by his enormous financial success as the first musical guru of America's youth. His only vices are chain-smoking and heavy drinking; he is very much a weary-looking, working-class, middle-aged, hairline-receding poor soul who "got lucky" by being in the right place at the right time--working nights at a big city radio station as a disc jockey who dared to defy management by playing the racially mixed, suggestively-worded, big-beat music America's "baby boom" children were more than ripe to respond to upon reaching puberty. The Alan Freed of AMERICAN HOT WAX enacts the role of the mythic visionary, the electronic pied piper who earned the adulation (and scorn) of millions by leading a generation out of the strait-laced conformity of one era and into the exciting and dangerous freedom of another. Just as this mystical imagery of rock-and-roll is evoked by the transcendent tragedy which concludes THE BUDDY HOLLY STORY ("And the rest is rock-and-roll ..."), Freed's prophetically triumphant remark to a Brooklyn policeman at the riotous conclusion of AMERICAN HOT WAX portends the dawning of a new age: "You can stop this show. You can stop me. But you can't stop rock-and-roll! Don't you <u>know</u> that?"

Just as the made-for-television motion picture has

taken the place of the Hollywood "program picture" and reworked most of the other successful film genres and story formulas of the past, the tailored-for-TV feature has (as has been shown here) extensively continued the half-century-old tradition of the show-business bio-film, employing time-tested, myth-infused narrative patterns in structuring both actual and invented events from a depicted celebrity's life. The passing of the years has led to the selecting of subject-hero figures from later eras in the history of commercial entertainment, however, as an indication that the target audience for these films is in a constant state of flux: the older members drop out and younger ones join the ranks of potential viewers. Because of the extended life of often-revived "film classics," certain stars from more than two generations earlier may yet be selected for portrayal--not only as nostalgic attractional factors, but as familiar, contemporary subjects for invocation, as noted earlier. Even personalities from a past too long gone to serve as first-hand nostalgia for even the oldest contemporary viewers are sometimes granted new life in the ongoing bio-film process if their enduring fame or compelling life stories are deemed sufficiently strong attractional factors by film makers.

In 1978 the over-arching cycle of the entertainer bio-film came full circle, with the showing of a made-for-television remake of the Oscar-winning 1936 production which, disregarding more tenuous starts, began the cycle in earnest by proving to the industry the viability of such films. The enduring fame of Florenz Ziegfeld certainly had faded a good deal in the public mind since the original picture's release, but it was still of sufficient intensity to merit this second full treatment of his life and career. With all major participants in the historical events safely gone to their rewards, no self-defensive disguising of characters or softening of motives was necessary for the film makers this time around. The way was clear for the telling of the Ziegfeld story without resort to either sentimentality or deception. The generic conventions of the bio-film exposé could be employed with ease.

ZIEGFELD: THE MAN AND HIS WOMEN takes as its structural model the studied fragmentation of viewpoint made famous by CITIZEN KANE, presenting flashback-styled, but in this case historically linear narrative segments dramatizing significant events in the showman's life. Each is introduced (in direct-to-the camera monologues) by one of the women playing major roles in the story.

Full circle: Paul Shenar as Florenz Ziegfeld, with Pamela Peadon as Marilyn Miller in ZIEGFELD: THE MAN AND HIS WOMEN (1978). Photo courtesy Capitol Communications.

Ziegfeld's mother tells of her boy's early years in Chicago; his witnessing the city's famous fire and thinking it quite a show; his disregarding his old-world father's ambition for the boy to become a serious musician; the boy's fledgling career as an exploitation promoter of freakish, P. T. Barnum-like stunts. Young Florenz Ziegfeld is seen telling his father, "the world is changing, and I've got my finger on the people's pulse. I know what they want-- sensation!" Then Mrs. Ziegfeld wistfully tells the film audience how her son first approached the business of putting on a show: "He never gave a thought for his discomfort or others'--only how well it played."

France's most famous singer-actress of the turn of the century, Anna Held, introduces the next segment, describing Ziegfeld, the man who brought her to America and made her his first wife: "He was unprincipled, cold, selfish. He wanted to please only himself. No woman who became involved with him emerged unscathed." Ziegfeld's private courtship and public promotion of Held is subsequently depicted, but decidedly less romantically than in THE GREAT ZIEGFELD. His decision to marry her even appears to be merely a part of his well-executed publicity campaign to keep both of their names in the headlines and thus attract more curious paying customers to her appearances on the musical comedy stage. "In Europe," says the cynical showman, "great artists are sought out by the discriminating--in America only publicity can make a star." Despite the conservative tenor of the times (circa 1905), Ziegfeld thinks nothing of requiring his wife to perform in the scandalously scantiest of garter-belted costumes ("They like Anna with or without clothes--but they like her a little better without!") or of arranging a quiet abortion for her when she becomes inconveniently pregnant ("Arrangements can be made ..."). "You've made me a freak," she exclaims, distraught over his endless publicity schemes, but Ziegfeld is unconcerned, having begun a new affair with the beautiful but talentless showgirl, Lillian Lorraine.

Lorraine, who could not be correctly named in THE GREAT ZIEGFELD and whose affair with her employer was shown in that film to be merely a "misunderstanding," self-satisfiedly tells the latter-day audience of ZIEGFELD: THE MAN AND HIS WOMEN, "He was a pushover, a pussycat. You could get anything you wanted out of him." In Lorraine's flashback Ziegfeld is seen constructing elaborate production numbers in which she is to star, although she can neither sing nor dance. Surrounded by opulence, all she needs to do is to be beautiful, thus exemplifying the famous Ziegfeld motto, "Glorifying the American girl."*

Ziegfeld's second wife, the gifted actress Billie Burke, introduces her portion of the story in a much more equivocal manner: "Flo was many men, but none could be manipulated. He was a genius. The ordinary rules of behavior didn't apply to him." Subsequently he is portrayed as the handsome, older man with a dangerous reputation whom she meets at a party and with whom she falls quickly in love and marries. His incurable sexual infidelity grieves her, but her love for him is too strong to allow her to leave. Instead, she has a child by him, retires from the stage, and resolves to stick with him until the end.

---

*Lorraine's lack of talent is exaggerated for dramatic effect; the actual historical character--indeed a famous beauty --sang and danced both in the "Follies" and in other producers' shows.

Marilyn Miller, Ziegfeld's biggest musical comedy star of the 1920s and another then-living performer whose character had to be name-disguised in THE GREAT ZIEGFELD, next speaks to the audience of the aging, quasi-gentleman who kept her name in lights for nearly a decade: "Florenz Ziegfeld was a hypocritical old goat who found the perfect way to be near a lot of young women." Denigrating not only his character, but his legendary talent as well, Miller adds, "Everything someone else did, he got credit for." Ziegfeld is then seen pursuing Miller both professionally and personally. First he accedes to her exorbitant financial terms in order to win her away from another theatrical producer; then he plies her with expensive gifts in hopes she will perform for him in private as well. Instead, she marries a man much nearer her own age. Her husband's sudden death in an auto accident renders her emotionally vulnerable, however, and the persistent Ziegfeld eventually comes to dominate both her mind and her career.

In two particularly repellent sequences the cruel nature of their relationship is depicted. Miller is informed of her husband's death just prior to her scheduled entrance in a nightly performance of her current Ziegfeld show. Although she protests through her tears that she cannot go on, her producer immediately spots this crucial chink in her emotional armor and callously proceeds to browbeat her into giving a performance against her wishes, replete with a wide array of her famous, cheery smiles, each one masking another heart-rending grimace of shock, pain, and sorrow. In a subsequent backstage encounter between producer and star, after his malevolent domination of her has become complete, Ziegfeld responds to her defiant cries of "I hate you," by demanding that she strip for him. Powerless in his presence, the humiliated girl does so in shame as Ziegfeld devours her flesh with his lust-filled, old man's eyes. Earlier, the imperious producer had responded with sheer scorn to his wife's concerned inquiry about Miller's ability to withstand the shock of her husband's death: "She's a puppet--I pull the string."

Eventually Miller manages to break free from Ziegfeld's Svengali-like hold over her, and she rushes to the scandal-sheet newspapers to reveal the hidden, evil nature of her former employer. Billie Burke reads one of the tabloid accounts of the affair to her husband and receives a far from comforting reply which synopsizes the nature of the multiple relationship referred to by the film's title.

Says Ziegfeld, "Women to me are like a flashing kaleidoscope of colors. They're all beautiful. I love them all! It has nothing to do with loyalty or fidelity. It has to do with stimulation, with renewing my creative juices ... I wish I could promise this won't happen again, but I can't."

The concluding segment of ZIEGFELD: THE MAN AND HIS WOMEN is introduced by an actress playing his daughter, Patty, who expresses a viewpoint quite in contradiction to the preceding narrative, but wholly in accord with the picture of her father successfully offered to the public in the original, 1936 bio-film: "There was a reason people called him 'The Great Ziegfeld.' He had the vision. He was a true pioneer, and he taught me the meaning of love. My father was a magnificent man--handsome, witty, and loving. His name will stand for spectacular beauty, imagination, and perfection as long as there is musical theater anywhere." The story of Ziegfeld's last years as a showman follows, recounting how his resounding failure in 1925, with four flop shows in a row, was more than compensated for by a string of the biggest hits of his career. With the sort of dialogue tinged with the irony of historical hindsight which has characterized so many bio-films, Ziegfeld observes, "Nineteen twenty-nine has been just about the best year I've had in my life." Then the stock market crashes, he is financially ruined, and many of his top stars defect to Hollywood and the new talkies.

Ziegfeld's last years are filled with dodging creditors and process servers, failed attempts at staging new shows, and a final move to Hollywood, to be near his loyal wife Billie, who has resumed her acting career (to pay off family bills) with successful performances in the films A BILL OF DIVORCEMENT and DINNER AT EIGHT. Still dreaming of another comeback for his own career, the broken old man dies in 1932.

ZIEGFELD: THE MAN AND HIS WOMEN invokes the familiar of long ago with considerably more facility and accuracy than was possible for THE GREAT ZIEGFELD, so much closer in historical proximity to the actual people and events. The overriding concern for maintaining audience sympathy which shaped the depicted motivations and actions of the hero of that film is, as if formulated in an inverse ratio, greatly diminished in the remake. ZIEGFELD: THE MAN AND HIS WOMEN rigorously includes impersonational linkage performances by each of the producer's well-remembered and bio-filmed stars (Fanny Brice, Will Rogers, Eddie Cantor, W. C. Fields, Nora Bayes, Marilyn Miller) across a historical time line which avoids the chronological confusion of the earlier film. In addition, the major Ziegfeld star whose own bio-film has often been planned, but never completed--black singer-comedian Bert Williams--is also portrayed in a rendition of his theme song, "Nobody." The fact that ZIEGFELD: THE MAN AND HIS WOMEN was produced on a television budget which in comparable dollars pales beside the studio outlay for the 1936 film is, however, visible in the lack of emphasis given to Ziegfeld's famous, lavish production numbers. Instead of building another towering spiral set similar to the one which dominates the visual impact of THE GREAT ZIEGFELD, the later film pegs its most spectacular number on a much more modest, linear staircase which is inundated by an avalanche of inexpensive, multi-colored balloons. Exterior shots in this film, which are kept to a bare minimum except for the archetypal reliance on a host of electrical theatre signs, appear to be lifted from stock footage of older, appropriate-looking period films. Authentic songs from Ziegfeld productions do, however, pepper the sound track, as do name-dropping, invocational dialogue references to even more celebrities of the period than were cited in the first film. Probably the only still-living v.i.p touched by the narrative of ZIEGFELD: THE MAN AND HIS WOMEN is near-centenarian composer Irving Berlin, who is briefly depicted in a sequence which immediately follows Ziegfeld's decision to commission music by George Gershwin. Berlin's character is seen expressing his hopes that Ziegfeld will respond favorably to the composer's new song, "A Pretty Girl Is Like a Melody."

The most significant difference between the two Ziegfeld bio-films, however, is not to be found in comparing their historical accuracy, production values, or intensity of familiarity invocation. The difference lies in their respective representations of how a discrete phenomenon of America's popular culture (the bio-film) tends to view a cohesive microcosm of its history (show business) across two widely different expanses of time. THE GREAT ZIEGFELD barely looked over its audience's shoulder, warmly remembering the man whose name meant the epitome of glamor in the popular entertainment of but a single generation grown to maturity. ZIEGFELD: THE MAN AND HIS WOMEN re-created an era which was fairly alien to much of its target audience, since original Broadway shows, unlike Hollywood movies, have not been blessed with the gift of late-show reincarnation. The

attractional factors of a bygone era of glamor, and of the
story of a powerful man and his subservient female harem,
were deemed sufficient by network authorities for them to
finance the film and grant it a single, three-hour prime-
time airing, but no perceived need for sentimental,
sympathy-arousing alterations of motives and actions appears to have been operant in the production process, nor
were the earlier, defensive distortions of THE GREAT
ZIEGFELD in need of repeating.

   Yet both films ultimately rely upon an ancient mythic
pattern in order to shape their depicted events into a dramatically effective fiction. It is the myth of the questor,
whose overwhelming drive to achieve his goal leads him to
a spectacular rise and a precipitous fall. The hero of THE
GREAT ZIEGFELD quested for beauty, in its most exquisite
forms, to be shared with the public. The later Ziegfeld
figure quests after physical sensation, and his elaborate
stage productions are also but a means to an end. While
the newer Ziegfeld bio-film grants the fallen showman no
ethereal renaissance, no visionary reunion with his triumphs of yesteryear, it does allow the Ziegfeld character
an opportunity to reflect on how the passing of the years
inexorably alters the perspective from which the public (or
its descendants) is able to view the once-cheered show business successes of an earlier day. In a sequence possibly
based on the personal remembrances of Patricia Ziegfeld
Stevenson, who served as the film's technical advisor, young
Patty Ziegfeld tells her father why she does not want to
grow up to be a "Ziegfeld girl." "I never wanted to be in
show business," she explains, "after I realized that stars
are like Christmas tree stars--made of tin, with price tags
on the back and glitter on the front." Waxing philosophical,
and perhaps explaining the shift in many bio-films of recent
years to the unsentimental, or if not, at least underlining the
major difference in the two Ziegfeld films, he replies, "It
wasn't always tin and price tags. There was a time when
this country was still young and innocent, and lived on
dreams. That was the time to be a showman. There were
real challenges then. You could capture the dreams of the
people and give them back as a gift--like a fine diamond,
perfect and glittering."

   This is not to say that the show-business biographical
films of today have a historical monopoly on relative truths,
for as has been shown, convenient conjunction of events,
mythic formulations based only on carefully selected facts,

condensation and omission of troublesome characters, and the arbitrary inclusion of invented incidents are still considered essential ingredients in the process of devising an entertaining narrative. As the brash young Ziegfeld explains to his father in an early sequence of the newer film, "Entertainment is not reality. If people wanted truth--they'd stay home!"

CONCLUSION

The show-business biographical film has now passed through a half-century of changing values, styles, technical innovations, and lessening legal and censorial restrictions. As a category of narrative film presentation it has been seen to encompass nearly as wide a variety of approaches as the war film or the detective story. While the entertainment bio-film may not possess as voluminous a body of completed productions as the other immediately recognizable genres, it nevertheless is firmly established, and is growing again, after a period of relative dormancy a decade ago. Made-for-television films have adopted its form with increasing regularity in recent seasons, and the commercial success of some of its latest theatrical examples suggests continued expansion and development on both fronts. The reflexive impulse, to construct (via universal mythic patterns) works of entertainment about the entertainers themselves, seems to be as strong as it ever was, judging by the future projects announced in the trade papers. Unless popular culture undergoes some radically unforeseen alteration, the show-business bio-film is likely to persist in one media form or another for an indefinite time, neither telling the "truth," something which is obviated by the selective, dramatic process, as shown in this book, nor telling the blatant lies of the genre's early years. Its future practitioners will continue to combine the naturalist illusion of reality (invoking that which audiences are likely to recognize) with dramatic employment of the eternal myths which so effectively structure and give meaning to the otherwise random complexities of the human experience.

FILMOGRAPHY

ACT ONE
(Moss Hart)
Warner Brothers 1963
W: Dore Schary (book by Moss Hart)
D: Dore Schary
C: George Hamilton (Hart), Jason Robards, Jr. (George S. Kaufman), Jack Klugman, Sam Levine, Ruth Ford, Eli Wallach.

THE ACTRESS
(Ruth Gordon)
Metro-Goldwyn-Mayer 1954
W: Ruth Gordon
D: George Cukor
C: Jean Simmons (Gordon), Spencer Tracy, Teresa Wright, Anthony Perkins, Ian Wolfe, Mary Wickes, Kay Williams (Hazel Dawn).

THE AMAZING HOWARD HUGHES
Roger Gimbel Productions/EMI 1977
W: John Gay (book by Noah Dietrich, Bob Thomas)
D: William A. Graham
C: Tommy Lee Jones (Hughes), Ed Flanders (Noah Dietrich), Tovah Feldshuh (Katharine Hepburn), Lee Purcell (Billie Dove), James Hampton (Wilbur Peterson), Marla Carlis (Jane Russell), Carol Bagdasarian (Jean Peters).

AMERICAN HOT WAX
(Alan Freed)
Paramount 1978
W: John Kaye
D: Floyd Mutrux
C: Tim McIntire (Freed), Fran Drescher, Jay Lena, Laraine Newman, plus Chuck Berry, Jerry Lee Lewis, Screamin' Jay Hawkins (themselves).

BELOVED INFIDEL
(F. Scott Fitzgerald)
Twentieth Century-Fox 1959
W: Sy Bartlett (book by Sheilah Graham, Gerold Frank)
D: Henry King
C: Gregory Peck (Fitzgerald), Deborah Kerr (Sheilah Graham), Eddie Albert, Philip Ober, Herbert Rudley, Karin Booth.

THE BENNY GOODMAN STORY
Universal 1955
W: Valentine Davies
D: Valentine Davies
C: Steve Allen (Goodman), Donna Reed, Berta Gersten, Herbert Anderson, Robert F. Simon, Harry James (himself), Gene Krupa (himself).

THE BEST THINGS IN LIFE ARE FREE
(Buddy DeSylva, Ray Henderson, Lew Brown)
Twentieth Century-Fox 1956
W: William Bowers, Phoebe Ephron (story by John O'Hara)
D: Michael Curtiz
C: Gordon MacRae (DeSylva), Dan Dailey (Henderson), Ernest Borgnine (Brown), Sheree North, Tommy Noonan, Norman Brooks (Al Jolson).

THE BIGGEST DANCER IN THE WORLD
(Isadora Duncan)
BBC Television 1966
W: Ken Russell (book by Sewell Stokes)
D: Ken Russell
C: Vivian Pickels (Duncan), Alexei Jawdokimov.

THE BIRTH OF THE BEATLES
Dick Clark Films Inc. 1979
D: Richard Marquand
C: Rod Culbertson (McCartney), Steve McKenna (Lennon), Jon Altman (Harrison), Ray Ashcroft (Starr), Ryan Michael (Best), Brian Jameson (Brian Epstein), David Wilkenson.

BOGEY
(Humphrey Bogart)
Charles Fries Productions 1979
W: Daniel Taradash (book by Joe Hyams)
D: Vincent Sherman
C: Kevin O'Connor (Bogart), Kathryn Harrold, Anne Wedgeworth, Patricia Barry, Donald May.

BOUND FOR GLORY
(Woody Guthrie)
United Artists 1976
W: Robert Getchell (book by Guthrie)
D: Hal Ashby
C: David Carradine (Guthrie), Ronnie Cox, Melinda Dillon, Gail Strickland, John Lehne, Ji-Tu Cumbaka.

BUD AND LOU
(Bud Abbott, Lou Costello)
Bob Banner Associates 1978
W: George Lefferts (book by Bob Thomas)
D: Robert C. Thompson
C: Harvey Korman (Abbott), Buddy Hackett (Costello), Michele Lee, Arte Johnson, Robert Reed, William Tregoe.

THE BUDDY HOLLY STORY
Columbia 1978
W: Robert Gittler (story by Steve Rash, Fred Bauer)
D: Steve Rash
C: Gary Busey (Holly), Don Stroud, Charles Martin Smith (the Crickets), Marla Richwine, Bill Jordan, Paul Mooney (Sam Cooke), Gilbert Melgar (Richie Valens), Gailard Sartain (J. P. "The Big Bopper" Richardson), George Simonelli (Dion).

THE BUSTER KEATON STORY
Paramount 1957
W: Sidney Sheldon, Robert Smith
D: Sidney Sheldon
C: Donald O'Connor (Keaton), Ann Blyth, Rhonda Fleming, Peter Lorre, Dave Willock (Joe Keaton), Claire Carleton.

CAN YOU HEAR THE LAUGHTER? THE STORY OF FREDDIE PRINZE
Roger Gimbel Productions/EMI 1979
W: Dalene Young (story by Peter S. Greenburg)
D: Burt Brinkerhoff
C: Ira Angustain (Prinze), Kevin Hooks, Julie Carmen, Ken Sylk (David Steinberg), Randee Heller, Stephen Elliot.

CHAMPAGNE CHARLIE
(George Leybourne)
Ealing 1944

W: Austin Melford, Angus MacPhail, John Dighton
D: Alberto Cavalcanti
C: Tommy Trinder (Leybourne), Stanley Holloway (the Great Vance), Betty Warren, Austin Trevor, Jean Kent, Guy Middleton.

COAL MINER'S DAUGHTER
(Loretta Lynn)
Universal 1980
W: Tom Rickman (book by Lynn)
D: Michael Apted
C: Sissy Spacek (Lynn), Tommy Lee Jones, Beverly D'Angelo (Patsy Cline), Levon Helm, Phyllis Boyens.

THE DAUGHTER OF ROSIE O'GRADY
(Tony Pastor)
Warner Brothers 1950
W: Jack Rose, Melville Shavelson, Peter Milne
D: David Butler
C: June Haver, Gordon MacRae (Pastor), James Barton, S. Z. Sakall, Jean Nelson, Debbie Reynolds.

DEAD MAN'S CURVE
(Jan and Dean)
Roger Gimbel Productions/EMI 1978
W: Dalene Young (story by Paul Morantz)
D: Richard Compton
C: Richard Hatch (Jan Barry), Bruce Davison (Dean Torrence), Pamela Bellwood, Floy Dean, Denise DuBarry, Dick Clark (himself), Wolfman Jack (the Jackal), the Beach Boys (themselves).

DEATH OF A CENTERFOLD: THE DOROTHY STRATTON STORY
MGM-TV/Wilcox Prod. 1981
W: Donald Stewart
D: Gabrielle Beaumont
C: Jamie Lee Curtis (Stratton), Bruce Weitz, Bibi Besch, Tracy Reed, Mitchel Ryan (Hugh Hefner), Mark Withers, Robert Reed.

DEEP IN MY HEART
(Sigmund Romberg)
Metro-Goldwyn-Mayer 1954
W: Leonard Spiegelgass (book by Elliott Arnold)
D: Stanley Donen
C: José Ferrer (Romberg), Merle Oberon (Dorothy

Donnelly), Helen Traubel, Doe Avedon, Walter Pidgeon
(J. J. Shubert), Paul Henreid (Florenz Ziegfeld), Tamara Tourmanova (Gaby Deslys).

DIXIE
(Dan Emmett)
Paramount 1943
W: Karl Tunberg, Darrell Ware, Claude Binyon (story by William Rankin)
D: A. Edward Sutherland
C: Bing Crosby (Emmett), Dorothy Lamour, Majorie Reynolds, Billy De Wolfe, Lynn Overman, Raymond Walburn, Eddie Foy, Jr.

THE DOLLY SISTERS
Twentieth Century-Fox 1945
W: John Larkin, Marian Spitzer
D: Irving Cummings
C: Betty Grable (Jenny), June Haver (Rosie), John Payne, S. Z. Sakall, Reginald Gardiner, Robert Middlemass (Oscar Hammerstein).

THE EDDIE CANTOR STORY
Warner Brothers 1954
W: Jerome Weidman, Ted Sherdeman, Sidney Skolsky (story by Sidney Skolsky)
D: Alfred E. Green
C: Keefe Brasselle (Cantor), Marilyn Erskine, Aline MacMahon, Arthur Franz, William Forrest (Florenz Ziegfeld), Hal March (Gus Edwards).

THE EDDY DUCHIN STORY
Columbia 1956
W: Samuel Taylor (story by Leo Katcher)
D: George Sidney
C: Tyrone Power (Duchin), Kim Novak, Victoria Shaw, James Whitmore, Rex Thompson, Larry Keating (Leo Reisman).

ELVIS!
Dick Clark Productions 1979
W: Anthony Lawrence
D: John Carpenter
C: Kurt Russell (Presley), Shelley Winters, Bing Russell, Robert Gray, Pat Hingle (Col. Tom Parker), Season Hubley (Priscilla Presley), Charles Cyphers (Sam Phillips), Will Jordan (Ed Sullivan), Galen Thompson (Hank Snow), Abi Young (Natalie Wood).

ELVIS AND THE BEAUTY QUEEN
David Gerber Company 1981
W: Julia Cameron
D: Gus Trikonas
C: Don Johnson (Elvis), Stephanie Zimbalist (Linda Thompson--Miss Tennessee), Ann Dusenberry (Jeannie LaMay--Miss Rhode Island), Rick Lenz, Ann Wedgeworth, Richard Herd.

EVEL KNIEVEL
Metro-Goldwyn-Mayer 1971
W: Alan Caillou, John Milius
D: Marvin Chomsky
C: George Hamilton (Knievel), Sue Lyon, Burt Fried, Rod Cameron.

F. SCOTT FITZGERALD IN HOLLYWOOD
Titus/Dan Goodman 1976
W: James Costigan
D: Anthony Page
C: Jason Miller (Fitzgerald), Tuesday Weld (Zelda), Julia Foster (Sheilah Graham), Dolores Sutton (Dorothy Parker), Susanne Benton, Michael Lerner, Tom Ligon (Alan Campbell), Tom Rosqui (Edwin H. Knopf).

THE FABULOUS DORSEYS
United Artists 1947
W: Richard English, Art Arthur, Curtis Kenyon
D: Alfred E. Green
C: Tommy Dorsey (himself), Jimmy Dorsey (himself), Janet Blair, William Lundigan, Sara Allgood, Arthur Shields, Paul Whiteman (himself), plus Charlie Barnet, Henry Busse, Mike Pingatore, Ziggy Elman, Bob Eberly, Helen O'Connell, Art Tatum, Stuart Foster, Ray Baudec (themselves).

FEAR ON TRIAL
(John Henry Faulk)
Alan Lansburg/MGM 1975
W: David W. Rintels (book by Faulk)
D: Lamont Johnson
C: William Devane (Faulk), George C. Scott (Louis Nizer), Dorothy Tristan, William Redfield, Milt Kogan, John Harkins (Vince Hartnett), Lois Nettleton ("Nan Claybourne"/Kim Hunter), David Suskind (himself), Mark Goodson (himself).

368 / Star Myths

THE FIVE PENNIES
    (Red Nichols)
Paramount 1959
W: Melville Shavelson, Jack Rose (story by Robert Smith)
D: Melville Shavelson
C: Danny Kaye (Nichols), Barbara Bel Geddes, Harry Guardino, Tuesday Weld, Louis Armstrong (himself), Bob Crosby, Ray Anthony (Jimmy Dorsey), Shelly Manne, Bobby Troup, Ray Daily (Glenn Miller).

FUNNY GIRL
    (Fanny Brice)
Columbia 1968
W: Isobel Lennart (book and play by Lennart)
D: William Wyler
C: Barbra Streisand (Brice), Omar Sharif (Nicky Arnstein), Kay Medford, Anne Francis, Walter Pidgeon (Florenz Ziegfeld), Lee Allen, May Questel.

FUNNY LADY
    (Fanny Brice)
Columbia 1975
W: Jay Presson Allen, Arnold Schulman (story by Schulman)
D: Herbert Ross
C: Barbra Streisand (Brice), James Caan (Billy Rose), Omar Sharif (Nicky Arnstein), Roddy McDowall, Carole Wells, Larry Gates (Bernard Baruch), Ben Vereen ("Bert Robbins"/Bert Williams).

GABLE AND LOMBARD
Universal 1975
W: Barry Sandler
D: Sidney J. Furie
C: James Brolin (Clark Gable), Jill Clayburgh (Carole Lombard), Allen Garfield (Louis B. Mayer), Red Buttons, Joanne Linville, Melanie Mayron.

THE GENE KRUPA STORY
Columbia 1960
W: Orin Jennings
D: Don Weiss
C: Sal Mineo (Krupa), Susan Kohner, James Darren, Celia Lovsky, Yvonne Craig, plus Red Nichols, Shelly Manne, Anita O'Day, Buddy Lester, Bobby Troup (in performance).

THE GEORGE RAFT STORY
Allied Artists 1961

W: Craine Wilbur
D: Joseph M. Newman
C: Ray Danton (Raft), Jayne Mansfield, Julie London, Barrie Chase, Herschel Bernardi, Frank Gorshin, Brad Dexter ("Bugsy" Siegel), Barbara Nichols (Texas Guinan), Neville Brand (Al Capone).

THE GIRL IN THE RED VELVET SWING
(Evelyn Nesbit)
Twentieth Century-Fox 1955
W: Walter Reisch, Charles Brackett
D: Richard Fleischer
C: Ray Milland (Stanford White), Farley Granger (Harry K. Thaw), Joan Collins (Nesbit), Glenda Farrell, Luther Adler, Cornelia Otis Skinner.

THE GLENN MILLER STORY
Universal 1954
W: Valentine Davies, Oscar Brodney
D: Anthony Mann
C: James Stewart (Miller), June Allyson, Charles Drake, George Tobias, Henry "Harry" Morgan, Barton MacLane (General "Hap" Arnold), plus Frances Langford, Louis Armstrong, Gene Krupa, Ben Pollack, the Archie Savage Dancers, the Modernaires (in performance).

GOLDEN GIRL
(Lotta Crabtree)
Twentieth Century-Fox 1951
W: Walter Bullock, Charles O'Neal, Gladys Lehman (story by Albert Louis, Arthur Louis, Edward Thompson)
D: Lloyd Bacon
C: Mitzi Gaynor (Crabtree), Dale Robertson, Dennis Day, James Barton, Una Merkel, Raymond Walburn, Carmen D'Antonio (Lola Montez).

THE GREAT CARUSO
Metro-Goldwyn-Mayer 1951
W: Sonya Levien, William Ludwig (story by Dorothy Caruso)
D: Richard Thorpe
C: Mario Lanza (Enrico Caruso), Ann Blyth, Dorothy Kirsten, Jarmila Novotna, Richard Hageman, Carl Benton Reid.

THE GREAT HOUDINIS
ABC Circle 1976
W: Melville Shavelson
D: Melville Shavelson

C: Paul Michael Glaser (Erich Weiss/Harry Houdini), Sally Struthers, Vivian Vance, Ruth Gordon, Adrienne Barbeau, Bill Bixby, Peter Cushing (Sir Arthur Conan Doyle).

THE GREAT VICTOR HERBERT
Paramount 1939
W: Russel Crouse, Robert Lively (story by Lively and Andrew L. Stone)
D: Andrew L. Stone
C: Walter Connolly (Herbert), Allan Jones, Mary Martin, Lee Bowman, Susanna Foster, Jerome Cowan.

THE GREAT WALLENDAS
Daniel Wilson Productions 1978
W: Jan Hartman
D: Larry Elikann
C: Lloyd Bridges, Britt Ekland, Taina Elg, Cathy Rigby, John Van Dreelin, Michael McGuire.

THE GREAT ZIEGFELD
Metro-Goldwyn-Mayer 1936
W: William Anthony McGuire
D: Robert Z. Leonard
C: William Powell (Florenz Ziegfeld, Jr.), Myrna Loy (Billie Burke), Luise Rainer (Anna Held), Frank Morgan, Virginia Bruce, Joseph Cawthorne, Ernest Cossart, A. A. Trimble (Will Rogers), Buddy Doyle (Eddie Cantor), Fanny Brice (herself), Harriet Hocter (herself), Paul Irving (Mr. Erlanger), Ray Bolger.

GYPSY
    (Gypsy Rose Lee)
Warner Brothers 1963
W: Leonard Spiegelgass (play by Arthur Laurents)
D: Mervyn LeRoy
C: Rosalind Russell (Mama Rose), Natalie Wood (Louise/Gypsy), Karl Malden, Paul Wallace, Parley Baer, Harry Shannon, Suzanne Caputo (Baby June), Ann Jillian (Dainty June).

HARLOW (I)
Magna Productions 1965
W: Karl Tunberg
D: Alex Segal
C: Carol Lynley (Jean Harlow), Ginger Rogers, Barry Sullivan, Efrem Zimbalist, Jr. ("William Mansfield"/William Powell), Lloyd Bochner, Jack Kruschen (Louis

B. Mayer), Hermione Baddeley (Marie Dressler), Hurd Hatfield (Paul Bern).

HARLOW (II)
Paramount 1965
W: John Michael Hayes (book by Irving Shulman)
D: Gordon Douglas
C: Carroll Baker (Jean Harlow), Red Buttons (Arthur Landow), Michael Connors ("Jack Harrison"/William Powell), Peter Lawford (Paul Bern), Martin Balsam ("Everett Redman"/Louis B. Mayer), Angela Lansbury, Raf Vallone.

HAYWIRE
  (Margaret Sullavan)
Warner Brothers Television 1980
W: Michael Tuchner (book by Brooke Hayward)
D: Michael Tuchner
C: Lee Remick (Sullavan), Jason Robards, Jr. (Leland Hayward), Deborah Raffin, Dianne Hull, Linda Gray, Dean Jagger.

THE HELEN MORGAN STORY
Warner Brothers 1957
W: Oscar Saul, Dean Reisner, Stephen Longstreet, Nelson Gidding
D: Michael Curtiz
C: Ann Blyth (Morgan), Paul Newman, Richard Carlson, Gene Evans, Cara Williams, Alan King, Walter Woolf King (Florenz Ziegfeld), Warren Douglas (Mark Hellinger), The De Castro Sisters, plus Jimmy McHugh, Rudy Vallee, Walter Winchell (themselves).

HOUDINI
Paramount 1953
W: Philip Yordan (book by Harold Kellock)
D: George Marshall
C: Tony Curtis (Harry Houdini), Janet Leigh, Torin Thatcher, Angela Clarke, Stefan Schnabel, Ian Wolfe.

THE I DON'T CARE GIRL
  (Eva Tanguay)
Twentieth Century-Fox 1953
W: Walter Bullock
D: Lloyd Bacon
C: Mitzi Gaynor (Tanguay), David Wayne, Oscar Levant, George Jessel (himself), Warren Stevens.

I DREAM OF JEANNIE
   (Stephen Foster)
Republic 1952
W: Allen Le May
D: Allan Dwan
C: Ray Middleton (E. P. Christy), Bill Shirley (Foster),
    Muriel Lawrence, Eileen Christy, Lynn Bari, Richard
    Simmons, Robert Neil, Louise Beavers, Percy Helton,
    Alfalfa Switzer.

I WONDER WHO'S KISSING HER NOW
   (Joe Howard)
Twentieth Century-Fox 1947
W: Lewis R. Foster
D: Lloyd Bacon
C: June Haver, Mark Stevens (Howard), Martha Stewart,
    Reginald Gardiner, Lenore Aubert, William Frawley.

I'LL CRY TOMORROW
   (Lillian Roth)
Metro-Goldwyn-Mayer 1955
W: Helen Deutsch, J. Richard Kennedy (book by Roth, Mike
    Connolly, Gerold Frank)
D: Daniel Mann
C: Susan Hayward (Roth), Richard Conte, Eddie Albert, Jo
    Van Fleet, Don Taylor, Ray Danton.

I'LL SEE YOU IN MY DREAMS
   (Gus Kahn)
Warner Brothers 1951
W: Melville Shavelson, Jack Rose
D: Michael Curtiz
C: Danny Thomas (Kahn), Doris Day, Frank Lovejoy,
    Patrice Wymore, James Gleason, Mary Wickes, William
    Forrest (Florenz Ziegfeld).

INCENDIARY BLONDE
   (Texas Guinan)
Paramount 1945
W: Claude Binyon, Frank Butler
D: George Marshall
C: Betty Hutton (Guinan), Arturo de Cordova, Charlie
    Ruggles, Albert Dekker, Barry Fitzgerald, Mary
    Phillips, Maurice Rocco (himself).

THE INCREDIBLE SARAH
   (Sarah Bernhardt)

Readers Digest Films 1976
W: Ruth Wolff
D: Richard Fleischer
C: Glenda Jackson (Bernhardt), Daniel Massey, Douglas Wilmer, David Langton, Simon Williams, John Castle.

INTERRUPTED MELODY
(Margery Lawrence)
Metro-Goldwyn-Mayer 1955
W: William Ludwig, Sonya Levien
D: Curtis Bernhardt
C: Eleanor Parker (Lawrence), Glenn Ford, Roger Moore, Cecil Kellaway, Peter Leeds, Leopold Sachse (himself).

IRISH EYES ARE SMILING
(Ernest R. Ball)
Twentieth Century-Fox 1944
W: Earl Baldwin, John Tucker Battle
D: Gregory Ratoff
C: Dick Haymes (Ball), June Haver, Monty Woolley, Anthony Quinn, Beverly Whitney, Maxie Rosenbloom.

IS EVERYBODY HAPPY?
(Ted Lewis)
Columbia 1943
W: Monte Brice
D: Charles Barton
C: Ted Lewis (himself), Larry Parks, Nan Wynn.

ISADORA/THE LOVES OF ISADORA
(Isadora Duncan)
Universal 1969
W: Melvyn Bragg, Clive Exton (books by Duncan, Sewell Stokes)
D: Karel Reisz
C: Vanessa Redgrave (Duncan), James Fox (Gordon Craig), Jason Robards, Jr. (Paris Singer), Ivan Tchenko, John Fraser, Bessie Love, Cynthia Harris (Mary Desti).

JAMES DEAN
The Jozak Company 1976
W: William Bast
D: Robert Butler
C: Stephen McHattie (Dean), Michael Brandon (Bast), Candy Clark, Meg Foster, Jayne Meadows, Dane Clark (James Whitmore).

THE JAYNE MANSFIELD STORY
Alan Landsburg Productions 1980
W: Charles Dennis, Nancy Gale, Steven Karpf, Elinor
   Karpf (book by Martha Saxton)
D: Dick Lowry
C: Loni Anderson (Mansfield), Arnold Schwarzenegger (Mickey
   Hargitay), Raymond Buktenica, Kathleen Lloyd, G. D.
   Spradlin.

JEANNE EAGELS
Columbia 1957
W: Daniel Fuchs, Sonya Levien, John Fante (story by Fuchs)
D: George Sidney
C: Kim Novak (Eagels), Jeff Chandler, Agnes Moorehead,
   Charles Drake, Larry Gates, Virginia Grey.

THE JOKER IS WILD
   (Joe E. Lewis)
Paramount 1957
W: Oscar Saul (book by Art Cohn)
D: Charles Vidor
C: Frank Sinatra (Lewis), Eddie Albert, Mitzi Gaynor,
   Jeanne Crain, Beverly Garland, Jackie Coogan.

JOLSON SINGS AGAIN
Columbia 1949
W: Sidney Buchman
D: Henry Levin
C: Larry Parks (Al Jolson), Barbara Hale, William
   Demarest, Ludwig Donath, Bill Goodwin, Tamara
   Shayne, Myron McCormick.

THE JOLSON STORY
Columbia 1946
W: Stephen Longstreet, Harry Chandler, Andrew Solt
D: Alfred E. Green
C: Larry Parks (Al Jolson), Evelyn Keyes ("Julie Benson"/
   Ruby Keeler), William Demarest, Ludwig Donath,
   Tamara Shayne, Bill Goodwin, Scotty Becket (Jolson as
   a boy), Edwin Maxwell (Oscar Hammerstein).

LADY SINGS THE BLUES
   (Billie Holiday)
Paramount 1972
W: Terrence McCloy, Chris Clark, Suzanne de Passe (book
   by Holiday and William Dufty)
D: Sidney J. Furie
C: Diana Ross (Holiday), Billy Dee Williams, Richard

Pryor, James Callahan, Paul Hampton, Sid Melton, Scatman Crothers.

THE LADY WITH RED HAIR
(Mrs. Leslie Carter, David Belasco)
Warner Brothers 1940
W: Charles Kenyon, Milton Krims (story by N. Brewster Morse, Norbert Falkner, book by Carter)
D: Kurt Bernhardt
C: Miriam Hopkins (Carter), Claude Rains (David Belasco), Richard Ainley, Laura Hope Crews, Helen Westley, John Litel.

A LADY'S MORALS
(Jenny Lind)
Metro-Goldwyn-Mayer 1930
W: Hans Kraly, Claudine West, John Meehan, Arthur Richman (story by Dorothy Farnham)
D: Sidney Franklin
C: Grace Moore (Lind), Reginald Denny, Wallace Beery P. T. Barnum), Gus Shy, Jobina Howland, Gilbert Emery.

LEADBELLY
(Huddie Ledbetter)
Paramount 1976
W: Ernest Kinoy
D: Gordon Parks
C: Roger E. Mosley (Ledbetter/Leadbelly), James E. Brodhead (John Lomax), John McDonald, Leonard Wrentz, Art Evans ("Blind Lemon" Jefferson), John Henry Faulk (Governor Pat Neff).

LEAVE 'EM LAUGHING
(Jack Thum)
Charles Fries Prod. 1981
W: Cynthia Mandelberg, Peggy Chandler Dick
D: Jackie Cooper
C: Mickey Rooney (Thum), Allen Goorwitz, Anne Jackson, Elisha Cook, Michael LeClair, William Windom (Smiley Jenkins), Red Buttons.

THE LEGEND OF VALENTINO
Spelling/Goldberg Productions 1975
W: Melville Shavelson
D: Melville Shavelson
C: Franco Nero (Rudolph Valentino), Suzanne Pleshette

(June Mathis), Judd Hirsh, Leslie Warren, Milton Berle (Jesse Lasky), Yvette Mimieux (Natacha Rambova), Alicia Bond (Nazimova), Michael Thoma (Rex Ingram).

LENNY
(Lenny Bruce)
United Artists 1974
W: Julian Barry (play by Julian Barry)
D: Bob Fosse
C: Dustin Hoffman (Bruce), Valerie Perrine (Honey Bruce), Jan Miner, Stanley Beck, Gary Morton, Guy Rennie.

LILLIAN RUSSELL
Twentieth Century-Fox 1940
W: William Anthony McGuire
D: Irving Cummings
C: Alice Faye (Russell), Don Ameche (Edward Solomon), Henry Fonda (Alexander Moore), Edward Arnold ("Diamond Jim" Brady), Warren William (Jesse Lewisohn), Leo Carillo (Tony Pastor), Nigel Bruce (William Gilbert), Claude Allister (Arthur Sullivan), Weber and Fields (themselves), Eddie Foy, Jr. (Foy, Sr.), Joseph Cawthorn (Leopold Damrosch), William Davidson (Grover Cleveland).

LITTLE EGYPT
(Betty Randolph)
Universal 1951
W: Oscar Brodney, Doris Gilbert (story by Brodney)
D: Frederick de Cordova
C: Rhonda Fleming ("Princess Izora"/"Little Egypt"/Betty Randolph), Mark Stevens, Nancy Guild, Charles Drake, Tom D'Andrea, Minor Watson.

LOOK FOR THE SILVER LINING
(Marilyn Miller)
Warner Brothers 1949
W: Phoebe and Henry Ephron, Marian Spitzer (story by Bert Kalmar, Harry Ruby)
D: David Butler
C: June Haver (Miller), Ray Bolger (Jack Donohue), Gordon MacRae, Charlie Ruggles, Rosemary DeCamp, Walter Catlett (himself), Will Rogers, Jr. (Rogers, Sr.).

LOUIS ARMSTRONG--CHICAGO STYLE
Charles Fries Productions 1975
W: James Lee

D: Lee Philips
C: Ben Vereen (Armstrong), Red Buttons, Margaret Avery, Janes MacLachlin, Lee DeBroux, Karen Jensen.

LOVE ME OR LEAVE ME
(Ruth Etting)
Metro-Goldwyn-Mayer 1955
W: Daniel Fuchs, Isobel Lennart (story by Fuchs)
D: Charles Vidor
C: Doris Day (Etting), James Cagney (Martin "The Gimp" Snyder), Cameron Mitchell, Robert Keith, Tom Tully, Harry Bellaver.

MAE WEST
Hill/Maldelker Prod. 1982
W: E. Arthur Kean
D: Lee Phillips
C: Ann Jillian (West), James Brolin, Roddy McDowall, Louise Giambalo, Chuck McCann, Lee DeBroux, Donald Hotton, Piper Laurie.

MAN OF A THOUSAND FACES
(Lon Chaney)
Universal 1957
W: R. Wright Campbell, Ivan Goff, Ben Roberts (story by Ralph Wheelwright)
D: Joseph Pevney
C: James Cagney (Chaney), Dorothy Malone, Jane Greer, Marjorie Rambeau, Jim Backus, Robert J. Evans (Irving Thalberg), Roger Smith (Creighton Chaney/Lon, Jr.) Clarence Kolb (himself), Danny Beck (Max Dill), Phil Van Zandt (George Loane Tucker).

MARILYN--THE UNTOLD STORY
(Marilyn Monroe)
Lawrence Schiller Prod. 1980
W: Dalene Young (book by Norman Mailer)
D: John Flynn, Jack Arnold
C: Catherine Hicks (Monroe), Jason Miller (Joe DiMaggio), Viveca Lindfors, Sheree North, Frank Converse (Arthur Miller), John Ireland, Richard Basehart (Laurence Olivier).

THE MIGHTY BARNUM
(P. T. Barnum)
Twentieth Century/United Artists 1934
W: Gene Fowler, Bess Meredyth

D: Walter Lang
C: Wallace Beery (Barnum), Adolphe Menjou, Virginia Bruce (Jenny Lind), Rochelle Hudson, Janet Beecher, Herman Bing.

MILLION DOLLAR MERMAID
(Annette Kellerman)
Metro-Goldwyn-Mayer 1952
W: Everett Freeman
D: Mervyn LeRoy
C: Esther Williams (Kellerman), Victor Mature, Walter Pidgeon, David Brian, Maria Tallchief (Anna Pavlova), Jesse White.

MOMMIE DEAREST
(Joan Crawford)
Paramount 1981
W: Frank Perry, Frank Yablans (book by Christina Crawford)
D: Frank Perry
C: Faye Dunaway (Crawford), Diana Scarwid (Christina Crawford), Rutanya Alda, Mara Hobel, Steve Forrest, Howard DaSilva (Louis B. Mayer), Jeremy Scott Reinbolt.

MOTHER WORE TIGHTS
(Burt and McKinley)
Twentieth Century-Fox 1947
W: Lamar Trotti (book by Miriam Young)
D: Walter Lang
C: Betty Grable (Myrtle McKinley), Dan Dailey (Frank Burt), Mona Freeman, Connie Marshall, Vanessa Brown, Robert Arthur.

MOVIEOLA: THE SILENT LOVERS; THE SCARLETT O'HARA WAR; THIS YEAR'S BLONDE
David Wolper 1980
W: Garson Kanin (book by Kanin)
D: John Erman
C: Kristina Wayborn (Greta Garbo), Barry Bostwick (John Gilbert), Harold Gould (Louis B. Mayer), Brian Keith (Mauritz Stiller), John Rubenstein (Irving Thalberg), Andra Lindley (Laura Hope Crews), Mackenzie Phillips (Lillian Gish), James Olson (Victor Seastrom), Tony Curtis (David O. Selznick), Joey Freeman (Walter Winchell), Jane Keane (Luella Parsons), Morgan Brittany (Vivien Leigh), Constance Forslund (Marilyn Monroe), Lloyd Bridges (Johnny Hyde).

MY GAL SAL
(Paul Dresser)
Twentieth Century-Fox 1942
W: Seton I. Miller, Darrel Ware, Karl Tunberg (story by Theodore Dreiser)
D: Irving Cummings
C: Victor Mature (Dresser), Rita Hayworth, Carole Landis, John Sutton, James Gleason, Phil Silvers, Walter Catlett.

MY WILD IRISH ROSE
(Chauncy Olcott)
Warner Brothers 1947
W: Peter Milne (book by Rita Olcott)
D: David Butler
C: Dennis Morgan (Olcott), Arlene Dahl, Andrea King (Lillian Russell), William Frawley (William Scanlan), George O'Brien ("Iron Duke" Muldoon), George Tobias, Alan Hale.

NIGHT AND DAY
(Cole Porter)
Warner Brothers 1946
W: Charles Hoffman, Leo Townsend, William Bowers, Jack Mofitt
D: Michael Curtiz
C: Cary Grant (Porter), Alexis Smith, Monty Woolley (himself), Ginny Simms, Jane Wyman, Eve Arden, Henry Stephenson, Mary Martin (herself).

THE NIGHT THAT PANICKED AMERICA
(Orson Welles)
Paramount 1975
W: Nicholay Meyer, Anthony Wilson
D: Joseph Sargent
C: Paul Shenar (Welles), Vic Morrow, Cliff DeYoung, Michael Constantine, Walter McGinn, Eileen Brennan, Tom Bosley, Will Geer, Merideth Baxter, Art Hannes.

NIJINSKY
Paramount 1979
W: unavailable (book by Romola Nijinsky, diary by her husband)
D: Herbert Ross
C: George de la Pena (Nijinsky), Alan Bates (Sergei Diaghilev), Leslie Browne.

OH YOU BEAUTIFUL DOLL
(Fred Fisher)
Twentieth Century-Fox 1949
W: Albert and Arthur Lewis
D: John M. Stahl
C: S. Z. Sakall (Alfred Breitenback/Fred Fisher), June Haver, Mark Stevens, Charlotte Greenwood, Gale Robbins, J. C. Flippen.

THE PATRICIA NEAL STORY
Lawrence Schiller & Assoc. 1981
W: Robert Anderson (book by Barry Farrell)
D: Anthony Harvey, Anthony Page
C: Glenda Jackson (Neal), Dirk Bogarde (Roald Dahl), Ken Kerschel, Jane Merrow, John Reilly, Mildred Dunnock (herself), Steve Eason (Frank Gilroy), Gloria Strook (herself), James Hayden (Martin Sheen).

THE PERILS OF PAULINE
(Pearl White)
Paramount 1947
W: P. J. Wolfson, Frank Butler (story by Wolfson)
D: George Marshall
C: Betty Hutton (White), John Lund, Billy De Wolfe, William Demarest, Constance Collier, Frank Faylen, plus William Farnum, Chester Conklin, Snub Pollard, James Finlayson, Creighton Hale, Hank Mann, Paul Panzer, Francis McDonald, Bert Roach, Heinie Conklin (themselves).

PRINCE OF PLAYERS
(Edwin Booth)
Twentieth Century-Fox 1955
W: Moss Hart (book by Eleanor Ruggles)
D: Philip Dunne
C: Richard Burton (Booth), Eva Le Gallienne, Maggie McNamara, John Derek (John Wilkes Booth), Raymond Massey, Charles Bickford.

RAINBOW
(Judy Garland)
Ten-Four Productions 1978
W: John McGreevey (book by Christopher Finch)
D: Jackie Cooper
C: Andrea McArdle (Garland), Don Murray, Michael Parks (Roger Edens), Rue McClanahan, Nicholas Pryor, Jack Carter, Martin Balsam (Louis B. Mayer), Moosie Drier

(Mickey Rooney), Johnnie Doran (Jackie Cooper), Philip Sterling (Arthur Freed).

RHAPSODY IN BLUE
(George Gershwin)
Warner Brothers 1945
W: Howard Koch, Elliot Paul (story by Sonya Levien)
D: Irving Rapper
C: Robert Alda (Gershwin), Joan Leslie, Alexis Smith, Charles Coburn, Herbert Rudley (Ira Gershwin), Eddie Marr (Buddy DeSylva), Oscar Loraine (Maurice Ravel), Hugo Kirchoffer (Walter Damrosch), plus Al Jolson, Oscar Levant, Paul Whiteman, George White, Hazel Scott, Anne Brown, Tom Patricola, John B. Hughes (themselves).

ST. LOUIS BLUES
(W. C. Handy)
Paramount 1958
W: Robert Smith, Ted Sherdeman
D: Allen Reisner
C: Nat King Cole (Handy), Eartha Kitt, Pearl Bailey, Cab Calloway, Mahalia Jackson, Ruby Dee, Juano Hernandez (Reverend Charles Handy), Billy Preston (young Handy), Ella Fitzgerald (herself).

SARAH
(Sarah Bernhardt)
Great Performances/PBS 1979
W: Suzanne Grossman
D: Waris Hussein
C: Zoe Caldwell (Bernhardt), Donald Davis, Jean LeClerc, Edward Atrienza, Olivette Thibault, Dawn Greenhalgh.

SCOTT JOPLIN
Universal 1977
W: Christopher Knopf
D: Jeremy Paul Kagan
C: Billy Dee Williams (Joplin), Art Carney (John Stark), Clifton Davis, Godfrey Cambridge, Seymour Cassell, Eubie Blake, Margaret Avery.

THE SEVEN LITTLE FOYS
(Eddie Foy)
Paramount 1955
W: Melville Shavelson, Jack Rose
D: Melville Shavelson

C: Bob Hope (Foy), Milly Vitale, George Tobias, Angela Clark, Herbert Heyes, James Cagney (George M. Cohan), plus Billy Gray, Lee Erickson, Paul De Rolf, Lydia Reed, Linda Bennett, Jimmy Baird, Tommy Duran (the children).

THE SEX SYMBOL
(Marilyn Monroe)
Screen Gems/Columbia 1974
W: Alvah Bessie (book by Bessie)
D: David Lowell Rich
C: Connie Stevens ("Kelly Williams"/"Emmaline Kelly"/Marilyn Monroe), Shelley Winters, Jack Carter, William Castle, Don Murray, James Olson.

SHINE ON HARVEST MOON
(Jack Norworth, Nora Bayes)
Warner Brothers 1944
W: Sam Hellman, Richard Weil, Francis Swann, James Kern (story by Weil)
D: David Butler
C: Ann Sheridan (Bayes), Dennis Morgan (Norworth), Jack Carson, Irene Manning, S. Z. Sakall, Marie Wilson.

SILENT VICTORY
(Kitty O'Neil)
The Channing-Debin-Locke Co. 1979
W: Steven Gethers
D: Lou Antonio
C: Stockard Channing (O'Neil), James Farentino, Colleen Dewhurst, Edward Albert, Brian Dennehey, Jim Antonio.

SO THIS IS LOVE
(Grace Moore)
Warner Brother 1953
W: John Monks, Jr. (book by Moore)
D: Gordon Douglas
C: Kathryn Grayson (Moore), Merv Griffin, Joan Weldon, Walter Abel, Rosemary DeCamp, Jeff Donnell, Douglas Dick, Mabel Albertson (Mary Garden), Roy Gordon (Otto Kahn).

SOMEBODY LOVES ME
(Blossom Seeley, Benny Fields)
Paramount 1952
W: Irving Brecher
D: Irving Brecher

C: Betty Hutton (Seeley), Ralph Meeker (Fields), Robert Keith, Billie Bird, Adelle Jergens, Henry Slate.

SOPHIA LOREN--HER OWN STORY
Roger Gimbel Productions/EMI 1980
W: Joanna Crawford (book by A. E. Hotchner)
D: Mel Stuart
C: Sophia Loren (herself, her mother), Armand Assante, Riza Braun, Teresa Saldani, John Gavin (Cary Grant), Rip Torn (Carlo Ponti), Edmund Purdom (Vittorio De Sica).

STAND BY YOUR MAN
(Tammy Wynette)
JNP Productions 1981
W: John Gay (book by Joan Dew)
D: Jerry Jameson
C: Annette O'Toole (Wynette), Cooper Huckabee, Helen Page Camp, Tim McIntire (George Jones), James Hampton.

STAR!
(Gertrude Lawrence)
Twentieth Century-Fox 1968
W: William Fairchild
D: Robert Wise
C: Julie Andrews (Lawrence), Richard Crenna, Michael Craig, Daniel Massey (Noel Coward), Robert Reed, Bruce Forsythe, Beryl Reid.

THE STAR MAKER
(Gus Edwards)
Paramount 1939
W: Frank Butler, Don Hartman, Arthur Caesar (story by Caesar, William A. Pierce)
D: Roy Del Ruth
C: Bing Crosby ("Larry Earl"/Edwards), Louise Campbell, Linda Ware, Ned Sparks, Janet Waldo, Walter Damrosch (himself).

STARS AND STRIPES FOREVER
(John Philip Sousa)
Twentieth Century-Fox 1952
W: Lamar Trotti (book by Sousa)
D: Henry Koster
C: Clifton Webb (Sousa), Debra Paget, Robert Wagner, Ruth Hussey, Finlay Currie, Roy Roberts.

THE STORY OF VERNON AND IRENE CASTLE
RKO 1939
W: Richard Sherman, Oscar Hammerstein II, Dorothy Yost (books by Irene Castle)
D: H. C. Potter
C: Fred Astaire (Vernon), Ginger Rogers (Irene), Edna May Oliver, Walter Brennan, Lew Fields (himself), Etienne Girardot.

THE STORY OF WILL ROGERS
Warner Brothers 1952
W: Frank Davis, Stanley Roberts (story by Mrs. Will Rogers)
D: Michael Curtiz
C: Will Rogers, Jr. (Rogers, Sr.), Jane Wyman, Carl Benton Reid, Eve Miller, James Gleason, Slim Pickins, Noah Beery, Jr. (Wiley Post), William Forrest (Florenz Ziegfeld), Earl Lee (Woodrow Wilson).

SWANEE RIVER
(Stephen Foster)
Twentieth Century-Fox 1939
W: John Taintor Foote, Philip Dunne
D: Sidney Lanfield
C: Don Ameche (Foster), Al Jolson (E. P. Christy), Andrea Leeds, Felix Bressart, Chick Chandler, Russell Hicks, The Hall Johnson Choir (minstrel singers).

THREE LITTLE WORDS
(Bert Kalmar, Harry Ruby)
Metro-Goldwyn-Mayer 1950
W: George Wells
D: Richard Thorpe
C: Fred Astaire (Kalmar), Red Skelton (Ruby), Vera-Ellen, Arlene Dahl, Keenan Wynn, Gloria De Haven (Mrs. Carter De Haven), Phil Regan (himself), Debbie Reynolds (Helen Kane), The Great Mendoza (himself).

TILL THE CLOUDS ROLL BY
(Jerome Kern)
Metro-Goldwyn-Mayer 1947
W: Myles Connolly, Jean Holloway, George Wells (story by Guy Bolton)
D: Richard Whorf
C: Robert Walker (Kern), Lucille Bremmer, Van Heflin, Paul Langton (Oscar Hammerstein), Paul Maxey (Victor Herbert), Judy Garland (Marilyn Miller), plus June

Allyson, Frank Sinatra, Virginia O'Brien, Angela Lansbury, Kathryn Grayson, Lena Horne, Tony Martin, Cyd Charisse, Gower Champion (themselves).

TONIGHT WE SING
(Sol Hurok)
Twentieth Century-Fox 1953
W: Harry Kurnitz, George Oppenheimer (book by Sol Hurok, Ruth Gode)
D: Mitchell Leisen
C: David Wayne (Hurok), Ezio Pinza (Feodor Chaliapin), Roberta Peters (Elisa Valdine), Tamara Toumanova (Anna Pavlova), Isaac Stern (Eugene Ysaye), Anne Bancroft.

TOO MUCH, TOO SOON
(Diana and John Barrymore)
Warner Brothers 1958
W: Art Napoleon (book by Diana Barrymore and Gerold Frank)
D: Art Napoleon
C: Dorothy Malone (Diana), Errol Flynn (John), Efrem Zimbalist, Jr., Neva Patterson, Martin Milner, Ray Danton, Murray Hamilton.

VALENTINO (I)
Columbia 1951
W: George Bruce (story by George Bruce)
D: Lewis Allen
C: Anthony Dexter (Valentino), Eleanor Parker, Richard Carlson, Patricia Medina, Joseph Calleia, Dona Drake.

VALENTINO (II)
United Artists 1977
W: Ken Russell, Mardik Martin
D: Ken Russell
C: Rudolf Nureyev (Valentino), Leslie Caron (Nazimova), Michelle Phillips (Natacha Rambova), Felicity Kendal (June Mathis), Seymour Castle (George Ullman), Peter Vaughan, Carol Kane, Huntz Hall (Jesse Lasky).

W. C. FIELDS AND ME
Universal 1976
W: Bob Merrill (book by Carlotta Monti, Cy Rice)
D: Arthur Hiller
C: Rod Steiger (Fields), Valerie Perrine (Monti), John Marley ("Harry Bannerman"/Adolph Zukor), Jack

Cassidy (John Barrymore), Paul Stewart (Florenz Ziegfeld), Bernadette Peters, Billy Barty, Dana Elcar, Allan Arbus (Gregory La Cava), Milt Kamen (Dave Chasen), Louis Zorich (Gene Fowler).

THE WINGS OF EAGLES
(Frank Wead)
Metro-Goldwyn-Mayer 1957
W: Frank Fenton, William Wister Haines (writings by Wead)
D: John Ford
C: John Wayne (Wead), Dan Dailey, Maureen O'Hara, Ward Bond ("John Dodge"/John Ford), Edmund Lowe, Ken Curtis.

WITH A SONG IN MY HEART
(Jane Froman)
Twentieth Century-Fox 1952
W: Lamar Trotti
D: Walter Lang
C: Susan Hayward (Froman), Rory Calhoun, David Wayne, Thelma Ritter, Robert Wagner, Una Merkel.

WORDS AND MUSIC
(Rodgers and Hart)
W: Fred Finklehoff (story by Guy Bolton, Jean Holloway)
D: Norman Taurog
C: Mickey Rooney (Lorenz Hart), Tom Drake (Richard Rodgers), Marshall Thompson (Herbert Fields), Janet Leigh, Betty Garrett, Ann Sothern, Perry Como, plus June Allyson, Judy Garland, Lena Horne, Gene Kelly, Vera-Ellen, Cyd Charisse (themselves).

YANKEE DOODLE DANDY
(George M. Cohan)
Warner Brothers 1942
W: Robert Buckner, Edmund Joseph (story by Buckner)
D: Michael Curtiz
C: James Cagney (Cohan), Joan Leslie, Walter Huston (Jerry Cohan), Richard Whorf (Sam Harris), George Tobias, Rosemary DeCamp, Jeanne Cagney, Eddie Foy, Jr. (Foy, Sr.), George Barbier (Mr. Erlanger), Minor Watson (Mr. Albee), Captain Jack Young (Franklin Delano Roosevelt).

YOUR CHEATIN' HEART
(Hank Williams)
Metro-Goldwyn-Mayer 1965

W: Stanford Whitmore
D: Gene Nelson
C: George Hamilton (Williams), Susan Oliver, Red Buttons, Arthur O'Connell (Fred Rose), Rex Ingram.

ZIEGFELD: THE MAN AND HIS WOMEN
(Florenz Ziegfeld)
Frankovich/Columbia 1978
W: Joanna Lee
D: Buzz Kulik
C: Paul Shenar (Ziegfeld), Samantha Eggar (Billie Burke), Barbara Parkins (Anna Held), Pamela Peadon (Marilyn Miller), Valerie Perrine (Lillian Lorraine), Gene McLaughlin (Will Rogers), Richard Shea (Eddie Cantor), Catherine Jacoby (Fannie Brice), David Downing (Bert Williams), Inga Swenson (Nora Bayes), Ron Hussman (Jack Norworth), Cliff Norton (Abe Erlanger), Frances Lee McCain, David Opatoshu, Nehemiah Persoff.

BIBLIOGRAPHY

Theoretical

Andrew, J. Dudley. The Major Film Theories: An Introduction. New York: Oxford Univ. Press, 1976.

Carr, Edward Hallett. What Is History? New York: Vintage Books, 1961.

Cawelti, John G. Adventure, Mystery, and Romance. Chicago: The Univ. of Chicago Press, 1976.

Edinger, Edward F. Ego and Archetype. Baltimore: Penguin Books, 1972.

Frye, Northrop. Anatomy of Criticism: Four Essays. Princeton, N.J.: Princeton Univ. Press, 1957.

_____. Fables of Identity: Studies in Poetic Mythology. New York: Harcourt, Brace & World, 1963.

Grant, Barry K., ed. Film Genre: Theory and Criticism. Metuchen, N.J.: Scarecrow Press, 1977.

Kaminsky, Stuart M. American Film Genres: Approaches to a Critical Theory of Popular Film. Dayton, Ohio: Pflaum Publishing, 1974.

McConnell, Frank. Storytelling and Mythmaking: Images from Film and Literature. New York: Oxford Univ. Press, 1979.

Propp, V. Morphology of the Folktale. Austin: Univ. of Texas Press, 1968.

Todorov, Tzvetan. The Fantastic: A Structural Approach to a Literary Genre. Ithaca, N.Y.: Cornell Univ. Press, 1973.

Historical

Barris, Alex. Hollywood According to Hollywood: How the Cinema World Has Seen Itself in Its Films. New York: A. S. Barnes, 1978.

Behlmer, Rudy, and Tony Thomas. Hollywood's Hollywood: The Movies About the Movies. Secaucus, N.J.: Citadel Press, 1975.

Bordman, Gerald. American Musical Theatre: A Chronicle. New York: Oxford Univ. Press, 1978.

Csida, Joseph, and June Bundy Csida. American Entertainment: A Unique History of Popular Show Business. New York: Watson-Guptill Publications, 1978.

Gilbert, Douglas. American Vaudeville: Its Life and Times. New York: Dover Publications, 1940.

Higham, Charles. Ziegfeld. Chicago: Henry Regnery, 1972.

Kobal, John. Gotta Sing Gotta Dance. New York: Hamlyn Publishing Group, 1971.

Meyers, Richard. Movies on Movies: How Hollywood Sees Itself. New York: Drake Publishers, 1978.

Palmer, Tony. All You Need Is Love: The Story of Popular Music. New York: Penguin Books, 1976.

Stallings, Penny. Flesh and Fantasy: The Truth Behind the Fantasy Behind the Truth. New York: St. Martin's Press, 1978.

Specialized Reference

Bronner, Edwin J. The Encyclopedia of the American Theatre, 1900-1975. London: The Tantivy Press, 1980.

Emmens, Carol A. Famous People on Film. Metuchen, N.J.: Scarecrow Press, 1977.

Franklin, Joe. Joe Franklin's Encyclopedia of Comedians. Secaucus, N.J.: Citadel Press, 1979.

Green, Stanley. Encyclopedia of the Musical Film. New York: Oxford Univ. Press, 1981.

Maltin, Leonard. The Great Movie Comedians. New York: Crown Publishers, 1978.

Marx, Kenneth S. Star Stats: Who's Who in Hollywood. Los Angeles: Price/Stern/Sloan, 1979.

Pickard, Roy. Who Played Who in the Movies: An A-Z. New York: Schocken Books, 1979.

Ragan, David. Who's Who in Hollywood, 1900-1976. New Rochelle, N.Y.: Arlington House--Publishers, 1976.

Shipman, David. The Great Movie Stars: The Golden Years. New York: Bonanza Books, 1970.

_____. The Great Movie Stars: The International Years. New York: St. Martin's Press, 1972.

INDEX

Part I: Celebrities Depicted in Show-Business Biographical Films

* denotes self-portrayal (?) denotes disguised portrayal

Abbott, Bud: BUD AND LOU
Adams, Franklin P.: ACT ONE
Albee, Edward Franklin: YANKEE DOODLE DANDY
Allyson, June: TILL THE CLOUDS ROLL BY*, WORDS AND MUSIC*
Arbuckle, Fatty: VALENTINO II
Armstrong, Louis: THE FIVE PENNIES*, THE GLENN MILLER STORY*, LOUIS ARMSTRONG--CHICAGO STYLE
Arnold, Gen. Hap: THE GLENN MILLER STORY
Arnstein, Nicky: FUNNY GIRL, FUNNY LADY
Arthur, Jean: MOVIEOLA

Ball, Ernest R.: IRISH EYES ARE SMILING
Bankhead, Tallulah: MOVIEOLA
Barnet, Charlie: THE FABULOUS DORSEYS
Barnum, Phineas T.: A LADY'S MORALS, THE MIGHTY BARNUM
Baruch, Bernard: FUNNY LADY
Barry, Jan: DEAD MAN'S CURVE
Barrymore, Diana: TOO MUCH, TOO SOON
Barrymore, John: ACT ONE, TOO MUCH, TOO SOON, W. C. FIELDS AND ME
Bayes, Nora: SHINE ON HARVEST MOON, YANKEE DOODLE DANDY, ZIEGFELD: THE MAN AND HIS WOMEN
Beach Boys: DEAD MAN'S CURVE
Belasco, David: THE LADY WITH RED HAIR
Benchley, Robert: ACT ONE, BELOVED INFIDEL (?)
Bennett, Joan: MOVIEOLA
Benny, Jack: GYPSY
Berlin, Irving: ZIEGFELD: THE MAN AND HIS WOMEN
Bern, Paul: HARLOW I, HARLOW II
Bernhardt, Sarah: THE INCREDIBLE SARAH, SARAH
Berry, Chuck: AMERICAN HOT WAX*, THE BUDDY HOLLY STORY
Best, Pete: THE BIRTH OF THE BEATLES
Bogart, Humphrey: BOGEY
Booth, Edwin: PRINCE OF PLAYERS
Booth, John Wilkes: PRINCE OF PLAYERS
Brady, "Diamond Jim": THE GREAT ZIEGFELD, LILLIAN RUSSELL

Brice, Fannie: ACT ONE, FUNNY GIRL, FUNNY LADY, THE GREAT ZIEGFELD*, ZIEGFELD: THE MAN AND HIS WOMEN
Broun, Haywood: ACT ONE
Brown, Anne: RHAPSODY IN BLUE*
Brown, Lew: THE BEST THINGS IN LIFE ARE FREE
Bruce, Lenny: LENNY
Burke, Billie: THE GREAT ZIEGFELD, ZIEGFELD: THE MAN AND HIS WOMEN
Burt, Frank: MOTHER WORE TIGHTS

Campbell, Alan: F. SCOTT FITZGERALD IN HOLLYWOOD
Cantor, Eddie: THE EDDIE CANTOR STORY, THE GREAT ZIEGFELD, THE STORY OF WILL ROGERS*
Carter, Mrs. Leslie: THE LADY WITH RED HAIR
Caruso, Enrico: THE GREAT CARUSO
Castle, Irene: THE STORY OF VERNON AND IRENE CASTLE
Castle, Vernon: THE STORY OF VERNON AND IRENE CASTLE
Catlett, Walter: LOOK FOR THE SILVER LINING*
Chaliapin, Feodor: TONIGHT WE SING
Champion, Gower: TILL THE CLOUDS ROLL BY*
Chaney, Lon: MAN OF A THOUSAND FACES
Chaplin, Charles: MOVIEOLA
Charisse, Cyd: TILL THE CLOUDS ROLL BY*, WORDS AND MUSIC*
Chasen, Dave: W. C. FIELDS AND ME
Christy, Edwin P.: HARMONY LAND, I DREAM OF JEANNIE, SWANEE RIVER
Clark, Dick: DEAD MAN'S CURVE*
Cleveland, Grover: BUFFALO BILL AND THE INDIANS, LILLIAN RUSSELL, STARS AND STRIPES FOREVER
Cline, Patsy: COAL MINER'S DAUGHTER
Cohan, George M.: THE SEVEN LITTLE FOYS, YANKEE DOODLE DANDY
Cohan, Jerry: YANKEE DOODLE DANDY
Conklin, Chester: PERILS OF PAULINE*
Conklin, Heinie: PERILS OF PAULINE
Cooke, Sam: THE BUDDY HOLLY STORY
Cooper, Jackie: RAINBOW
Cornell, Katharine: ACT ONE
Costello, Lou: BUD AND LOU
Coward, Noel: STAR!
Crabtree, Lotta: GOLDEN GIRL
Crawford, Joan: MOMMIE DEAREST, MOVIEOLA
Crews, Laura Hope: MOVIEOLA
Craig, Gordon: ISADORA
Cukor, George: MOVIEOLA
Curtis, King: THE BUDDY HOLLY STORY

Dahl, Roald: THE PATRICIA NEAL STORY
Damrosch, Leopold: LILLIAN RUSSELL
Damrosch, Walter: RHAPSODY IN BLUE, THE STAR MAKER*

Davis, Bette: MOVIEOLA
Dawn, Hazel: THE ACTRESS
Dean, James: JAMES DEAN
DeHaven, Mrs. Carter: THREE LITTLE WORDS
DeSica, Vittorio: SOPHIA LOREN: HER OWN STORY
Deslys, Gaby: DEEP IN MY HEART
De Sylva, Buddy: THE BEST THINGS IN LIFE ARE FREE, RHAPSODY IN BLUE
Diaghilev, Sergei: NIJINSKY
Dion: THE BUDDY HOLLY STORY
Dolly, Jenny: THE DOLLY SISTERS
Dolly, Rosie: THE DOLLY SISTERS
Domino, Fats: THE BUDDY HOLLY STORY
Donnelly, Dorothy: DEEP IN MY HEART
Donohue, Jack: LOOK FOR THE SILVER LINING
Dorsey, Jimmy: THE FABULOUS DORSEYS*, THE FIVE PENNIES, THE GENE KRUPA STORY
Dorsey, Tommy: THE FABULOUS DORSEYS*, THE GENE KRUPA STORY
Dove, Billie: THE AMAZING HOWARD HUGHES
Dresser, Paul: MY GAL SAL
Dressler, Marie: HARLOW I
Duchin, Eddy: THE EDDY DUCHIN STORY
Duchin, Peter: THE EDDY DUCHIN STORY
Duncan, Isadora: BIGGEST DANCER IN THE WORLD, ISADORA
Dunnock, Mildred: THE PATRICIA NEAL STORY*
Durante, Jimmy: THE EDDIE CANTOR STORY

Eagels, Jeanne: JEANNE EAGELS
Eberly, Bob: THE FABULOUS DORSEYS*
Edens, Roger: RAINBOW
Edwards, Gus: THE EDDIE CANTOR STORY, THE STAR MAKER (?)
Edwards, Ralph: I'LL CRY TOMORROW
Emmett, Dan: DIXIE
Epstein, Brian: THE BIRTH OF THE BEATLES
Erlanger, Abe: THE GREAT ZIEGFELD, YANKEE DOODLE DANDY
Etting, Ruth: LOVE ME OR LEAVE ME

Farnum, William: THE PERILS OF PAULINE*
Faulk, John Henry: FEAR ON TRIAL
Faye, Alice: BELOVED INFIDEL (?)
Ferber, Edna: ACT ONE
Fields, Benny: SOMEBODY LOVES ME
Fields, Herbert: WORDS AND MUSIC
Fields, Lew: LILLIAN RUSSELL*, THE STORY OF VERNON AND IRENE CASTLE*
Fields, W. C.: MAE WEST, W. C. FIELDS AND ME
Finlayson, James: THE PERILS OF PAULINE*
Fisher, Fred: OH YOU BEAUTIFUL DOLL
Fitzgerald, Ella: ST. LOUIS BLUES*
Fitzgerald, F. Scott: BELOVED INFIDEL, F. SCOTT FITZGERALD

IN HOLLYWOOD
Ford, Frankie: AMERICAN HOT WAX*
Ford, Henry: THE STORY OF WILL ROGERS
Ford, John: THE WINGS OF EAGLES (?)
Foster, Stephen: HARMONY LANE, I DREAM OF JEANNIE, SWANEE RIVER
Fowler, Gene: W. C. FIELDS AND ME
Foy, Eddie: LILLIAN RUSSELL, THE SEVEN LITTLE FOYS, YANKEE DOODLE DANDY
Freed, Alan: AMERICAN HOT WAX
Freed, Arthur: RAINBOW
Froman, Jane: WITH A SONG IN MY HEART

Gable, Clark: GABLE AND LOMBARD, MOVIEOLA
Garbo, Greta: MOVIEOLA
Garden, Mary: SO THIS IS LOVE
Garland, Judy: RAINBOW, WORDS AND MUSIC*
Gershwin, George: ACT ONE, RHAPSODY IN BLUE, SO THIS IS LOVE
Gershwin, Ira: RHAPSODY IN BLUE
Gilbert, John: MOVIEOLA
Gilbert, William: THE GREAT GILBERT AND SULLIVAN, LILLIAN RUSSELL
Gish, Lillian: MOVIEOLA
Goddard, Paulette: MOVIEOLA
Goodman, Benny: THE BENNY GOODMAN STORY
Goodson, Mark: FEAR ON TRIAL*
Gordon, Ruth: THE ACTRESS
Graham, Sheilah: BELOVED INFIDEN, F. SCOTT FITZGERALD IN HOLLYWOOD
Grant, Cary: MAE WEST, SOPHIA LOREN: HER OWN STORY
Grayson, Kathryn: TILL THE CLOUDS ROLL BY*
Guinan, Texas: THE GEORGE RAFT STORY, INCENDIARY BLONDE
Guthrie, Woody: BOUND FOR GLORY

Hale, Creighton: THE PERILS OF PAULINE*
Hammerstein, Oscar: THE DOLLY SISTERS, THE JOLSON STORY
Hammerstein, Oscar II: TILL THE CLOUDS ROLL BY
Handy, W. C.: ST. LOUIS BLUES
Hardy, Oliver: HARLOW II
Harlow, Jean: HARLOW I, HARLOW II
Harris, Sam: YANKEE DOODLE DANDY
Harrison, George: THE BIRTH OF THE BEATLES
Hart, Lorenz: WORDS AND MUSIC
Hart, Moss: ACT ONE
Havoc, June: GYPSY
Hawkins, Screamin' Jay: AMERICAN HOT WAX*
Hayes, Helen: ACT ONE
Hayward, Leland: HAYWIRE
Hefner, Hugh: DEATH OF A CENTERFOLD
Held, Anna: THE GREAT ZIEGFELD, ZIEGFELD: THE MAN AND

HIS WOMEN
Hellinger, Mark: THE HELEN MORGAN STORY
Henderson, Ray: THE BEST THINGS IN LIFE ARE FREE
Hepburn, Katharine: THE AMAZING HOWARD HUGHES
Herbert, Victor: THE GREAT VICTOR HERBERT, THE GREAT ZIEGFELD, TILL THE CLOUDS ROLL BY
Hochter, Harriet: THE GREAT ZIEGFELD*
Holiday, Billie: LADY SINGS THE BLUES
Holly, Buddy: THE BUDDY HOLLY STORY
Hopkins, Miriam: MOVIEOLA
Horne, Lena: TILL THE CLOUDS ROLL BY*, WORDS AND MUSIC*
Houdini, Harry: THE GREAT HOUDINIS, HOUDINI
Howard, Joe: I WONDER WHO'S KISSING HER NOW
Howard, Leslie: ACT ONE
Howard, Sidney: MOVIEOLA
Hudson, Rock: THE PATRICIA NEAL STORY*
Hughes, Howard: THE AMAZING HOWARD HUGHES
Hughes, John B.: RHAPSODY IN BLUE*
Hunter, Kim: FEAR ON TRIAL (?)
Hurok, Sol: TONIGHT WE SING
Hyde, Johnny: MOVIEOLA

Ingram, Rex: THE LEGEND OF VALENTINO

Jack, Wolfman: DEAD MAN'S CURVE
James, Harry: THE BENNY GOODMAN STORY*
Jefferson, Blind Lemon: LEADBELLY
Jessel, George: THE I DON'T CARE GIRL*
Jolson, Al: THE BEST THINGS IN LIFE ARE FREE, HARLOW I, JOLSON SINGS AGAIN, THE JOLSON STORY, RHAPSODY IN BLUE*
Jones, George: STAND BY YOUR MAN
Joplin, Scott: SCOTT JOPLIN

Kahn, Gus: I'LL SEE YOU IN MY DREAMS
Kahn, Otto: SO THIS IS LOVE
Kalmar, Bert: THREE LITTLE WORDS
Kaufman, George S.: ACT ONE
Keaton, Buster: THE BUSTER KEATON STORY
Keaton, Joe: THE BUSTER KEATON STORY
Keeler, Ruby: THE JOLSON STORY (?)
Kellerman, Annette: MILLION DOLLAR MERMAID
Kelly, Gene: WORDS AND MUSIC*
Kern, Jerome: THE GREAT ZIEGFELD, TILL THE CLOUDS ROLL BY
Knievel, Evel: EVEL KNIEVEL, VIVA KNIEVEL
Knopf, Edwin H.: F. SCOTT FITZGERALD IN HOLLYWOOD
Kolb, Clarence: MAN OF A THOUSAND FACES*
Krupa, Gene: THE BENNY GOODMAN STORY, THE GENE KRUPA STORY, THE GLENN MILLER STORY*

LaCava, Gregory: W. C. FIELDS AND ME
Langford, Frances: THE GLENN MILLER STORY*
Lansbury, Angela: TILL THE CLOUDS ROLL BY*
Laurel, Stan: HARLOW I
Lasky, Jesse: THE LEGEND OF VALENTINO, VALENTINO II
Lawrence, Gertrude: STAR!
Lawrence, Marjorie: INTERRUPTED MELODY
Ledbetter, Huddie: LEADBELLY
Lee, Gypsy Rose: GYPSY
Leigh, Vivien: MOVIEOLA
Lennon, John: THE BIRTH OF THE BEATLES
Lester, Buddy: THE GENE KRUPA STORY*
Levant, Oscar: RHAPSODY IN BLUE*
Lewis, Jerry Lee: AMERICAN HOT WAX*
Lewis, Joe E.: THE JOKER IS WILD
Lewis, Ted: IS EVERYBODY HAPPY?*
Lewisohn, Jesse: LILLIAN RUSSELL
Leybourne, George: CHAMPAGNE CHARLIE
Lind, Jenny: A LADY'S MORALS, THE MIGHTY BARNUM
Lomax, John: LEADBELLY
Lombard, Carole: GABLE AND LOMBARD, MOVIEOLA
Loren, Sophia: SOPHIA LOREN--HER OWN STORY
Lorraine, Lillian: THE GREAT ZIEGFELD (?), ZIEGFELD: THE MAN AND HIS WOMEN
Lynn, Loretta: COAL MINER'S DAUGHTER

McCarthy, Charlie: MAE WEST
McCartney, Paul: THE BIRTH OF THE BEATLES
McCormick, John: SO THIS IS LOVE
McDonald, Francis: THE PERILS OF PAULINE
McHugh, Jimmy: THE HELEN MORGAN STORY*
McKinley, Myrtle: MOTHER WORE TIGHTS
Mann, Hank: THE PERILS OF PAULINE
Manne, Shelly: THE GENE KRUPA STORY*
Mansfield, Jayne: THE JAYNE MANSFIELD STORY
Martin, Mary: NIGHT AND DAY*
Martin, Tony: TILL THE CLOUDS ROLL BY*
Mathis, June: THE LEGEND OF VALENTINO, VALENTINO II
Mayer, Louis B.: GABLE AND LOMBARD, HARLOW I, HARLOW II (?), MOVIEOLA, MOMMIE DEAREST, RAINBOW
Mendoza, The Great: THREE LITTLE WORDS*
Milestone, Lewis: THE AMAZING HOWARD HUGHES
Miller, Arthur: MARILYN: THE UNTOLD STORY
Miller, Glenn: THE FIVE PENNIES, THE GLENN MILLER STORY
Miller, Marilyn: THE GREAT ZIEGFELD (?), LOOK FOR THE SILVER LINING, TILL THE CLOUDS ROLL BY, ZIEGFELD: THE MAN AND HIS WOMEN
Monroe, Marilyn: MARILYN: THE UNTOLD STORY, MOVIEOLA, THE SEX SYMBOL (?)
Montez, Lola: GOLDEN GIRL
Monti, Carlotta: W. C. FIELDS AND ME
Moore, Alexander: LILLIAN RUSSELL

Moore, Grace: SO THIS IS LOVE
Morgan, Helen: THE HELEN MORGAN STORY

Nathan, George Jean: ACT ONE
Nazimova: THE LEGEND OF VALENTINO, VALENTINO II
Neal, Patricia: THE PATRICIA NEAL STORY
Nesbit, Evelyn: THE GIRL IN THE RED VELVET SWING
Nichols, Red: THE FIVE PENNIES, THE GENE KRUPA STORY*
Nijinsky: NIJINSKY
Norworth, Jack: SHINE ON HARVEST MOON, ZIEGFELD: THE MAN AND HIS WOMEN

O'Brien, Virginia: TILL THE CLOUDS ROLL BY*
O'Day, Anita: THE GENE KRUPA STORY*
O'Neil, Kitty: SILENT VICTORY
Olcott, Chauncey: MY WILD IRISH ROSE
Olivier, Laurence: MARILYN: THE UNTOLD STORY

Panzer, Paul: THE PERILS OF PAULINE
Parker, Dorothy: ACT ONE, F. SCOTT FITZGERALD IN HOLLYWOOD
Parker, Colonel Tom: ELVIS!
Parsons, Louella: MOVIEOLA
Pastor, Tony: THE DAUGHTER OF ROSIE O'GRADY, LILLIAN RUSSELL
Patricola, Tom: RHAPSODY IN BLUE*
Pavlova, Anna: MILLION DOLLAR MERMAID, TONIGHT WE SING
Peters, Jean: THE AMAZING HOWARD HUGHES
Pollack, Ben: THE GLENN MILLER STORY*
Pollard, Snub: THE PERILS OF PAULINE*
Ponti, Carlo: SOPHIA LOREN--HER OWN STORY
Porter, Cole: NIGHT AND DAY
Post, Wiley: THE STORY OF WILL ROGERS
Powell, William: HARLOW I (?), HARLOW II (?)
Presley, Elvis: ELVIS!, ELVIS AND THE BEAUTY QUEEN
Presley, Priscilla: ELVIS!
Prinze, Freddie: CAN YOU HEAR THE LAUGHTER?

Raft, George: THE GEORGE RAFT STORY, MAE WEST
Rambova, Natacha: THE LEGEND OF VALENTINO, VALENTINO II
Randolph, Betty: THE GREAT ZIEGFELD, LITTLE EGYPT
Ravel, Maurice: RHAPSODY IN BLUE
Regan, Phil: THREE LITTLE WORDS*
Reisman, Leo: THE EDDY DUCHIN STORY
Reynolds, Debbie: THREE LITTLE WORDS
Richardson, J. P. "The Big Bopper": THE BUDDY HOLLY STORY
Roach, Bert: THE PERILS OF PAULINE
Rocco, Maurice: INCENDIARY BLONDE*
Rockefeller, John D.: THE STORY OF WILL ROGERS

Rodgers, Richard: WORDS AND MUSIC
Rogers, Ginger: THE AMAZING HOWARD HUGHES
Rogers, Will: THE GREAT ZIEGFELD, LOOK FOR THE SILVER LINING, THE STORY OF WILL ROGERS, ZIEGFELD: THE MAN AND HIS WOMEN
Romburg, Sigmund: DEEP IN MY HEART
Rooney, Mickey: RAINBOW
Roosevelt, Franklin D.: THE EDDIE CANTOR STORY, YANKEE DOODLE DANDY
Rose, Billy: FUNNY LADY
Roth, Lillian: I'LL CRY TOMORROW
Ruby, Harry: THREE LITTLE WORDS
Russell, Jane: THE AMAZING HOWARD HUGHES
Russell, Lillian: THE GREAT ZIEGFELD, LILLIAN RUSSELL, MY WILD IRISH ROSE

Sachse, Leopold: INTERRUPTED MELODY*
Scanlan, William: MY WILD IRISH ROSE
Schenck, Joseph: VALENTINO II
Scott, Hazel: RHAPSODY IN BLUE*
Seastrom, Victor: MOVIEOLA
Seeley, Blossom: SOMEBODY LOVES ME
Selznick, David O.: MOVIEOLA
Selznick, Myron: MOVIEOLA
Sheen, Martin: THE PATRICIA NEAL STORY
Sherwood, Robert: ACT ONE
Shubert, J. J.: DEEP IN MY HEART
Siegel, Bugsy: THE GEORGE RAFT STORY
Sinatra, Frank: TILL THE CLOUDS ROLL BY*
Snow, Hank: ELVIS!
Snyder, Martin "The Gimp": LOVE ME OR LEAVE ME
Solomon, Edward: LILLIAN RUSSELL
Sousa, John Philip: STARS AND STRIPES FOREVER
Starr, Ringo: THE BIRTH OF THE BEATLES
Steinberg, David: CAN YOU HEAR THE LAUGHTER?
Stiller, Mauritz: MOVIEOLA
Stratton, Dorothy: DEATH OF A CENTERFOLD
Stravinsky, Igor: NIJINSKY
Sullavan, Margaret: HAYWIRE, MOVIEOLA
Sullivan, Arthur: THE GREAT GILBERT AND SULLIVAN, LILLIAN RUSSELL
Sullivan, Ed: THE BUDDY HOLLY STORY, ELVIS!
Sunday, Billy: ISADORA (?)
Susskind, David: FEAR ON TRIAL*

Tanguay, Eva: THE I DON'T CARE GIRL
Templeton, Fay: YANKEE DOODLE DANDY
Thalberg, Irving: MAN OF A THOUSAND FACES, MOVIEOLA
Thaw, Harry K.: THE GIRL IN THE RED VELVET SWING
Thum, Jack: LEAVE 'EM LAUGHING
Torrence, Dean: DEAD MAN'S CURVE

Troup, Bobby: THE GENE KRUPA STORY*
Tucker, George Loane: MAN OF A THOUSAND FACES
Tucker, Sophie: THE JOKER IS WILD
Turner, Lana: MOVIEOLA

Ullman, George: VALENTINO II

Valdine, Elisa: TONIGHT WE SING
Valens, Richie: THE BUDDY HOLLY STORY
Valentino, Rudolph: THE LEGEND OF VALENTINO, VALENTINO I, VALENTINO II
Vallee, Rudy: THE HELEN MORGAN STORY*
Vance, The Great: CHAMPAGNE CHARLIE
Vera-Ellen: WORDS AND MUSIC*

Wallenda (family): THE GREAT WALLENDAS
Wead, Frank: THE WINGS OF EAGLES
Weber, Joe: LILLIAN RUSSELL*
Welles, Orson: THE NIGHT THAT PANICKED AMERICA
West, Mae: MAE WEST
White, George: RHAPSODY IN BLUE*
White, Pearl: THE PERILS OF PAULINE
White, Stanford: THE GIRL IN THE RED VELVET SWING
Whiteman, Paul: THE FABULOUS DORSEYS*, RHAPSODY IN BLUE*
Williams, Bert: FUNNY LADY (?), ZIEGFELD: THE MAN AND HIS WOMEN
Williams, Hank: YOUR CHEATIN' HEART
Wilson, Woodrow: THE STORY OF WILL ROGERS
Winchell, Walter: THE HELEN MORGAN STORY*, MOVIEOLA
Wood, Natalie: ELVIS!
Woolcott, Alexander: ACT ONE
Woolley, Monty: NIGHT AND DAY*
Wynette, Tammy: STAND BY YOUR MAN

Ysaye, Eugene: TONIGHT WE SING

Ziegfeld, Florenz: DEEP IN MY HEART, THE EDDIE CANTOR STORY, FUNNY GIRL, THE GREAT ZIEGFELD, THE HELEN MORGAN STORY, I'LL SEE YOU IN MY DREAMS, THE STORY OF WILL ROGERS, W. C. FIELDS AND ME, ZIEGFELD: THE MAN AND HIS WOMEN
Zukor, Adolph: W. C. FIELDS AND ME (?)

Part II: Motion Pictures Cited in the Text

Extended descriptions are underscored [for example, 155]
Illustrations are marked with a dagger [for example, 347†]

ABRAHAM LINCOLN, 7
ACT ONE, 339
ACTRESS, THE, 217-218, 339
AL CAPONE, 230
ALEXANDER'S RAGTIME BAND, 45, 62, 63, 95, 102, 164
ALWAYS LEAVE 'EM LAUGHING, 294-295
AMAZING HOWARD HUGHES, THE, 346-349, 347†
AMERICAN HOT WAX, 350-352
ANNIE GET YOUR GUN, 342
ANNIE OAKLEY, 342
ASPHALT JUNGLE, THE, 256, 259

BABY FACE NELSON, 230
BE YOURSELF, 2
BEAU BRUMMEL (1924), 52
BENNY GOODMAN STORY, THE, 138, 140-143, 141†, 148
BEST THINGS IN LIFE ARE FREE, THE, 114-115, 121-124, 122†, 129, 187
BIGGEST DANCER IN THE WORLD, 288-291
BILL OF DIVORCEMENT, A, 357
BIRTH OF THE BEATLES, THE, 152-157, 155†, 198, 206, 322, 339
BOGEY, 248-249
BOLERO, 230
BOUND FOR GLORY, 193-194, 195-197, 196†, 199
BROADWAY MELODY, THE, 9
BROADWAY THROUGH A KEYHOLE, 17
BROADWAY TO HOLLYWOOD, 159
BUD AND LOU, 321-323
BUDDY HOLLY STORY, THE, 152, 198-201, 204, 352
BUFFALO BILL, 342
BUFFALO BILL AND THE INDIANS, or SITTING BULL'S HISTORY LESSONS, 342-344
BUSTER KEATON STORY, THE, 303-306, 304†, 313

CAMILLE (1936), 250
CAN YOU HEAR THE LAUGHTER?, 323-325, 324†
CAN'T STOP THE MUSIC, 292

CATCH US IF YOU CAN, 152
CHAMPAGNE CHARLIE, 162-163
CITIZEN KANE, 284, 316, 353
COAL MINER'S DAUGHTER, 209-210
COLLEGE, 306
COPS, 305

DAMES, 165
DANCE OF LIFE, THE, 56
DAUGHTER OF ROSIE O'GRADY, THE, 345
DEAD MAN'S CURVE, 201-203, 207
DEATH OF A CENTERFOLD, 264-266
DEATH TRAP, 107
DEEP IN MY HEART, 130-132, 187
DESERT SONG, THE, 130
DINNER AT EIGHT, 357
DIXIE, 100-102
DOLLY SISTERS, THE, 163, 176
DON'T KNOCK THE ROCK, 152

EDDIE CANTOR STORY, THE, 153, 298-301, 299†, 302
EDDY DUCHIN STORY, THE, 138, 143-146, 143†, 221, 249
ELVIS!, 203-207, 205†, 210
ELVIS AND THE BEAUTY QUEEN, 207-209
EVEL KNIEVEL, 340

F. SCOTT FITZGERALD AND THE LAST OF THE BELLES, 336
F. SCOTT FITZGERALD IN HOLLYWOOD, 336-338
FABULOUS DORSEYS, THE, 135-138, 251
FAME, 292
FATHER OF THE BRIDE, 217
FEAR ON TRIAL, 319-321, 320†
FERRY CROSS THE MERSEY, 152
FIVE PENNIES, THE, 138, 146-148, 146†, 151, 165
FLESH AND THE DEVIL, 250
FORTY-SECOND STREET, 165
FOX, THE, 107
FRONT PAGE, THE (1931), 348
FROZEN NORTH, THE, 306
FUNNY GIRL, 307-310
FUNNY LADY, 310-311

GABLE AND LOMBARD, 236-240, 249, 336
GALAXINA, 264
GENE KRUPA STORY, THE, 138, 148-150, 152
GEORGE RAFT STORY, THE, 229-232, 306, 336
GERTIE WAS A LADY -- see STAR!
GIRL IN THE RED VELVET SWING, THE, 218
GLENN MILLER STORY, 137-140, 139†, 145, 151

GO INTO YOUR DANCE, 165
GOLD DIGGERS (series), 9
GOLDEN GIRL, 276-279, 277†, 281, 283
GONE WITH THE WIND, 240, 350
GOODBYE, NORMA JEAN, 255-256
GREAT CARUSO, THE, 174-175, 187, 188, 194, 345
GREAT GILBERT AND SULLIVAN, THE, 128-130
GREAT HOUDINIS, THE, 335-336
GREAT VICTOR HERBERT, THE, 61, 61-63, 64, 66, 95, 116, 124, 129
GREAT WALLENDAS, THE, 340-341
GREAT WALTZ, THE, 44, 69
GREAT ZIEGFELD, THE, 17, 19-43, 31†, 39†, 44-46, 50, 52-53, 57, 60, 63-64, 78-79, 81-83, 88, 92, 104, 160-161, 166, 194, 276, 279, 308, 332, 355-359
GYPSY, 198, 286-288, 287†, 330

HARD DAY'S NIGHT, A, 292
HARLOW I (Electronovision), 232-233, 336
HARLOW II, 232, 233-235, 236, 256, 261, 268, 336
HARMONY LANE, 118
HAYWIRE, 266-270, 268†
HEAT'S ON, THE, 332
HELEN MORGAN STORY, THE, 183, 184-187, 185†, 207
HELL DIVERS, 339
HELL'S ANGELS, 233, 348
HOLLYWOOD CAVALCADE, 53, 214, 283
HOUDINI, 222, 334†, 335

I DON'T CARE GIRL, THE, 284-285, 316
I DREAM OF JEANNIE, 118-121
I WONDER WHO'S KISSING HER NOW, 113, 114†, 115, 121, 284
I'LL CRY TOMORROW, 182-184, 187, 197, 226, 323
I'LL SEE YOU IN MY DREAMS, 114-115, 117-118
INCENDIARY BLONDE, 344-345
INCREDIBLE SARAH, 246-248, 246†
INDISCREET (1931), 123
INTERRUPTED MELODY, 179-181, 180†, 182, 202-203, 252
IRISH EYES ARE SMILING, 102-103, 113, 115, 131, 170
IRON MASK, THE, 52
IS EVERYBODY HAPPY? (1929), 2
IS EVERYBODY HAPPY? (1943), 133-135, 134†, 162, 164, 321
ISADORA -- see THE LOVES OF ISADORA

JAMES DEAN, 244-246
JAMES DEAN STORY, THE, 255
JAMES DEAN: THE FIRST AMERICAN TEENAGER, 255
JAYNE MANSFIELD STORY, THE, 261-264, 262†
JAZZ SINGER, THE, 1, 165
JEANNE EAGELS, 223-226, 224†

Index / 403

JOKER IS WILD, 306-307, 315
JOLSON SINGS AGAIN, 170-174, 176, 184, 203, 207, 284, 301
JOLSON STORY, THE, 164-167, 166†, 169, 172, 174, 176, 194, 260, 301, 310, 336, 352
JUST IMAGINE, 123

KATIE: PORTRAIT OF A CENTERFOLD, 265

LADY OF BURLESQUE, 294
LADY SINGS THE BLUES, 151, 191-193, 195, 207, 234
LADY WITH RED HAIR, THE, 76, 79-82, 80†, 212
LADY'S MORALS, A, 2-7, 8-9, 11, 43, 46, 65, 121
LEADBELLY, 151, 193-195, 199
LEAVE 'EM LAUGHING: THE STORY OF JACK THUM, 325-327, 326†
LEGEND OF VALENTINO, THE, 240-242, 243, 252
LENNY, 316-319, 317†, 323, 328
LIFE OF BUFFALO BILL, THE, 1
LILAC TIME, 9
LILLIAN RUSSELL, 76-79, 77†, 82, 86
LITTLE EGYPT, 279-281, 280†, 283
LOOK FOR THE SILVER LINING, 34, 204, 274-276, 275†
LOUIS ARMSTRONG--CHICAGO STYLE, 150-152, 234, 306
LOVE ME OR LEAVE ME, 181-182, 184, 186-187
LOVES OF ISADORA, 288-291
LUCKY BOY, 1

MACHINE GUN KELLY, 230
MAE WEST, 328-333
MAKING LOVE, 107
MAN OF A THOUSAND FACES, 220-223, 222†, 249, 271, 303, 306
MARCH OF TIME, 159
MARILYN: THE UNTOLD STORY, 256-261, 257†
MIGHTY BARNUM, THE, 11-16, 23, 28, 43, 46, 50, 53-54, 57, 60, 65-66, 71-72, 81, 101, 104, 121, 123, 150, 167
MILLION DOLLAR MERMAID, 281-284, 282†
MOMMIE DEAREST, 266-270, 269†
MOTHER WORE TIGHTS, 272†, 273-274
MOVIEOLA -- see THE SCARLETT O'HARA WAR, THE SILENT LOVERS, and THIS YEAR'S BLONDE
MURDER, INC., 230
MY GAL SAL, 94-95, 99-100, 102-103, 113, 127, 131
MY LITTLE CHICADEE, 331
MY WILD IRISH ROSE, 167-170, 169†

NEW WINE, 106
NIGHT AFTER NIGHT, 331
NIGHT AND DAY, 104, 107-110, 108†, 140
NIGHT THAT PANICKED AMERICA, THE, 350-351
NIJINSKY, 107, 292-293

OH, YOU BEAUTIFUL DOLL, 113, <u>115-116</u>, 124, 127, 142, 284
OUTLAW, THE, 349

PATRIA, 52
PATRICIA NEAL STORY, 252-255
PERILS OF PAULINE, THE (1947), <u>212-214</u>, 216, 284, 306
PORTRAIT OF A MOBSTER, 230
PRIDE AND THE PASSION, THE, 252
PRINCE OF PLAYERS, <u>218-220</u>, 219†, 271

QUEEN ELIZABETH, 2
QUEEN OF THE NIGHTCLUBS, 1

RAINBOW, <u>197-198</u>, 339
RECKLESS, 17
RHAPSODY IN BLUE, <u>103-107</u>, 105†, 109-110, 127, 136, 140, 203
RISE AND FALL OF LEGS DIAMOND, 230
ROCK AROUND THE CLOCK, 152, 292
ROSE OF WASHINGTON SQUARE, 44, 307

ST. LOUIS BLUES, <u>126-128</u>, 126†, 149, 151, 191
SARAH, <u>246-248</u>
SATURDAY NIGHT FEVER, 291
SCARFACE, 230-231, 348
SCARLETT O'HARA WAR, THE, <u>349-350</u>
SCOTT JOPLIN, <u>128-129</u>
SEVEN LITTLE FOYS, THE, <u>302-303</u>, 302†
SEVENTH HEAVEN, 9
SEX SYMBOL, THE, <u>255</u>
SHE DONE HIM WRONG, 331
SHEIK, THE, 216, 243
SHERLOCK HOLMES, 2
SHINE ON HARVEST MOON, <u>159-162</u>, 161†, 163, 172, 273
SHIPMATES FOREVER, 165
SILENT LOVERS, <u>250-251</u>
SILENT VICTORY: THE KITTY O'NEIL STORY, <u>341-342</u>, 341†
SINGIN' IN THE RAIN, 230
SINGING FOOL, 123
SO THIS IS LOVE, 153, <u>178-179</u>, 204, 339
SOME LIKE IT HOT, 231
SOMEBODY LOVES ME, <u>177-178</u>
SOMETHING'S GOT TO GIVE, 260
SON OF THE SHEIK, 241
SONG OF MY HEART, 2
SOPHIA LOREN--HER OWN STORY, <u>251-252</u>
SOUND OF MUSIC, 235
SOUTH OF DIXIE, 172
STAND BY YOUR MAN, 209, <u>210-211</u>, 252
STAR!, <u>235-236</u>, 237†

STAR 80, 266
STAR IS BORN, A, (1937), 63
STAR MAKER, THE, 53, 54-60, 62-64, 70, 72, 82, 159, 164
STARS AND STRIPES FOREVER, THE, 124-126, 125†, 128
STORY OF VERNON AND IRENE CASTLE, 45-53, 47†, 54, 63, 72, 82, 87, 90-91, 140, 273
STORY OF WILL ROGERS, THE, 295-298, 296†, 300
STUDENT PRINCE, THE, 130
SUNDAY, BLOODY SUNDAY, 107
SUNNYSIDE UP, 123
SWANEE RIVER, 63-75, 68†, 87, 90, 94-95, 100-102, 107, 111, 115, 118-119, 121, 128, 140

THAT CERTAIN SUMMER, 107
THIN MAN, THE, 39
THIS IS ELVIS, 266
THIS YEAR'S BLONDE, 256, 259, 261
THOSE WERE THE HAPPY TIMES -- see STAR!
THREE LITTLE WORDS, 114-115, 116-117, 120-121, 123, 129, 276
TILL THE CLOUDS ROLL BY, 110-113, 112†, 114, 140, 204, 274
TO HELL AND BACK, 220
TONIGHT WE SING, 284, 345-346, 346†
TOO MUCH, TOO SOON, 226-229, 227†
TOPPER, 39
TWO ARABIAN NIGHTS, 348

VALENTINO I (1951), 214-217, 215†, 222, 229, 244, 251, 268, 306, 313
VALENTINO II (1977), 242-244, 243†, 245, 292
VIVA KNIEVEL, 340

W. C. FIELDS AND ME, 311-316, 312†, 319, 336
WHAT PRICE GLORY?, 9
WHAT PRICE HOLLYWOOD?, 17
WHOOPIE, 118
WINGS OF EAGLES, THE, 338-339
WITH A SONG IN MY HEART, 175-177, 202
WIZARD OF OZ, 198
WORDS AND MUSIC, 110-113, 112†, 129, 140, 322

YANKEE DOODLE DANDY, 83-94, 84†, 99, 124-125, 147, 159, 165, 303
YOUNG MAN WITH A HORN, 181
YOUNG PEOPLE, 159
YOUR CHEATIN' HEART, 188-191, 190†, 210, 234

ZIEGFELD FOLLIES, THE, 43
ZIEGFELD: THE MAN AND HIS WOMEN, 353-360, 354†

ABOUT THE AUTHOR

Motion picture historian Robert Milton Miller holds an M. A. in film from Kansas University and a Ph. D. in film from Northwestern. During the past 15 years he has programmed over a thousand vintage silent and sound features for various film societies and college courses. Former editor of the Northwestern Film Guide and founder of the Northwestern Film Board, he is currently Vice President of the National Society for Cinephiles and Assistant Professor of Communication Studies at Northern Illinois University.